National Socialist Cultural Policy

Edited by
Glenn R. Cuomo

St. Martin's Press
New York

NATIONAL SOCIALIST CULTURAL POLICY
Copyright © 1995 by Glenn R. Cuomo
All rights reserved. Printed in the United States of America.
No part of this book may be used or reproduced in any manner whatsoever without written permission except in the cases of brief quotations embodied in critical articles or reviews. For information, address St. Martin's Press, Scholarly and Reference Division, 175 Fifth Avenue, New York, N.Y. 10010

Design by Acme Art, Inc.

ISBN 0-312-09094-3

Library of Congress Cataloging-in-Publication Data

National Socialist cultural policy / [edited by] Glenn R. Cuomo.
    p.   cm.
  Includes bibliographical references and index.
  ISBN 0-312-09094-3 (alk. paper)
  1. Germany—Cultural policy—History—20th century. 2. National socialism. 3. Germany—Intellectual life—20th century.
4. Germany—Politics and government—1933-1945. 5. National socialism and art. I. Cuomo, Glenn R.
DD256.5.N317 1995
943.08—dc20   95-9565
                                                                       CIP

First Edition: October 1995
10 9 8 7 6 5 4 3 2 1

Contents

List of Tables iv

    Introduction
        Glenn R. Cuomo 1

1. Nazi Cultural Politics: Intentionalism vs. Functionalism
    Ehrhard Bahr 5

2. Cultural Eugenics: Social Policy, Economic Reform,
   and the Purge of Jews from German Cultural Life
    Alan E. Steinweis 23

3. The Nazi "Seizure" of the Berlin Philharmonic,
   or the Decline of a Bourgeois Musical Institution
    Pamela M. Potter 39

4. The Foundations of Theater Policy in Nazi Germany
    Bogusław Drewniak 67

5. Nazi Film Policy: Control, Ideology, and Propaganda
    David Welch 95

6. A Guide through the Visual Arts Administration
   of the Third Reich
    Jonathan Petropoulos 121

7. Literary Policy in the Third Reich
    Jan-Pieter Barbian 155

8. The Diaries of Joseph Goebbels as a Source for the
   Understanding of National Socialist Cultural Politics
    Glenn R. Cuomo 197

Notes on the Contributors 246

Index 248

List of Tables

Table 1: Reich Subsidies (in Reichsmark) for German Theaters 78
Table 2: Percentage of Films Exhibited, 1934-1944 108

Introduction

Glenn R. Cuomo

Over 60 years have passed since Adolf Hitler assumed the chancellorship in Germany and his National Socialist Party implemented its plan for a "renewal" of German culture. Some of the forms this program took remain an indelible feature in the legacy of European fascism. The book burnings on 10 May 1933 created an international sensation,[1] as did the mass flight into exile of many of Germany's most talented actors, artists, authors, directors, and critics. The Hitler regime further scandalized the civilized world with the "Degenerate Art Exhibition" of 1937 and subsequent "educational displays," where it pilloried the "decadent" art that had flourished during the Weimar Republic. At the same time the National Socialists publicly rejected the modernist art of the recent past, they attempted to regiment all those artists who elected to remain in the "Third Reich." The establishment of the Reich Chamber of Culture as a compulsory organization covering all sectors of cultural activity served to exclude "undesirables"—Jews and other "politically unreliable" artists—from practicing their profession.

To be sure, these manifestations of overt suppression and control were undeniable features of the cultural policy practiced under National Socialism. But the actual conditions of cultural life were far more complex and contradictory than the situation one would have expected to prevail under a totalitarian government. Here we need only to turn to Hans Dieter Schäfer's pioneering study of popular culture in Germany from 1933 to 1945. With the help of advertisements, cinema and broadcasting programs, and popular magazines, Schäfer demonstrated that the everyday reality of cultural life under Hitler not only was quite diverse and remarkably "liberal" in some areas, but also often at odds with the values promoted by the National Socialist ideology.[2]

Such contradictions were the inevitable consequences of the Janus-faced cultural policy that emerged from the competing ideological, economic, and personal agendas pursued by the leading members of the Nazi hierarchy and the network of state, police, and Nazi Party agencies, ministries, and departments they controlled. Only in the last decades, after thousands of archival documents produced by these agencies have been scrutinized, have we begun to understand the full dimensions of the National Socialist apparatus for cultural control. With its overlapping purviews and rivaling interests, this apparatus operated in what Volker Dahm aptly labeled a "state of authoritarian anarchy" (*autoritäre Anarchie*) and provided one more example that refutes the notion that Hitler's Third Reich ever had been an efficiently functioning "perfect monolithic order."[3]

As we shall see in the following chapters by scholars from four countries in German history, cultural studies, musicology, and literature, the cultural policy put in practice by the National Socialist regime encompassed many principles that seemed to be incompatible. On the one hand, Hitler and the Party leadership promoted an aesthetics of representational art rooted in the realism and neoclassicism of the previous century. On the other hand, they also were willing to embrace the most recent technological advances in the new mass media of broadcasting and film. When "purging" the ranks of Germany's artists of "undesirables," the regime applied radical racial and ideological criteria, while simultaneously trying to avoid damage to the German economy and any loss of international prestige as a leading representative of Western culture.

The following analyses also show that not all effects of the comprehensive governmental intervention in the cultural sector were negative. For example, the Berlin Philharmonic Orchestra did not experience fiscal security until after the National Socialist takeover. With the regimentation of the theater sector came the first pensions and other social programs for people in theater, as well as the standardization of salaries. In a similar vein, the Reich Literature Chamber enacted guidelines for contractual agreements between authors and publishers and provided stipends for needy members. For the leaders of the book trade, National Socialism's anti-Semitic measures helped eliminate the competition posed by "non-Aryan" publishing houses.

Moreover, the vacuum created by massive emigration and large-scale expulsions from the Reich Chamber of Culture created opportunities for those German artists who possessed the requisite "racial" and political qualifications to pursue careers under Hitler's regime. Here we must not forget that the period of the Third Reich did not encompass the entire productive and highly lucrative careers of individuals condemned after 1945 for their cooperation with the Nazi regime: the film directors Leni Riefenstahl and Veit Harlan, the actor Emil Jannings, the author Hanns Johst, and the sculptor Arno Breker. These same 12 years also saw significant professional accomplishments within Hitler's Reich by prominent figures we often identify with the cultural achievements of the German Federal Republic: the conductor Herbert von Karajan, the publisher Peter Suhrkamp, the actors Bernhard Minetti and Heinz Rühmann, and authors such as Alfred Andersch, Günter Eich, and Hans-Erich Nossack.

Since the following analyses provide overviews of current scholarship on the topics in addition to relevant published and unpublished sources, no effort was made to reduce the number of endnotes. At the same time, however, citations in the German original were kept to an absolute minimum in both the text and the notes in order to render this collection accessible to a nonspecialized readership. The detailed documentation of sources therefore will serve readers interested in consulting the original materials. Even though certain sources receive multiple citations throughout the volume, full bibliographical data are given in the notes following each contribution because it is likely that these contributions might be read separately. For this same reason allowances have been made for some overlap in the discussions of key aspects and figures in National Socialist cultural policy, although each time a different focus applies. One example is the rivalry between Alfred Rosenberg and Joseph Goebbels over cultural policy. This conflict manifested itself particularly in theater and literary matters and is analyzed in these two contexts, as well as with respect to Goebbels' diaries.

Notes

1. Cf. Guy Stern, "The Book Burning: Widerschein in Amerika," in *"Das war ein Vorspiel nur . . ." Bücherverbrennung Deutschland 1933: Voraussetzungen und Folgen,* eds. Hermann Haarmann, Walter Huder, and Klaus Siebenhaar (Berlin: Medusa Verlagsgesellschaft, 1983), pp. 97-107.

2. Hans Dieter Schäfer, "Das gespaltene Bewußtsein: Über die Lebenswirklichkeit in Deutschland 1933-1945," in H. D. Schäfer, *Das gespaltene Bewußtsein: Deutsche Kultur und Lebenswirklichkeit 1933-1945* (München: Carl Hanser, 1981), pp. 114-62.

3. Volker Dahm, *Das jüdische Buch im Dritten Reich. Erster Teil: Die Ausschaltung der jüdischen Autoren, Verleger und Buchhändler* (Frankfurt/Main: Buchhändler-Vereinigung, 1979), p. 6. On the imperfect reality that resulted

from the National Socialists' attempt to organize all aspects of political and social life in Germany, see Karl Dietrich Bracher, *The German Dictatorship: The Origins, Structure, and Effects of National Socialism* (New York: Praeger Publishers, 1970), pp. 345-46.

1

Nazi Cultural Politics: Intentionalism vs. Functionalism

Ehrhard Bahr

For more than 60 years, global interpretations of fascism have described National Socialist culture as an aesthetic phenomenon, examining its social functions and moral implications. Before and during the Third Reich period, this stance was expressed in essays by Bertolt Brecht and Ernst Bloch, by Thomas Mann and Walter Benjamin. Best known is Benjamin's definition of fascism as "the situation of politics [rendered] aesthetic."[1] This tradition established in the 1930s and 1940s has been continued into the 1990s, as evidenced by Peter Reichel's recent book explaining Hitler's rule as an identification of the sociopolitical sphere with the aesthetic: "Hitler understood aestheticization in real, though superficial, terms as 'beautification of life,' as production of a pseudo-reality which was supposed to influence the perception as well as the image of reality of millions and concede to them visually and symbolically what was denied to them in reality."[2] Such an interpretation disregards the racist basis of Nazi cultural politics and the fact that Nazi anti-Semitic legislation was perhaps nowhere as consistently enforced between 1933 and 1939 as in the area of culture. In contrast to Reichel, my purpose is to provide an analysis of Nazi cultural politics and their underlying intentions in terms of the "racial state" instituted by the Nazi government[3]; to put forward in the form of theses a critique of the interpretative tradition explaining Fascist culture as an aesthetic phenomenon; and to apply the interpretations of the international historiography of the Nazi genocide of the Jews to the area of Nazi cultural politics. It is my thesis that the same principles operative in Nazi racial politics also determined their cultural politics. Furthermore, I propose that the interpretations of the Holocaust have the same validity here as in any other area controlled by Nazi decision making and implementation of policy.

This chapter was conceived as a lecture for the Los Angeles County Museum of Art exhibition entitled "Degenerate Art: The Fate of the Avant-Garde in Nazi Germany" (February 17-May 12, 1991). One of this exhibit's most disturbing items was a profoundly shocking videotape in the literature gallery, showing film clips of the burning of the books on 10 May 1933. The videotape, edited by Erwin Leiser, ends with a film showing women and children in the nude, waiting for their turn in the execution line. The film's final image is the open door of an oven in a crematorium, revealing the remains of a human skeleton. Using a quote from the nineteenth-century German-Jewish poet Heinrich Heine—"Where men burn books, / They will burn people also in the end"—Leiser relates the events of May 1933 to the Nazi pogroms of November 1938, the infamous "crystal night" (Kristallnacht), and to the extermination camps of 1942 by including film clips of burning synagogues from 1938 and gas chambers from 1942. The videotape makes a legitimate historical statement and provides an interpretation of the exhibit: What was started in May 1933 by the burning of the books and was continued in 1937 by the exhibit of "Degenerate Art" in Munich culminated after 1942 in the German extermination camps in Poland. By establishing a direct relationship between the National Socialists' cultural and racial policies, the videotape opens a window to the understanding of Nazi cultural politics and their underlying intentions.

With the burning of the books in 1933, the National Socialists tried to demonstrate what they considered to be German, what they considered to be un-German, and what they intended to do with whatever or whomever they perceived as un-German. They began with the burning of books and they ended, as Heine predicted in 1821, with "the burning of people."[4] One may question this interpretation with reference to the fact that of the 112 artists included in the "Degenerate Art" exhibition in Munich in 1937, only six were Jewish,[5] but such a reference disregards the anti-Semitic signifiers in the exhibition's posters and graffiti.[6] It is important to understand that the word "degenerate" is by itself an anti-Semitic term of the Nazi vocabulary. Furthermore, the purges in literature, music, and film were largely anti-Semitic, although not all exiles from Hitler's Germany were Jewish (consider Bertolt Brecht, Heinrich Mann, and Paul Hindemith). In 1936, Thomas Mann took issue with an article in the *Neue Züricher Zeitung* that claimed that only Jewish authors had left Germany and declared his solidarity with the German-Jewish authors in exile.[7]

The Nazis' definition of what was German was based on a biomedical worldview that posited a fictitious German norm and resulted in the argument that anything deviating from this norm was to be "removed" like a cancer from the fictitious body of a German people, or *Volk*. Nineteenth-century pseudoscience provided the Nazis with a term for this norm and the deviation therefrom: the German words *Art*, or "genus," and *Entartung*, or "degeneration." While the Nazi usage of both the terms "race" and "Aryan" was totally unscientific and derived from pseudoscientific publications of the nineteenth century, the terms had the aura of scientific respectability not only among the masses but also among the educated middle class. The link between degeneration and the Jews was one of the standard associations of Nazi propaganda. Although Jews had settled in Germany for over 1,000 years, they were now considered as not fitting the fictitious German norm, and they were designated as degenerate—deviating from and harmful to the norm. Therefore, according to Nazi ideology, they had to be removed from the body of the German people, and this body had to be protected from or immunized against the influence of "degeneration."[8]

International historiography has traced the links between the National Socialists' racial ideology and its implementation in the form of persecution and extermination. During the early 1980s, the British historian Tim Mason introduced the terms "intentionalism" and "functionalism" to the interpretation of the Nazi regime in international historiography.[9] The term "intentionalism" or "intentionalist" was applied to the traditional school of interpretation that claimed a direct relationship between Hitler's ideology and master plan, as expounded in *Mein Kampf* of 1925/26, and the Nazi policies implemented after 1933. According to Saul Friedländer, who has analyzed the methodologies of the intentionalist and functionalist schools, the traditional school perceived "initial aims" and subsequent "steps" that "were taken systematically to implement those aims."[10] The axiomatic premise of the intentionalists was "the absolute centrality of Adolf Hitler within the system."[11] The functionalist interpretation, on the other hand, is based on the premise "that there is no necessary relationship between the ideological dogmas of Nazism and the policies of the Third Reich." According to Friedländer's analysis, the functionalists perceived Nazi decisions as "functionally linked to one another" and not following "a preestablished plan." The functionalist argument is based on the assumption that "the constant interaction and the constant pressures exercised by multiple agencies within the system necessarily limit the role of the central decision maker" and that "his decisions take the aspect of a planned policy with clear aims only through the artifices of propaganda or, for the historian, in retrospect."[12]

The historiographical differences between these schools have been at the center of the interpretation of the genesis and implementation of the policies of the Nazi genocide. Both of these terms—intentionalism and functionalism—are expressions of the historians' dilemma of explaining the most traumatic event of modern German and European history. At the same time, these interpretative patterns, resulting from the historiography of the Holocaust, apply to other areas of Nazi planning, decision making, and implementation of policies. The following analysis will treat the cultural politics of the National Socialist government on an interdisciplinary level and apply the intentionalist and the functionalist interpretations to this area of Nazi politics. Although the Nazis' cultural politics do not have the same dimensions as those policies regarding the Holocaust or the Shoah, as it is called in Hebrew, they have the same implications. There were thousands of victims, and the loss of lives and creativity is still felt today. We expect to find that similar patterns of policymaking were observed and that the same principles underlying the implementation of the Holocaust also were operative in Nazi cultural politics.

The intentionalist interpretation of Nazi cultural politics will focus on Hitler's early statements on anti-Semitism and the first Party program of the German Workers' Party of February 1920, which was the forerunner of the National Socialist German Workers' Party (NSDAP). Hitler's early statements on anti-Semitism are crucial, because he never changed his mind on this subject. A letter by Hitler of September 1919 documents his special brand of anti-Semitism. The ultimate goal, he said at that time, must be "the elimination *(Entfernung)* of the Jews altogether."[13]

The 25-point Party program of 1920 was written by Hitler and Anton Drexler, one of the early founders of the Nazi Party. Among other things, point 23 demanded "legal action against a tendency in art and literature which undermines our national life, and the closing of cultural events violating the preceding demands." This point contains the program of Nazi cultural politics in a nutshell. A certain tendency in art and literature was identified as "undermining the [German] national life," and cultural events that were perceived as violating the Nazis' demands were targeted for suppression. Only the criteria for such undermining influence were not yet listed and the means of suppression were not yet spelled out. These demands were accompanied by a declaration of war against "deliberate political mendacity and its dissemination in the press." To facilitate a press sympathetic to national concerns, the Nazi Party of 1920 demanded that "all editors of, and contributors to, newspapers appearing in the German language must be members of the *Volk (Volksgenossen)*." Additional demands were made with regard to non-German newspapers and non-German ownership, with the term "non-German" being used as a euphemism for Jewish.

"Non-German newspapers [shall] require the express permission of the State for their publication. They are not allowed to be printed in the German language.... [N]on-Germans shall be prohibited by law from any financial involvement in or influence on German newspapers...."[14] These demands for new press legislation can be shown to contain a blueprint for the anti-Jewish legislation of 1935, the so-called Nuremberg Laws, which distinguished between two categories: Reich Citizen for members of the German nation and State Subject for German Jews. The same distinction was made in points 4 and 5 of the Party program of 1920. These points demanded that all civil rights for the Jews be abolished (point 4) and that they be placed under the jurisdiction applying to all aliens (point 5).

The next important source for an intentionalist interpretation of Nazi cultural politics is Hitler's book *Mein Kampf.* Written in prison, after Hitler was convicted of high treason as a result of the unsuccessful putsch of November 1923, this book provides a summary of Hitler's ideas about race and culture as well as the biomedical arguments on which they were based. In the central chapters of the first volume, Hitler identified the causes of the collapse of the German Empire in 1918. This collapse was not attributed to the military defeat but to "a large number of symptoms of disease and their causes."[15] Hitler perceived the collapse in terms of "diseases of the national body" (*Mein Kampf,* p. 233; all subsequent page references are cited in parentheses in the text). Among the diagnosed symptoms of decay, Hitler listed industrialization, urbanization, the aimlessness of German policy, parliamentary half measures, and psychological errors of the monarchy. But more important than these symptoms undermining the health of the national body were, according to Hitler, two other causes: syphilis and degenerate culture, or as he put it, the poisoning of the soul by "big city 'civilization'" (254). While the fight against prostitution is recommended as a remedy against syphilis, the "cleansing of our culture" is demanded as an antidote to urban civilization. This cleansing of culture is projected to extend to nearly all fields: "Theater, art, literature, cinema, press [...] must be cleansed of all manifestations of our rotting world and placed in the service of a moral, political, and cultural idea" (255). The equation of syphilis and culture is the best indication of the biomedical argument of Hitler's cultural politics.

That the term "degeneration" is part of this vocabulary becomes evident in the further development of the argument. Hitler believed he had found an element intruding into German art that up to the turn of the century would have been regarded as foreign. This foreign element was for him indicative of "a spiritual degeneration that had reached the point of destroying the spirit" (258). Concluding that the political collapse of 1918 was culturally anticipated in this "degeneration," Hitler delivered a harangue against modernist art as "art Bolshevism." Sixty years ago, he commented, such a cultural collapse, as it manifested itself in futurist, cubist, and dadaistic works, "would have seemed simply impossible and its organizers would have ended up in a madhouse" (258). As Hitler said, he saw these diseases "in nearly every field of art and culture" in Germany between 1900 and 1925. The "Bolshevist present" was for him "embodied in a cubist monstrosity," and he questioned whether it was "permissible to dish up the hallucinations of lunatics or criminals to the healthy world" (262). What makes this tedious harangue so important for the intentionalist interpretation is the fact that it provides the complement of terms later used to designate modernist art as a special kind of cultural degeneration.

Hitler attributed the ultimate reason for the decline of Imperial Germany, however, to its failure to recognize the racial problem in Germany. For him, history was determined by "the survival of the fittest," a popularized version of Social Darwinism. In Hitler's terminology, this reads as "the self-preservation and propagation of the species and the race . . . subject to the laws of Nature" (283). Consequently, Hitler also sought to provide a racial justification of his cultural politics in *Mein Kampf.* For him, the "Aryan" was the founder and custodian of culture (290, 383), whereas the Jewish people were declared to be a people "without any true culture, especially without a culture of its own" (302). Hitler maintained that "there has never been a Jewish art and accordingly there is none today either" (303). This pernicious demagoguery reveals the racist basis of Hitler's concept of cultural degeneration and the claim for a mandate to excise this "disease of degeneration" from the German national body.

The first instance of implementation of Nazi cultural politics that we shall turn to is the coalition government in the state of Thuringia in 1930. After the local Nazi Party had won a plurality in the state elections of January 1930, Wilhelm Frick, one of Hitler's loyal deputies, joined the state government as minister of the interior, in which role he supervised the state police and education. One of Frick's first political actions was to introduce a regulation called "Ordinance against Negro Culture," which was to rid Thuringia of all "immoral and foreign racial elements in the arts."[16] This ordinance resulted in the blacklisting of books, the censorship of theater, cinema, and concert stage as well as a purge of modernist art from the Weimar Ducal Museum. This 1930 purge, which took place three years before Hitler came to power, included works by Ernst Barlach, Otto Dix, Lyonel Feininger, Erich Heckel, Wassily Kandinsky, Paul Klee, Oskar Kokoschka, Wilhelm Lehmbruck, Franz Marc, Emil Nolde, Oskar Schlemmer, and Karl Schmidt-Rottluff.[17] Since it was the declared goal of the Nazi members of the Thuringian government to pave the way for the Third Reich, it is not surprising to find the same artists and their works in the "Degenerate Art" exhibition of 1937. In addition to carrying out these purges, Frick appointed two notorious racists to key positions: Hans F. K. Günther, the author of *Rasse und Stil* (Race and style), and Paul Schultze-Naumburg, the author of *Kunst und Rasse* (Art and race). Both men were among the intellectuals to provide the ideological basis for the 1937 exhibition. These early actions made Thuringia the rehearsal stage of Nazi cultural policies. Even though Frick had to resign in April of 1931, his actions were praised throughout the Party press.[18] They were a prelude to the cultural policies to be implemented after 1933.

After Hitler had been appointed chancellor in January 1933, the various stages of his cultural policies were implemented in rapid succession. In February 1933, two members of the Prussian Academy of Arts who were critical of the Nazi Party were forced to resign: Käthe Kollwitz and Heinrich Mann. Thirteen other members resigned in protest, including Ricarda Huch, Thomas Mann, and Alfred Döblin. In early March 1933, Hitler was able to enlarge his cabinet to include Joseph Goebbels as minister of popular enlightenment and propaganda. In early April, Hitler issued the "Law for the Restoration of the Civil Service," which regulated the dismissal of Jews and persons considered "politically unreliable" from the civil service. This law retroactively validated the dismissal of Arnold Schoenberg by the Prussian Academy of Arts, and of Max Beckmann, Otto Dix, Paul Klee, and Oskar Schlemmer by the art academies in Berlin, Dresden, Düsseldorf, and Frankfurt. In May 1933, the burning of books at public ceremonies was organized in most university cities in Germany. In Berlin, Joseph Goebbels presided over the ceremony in front of the university. He opened his speech on the Opernplatz by proclaiming the end of "the age of overblown Jewish intellectualism" and specifically targeted the works of Jewish *Asphaltliteraten* (decadent, metropolitan men of letters).[19] During the same month, the first blacklists for lending libraries and bookstores were issued, including more than 150 "unacceptable" authors.[20] In July, the Bauhaus school of architecture was closed in Berlin. In September 1933, the establishment of the Reich Chamber of Culture (Reichskulturkammer) was proclaimed. In October 1933, Hitler went to Munich to lay the cornerstone of the House of German Art, the museum that was inaugurated in July 1937 as a counterpart to the exhibition of "Degenerate Art." Finally, in November 1933, the Reich Chamber of Culture was instituted as a branch of the Ministry of Propaganda under Goebbels' presidency. Divided into seven chambers—film, theater, music, visual arts, radio, press, and literature—this new institution began to exercise firm control over the cultural and intellectual activities of its members. All artists, actors, composers, journalists, musicians, and writers who wished to practice their professions had to become members of the appropriate section of the chamber. Although the original Chamber of Culture legislation did not include an "Aryan Paragraph," the chamber could determine a person's "suitability," and both racial and political criteria were cited routinely as grounds for the rejection or expulsion of "unsuitable" artists. According to its mandate, the chamber also supervised and directed creative productions by the members of the various subchambers. The goal was to achieve a uniform national culture under the leadership and control of the Nazi Party and government.[21]

I have listed these activities of the Nazi government in 1933 month by month in order to indicate the great number of cultural policies enacted during the first year and to characterize briefly their suppressive nature. The pace and direction of the cultural policies confirm the intentionalist interpretation. The inauguration of the House of German Art in 1937 clearly marks the culmination of Hitler's cultural aspirations of his first years of rule. In his government proclamation of 1 February 1933, Hitler had appealed to the German nation to give him four years' time. In 1937, he expected the nation to confirm and applaud the fulfillment of his program.

The functionalist interpretation will focus on the issues and events that appear as interference or deceleration of Hitler's cultural policies between 1933 and 1937. The first important event to be introduced under this heading is the burning of the books. This event, usually believed to have been conceived and organized by Goebbels, was actually the creation of a non-Nazi organization: the German Students' Association.[22] This association, which was founded in 1919 to represent the students at German universities at the national level, designed and conducted the propaganda campaign "Against the un-German Spirit" in April 1933, which was to culminate in the burning of books at German universities in early May. The campaign, featuring a vicious anti-Semitic poster and a script for the ceremony of the burning of the books, was carefully orchestrated by a special press and propaganda office. Although Goebbels welcomed and supported the campaign, he was only an invited speaker at the official ceremony in Berlin. Recent research has emphasized that Hitler never referred to the event in his speeches and that Nazi ideology did not mark it as a central date of the Party's history.[23] This deemphasis may perhaps be attributed to the negative press reaction abroad, but it is not an indication of a policy change. Furthermore, it is important to note that non-Nazi organizations, such as the German Students' Association, were eager to preempt the policies of rival Nazi organizations. The film clips of the book burning show that not only brownshirts were engaged in throwing books into the fire, but also members of the fencing fraternities. The central Nazi administration did not hesitate to exploit such rivalries for its own purposes. In this particular case, the competition between the German Students' Association and the Nazi Students' Association may have resulted in a more radical policy than originally planned.

Nazi rule was a polycratic system and its cultural policies were no exception. On the contrary, the interagency rivalry was perhaps more evident here than in any other area. Goebbels' ministry and the Reich Chamber of Culture under his presidency had a rival in the Combat League for German Culture (Kampfbund für deutsche Kultur) under the leadership of Alfred Rosenberg, the author of *Der Mythus des 20. Jahrhunderts* (1930). Founded in 1929, this organization gathered not only Nazi writers, artists, and scholars, but also other nationalists, ultraconservatives, and pan-German racists of various colors. In January 1934, Hitler created a new department for the supervision of the ideological training of the Party, known as the Office for the Supervision of Ideological Training and Education of the Nazi Party, with Rosenberg as its head. This move institutionalized the rivalry between the two top Nazi officials in the area of cultural politics. The interoffice infighting did not neutralize the negative effects of Nazi cultural politics but radicalized them. In many instances, Rosenberg forced Goebbels' hand in cultural policies. Many of the ideologists of the concept of degenerate art were recruited from the Combat League for German Culture rather than from Goebbels' Ministry of Popular Enlightenment and Propaganda, which promoted a pro-modernist policy at the beginning in 1933/34. Likewise, the precursor exhibitions of the 1937 "Degenerate Art" exhibition in Munich were mainly inspired by the ideology of Rosenberg's Combat League.[24]

In 1933, a faction of the Berlin Nazi Students' Association espoused expressionism as *the* German revolutionary art most appropriate to express the revolutionary political movement of the Nazi Party. So did the expressionist poet Gottfried Benn in his article on expressionism of November 1933; he advocated its Nordic or German character and confirmed that Kandinsky, Kokoschka, Klee, Hofer, Belling, Kirchner, and Schmidt-Rotluff were "Aryans."[25] In July 1933, the Berlin Nazi Students' Association sponsored a public panel discussion of modernist art at the University of Berlin and an exhibition, entitled "Thirty German Artists," which featured the works of Barlach, Heckel, Lehmbruck, Macke, Marc, Marcks, Müller, Nolde, Pankok, Pechstein, Rohlfs, and Schmidt-Rottluff. Three days later, the exhibition was closed on orders of Wilhelm Frick, minister of the interior, who had purged the Weimar museum of modernist art in 1930. But a week later the Berlin exhibition was reopened—although without the sponsorship of the Nazi Students' Association. The student leaders responsible for the exhibition were expelled from that group. During the following year, there was another oppositional wave, triggered by an exhibition of Italian Futurist Art in Berlin in March 1934. In the presence of Goebbels, Göring, Hess, and Röhm on the one hand and members of the Bauhaus and Dadaism on the other (Ladislaus Moholy-Nagy, Kurt Schwitters), Gottfried Benn welcomed Filippo Tommaso Marinetti and hailed futurism as the artistic basis of Italian fascism.[26] Art historians have identified a considerable number of events and institutions—such as the art journal *Kunst der Nation*—that promoted a pro-modernist course during the early Nazi period and enjoyed Goebbels' official approval.[27] In April 1933, Goebbels promised that "every genuine artist is free to experiment," and in his speech at the opening of the Reich Chamber of Culture, he declared: "German art needs fresh blood. We live in a young era. Its supporters are young, and their ideas are young. They have nothing more in common with the past, which we have left behind us. The artist who seeks to give expression to this age must also be young and he must create new forms."[28]

In May 1933, Goebbels defined the "new" German art in terms of the "New Objectivity" of the 1920s as "objective" and "unsentimental."[29] When his Propaganda Ministry prepared an exhibition of German art to be sent to the Chicago "Century of Progress" exposition in mid-1933, works of Ernst Barlach and Emil Nolde were included.[30]

These pro-modernist pronouncements caused counterattacks by Alfred Rosenberg and the Combat League for German Culture. Rosenberg portrayed the position of the progressive Berlin faction as a political revolt in the guise of an artistic revolution, while members of the Combat League characterized the events organized by the Berlin Nazi Students' Association as acts of sabotage and an attack on the Party leadership.[31] The *Völkischer Beobachter,* edited by Rosenberg, relentlessly attacked any pro-modernist statement as "cultural Bolshevism" and branded the opposition as a dangerous resistance movement against the new ideal of a racially determined art as prescribed by Hitler and the Nazi Party.

This kind of infighting was typical for the evolvement of many Nazi institutions and policies, and the cultural policies were no exception. A process of "cumulative radicalization," as it has been called by Hans Mommsen,[32] also can be observed in the realm of cultural politics. This radicalization occurred whenever the various competing Nazi agencies fought for positions of power within the system. But the "cumulative radicalization" of the cultural politics was mainly due to Hitler's intervention and not the result of the interaction of various agencies. The balance of power between Goebbels and Rosenberg was controlled by Hitler's firm leadership in matters of cultural politics between 1933 and 1939.

Although Nazi cultural politics provide evidence that "the Nazi regime was anything but monolithic,"[33] and was even chaotic at times, the direction of Hitler's real intentions emerges very clearly. The functionalist or structuralist interpretation finds its most legitimate usage in the initial phases of implementation of cultural policy. But the problem of interpretation cannot be solved by a synthesis between the intentionalist and functionalist approach.[34] The evidence shows that the functionalist interpretation fails in its application to long-term developments.

At the beginning of his regime, Hitler was relatively ambiguous in his pronouncements on art. His first public statement on art in 1933 seemed to appease both the Goebbels and Rosenberg factions. He condemned modernist art, but asserted that "today's tasks require new methods."[35] This statement was considered a rejection of the position of the Combat League for Culture, while the condemnation of modernism was taken as a repudiation of the rebellious Berlin faction. Goebbels' appointment as president of the Reich Chamber of Culture was seen as a step in the right direction toward restraining the dogmatism of Rosenberg and his Combat League for German Culture. By September 1934, however, Hitler defined and set the course of the cultural policies for the years to come. At the annual Nazi Party Rally in Nuremberg, he identified two cultural dangers threatening National Socialism. First, the modernists, whom he described as "the cubists, futurists, and Dadaists," were targeted as "the corrupters of art." There was no place in Germany for modernist art, he claimed, declaring that such "charlatans are mistaken that the creators of the Third Reich are foolish or cowardly enough to let themselves be . . . intimidated by their chatter." He would not tolerate any "cultural assistance to political destruction," and he demanded that art be integrated as part of the Nazi political program. The other cultural danger he perceived were the traditionalists. In this case, Hitler attacked the historicist followers of Rosenberg and the Combat League for German Culture. He ridiculed the representatives of a revival of Teutonic art and ordered such revivalist activities to cease. These policies, outlined in Hitler's speech of 1934, became the official program of Nazi cultural politics, and "there was to be no significant deviation from the direction pointed by Hitler."[36]

Rosenberg and the Combat League for German Culture were prevented from gaining further control in cultural affairs. By 1935, the Combat League was incorporated into the Nazi Labor Front and had lost its significance within the Nazi system, while Rosenberg shifted his activities to other areas. Goebbels, on the other hand, was forced to retrench his more progressive program and to withdraw to a more reactionary approach to culture. His main concern in 1933/34 had been international public relations and opportunism. Goebbels wanted the Nazi state to "appear creative, rather than restrictive," and its cultural policies to be perceived as progressive abroad.[37] At home, his aim was to obtain total control over cultural affairs and to exclude Rosenberg from any position of effective influence in this area. Goebbels made any concession necessary to achieve his goals.

In 1935, a phase of generally increasing radicalization set in. It has been described as the second stage of cultural *Gleichschaltung* (coordination), lasting until the Great German Art Exhibition of July 1937 and the exhibition "Degenerate Art" as its counterpart. In spring 1935, the progressive art journal *Kunst der Nation* was discontinued. After 10 April 1935, art exhibitions required a permit and approval by the president of the Reich Chamber for Visual Arts. In October 1936, the Berlin National Gallery, which had shown expressionist paintings with Goebbels' approval, had to close down its modern art collection. And at the end of November 1936, Goebbels prohibited art criticism.[38]

In spite of Goebbels' early pro-modernist leaning, it would be false to portray him as a defender of the avant-garde. He was more interested in power and control than in the welfare of the arts, literature, and music—be they avant-garde or not. In the end, it was Goebbels who initiated the exhibition of "Degenerate Art" in Munich in July 1937, thus emulating the earlier exhibits of "infamy" *(Schandausstellungen)* inspired or organized by Rosenberg's Combat League. Goebbels' diaries indicate that he made this move in order to consolidate his power base and to make "his contribution," as he said, to Hitler's cultural policies.[39] The propaganda minister did not hesitate to invite two former associates of Rosenberg's Combat League for German Culture to develop the concept for the installation of the exhibit: Wolfgang Willrich and Walter Hansen. Both were known as fanatic enforcers of the Party line in cultural affairs and as notorious informers even by Nazi standards. Even Heinrich Himmler, chief of the German police and the SS, had to restrain Hansen and Willrich in their attacks on artists and writers whom they had accused of "cultural Bolshevism,"[40] while Goebbels probably selected them on the same grounds for purely opportunistic reasons. Willrich had just published a book that appeared to be a perfect expression of Hitler's ideas about the racial regeneration of German art. The book, entitled *Säuberung des Kunsttempels* (Cleansing the temple of art), contained almost verbatim the program for the exhibition of "Degenerate Art." Goebbels also appointed the commission under the chairmanship of Adolf Ziegler to confiscate the works of art from German museums for the exhibition. Finally, he supervised the sales and the destruction of modernist art in 1938.

By August 1937, the definitive Nazi cultural politics were in place and enforced in all areas. An example of this third phase, in which the antimodern and more radical forces prevailed, is the "Degenerate Music" exhibition, which was staged in Düsseldorf in 1938 in conjunction with the national musical festival, the Reichsmusiktage, and prepared by the Reich Chamber for Music under Goebbels' close supervision.[41] Of course, Goebbels secured Hitler's authorization for all these measures. Nothing was done without Hitler's approval. The appropriate legislation was issued in the name of the Führer and chancellor of the Reich. Hitler called 1937 the "turning point" in German art and culture in Munich; at this time his cultural policies were fully implemented. In contrast to documents relating to the Holocaust, Hitler's signature can be found on the major documents relating to the cultural policies.

Even an apparent anomaly as the Kulturbund deutscher Juden, or the Jüdischer Kulturbund (The Jewish Cultural League), which conducted an extensive cultural program in some of the major German cities under the supervision of Goebbels' Propaganda Ministry between 1933 and 1938, can be explained as total racial segregation in terms of Hitler's cultural policies.[42] The fact that Franz Kafka's works were published by Schocken in Germany until 1935 is no argument against the intentionalist interpretation. Goebbels put a stop to Kafka's publication in Nazi Germany after Klaus Mann reminded him in an exile journal *(Die Sammlung)* from Holland that the works of the greatest German-Jewish writer were being published under his very own nose.[43]

In conclusion, modernist art, such as expressionism, could never have functioned within Hitler's cultural policies as some revolutionary factions within the Nazi Party had suggested in 1933/34. In his speech at the opening of the Great German Art Exhibition on 19 July 1937, Hitler reiterated his aversion to modernist art in strong terms and demanded what he called "eternal standards of beauty" for art. "For true art is and remains eternal in its achievements," he said. Yet since the beginning of the nineteenth century, artists and writers had realized that art was no longer to be determined by the timeless standards of classicism, but by actuality or modernity. Styles would change with the accelerated pace of modernity. Hitler was protesting against this pace and the multiplicity of styles, comparing art before National Socialism to fashion: "There was a new fashion almost every year. One year Impressionism, then Futurism, Cubism, but perhaps also Dadaism, etc. . . . National Socialist Germany, however, means to have a *German* art again, and this . . . must and will be an *eternal* art."[44]

For Hitler, art was not determined by history but by race. History was transitoriness, while race provided Hitler with a fixed point of reference within the changes of time. Art was for him an expression of race, "an eternal monument to survive the changes of history."[45] Therefore Hitler rejected terms such as "modern" or "traditional" for art and acknowledged only the standards "eternal" *(ewig)* and "transitory" *(vergänglich)*. He claimed a special relationship between German and classical Greek art, establishing a new type of classicism. Neither medieval art nor expressionism could serve as models, but only classical Greek art as an expression of an "Aryan" race, of a "healthier and stronger" human type. Hitler considered it his task to protect the German race and its art from destruction or, as he put it, "degeneracy." Artists who painted "meadows in blue, the sky in green, and the clouds in yellow," or presented members of the German nation as "cretins," were to be considered as either sick or charlatans.[46] Neither the perpetuation of such artists' hereditary "defects" nor any deliberate deception of the German people was to be tolerated. Therefore Hitler wanted those whom he perceived as dangerous to German art to be segregated, ghettoized, deported, and finally exterminated. His speech of 1937 clearly demonstrates that the cultural politics of the Third Reich implemented his intentions and that they constituted an integral part of his racial policies.

Notes

1. Walter Benjamin, "The Work of Art in the Age of Mechanical Reproduction," in *Illuminations,* ed. Hannah Arendt, trans. Harry Zohn (New York: Schocken, 1969), p. 242.
2. Peter Reichel, *Der schöne Schein des Dritten Reiches: Faszination und Gewalt des Faschismus* (Munich: Hanser, 1991), p. 372.
3. See Michael Burleigh and Wolfgang Wippermann, *The Racial State: Germany 1933-1945* (Cambridge: Cambridge University Press, 1991), pp. 304-7.
4. Heinrich Heine, "Almansor," in *Sämtliche Schriften,* ed. Klaus Briegleb, vol. 1 (München: Hanser, 1968), pp. 284-85.
5. Stephanie Barron, "1937: Modern Art and Politics in Prewar Germany," in *"Degenerate Art": The Fate of the Avant-Garde in Nazi Germany,* ed. Stephanie Barron (Los Angeles: Los Angeles County Museum of Art, 1991), p. 9.
6. See illustrations in Christoph Zuschlag, "An 'Educational Exhibition': The Precursors of *Entartete Kunst* and Its Individual Venues," in Barron, ed., *"Degenerate Art,"* pp. 82-103, and the facsimile of the *"Entartete Kunst"* brochure in ibid., pp. 357-90.
7. Thomas Mann, "[An Eduard Korrodi]," *Gesammelte Werke in dreizehn Bänden,* 2nd rev. ed. (Frankfurt/Main: Fischer, 1974), vol. 11, pp. 788-93.
8. See Sander L. Gilman, *Difference and Pathology: Stereotypes of Sexuality, Race and Madness* (Ithaca, NY: Cornell University Press, 1985), pp. 217-38.

9. Tim Mason, "Intention and Explanation: A Current Controversy about the Interpretation of National Socialism," in *Der "Führerstaat": Mythos und Realität: Studien zur Struktur und Politik des Dritten Reiches* / *The "Führer State": Myth and Reality: Studies on the Structure and Politics of the Third Reich*, eds. Gerhard Hirschfeld and Lothar Kettenacker, intro. Wolfgang J. Mommsen (Stuttgart: Klett-Cotta, 1981), pp. 23-42.
10. Saul Friedländer, introduction to, *Hitler and the Final Solution*, by Gerald Fleming (Berkeley: University of California Press, 1984), p. ix.
11. Klaus Hildebrand, "Monokratie oder Polykratie? Hitlers Herrschaft und das Dritte Reich," in *Der Führerstaat*, ed. Hirschfeld and Kettenacker, p. 75.
12. Friedländer, pp. ix-x.
13. Cited by Eberhard Jäckel, *Hitler's World View: A Blueprint for Power*, trans. Herbert Arnold, foreword Franklin L. Ford (Cambridge, MA: Harvard University Press, 1981), p. 48. See also Werner Maser, *Hitlers Briefe und Notizen: Sein Weltbild in handschriftlichen Dokumenten* (Düsseldorf: Econ, 1973), pp. 223-87.
14. Ernst Deuerlein, ed., *Der Aufstieg der NSDAP in Augenzeugenberichten* (Düsseldorf: Karl Rauch, 1968), p. 111. For a relatively accurate English translation of the NSDAP platform, see Jeremy Noakes and Geoffrey Pridham, eds., *Nazism, 1919-1945: A History in Documents and Eyewitness Accounts*, vol. 1 (New York: Schocken, 1990), p. 16.
15. Adolf Hitler, *Mein Kampf*, trans. Ralph Manheim (Boston: Houghton Mifflin, 1971), p. 231.
16. Barbara Miller Lane, *Architecture and Politics in Germany 1918-1945*, with a new preface by the author (Cambridge, MA: Harvard University Press, 1985), pp. 156-57.
17. Hildegard Brenner, *Die Kunstpolitik des Nationalsozialismus* (Reinbek: Rowohlt, 1963), p. 33.
18. Miller Lane, p. 157. See also Günter Neliba, *Wilhelm Frick: Der Legalist des Unrechtstaates: Eine politische Biographie* (Paderborn: Schöningh, 1992), pp. 57-64.
19. Helmut Heiber, ed., *Goebbels-Reden. Band 1: 1932-1939* (Düsseldorf: Droste, 1971), pp. 108-9.
20. The first blacklists compiled in May 1933 were of a semiofficial nature. There was a recommendation for the "cleansing" of public libraries by the *Börsenblatt für den Deutschen Buchhandel* of 16 May 1933 and a mimeographed blacklist put together by the *Kampfbund für Deutsche Kultur*. The official *Liste des schädlichen und unerwünschten Schrifttums*, edited by the Reich Chamber for Literature, was not circulated until 1935. See Volker Dahm, "Die nationalsozialistische Schrifttumspolitik nach dem 10. Mai 1933," in *10. Mai 1933: Bücherverbrennung in Deutschland und die Folgen*, ed. Ulrich Walberer (Frankfurt/Main: Fischer, 1983), pp. 36-83.

21. Volker Dahm, "Anfänge und Ideologie der Reichskulturkammer: Die 'Berufsgemeinschaft' als Instrument kulturpolitischer Steuerung und sozialer Reglementierung," *Vierteljahrshefte für Zeitgeschichte* 34 (1968): 53-84.
22. On the history of the formation of National Socialist student groups, the emerging role of the National Socialist Student Association, and its seizure of the German Students' Union, see Geoffrey J. Giles, *Students and National Socialism in Germany* (Princeton, NJ: Princeton University Press, 1985), pp. 26-43, 44-72, 129-33. Giles attributes the competition between the German Students' Union and the National Socialist Student Association to the dualist structure of the student leadership, where the German Students' Union was responsible to the state and the National Socialist Student Association to the Nazi Party (129). The German Students' Association kept the book burning campaign secret from the National Socialist Student Association until the last moment (130). See also Hans-Wolfgang Strätz, "Die studentische 'Aktion wider den undeutschen Geist' im Frühjahr 1933," *Vierteljahrshefte für Zeitgeschichte* 16 (1968): 347-72; Anselm Faust, *Der Nationalsozialistische Deutsche Studentenbund: Student und Nationalsozialismus in der Weimarer Republik*, 2 vols. (Düsseldorf: Schwann, 1973); Michael H. Kater, *Studentenschaft und Rechtsradikalismus in Deutschland 1918-1933: Eine sozialgeschichtliche Studie zur Bildungskrise in der Weimarer Republik* (Hamburg: Hoffmann & Campe, 1975).
23. Gerhard Sauder, ed., *Die Bücherverbrennung: Zum 10. Mai 1933*, 2nd ed. (München: Hanser, 1983), pp. 261-68.
24. Zuschlag, pp. 98-101.
25. Gottfried Benn, "Bekenntnis zum Expressionismus [5 November 1933]," in *Gottfried Benn 1886-1956: Eine Ausstellung des Deutschen Literaturarchivs im Schiller-Nationalmuseum Marbach am Neckar*, ed. Ulrich Ott (Marbach: Deutsche Schillergesellschaft, 1986), pp. 216-18.
26. Gottfried Benn, "Gruß an Marinetti [30 March 1934]," in Ott, pp. 223-24; see also pp. 224-26. See also Peter Demetz, *Worte in Freiheit: Der italienische Futurismus und die deutsche literarische Avantgarde 1912-1934* (München: Piper, 1990), pp. 145-51.
27. Stefan Germer, "Kunst der Nation: Zu einem Versuch, die Avantgarde zu nationalisieren," in *Kunst auf Befehl?: Dreiunddreißig bis Fünfundvierzig*, eds. Bazon Brock and Achim Preiß (München: Klinkhardt and Biermann, 1990), pp. 21-40.
28. Heiber, vol. 1, p. 139.
29. Miller Lane, p. 176.
30. See Brenner, pp. 63-86; Miller Lane, pp. 169-84; Elaine S. Hochman, *Architects of Fortune: Mies van der Rohe and the Third Reich* (New York: Fromm International Pub. Corporation, 1990), pp. 159-74.

31. Hochman, p. 167.
32. Hans Mommsen, untitled paper, in *Totalitarismus und Faschismus: Eine wissenschaftliche Begriffskontroverse: Kolloquium im Institut für Zeitgeschichte am 24. November 1978,* ed. Institut für Zeitgeschichte (München: Oldenbourg, 1980), p. 25; Hans Mommsen, "Hitlers Stellung im nationalsozialistischen Herrschaftssystem," in *Der "Führerstaat,"* eds. Hirschfeld and Kettenacker, pp. 56-66.
33. Saul Friedländer, "From Anti-Semitism to Extermination: A Historiographical Study of Nazi Policies toward the Jews and an Essay in Interpretation," in *Unanswered Questions: Nazi Germany and the Genocide of the Jews,* ed. François Furet (New York: Schocken, 1989), p. 19.
34. Ibid., p. 18.
35. Miller Lane, p. 180.
36. Henry Grosshans, *Hitler and the Artists* (New York: Holmes & Meier, 1983), pp. 74 f.
37. Miller Lane, p. 177.
38. Germer, in *Kunst auf Befehl,* ed. Brock and Preiß, pp. 39-40.
39. Elke Fröhlich, ed., *Die Tagebücher von Joseph Goebbels: Sämtliche Fragmente,* vol. 3 (München, New York: Saur, 1987), p. 198. See also pp. 189-90, 192, 198, 211, 215, 325, 401, 403, 445, 449, 547, 561. For a discussion of Goebbels' role in organizing the exhibition of "Degenerate Art," see Klaus Backes, *Hitler und die bildenden Künste: Kulturverständnis und Kulturpolitik im Dritten Reich* (Köln: Dumont, 1988), pp. 73-77; Ralf Georg Reuth, *Goebbels* (München: Piper, 1990), pp. 366-69.
40. Wolfgang Willrich was a painter in the "realist" style promoted by the Nazis. His book *Säuberung des Kunsttempels: Eine kunstpolitische Kampfschrift zur Gesundung deutscher Kunst im Geiste nordischer Art* (München: J. F. Lehmann, 1937) represented an attack on all former expressionists still involved in German cultural life, as, for example, Hanns Johst, a former expressionist and contributor to *Die Aktion,* now president of the Reich Chamber for Literature. Johst had been offering Benn protection from Party hard-liners. Willrich wanted to get rid of Johst just as much as he was after Benn and others. See Glenn R. Cuomo, "Purging an 'Art Bolshevist': The Persecution of Gottfried Benn in the Years 1933-38," *German Studies Review* 9 (1986): 85-105. Ott includes the correspondence exchanged between Hanns Johst and Benn, and Johst and Himmler regarding Willrich's attack on Benn (240-45).
41. The *Entartete Musik* ("Degenerate Music") exhibition presented attacks on American jazz, the "musical Bolshevist" *Threepenny Opera* of Kurt Weill, the jazz opera *Jonny spielt auf* of Ernst Krenek, and the 12-tone·music of Arnold Schoenberg as alien, racially degenerate elements to be purged from German

music. See Fred K. Prieberg, *Musik im NS-Staat* (Frankfurt/Main: Fischer, 1982); Michael Meyer, *The Politics of Music in the Third Reich* (New York: Lang, 1990), and "A Musical Facade for the Third Reich," in *"Degenerate Art,"* ed. Barron, pp. 171-83.

42. See Henryk M. Broder and Eike Geisel, eds., *Premiere und Pogrom: Der Jüdische Kulturbund 1933-1941: Texte und Bilder* (Berlin: Siedler, 1992).
43. Klaus Mann, "Dank für die Kafka-Ausgabe," *Die Sammlung: Literarische Monatsschrift* 2, No. 11 (July 1935): 664. See Volker Dahm, *Das jüdische Buch im Dritten Reich*, vol. 2 (Frankfurt/Main: Buchhändler-Vereinigung, 1982), pp. 558-67.
44. Adolf Hitler, "Rede zur Eröffnung der 'Großen Deutschen Kunstausstellung' 1937," in *Die "Kunststadt" München 1937: Nationalsozialismus und "Entartete Kunst,"* ed. Peter-Klaus Schuster, 3rd ed. (München: Prestel, 1988), p. 244.
45. Ibid., p. 246.
46. Ibid., p. 250.

2

Cultural Eugenics: Social Policy, Economic Reform, and the Purge of Jews from German Cultural Life

Alan E. Steinweis

The persecution of Jews by the Nazi regime has generated an immense, and constantly growing, body of scholarship.[1] Recent years have also seen a spate of books and articles on the theme of professionalization in German history,[2] as well as increased attention to the Nazi regime's approach to social welfare concerns.[3] Meanwhile, the complex relationship between the arts and National Socialism has also come under increasing scholarly scrutiny. In this chapter I hope to bring together these often disparate trends in recent historiography by examining the policies of the National Socialist regime in the areas of professionalization and social policy in the artistic-cultural sphere, and clarifying how those policies intersected with the purge of Jews and other persons deemed undesirable by National Socialism. An analysis of these issues will not only shed light on the cultural priorities of the Nazi regime, it will also enhance our understanding how German artists made the transition from democracy to dictatorship.

In September 1933, the Nazi-controlled cabinet of the German Reich, acting on the initiative of the propaganda minister, Joseph Goebbels, created the Reich Chamber of Culture (Reichskulturkammer). Under Goebbels' supervision, the chamber served until 1945 as the exclusive, officially recognized, compulsory professional corporation for the arts, entertainment, and the media. Divided into subchambers for music, theater, the visual arts, literature, film, radio,[4] and the press, this organization encompassed several hundred thousand professionals, influenced the activities of millions of amateur artists and musicians, and made a profound impact on millions of Germans who in one way or another were consumers of culture.

Goebbels designed the chamber system according to corporatist principles that had attained broad currency in interwar Germany (indeed in interwar Europe) during the crisis of liberalism. The occupational interests of German artists were now to be served by a single state-acknowledged mass organization, rather than by a multiplicity of interest groups. Hence, the numerous cultural unions and occupational associations active in the Weimar era were forcibly integrated into the new chamber system during 1933 and 1934. The fractiousness and adversarialism characteristic of these old organizations had supposedly reflected the decay of the liberal order; they were now forced to merge into an "organic whole." German artists were to become an "estate" *(Stand)*.

The chamber's stated mission was to "promote German culture on behalf of the German Volk and Reich" and to "regulate the economic and social affairs of the culture professions."[5] The strategy pursued was two-pronged: It entailed both the "promotion of creative and productive forces" as well as the "eradication of unworthy and dangerous elements."[6] In essence, this strategy constituted a form of cultural eugenics, simultaneously nourishing the "healthy" and weeding out the "unhealthy." Most research on the chamber relates to the latter function, which assumed the form of massive racial-political purges and an intrusive artistic-intellectual censorship.[7] However, the economic, social, and professional dimensions of chamber policy—the so-called promotion of ideologically acceptable persons, aesthetics, and values—has received little attention from historians.[8] In the areas of work creation, professional education, certification, wage and benefits policy, and social insurance, the chamber system formulated numerous measures designed to alleviate poverty, unemployment, and underemployment among its members.

The creation of the Chamber of Culture arose from the convergence of several factors. First, the National Socialist regime required a mechanism to regulate access to participation in the nation's cultural life. The chamber's membership guidelines, as they evolved up to the outbreak of war in 1939, allowed it to decline membership to Jews, Communists, homosexuals, Gypsies, and members of other "racial," political, or social groups condemned to ostracism by the dictates of Nazi ideology. Yet it would be simplistic to conceive of the chamber exclusively as a tool employed by a totalitarian state to enforce a sinister ideology and to terrorize powerless artists and entertainers. Rather, the creation of the chamber also reflected an attempt by the new regime to ingratiate itself with artists and entertainers who for years had been calling for a major overhaul in the structure of their professions.

Indeed, the professional, economic, and social agenda of the chamber during most of its 11-year existence stemmed from a widely accepted diagnosis of the disastrous financial conditions prevailing in the German cultural establishment during the Weimar Republic. The Depression and resultant government austerity measures had severely undermined the financial position of artists. This is not to imply, however, that the situation had been entirely satisfactory during the so-called Golden Years of the Weimar Republic before 1930. On the contrary, the Depression had merely exacerbated a bad situation, reinforcing a commonly held conviction that fundamental structural reform of the arts would be necessary.

Many experts attributed the troubles of German artists to the liberal structure of German cultural life.[9] They claimed that the cultural marketplace was simply too free for its own good. The problem ostensibly stemmed from inadequate provisions for cultural activity in the Reich Commercial Code and from the historical failure of artists to professionalize as aggressively as did members of other occupations. Fundamental to this critique was the absence of a central authority capable of enforcing an equitable, socially responsible distribution of income. Left to the vicissitudes of a free market, theaters, orchestras, and other cultural institutions competed among themselves for talent, resulting in a "star system"—the polarization of artists into a large proletariat and a small cadre of high-salaried stars. The system's inability to prevent the unqualified and the untalented from entering the employment pool further aggravated the situation. The unqualified dilettantes who populated the cultural proletariat kept salaries and wages low even for the genuinely talented and often deprived truly deserving artists of work altogether. A further structural deficiency exacerbated the problems connected with this so-called dilettantism: The arts lacked central leadership in matters of education and training. It was often alleged that inferior academies, poor teachers, and charlatans were churning out too many inferior artists and performers.[10]

Unsatisfactory professional structures were also widely blamed for the absence of an adequate pension system for artists. The fact that thousands of artists and performers lived in indigent retirement did not speak well for Germany's reputation as a land of culture. Experts on the economics of culture had attributed the absence of a satisfactory pension system to two factors: the decentralized structure of the art profession, and the highly skewed distribution of wealth among artists. Widespread poverty, on the one hand, and the inability to compel subscription by the financially comfortable, on the other, had combined to prevent the formation of a pension insurance pool that could pass actuarial muster. Furthermore, theater people and musicians employed by public companies and orchestras, who generally were well paid, had already been integrated into local or provincial pension systems for civil servants. Support from philanthropic foundations, such as the Schiller Foundation, made old age more comfortable for some who fell through this system's numerous cracks, but philanthropy could hardly begin to address the broader, systemic problem.[11] Especially after the onset of the Depression, Nazis and others on the right wing tended increasingly to merge the foregoing structural analysis with xenophobic, anti-Semitic views. They bemoaned the supposed flooding of the German cultural marketplace with Jews and foreigners. Their critique was internally coherent, in that it perceived artistic-cultural renewal and structural deliberalization as two sides of the same coin.[12] "Non-Germans" were depriving "Germans" of jobs, and the "alien" influences on German culture were scaring audiences away from galleries, theaters, and concert halls.[13] A genuine economic crisis facing the German art world was explained in terms that made sense to Germans who eschewed cultural modernism and who were predisposed to subscribe to notions about Jewish conspiracies.

Hence, from the Nazi point of view, the Chamber of Culture was designed to address a set of interrelated cultural and structural problems. In 1933, Nazis and their sympathizers could doubly applaud the advent of the Chamber of Culture, first, as a blow against economic liberalism, and second, as a mechanism for ridding the German theater of the "Jewish-Bolshevist virus," which supposedly thrived in liberal host environments. Many who did not subscribe to the Nazi assessment of the situation in its entirety nevertheless sympathized with the need for an activist official policy toward the arts. Richard Strauss, then the greatest living luminary of German music, exemplified this attitude. After accepting the presidency of the new Chamber of Music, he publicly praised the Nazi regime, claiming that "the new Germany is unwilling to let artistic matters slide, as it did more or less up to now."[14] The point here is not that Strauss and many others who looked to the state for solutions to the financial-structural crisis of German culture were Nazis; most were not. Rather, a significant common ground existed between the Nazi movement and non-Nazi advocates of structural reform of German cultural life. Both favored centralization, deliberalization, and professionalization of the arts. During the crucial founding phase of Nazi rule, this common ground proved sufficient to win legitimacy (if not popularity) for the regime in broad segments of the German cultural establishment. Furthermore, by actively addressing several of the major financial and structural problems plaguing German culture, the regime attenuated much of the psychological distress generated by political intervention, censorship, and purges.

Nevertheless, the chamber system contained the roots of a fundamental tension between party-state officialdom and the cultural establishment. Who would formulate and supervise the reform process? Where did political authority end and professional authority begin? How could the totalitarian impulse of Nazi leaders be reconciled with the corporatist aspirations of artists?

The authoritarian structure of the Chamber of Culture and its subchambers, based on the National Socialist "leadership principle" *(Führerprinzip)*,[15] enabled the regime to regulate all aspects of professional existence in the cultural sphere. As a Chamber of Culture legal expert put it, the chamber system forced artists into a "compulsory working relationship with the state leadership."[16] In practice, the application of this principle led to a fundamental distinction between two parallel levels of activity in the cultural sphere. The concept "culture-political" *(kulturpolitisch)* applied to the substantive qualities of art and performance and to the political and "racial" background of artistic personnel. In contrast, the concept "culture-professional" *(kulturberuflich)* pertained to the technical, organizational, and financial aspects of cultural life. Generally speaking, officials in the Ministry of Propaganda, as well as their political agents in the chamber central offices, most of whom possessed solid National Socialist credentials, closely supervised developments in the "culture-political" realm. At the same time, they entrusted matters in the "culture-professional" area to experts with roots in the art community, many of whom had served in artistic unions and occupational associations prior to 1933.

The cultural purge and reform of the economics of cultural life must be seen as inextricably interconnected dimensions of a single process, although for understandable reasons of explanatory clarity they often have been presented as entirely separate chronologies. The policies intersected at several points. In the early years of the Nazi regime, preoccupation with economic issues among the rank-and-file of professional artists helped give the regime a free hand to move forward on the purge front against a minority of Jewish and other ideologically objectionable artists, the removal of whom would create new opportunities. By the time that the Nazi regime had halted progress, or even reversed itself, in key areas of culture-economic reform, the "purification" measures had already eliminated the vast majority of Jewish artists from the German cultural "estate." Temporarily exempted from the purge were a small number of Jews, and others who by virtue of partial Jewish ancestry or marriage to Jews were regarded as "tainted," whose continued participation in German cultural life was seen as economically necessary. In one area where the regime's commitment to reform was consistent—improving the social safety net for retired artists—Jews were excluded from the outset.

Meanwhile, after 30 January 1933, with the backing of a ruthless regime, reformers moved aggressively on the culture-professional front, instituting an overhaul of occupational rules, procedures, and structures that had eluded them in the Weimar era. They were confident that the chamber would accomplish in authoritarian fashion what the sloppy, fractious system of occupational representation of the liberal-democratic Weimar period had proved unable to achieve. The subsidiary chambers of the Chamber of Culture promulgated numerous orders in attempting to establish meaningful boundaries of the cultural "estate."[17] The Music Chamber imposed rigid restrictions on public performances by amateur and avocational musicians,[18] erected new barriers in the way of foreign musicians who wished to perform in Germany,[19] and implemented a comprehensive system for testing aptitude among existing professional musicians. The other individual chambers took similar steps, the specific stipulations being determined by the unique structural characteristics of each artistic occupation.

Concurrent to such measures, preparatory steps were taken for the massive purge of political opponents, Jews, and other so-called non-Aryans. Artists connected in one way or another to the Communist movement were the first to be rounded up, summarily incarcerated in prisons or concentration camps, and, in a few cases, killed. All of this was made possible by the emergency decree promulgated by President Paul von Hindenburg in the wake of the Reichstag fire. The sequence of Nazi measures against artists, in which the assault on Communists preceded that against Jews, ought not be interpreted as proof of a recently reiterated view that anticommunism was a higher Nazi priority than anti-Semitism, and that the latter was merely an outgrowth of the former.[20] Rather, the sequence was simply the product of legal contingencies and of what was administratively and politically possible in 1933. Later in the 1930s, the regime extended clemency to contrite ex-Communists at precisely the time that it was intensifying restrictions against Jews.[21]

In the spring of 1933, the new Nazi Civil Service Law had caused the dismissal of many Jewish artists and performers who held civil service positions—personnel employed by state or municipally owned theaters, orchestras, museums, and radio broadcasters. Not until the creation of the Chamber of Culture later in 1933 did the regime have at its disposal a means for purging self-employed Jewish artists or those employed by nongovernment entities. Goebbels was extremely anxious to get rid of these Jews as well, and in February 1934, he announced his intention to do so.[22] This purge did not take place until the middle months of 1935, however, in part because the process of establishing ancestry through a system of questionnaires and ancestry documents was inherently time-consuming, but primarily because the economics minister, Hjalmar Schacht, convinced Hitler to postpone a potentially economically disruptive occupational purification. During this brief hiatus, many Jewish artists suffered harassment at the hands of the Chamber of Culture and other government officials. Once the 1935 purge went forward, the only Jews to receive special dispensations from Goebbels were those whose activities generated significant amounts of foreign currency and those upon whom a large number of "Aryan" employees depended for their jobs. With only a very tiny number of exceptions, these special dispensations had been rescinded by the outbreak of war in September 1939.

As the persecution of Jewish artists intensified, the regime fundamentally changed its attitude toward structural reform of the arts. Beginning in the mid-1930s, pressure from the Propaganda Ministry forced the chambers to relax many of their restrictions on amateur activity. Organizations such as the Hitler Youth and the Storm Troops (SA) complained that Music Chamber guidelines impinged on their freedom to conduct marches and rallies at which music formed a central component. Similarly, amateur village theater ensembles in the German province complained that regulations promulgated by the Theater Chamber inhibited participatory events that had long been woven into the fabric of local culture.[23] Indeed, by the late 1930s, the culture chambers had been forced to dismantle or water down many of the professionalization measures that they had instituted earlier, a retreat that engendered tremendous bitterness among professional artists who felt betrayed by a regime that had promised them unprecedented protection.[24]

Goebbels himself was largely responsible for the backtracking. The propaganda minister insisted on eliminating, or at least holding to a minimum, what he regarded as artificial distinctions between "professional" and "amateur." If, as Goebbels contended, it was the aim of the Nazi regime "once again to place the artist in a direct union with the driving forces of modern German development, and thereby to restore that close touch with the German people that the artist, much to his own detriment, has lost," then aptitude exams, certification guidelines, indeed the entire range of measures designed to circumscribe a cultural "estate," were counterproductive. Pointing to the difficulties inherent in distinguishing years in advance between "the future dilettante" and "the future genius," Goebbels asserted that mistakes, "shortsightedness, envy, or jealousy" may "all too easily exclude a future genius from the chamber."[25] It should be emphasized in this context that one of the profound personal disappointments in Hitler's youth had been his rejection by the Art Academy in Vienna on the basis of a formal assessment of artistic aptitude. Although we have no direct evidence that Hitler determined Goebbels' position on this question, it is more than likely that the two men discussed the issue at length. Goebbels' personal diaries are replete with instances of detailed discussions between the two men concerning technical aspects of cultural policy, ranging from retirement pensions for artists to the fates of individual German artists who had committed "racial disgrace" through sexual relations with "non-Aryans."[26]

In contrast to his reversals on professionalization, Goebbels remained true to his word when it came to extending and improving the pension system for artists.[27] The minister's diaries reflect the sincerity of this effort, even if Goebbels was simultaneously motivated by a more cynical desire to enhance his and the regime's legitimacy in cultural circles.[28] Moreover, the diaries also suggest that this project had Hitler's backing.[29] Some contextualization is necessary here. Like the German Empire and the Weimar Republic that preceded it, as well as the Federal and German Democratic republics that followed it, the Nazi regime presided over an expansion of the German system of social security. In this particular respect the Third Reich must be understood as part of the longer trajectory of German history in the age of industrial society. From the perspective of Nazi leaders, social security programs were consistent with the populist paternalism of National Socialist ideology, alleviating the inflationary pressures generated by full employment by channeling personal income into forced savings, in the process building financial reserves that could be tapped by the Reich to finance a host of state construction projects.[30]

While much of the detailed work on the pension system was carried out by cultural functionaries with experience in such matters, Goebbels devoted considerable energy to overcoming bureaucratic obstacles, especially those erected by what he called the "little philistines in the Finance Ministry."[31] The final product fell far short of expectations, however. By the outbreak of war, universal pensions had been extended only to orchestral musicians and theater professionals. After the advent of hostilities in September 1939, more urgent matters took precedence. Despite the modest dimensions of the pension scheme actually put in place, Goebbels felt little compunction in touting it as a "cultural deed" unique in world history.[32]

It is in the activity of Goebbels that the intersection between the economic reform of German cultural life and the purge of "undesirable" artists is most obviously visible. As we have seen, Goebbels intervened with profound results both to hinder professionalization and to promote pensions. At the same time, he kept close watch on the so-called process of cultural "de-Jewification." Whenever pragmatic obstacles to the purge of Jews and those "tainted" by Judaism arose within the chambers, Goebbels maintained constant pressure to accelerate the process.[33]

Although after September 1939 wartime conditions created a manpower drain in the cultural world, the regime was loathe to address shortages of entertainers through compromise in the area of de-Jewification. Indeed, the war brought about an expansion and intensification of the cultural purge. Germans who had been convicted repeatedly of violating Paragraph 175 of the Reich Criminal Code, which banned homosexual relations among men, had already been expelled from the cultural chambers before the war; after the onset of hostilities, the chambers showed even less tolerance for homosexuality. Concurrently, the chambers actively participated in the cultural Germanization of Polish and Czech territories that had been annexed by the German Reich. Persons of Polish ancestry were subjected to an especially thoroughgoing purge in order both to purify cultural institutions of "inferior Slavs" and to create new job opportunities for unemployed and underemployed Germans. Czechs, who ranked somewhat higher on the Nazi racial scale, were treated less harshly.[34] In the latter stages of the war, the chambers stepped up expulsions of German artists suspected of defeatism, which in many cases amounted to little more than a casual pessimistic comment to an acquaintance.

In his monumental study of the German bureaucracy that launched and executed the so-called Final Solution of the Jewish question, Raul Hilberg has shown how participation in the process of disenfranchisement and genocide extended to almost every agency of the German state.[35] We have already seen how the cultural chambers deprived German-Jewish artists of their livelihoods. During the war, the chambers went one step further, facilitating the transfer of dwellings from Jews to "Aryan" artists who had been bombed out of their homes or apartments and supervising the "Aryanization" of art objects from Jews prior to deportation. These practices embodied cultural eugenics in a particularly direct form.

How did the majority of German artists respond to such measures? The surviving documentation contains very few references to objections, protests, or surreptitious attempts to undermine or circumvent the purge. And it should be emphasized that the sources are hardly silent when it comes to the opinions of German artists about matters such as chamber economic regulation. German artists complained frequently about the inadequacy of chamber professionalization measures, burdensome paperwork, and insufficient job opportunities. Dissatisfaction over these and other issues was routinely cited in reports to Berlin by regional and local chamber officials, as well as in periodic domestic morale reports compiled by the Security Service (SD). Officials who were in charge of formulating and enforcing racial policy certainly would have been alert to dissent and would have discussed its manifestations. Yet the historian immersed in the documentation of the cultural chambers cannot help but notice the deafening silence with which German artists responded to the purge of thousands of their colleagues.

In explaining this response, the economic situation of the German art world must be considered. National Socialism had come to power promising to implement bold measures to end the crisis of unemployment. In the Great Depression, German artists suffered from levels of unemployment and underemployment surpassing that afflicting industrial workers. The advent of the Nazi regime presented an opportunity. For two years after the creation of the Chamber of Culture, the regime seemed to be living up to the promise of professional reform in the arts. The most comprehensive purge of Jews from German cultural life coincided with this phase of economic reform. Although Goebbels later forced the chambers to rescind or scale back professionalization efforts, the overall improvement in the German economy created new employment opportunities in the cultural fields and led to a general increase in the incomes of artists.[36] Simultaneously, Goebbels promoted the expansion of the pension system.

While a number of anti-Semitic and otherwise ideologically motivated artists undoubtedly welcomed the purges as a culturally and demographically positive measure, it would not be fair to conclude that the majority of German artists actively welcomed them. German artists, in effect, accepted a Faustian trade-off, which held out the promise of enhanced material security to the majority at the expense of the civil rights of a minority. More than a few took advantage of the occupational mobility created by widespread dismissals.[37]

A further factor that must be considered in assessing the response of the majority is the actual fate of Jewish artists who were purged from the chambers. This factor has very often been overlooked by scholars of Nazi cultural policy, for once the Jews had been removed from the German cultural mainstream they moved into a field of activity the study of which has been primarily the domain of Jewish historiography. The legal and occupational disenfranchisement of Jews in the 1930s was widely understood to be a reversal of the emancipation process of previous decades, rather than a prelude to mass murder. Partly on their own initiative, and partly in response to pressures from the Nazi regime, German Jews reverted to a tradition of communal self-help that had been the norm prior to emancipation. A distinctly Jewish social and cultural infrastructure had survived assimilation and now, in the face of Nazi persecution, could be expanded and relied upon for physical and spiritual survival.

Jewish cultural activity in Nazi Germany was concentrated in a Jewish Cultural League.[38] This organization was founded in 1933, after the Civil Service Law had led to the dismissal of many Jewish theater performers and orchestral musicians. The league was to serve as a Jewish cultural ghetto; it would produce performances by Jewish artists for Jewish audiences. The ranks of Jewish artists who depended on the league beginning in 1933 swelled considerably once the Chamber of Culture initiated its purge in 1935.

By no means could the league provide work for the thousands of Jewish artists who had been cut off from the mainstream of German culture. But while the economic reality of Jewish artists was catastrophic, the very existence of an organized, segregated Jewish culture may well have facilitated the psychological accommodation of some non-Jewish artists to the purge of their Jewish colleagues. After all, it was not to concentration camps or to literal ghettos that Jewish artists were being sent in 1933 and 1935. Years later, when such a fate did indeed befall German Jews, most Germans had other matters foremost in mind, and it had become far riskier to criticize the regime.

In the final analysis, the majority of German artists responded to Nazi anti-Jewish policies much as did the majority of other Germans. A combination of indifference, fear, and opportunism led most to look away, leaving active persecution to a small minority and active opposition to an even smaller one. The important question to ask is whether more should have been expected of artists than of other Germans whose daily preoccupations were more mundane. The answer, if there is one, cannot be provided here.

Notes

1. The arguments made in this chapter summarize themes developed more fully in my recent book: Alan E. Steinweis, *Art, Ideology, and Economics in Nazi Germany: The Reich Chambers of Music, Theater and the Visual Arts* (Chapel Hill: University of North Carolina Press, 1993).
2. See especially Konrad H. Jarausch, *The Unfree Professions: German Lawyers, Teachers, and Engineers, 1900-1959* (Oxford: Oxford University Press, 1990), and Konrad H. Jarausch and Geoffrey Cocks, eds., *German Professions 1800-1950* (New York: Oxford University Press, 1990).
3. Two pathbreaking studies are Rainer Zitelmann, *Hitler: Selbstverständnis eines Revolutionärs* (Stuttgart: Klett-Cotta, 1987), and Ronald Smelser, *Robert Ley: Hitler's Labor Front Leader* (Oxford: Berg, 1989).
4. The Radio Chamber was dissolved in 1939. As most German radio employees had a single employer, the Reichsrundfunkgesellschaft, a professional organization for purposes of integration, representation, and control, was ultimately deemed superfluous.
5. "Erste Verordnung zur Durchführung des Reichskulturkammergesetzes," 1 November 1933, Par. 3, in *Das Recht der Reichskulturkammer: Sammlung der für den Kulturstand geltenden Gesetze und Verordnungen, der amtlichen Anordnungen und Bekanntmachungen der Reichskulturkammer und ihrer*

Einzelkammern, 1st ed., 5 vols., ed. Karl-Friedrich Schrieber (Berlin: Junker und Dünnhaupt, 1935-37) (hereafter cited as *RdRKK*-1); 2nd ed., 2 vols., eds. Karl-Friedrich Schrieber, Alfred Metten, and Herbert Collatz (Berlin: de Gruyter, 1943) (hereafter cited as *RdRKK*-2); 1st ed., vol. 1, pp. 2-8.

6. Hans Pfundtner and Reinhard Neubert, eds., *Das neue Deutsche Reichsrecht: Ergänzbare Sammlung des geltenden Rechts seit dem Ermächtigungsgesetz mit Erläuterungen* (Berlin: Spaeth und Linde, 1933 and periodic updates). The commentary on the Chamber of Culture is found under the heading I. Öffentliches Recht, d) Kulturwesen, 6: Reichskulturkammergesetz.

7. The purge of Jews from the Literature Chamber has been the most thoroughly examined. See Volker Dahm, "Das jüdische Buch im Dritten Reich. Teil 1: Die Ausschaltung der jüdischen Autoren, Verleger und Buchhändler," *Archiv für Geschichte des Buchwesens* 20 (1979): 1-300.

8. See Volker Dahm's appeal for closer focus on cultural policy in "Die Reichskulturkammer als Instrument kulturpolitischer Steuerung und sozialer Reglementierung," *Vierteljahrshefte für Zeitgeschichte* 34 (January 1986): 53-84. The standard works on Nazi cultural policy tend to treat the Chamber of Culture either superficially or anecdotally. See, e.g., Fred K. Prieberg, *Musik im NS-Staat* (Frankfurt: Fischer, 1982); Bogusław Drewniak, *Das Theater im NS-Staat* (Düsseldorf: Droste, 1983); Otto Thomae, ed., *Die Propaganda-Maschinerie: Bildende Künste und Öffentlichkeitsarbeit im Dritten Reich: Eine Dokumentation* (Berlin: Gebr. Mann, 1978); and the four-volume document series edited by Joseph Wulf, *Kunst und Kultur im Dritten Reich* (Gütersloh: Sigbert Mohn, 1963-64; Frankfurt: Ullstein, 1983), which contains individual volumes on the arts, literature, music, and theater and film. A more sophisticated treatment can be found in Michael Kater, *Different Drummers: Jazz in the Culture of Nazi Germany* (New York: Oxford University Press, 1992).

9. For a more thorough discussion of this critique see Steinweis, *Art,* chap. 1.

10. Dr. Wagner-Roemmich, "Durch Theaterkrisen zur Theaterreform," *Der Neue Weg* (hereafter cited as *DNW*), 1 March 1930; "Theaternot," *DNW,* 1 April 1930; "Dilettanterei," *DNW,* 1 February 1931; "Bochum und die Theaterplanwirtschaft," *DNW,* 16 September 1931; Heinz Dietrich Kenter, "Neuregelung der deutschen Schauspielschulen," *Deutsche Kultur-Wacht* (hereafter cited as *DKW*), 23 September 1933. Many of these were later synthesized in Fritz Herterich, *Theater und Volkswirtschaft* (München: Duncker und Humblot, 1937).

11. "Selbsthilfe der Schauspieler," *DNW,* 16 March 1930; "Die Altersversorgung ist gesichert!" *Deutsches Bühnen Jahrbuch,* 1938, pp. 1-10, and "Vermerk" by Reimer, 27 July 1944, Bundesarchiv Koblenz (hereafter cited as BAK),

Bestand R 55 (Reichsministerium für Volksaufklärung und Propaganda; hereafter cited as RMfVuP), file 125.
12. Franz Lawaczeck, "Kultur und Wirtschaft," *DKW,* 1933, Heft 1, no date (probably January); Hans Scheller, "Deutsches Theater," *DKW,* 1933, Heft 5, no date (probably February); Hans Esdras Mutzenbecher, "Rede an die deutschen Bühnenvorstände," *DKW,* 1933, Heft 12, no date (June or July); Dr. Schroeder, "Ein Beitrag zur Reform des deutschen Theaters," *DKW,* 8 July 1933; Friedrich Billerbeck-Gentz, "Die Ausschaltung des Liberalismus am deutschen Theater," *DKW,* 28 October 1933. Kampfbund calls for the purging of foreigners were loud and very frequent. For a typical example see "Kampf der Überfremdung," *DKW,* 1932, Heft 1, no date (probably October or November).
13. See, e.g., Hans Hinkel, "Deutsches Kunstschaffen," *Freiheitskampf,* 27 May 1934, in BAK/R 56 I (Reichskulturkammer-Zentrale)/71.
14. Richard Strauss, speech of 13 February 1934 at the first meeting of the Reich Music Chamber, excerpted in Joseph Wulf, *Musik im Dritten Reich: Eine Dokumentation* (Frankfurt/Main: Ullstein, 1983), p. 195; Wulf mistakenly assigns the date 13 February 1933 to this speech.
15. The president of the Chamber of Culture (Goebbels) appointed all presidents of the subchambers and also reserved the right to veto all decisions made by the subchambers. "Erste Verordnung zur Durchführung des Reichskulturkammergesetzes," 1 November 1933, *RdRKK*-1, vol. 1, pp. 2-8, paragraphs 13, 22.
16. Hans Schmidt-Leonhardt, "Die Reichskulturkammer," part 2, section 2, pp. 7-8, in *Grundlagen, Aufbau und Wirtschaftsordnung des nationalsozialistischen Staates,* 3 vols., ed. Fritz Müssigbrodt. Vol. 1: *Die weltanschaulichen Grundlagen des nationalsozialistischen Staates* (Berlin: Spaeth und Linde, 1938).
17. Most of these orders can be found in *RdRKK*-1, vol. 1. Notably, the term "protection" (*Schutz)* was employed in the titles of the orders issued by the Visual Arts Chamber (thus, for example, "Erste Anordnung betr. Schutz des Berufes und die Berufsausübung der Gartengestalter," 1 September 1934, *RdRKK*-1, vol. 1, pp. 143-45). More than a manifestation of sarcastic totalitarian obfuscation—note the use of the word *Schutz* in the Reichstag Fire Decree of February 1933—the employment of this term in this context connoted a belief in the positive value of state regulation that was at the heart of the chamber concept.
18. Reichskartell der deutschen Musikerschaft to RMfVuP, 24 July 1933, BAK: R 55/1141; "Bekanntmachung der Vereinbarung zwischen der Reichsmusikkammer und der Reichsleitung des Arbeitsdienstes," 1 March 1934, *RdRKK*-1, vol. 1, pp. 89-90; "Richtlinien für das Verhältnis der

Berufsmusiker zu den Laien-Instrumentalvereinen," 7 May 1934, *RdRKK*-1, vol. 1, pp. 92-93; "Richtlinien für die Mitglieder der Fachschaft Volksmusik," 28 October 1935, *RdRKK*-1, vol. 3, pp. 45-47; "Verfügung zu Par. 6 der III. Anordnung zur Befriedung der wirtschaftlichen Verhältnisse im deutschen Musikleben," 21 May 1937, *RdRKK*-2, Reichmusikkammer, II, 7; "Zweite Anordnung zur Befriedung der wirtschaftlichen Verhältnisse im deutschen Musikleben," 26 April 1934, *RdRKK*-1, vol. 1, pp. 91-92.

19. Reichsmusikkammer (hereafter cited as RMK) to RMfVuP, 25 April 1934, BAK: R 55/1183; RMK, Amt f. Chorwesen u. Volksmusik, to RMfVuP, 12 July 1935, BAK: R 55/1186; RMK to RMfVuP, 1 August 1935, BAK: R 55/1186; RMK to RMfVuP, 27 May 1935, RMfVuP to RMK, 3 June 1935, RMK to RMfVuP, 2 August 1935, and RMfVuP to Heller, 7 August 1935, all in BAK: R 55/1185.

20. Arno J. Mayer, *Why did the heavens not darken? The "final solution" in history* (New York: Pantheon Books, 1988).

21. Steinweis, *Art*, pp. 127-28.

22. Speech of 7 February 1934 contained in Deutsches Nachrichtenbüro release of 8 February 1934, BAK: R 43 II/1241. For further analysis see Steinweis, p. 108.

23. Steinweis, pp. 88, 137.

24. See, e.g., "Jahresbericht 1938—Ausweisabteilung," 30 December 1938, as well as supporting documents in the Berlin Document Center, RMK, Binder: "Rundschreiben sowie Tätigkeitsberichte"; "Jahreslagebericht," 1938; in Heinz Boberach, ed., *Meldungen aus dem Reich: Die geheimen Lageberichte des Sicherheitsdienstes der SS, 1938-1945*, 17 vols. (Herrsching: Pawlak, 1984) (hereafter cited as *Meldungen*), vol. 2, pp. 11, 114; "Vierteljahresbericht," 1939, *Meldungen*, vol. 2, p. 276.

25. Goebbels' speech of 15 November 1935, in *Dokumente der deutschen Politik*, vol. 3, doc. 48.

26. Steinweis, *Art*, pp. 117-18; Adolf Hitler, *Mein Kampf*, trans. Ralph Mannheim (Boston: Houghton Mifflin, 1943; 1971), p. 20.

27. Goebbels' speech of 26 November 1937, in *Dokumente der deutschen Politik*, vol. 5, doc. 77.

28. *Goebbels-Tagebücher*, entries for 5 November 1936, 29 January 1937, 8 April 1937, 5 June 1937.

29. Ibid., entry for 29 January 1937.

30. Volker Hentschel, *Geschichte der deutschen Sozialpolitik, 1880-1980: soziale Sicherung und kollektives Arbeitsrecht* (Frankfurt/Main: Suhrkamp, 1983), pp. 136-44, Claude W. Guillebaud, *The Social Policy of Nazi Germany* (Cambridge: Cambridge University Press, 1941), pp. 84-93. For a Nazi perspective see *Deutsche Sozialpolitik: Bericht der Deutschen Arbeitsfront, Zentralbüro*,

Sozialamt (Zeit: 1. Januar 1938 bis 31. Dezember 1938) (Berlin: Verlag d. Deutschen Arbeitsfront, 1939), pp. 209-54.
31. *Goebbels-Tagebücher,* entries for 22 September 1937, 24 December 1937. The quotation is from the latter entry.
32. Goebbels as quoted in "Die Altersversorgung für Bühnenschaffende ist gesichert!" *Deutsches Bühnen Jahrbuch,* 1938, p. 5.
33. Steinweis, *Art,* pp. 112-13.
34. For further details see Alan E. Steinweis, "German Cultural Imperialism in Czechoslovakia and Poland, 1938-1945," *International History Review* (August 1991): 466-80.
35. Raul Hilberg, *The Destruction of the European Jews,* 2nd ed., 3 vols. (New York: Holmes & Meier, 1985).
36. See analysis of artists' incomes in Steinweis, *Art,* pp. 94-98.
37. Ernst Piper, "Nationalsozialistische Kulturpolitik und ihre Profiteure: Das Beispiel München," in *"Niemand war dabei und keiner hat's gewußt": Die deutsche Öffentlichkeit und die Judenverfolgung 1933-1945,* ed. Jörg Wollenberg (München: Piper, 1989), pp. 129-57.
38. The best treatment of this important but relatively neglected subject is Volker Dahm, "Kulturelles und geistiges Leben," in *Die Juden in Deutschland 1933-1945: Leben unter nationalsozialistischer Herrschaft,* ed. Wolfgang Benz (München: Beck, 1988), pp. 75-267.

3

The Nazi "Seizure" of the Berlin Philharmonic, or the Decline of a Bourgeois Musical Institution

Pamela M. Potter

The bibliography of cultural history of the Nazi period has revealed a curious lacuna: Scattered among the impressive number of titles dedicated to architecture, painting, literature, and film are surprisingly few works dedicated to music, the area Goebbels had dubbed "the most German of the arts." This gap in scholarship can be explained in part by the uninterrupted success of prominent musical figures before and after 1945 and their efforts to suppress investigations into their roles under Hitler. It is also due to the reluctance of music historians to confront the complexity of the interconnections between music and politics in the Third Reich, as well as their late start in incorporating twentieth-century music into the canon of music history. In any event, this lacuna has apparently left us with no alternative but to plug music into the variables of the Weimar-culture-turned-Nazi-culture formula, a formula that implies that the thriving free experimentation in the arts under the Weimar Republic was carried out by artists with socialist leanings. They were attacked by nationalist reactionaries and then purged by the Nazi government and substituted with a crass, backward, nationalistic, and militaristic culture.

The application of this "Weimar culture/Nazi culture" polarity to the area of music has led us to a number of misconceptions. One is that the musical counterparts of expressionism—atonality, dodecaphony, neoclassicism, primitivism, and so on—had become widely accepted as the musical taste of the

Weimar period. Another is that they were eradicated from above with a sweeping gesture of bans and purges on 30 January 1933 and were replaced with the officially sanctioned musical aesthetic typified by *Kampflieder,* marches, and Wagner imitations. A further misconception is the generalization that artistic trends fell into two distinct political camps, such that experimentation was tied to the left and reaction to the right.[1]

Individual studies have already begun to chip away at these assumptions. With regard to bans and the imposition of a Nazi musical aesthetic, it is difficult to demonstrate the existence of a National Socialist "music police" that exercised rigid controls on the performance of ideologically undesirable music. Closer investigations of jazz under the Nazis have revealed that far-reaching bans could never be enforced completely; personal recollections attest to the failure to remove the works of Mendelssohn and other renowned Jewish composers from the repertoire; and a critical assessment of the compositions produced between 1933 and 1945 fail to conform to any consistent "Germanic," "Nazi," or antimodern aesthetic.

Second, looking back prior to 1933, we find it equally problematic to accept the "Weimar culture" paradigm for music and to assume that experimentation was encouraged and enjoyed by the public. The proliferation of music making in amateur groups, at home, and in paramilitary and political movements in the Weimar years and beyond was part of a widespread movement to bring music "back to the *Volk*"—to reject the bourgeois institutions of virtuosity, monumentality, complexity, and alienation that characterized nineteenth-century Romanticism as well as the "intellectual" music of Schoenberg and his school. Musical tastes were turning more toward early music (in the *Hausmusik* revival), folk music (in the *Jugendmusikbewegung*), and all other categories of music that were meaningful for audiences and "performance-ready" for amateurs, while the relatively simple tunes of the cabaret and imported American entertainment music filled the nightclubs and airwaves. As a composer Arnold Schoenberg attracted attention largely within academic circles and could not compete on the open market with popular trends. He insisted that modern works be performed only within private societies in the absence of critics[2] but at the same time made feeble attempts to compose cabaret songs and regretted throughout his life that he could never reach the public at large.

Finally, it is inaccurate to assume that experimenters pursued liberal politics while musical conservatives were unequivocally nationalistic and paved the way for cultural policies after 1933. Schoenberg came across in many of his writings as unabashedly nationalistic and viewed himself as the heir to the legacy of Beethoven and Wagner. The workers' movement, on the other hand, promoted music that was traditional, accessible, and even nationalistic. The repertoire of workers' choral groups consisted largely of German folk songs, Romantic Lieder, and selections from operas and operettas.[3] Similarly, Kurt Weill, in his collaborations with Bertolt Brecht, strove to break away from the music of intellectual progressives, which appealed only to a small segment of society, and he sought to reach the broader audience with clarity and simplicity of style.[4]

The nazification of music can be observed more easily on an institutional level: the *Gleichschaltung* (coordination) of musical life through such actions as the establishment of the Reich Chamber of Culture and the automatic nationalization of subsidized orchestras, opera houses, and conservatories. Even where institutions are concerned, however, certain misconceptions can arise in an effort to sustain the idea of a Weimar culture/Nazi culture polarity. We cannot assume, for instance, that the Weimar government was particularly sympathetic to the musical avant-garde. The Kroll Opera, which stood out as one of the most important outlets for staging contemporary works and experimental productions, had to close its doors in 1930 when the Prussian government cut off its support. Even the Kroll staged relatively few modern works and concentrated on new interpretations of more traditional repertoires.[5]

The image of brown-shirted thugs beating down doors of concert halls and opera houses, invading management offices, and taking control of personnel and programming decisions also loses credibility on closer investigation. It has already been observed that the Nazis' regulation of cultural life was a welcome innovation for many starving artists and performers. Such a warm reception emanated from struggling institutions as well. In the case of the Berlin Philharmonic Orchestra, the *Gleichschaltung* (coordination) did involve a shift in power and an unprecedented degree of outside interference in the inner workings of the organization, but the orchestra did not consider such a reorganization as invasive. Rather, the change was welcome and long overdue. The *Gleichschaltung* offered a guarantee for the Philharmonic's survival after it had attempted unsuccessfully for years to become a government-sponsored organization.

The Berlin Philharmonic Orchestra was founded in 1882 as a private corporation when the concert agent Hermann Wolff amassed support from private patrons. A corporate contract, drawn up in 1903, required every musician to pay in 600 Reichsmark (RM) for one share of the corporation.[6] The organization was completely independent, determining its own policies on membership, conductors, and repertoire. Nevertheless, in January 1934, the orchestra came under the control of Nazi propaganda minister Joseph Goebbels as an official "Reich orchestra." Since it had not been a Reich, Prussian, or municipal orchestra but a private corporation, its transformation into a government institution required more than the usual pro forma procedure, and one is tempted to see its transformation as a "capitulation" or a Nazi "coup."

Although the Philharmonic saga may resemble the traditional image of the omnipotent National Socialist cultural machinery overwhelming even the most self-sufficient entities, a closer look at the history of the orchestra prior to the Third Reich presents quite a different scenario. By 1933, the Philharmonic, despite its world fame, was on the brink of financial ruin. It had already been engaged in negotiations with the Berlin, Prussian, and Reich governments for at least ten years. These appeals aimed at emergency aid as well as an eventual takeover of the orchestra by some branch of the government.

It was clear almost at the time of the founding of the corporation that the Berlin Philharmonic could not sustain itself forever. The unique status of orchestra-as-corporation worked as a strategy for securing artistic autonomy, but its practicality became questionable in times of economic stress, reduced concert attendance, and rising maintenance costs. The various attempts over the years at securing private support—the ill-fated Philharmonische Gesellschaft and the few emergency contributions from private families—had had little success. The orchestra felt the need to turn to government sources as early as 1912, and the city of Berlin came through with a large subsidy in return for a series of public concerts.[7]

The First World War caused additional setbacks for the orchestra,[8] while the worst blows to its financial situation followed in the period of inflation, when it fell victim to exploitation by certain private interests.[9] It became imperative to dissolve disadvantageous contracts in order to get the organization back on its feet.[10] This required the intervention of experienced lawyers and legislators from the city council who could negotiate on behalf of the orchestra and arrive at better terms.[11] The inflation also depleted the orchestra's pension fund, which had been very substantial at the end of the war, and the city council considered stepping in to take over its pension.[12]

The government of the city of Berlin was the mainstay of assistance for the Berlin Philharmonic for many years. The city's willingness to support the orchestra was based on a tacit understanding: The Philharmonic had played a leading role in raising Berlin to a world music center,[13] and the legislators saw their obligation to the orchestra as "more than a moral one."[14] From 1911 to 1923, the city agreed to furnish an annual subsidy, which rose accordingly as the orchestra became less capable of sustaining itself.[15] Being the main contributor, the city government naturally took an active interest in the orchestra's financial management. From the early 1920s, it functioned not only as a sponsor for the orchestra but also as an advisor in management and eventually a spokesman in negotiations with the other levels of government. The city's influence in orchestra matters ended there, however, and did not invade the internal workings of the organization.

The city would continue to be the Philharmonic's staunchest supporter in times of need, but by 1927 legislators had to respond to wider budgetary setbacks. Unable to maintain their annual subsidy to the Berlin Philharmonic while simultaneously supporting the Berlin Symphony Orchestra, city officials informed the Reich and Prussian governments that "the Berlin Philharmonic Orchestra, Inc. assumes a commanding position not only in Berlin musical life, but even more so with its numerous concerts abroad in the post-war years has it contributed to regaining for German art its old image. Therefore the preservation of the orchestra must be a common affair for the Reich, the *Land* [Prussia] and the Reich capital."[16] Thus for the 1927 season, the city offered to provide only 105,000 Reichsmark (RM), slightly more than half of its normal subsidy, and expected the Reich and Prussia to contribute the rest of the needed 95,000 RM. Prussia refused outright, and after much deliberation the Reich Ministry of Finance declined to assist,[17] whereas the Ministry of the Interior went and used the money it had set aside for the Philharmonic for another purpose.[18]

The situation in 1928 was not much better. The Prussian minister for science, art and popular education and the Reich minister of finance decided that the city alone should subsidize the orchestra.[19] City officials opted for a new approach and attempted to interest the Reich and Prussia in the prospect of restructuring the financial base of the orchestra by suggesting they purchase shares of the corporation. They used the term "reorganization," perhaps as a euphemism for a "takeover" or "nationalization," or perhaps to underline the city's intentions to preserve the corporation's autonomous nature. Involving the city, Reich, and Prussian governments as shareholders in such a risky venture was controversial but seemed the only way to generate their active interest.

The idea of reorganizing the Philharmonic had come up earlier on isolated occasions,[20] but not in any concrete terms. The new plan had its beginnings at a meeting of the lord mayor Gustav Böss, Lange (member of the city parliament and the orchestra's supervisory board), Kestenberg (the administrator of musical affairs in the Prussian Ministry for Science, Art and Popular Education), and a representative of the Reich Ministry of the Interior, Donnevert, in December 1928 and was pursued throughout most of the following year. In order to cover the deficit of 370,000 RM, the city would contribute 250,000 RM, and the Reich and Prussia would contribute the rest: "The intention would be to establish a corporation whose major shareholders should be the three above-named contributors, while the shareholders of the existing corporation should be taken into the new company following the dissolution of the former one, however in such a manner that the first three named retain the majority."[21] The three parties would add to the capital of the orchestra in predetermined proportions, such that the capital would be more than doubled and the government shareholders would own 51 percent of the total shares.[22] An executive board would consist of four members chosen by the orchestra, five by the city council, two by the city magistrate, and two by the Reich Ministry of the Interior.[23]

The plan was designed to preserve the corporation status, maintain the artistic autonomy of the orchestra, and still have enough government influence in financial matters to keep the corporation solvent. Reactions in the press were somewhat skeptical and questioned the benefactors' real intentions. On 29 September 1929, the *Vossische Zeitung* reported the details of the plans with some doubts about the city's goodwill:

> Pure, boundlessly generous patronage has never existed in practice, ever since the beginnings of patronage, and the city of Berlin is no exception. It hopes to accomplish initiatives, fortunately until now almost exclusively organizational and business initiatives. It requires the complete control of the business management, and in order to facilitate this control effectively, it has demanded to possess, together with the Reich, a majority of the Philharmonic Orchestra company. A business that stands in such a sharp deficit cannot say no to the wishes of its largest investor. The 95 members of the Philharmonic Orchestra, who up to now owned the shares of the company exclusively, have therefore had to come to terms with the fact that through an increase in capital the city and the Reich become the strongest shareholders, that they will take over the majority of the board of directors—the post of chairman will probably go to Stadtsyndikus Lange—that in practicality the city will handle the more important contract negotiations and will also have a significant influence on the artistic aspect.[24]

The reorganization plan seemed all but certain to go forward, when the Reich government suddenly had a change of heart. Opinions differed on the reasons for the withdrawal. Lange blamed the failure on the "intolerance of the Reich Ministry of the Interior and the rejecting behavior of the Prussian bureaucracy,"[25] while orchestra director Wilhelm Furtwängler attributed the Reich's actions to economic emergency measures.[26] Furtwängler attempted unsuccessfully to use his international reputation to appeal to Chancellor Brüning to annul the emergency measures, drawing attention to the cultural importance of the orchestra abroad. He also pointed out that he had passed up attractive offers in Vienna and America to make himself available to Berlin musical life with the understanding that the city and the Reich would guarantee the needed subsidies.[27]

An interim solution came about in 1931 when the press publicized the irony of sustaining a lesser-known group, the Berlin Symphony Orchestra, at the expense of the world-renowned Philharmonic and called for the realization of a three-year-old plan to merge the two orchestras.[28] Adopting the merger plan, the city council agreed forthwith to dissolve the Berlin Symphony in order to sustain the Philharmonic and promised a very substantial yearly subsidy.[29] The orchestra agreed to give a number of public performances in return.[30] By the beginning of the 1932/33 season, the merger was complete, and the Berlin Philharmonic took on 23 new members from the former Symphony Orchestra.[31]

The city still hoped for a more substantial contribution from the Reich and more interest from Prussia, which up to that time had undertaken no obligations.[32] When the city and the orchestra renewed the appeal to the Reich to take on a portion of the corporation in 1932, the Ministry of Finance rejected the plan once again.[33] The city made one last desperate attempt to extract at least a symbolic contribution from the Reich, reducing the request from 90,000 RM to only 6000 RM. Their pleas stressed "that the situation of the orchestra is so serious, that this amount cannot be renounced," and "the Reich has a special interest in the preservation of our orchestra not only for general reasons, but also for very noteworthy reasons of foreign policy."[34] It was already quite clear that the amount of cooperation needed from the Reich government to secure the future of the orchestra would not be forthcoming under the current administration.

The failure to nationalize the Berlin Philharmonic Orchestra prior to Hitler's rise to power was due to a lack of cooperation from all government branches concerned. Although Lange had blamed the Reich and Prussia for the failure of the 1929 reorganization plan by virtue of their "rejecting nature," some of his own colleagues in the city legislature also contributed to the opposition. The left, and particularly the members of the Communist Party, had been against lavishing support on the Philharmonic for some years, initially because they considered the orchestra to carry a high snob factor and to render itself inaccessible to the middle and working classes.[35] In 1929, Communists' criticisms centered on the argument that the money could be better used for social services. The Center Party joined in the opposition for so-called nationalistic reasons, probably because of the high salary Furtwängler was to receive in spite of the depths to which the economy and services had fallen.[36] Then in 1931, Lange expressed astonishment in his diary at a decision to cut back funding from the Philharmonic and offered a surprising explanation: "14.11. On the advice of the so-called emergency program the budget committee unexpectedly affirmed the previously rejected subsidy for the Berlin Symphony Orchestra but denied assistance for the Philharmonic Orchestra. The reason I was given was that the Philharmonic Orchestra was thought to be infested with National-Socialists." He dismissed this and attributed the decision more to the disappointment of the left when Furtwängler refused to conduct the public concerts.[37]

The long-standing lack of cooperation from Prussia posed a second impediment to reorganization. Prussian officials usually argued that the Philharmonic was not a Prussian concern and that a city like Berlin should be in a position to support it alone just as any large city takes responsibility for its municipal orchestra.[38] Leo Kestenberg of the Prussian Ministry for Science, Art, and Popular Education even questioned the seriousness of the situation and believed that the orchestra had a very good income.[39] There was also the feeling that Prussia should offer support instead to the orchestras in the "endangered border areas" of the Reich.[40] Philharmonic advocates tried to play on these sentiments in their direct appeals to Prussia, arguing

> that the Berlin Philharmonic Orchestra has fulfilled a high cultural mission for decades as the leading orchestra in Germany through its concerts in Prussia and therefore represents an unchallenged important factor in the cultural life of Germany beyond the framework of its Berlin activities. We refer especially to our concert tours in the threatened border areas. Already at the time of the occupation we concertized in the Rhine and Saar regions. The enthusiastic reception by the population of these regions showed us that the concerts of the orchestra from the Reich capital were considered a symbol of loyalty to the Fatherland and the community of all German tribes.[41]

But even this tactic failed to soften Prussia's obstinacy.

Finally, the Reich's refusal to cooperate—the linchpin in the failure to nationalize the orchestra—was due in part to the absence of a responsible office in the Reich government, a problem that caused the Philharmonic endless frustration. Unlike Berlin and Prussia, the Reich had no administrative body for cultural affairs. The Philharmonic usually approached the Ministry of the Interior and the Ministry of Finance, shuttling back and forth between the two with its requests for emergency aid. The Ministry of the Interior, although formally responsible for matters concerning the Philharmonic, cooperated only to the extent that the individual assigned to the matter had an interest in preserving the orchestra. By late 1927, the "sympathetic ear" in that ministry, an official named Külz, had been replaced. His successors refused to honor any promises of subsidies, making negotiations between the city and the Reich that much more difficult.⁴² The Ministry of Finance considered the orchestra's situation only upon the recommendations from the Ministry of the Interior. It then had only to approve or reject aid in the context of the budget of the entire Reich and had no interest in participating in a reorganization plan.⁴³

The Nazis' assumption of power on 30 January 1933 would prove to be a fortuitous development for the survival of the Philharmonic, mainly because of the creation of the Propaganda Ministry. The new ministry represented the most viable potential patron for the orchestra after its decade of frustrations with the Reich Ministry of Finance and the Ministry of the Interior. The "overadministrating" of cultural affairs by the Propaganda Ministry, the Amt Rosenberg, and the Deutsche Arbeitsfront was a welcome imposition in a country that had had virtually no central program for cultural administration.

Goebbels must have been very interested in assuming control over the Berlin Philharmonic, but obviously realized that the utmost caution was required. According to a secondhand account, Furtwängler immediately recognized the Propaganda Ministry's potential and approached Goebbels directly for an increased subsidy. Goebbels reportedly expressed to him an interest in "claiming responsibility for the Philharmonic Orchestra within his ministry."⁴⁴ Mostly, however, Goebbels restrained himself from appearing too eager to assume responsibility for the Berlin Philharmonic. The first open recommendation did not emanate from the propaganda minister himself but rather from a third party. Pfundtner, the secretary of the Reich Ministry of the Interior, invited representatives from the Reich Ministry of Finance and the Prussian Ministry for Science, Art and Popular Education, the lord mayor of Berlin, Furtwängler, and the business staff of the orchestra to a meeting on 12 April to discuss the orchestra's reorganization.

Prussian and city representatives opened the meeting by expressing outright their inability to provide additional subsidies. A representative of the city council declared that the proposed management of the orchestra by several administrative bodies was inefficient. He recommended that one Reich ministry, such as the Ministry of the Interior, provide the total subsidy of the orchestra. A handwritten note on the report of the meeting comments: "the [Reich Ministry of the Interior] and the RFM do nothing? There is also the possibility that the new Propaganda Ministry may help."⁴⁵ The new seed for reorganization had been planted, but Goebbels still kept a low profile.

The Propaganda Ministry would come to the rescue only after the orchestra had been plagued by a variety of external and internal pressures. The first round of outside pressures on the orchestra arose as it came under public scrutiny for its association with Jews. Bruno Walter, the renowned Jewish conductor, had been forbidden to conduct a scheduled concert at the Gewandhaus in Leipzig. Storm Troopers had allegedly threatened to cause a disturbance at the concert hall if Walter appeared at his upcoming concert with the Philharmonic.[46] When he tried to secure police protection, Walther Funk of the Propaganda Ministry recommended that an "Aryan" conductor be sought instead, and Richard Strauss agreed to take Walter's place.[47] Attention was focused on the Philharmonic again when Furtwängler wrote a letter to Goebbels in which he protested the treatment of Jewish musicians, calling for artistic judgment on the basis of good or bad, not Aryan or Jewish. Goebbels reciprocated by convincing Furtwängler to allow the letter to be printed in the *Vossische Zeitung* on 11 April. Without informing Furtwängler, he published his own unctuous response simultaneously in the *Berliner Lokal-Anzeiger*.[48]

Days later, the Philharmonic received orders from the city government to conform to racial restrictions. Since the city contributed the most financial support and had direct influence on the orchestra, it did not hesitate to attempt to instigate anti-Semitic purges after Nazis had taken over important municipal offices. On 22 April 1933 the orchestra received a letter from Hafemann[49] in the mayor's office demanding a list of the Jews and half Jews under contract with the orchestra in order to decide on their dismissal. The orchestra responded by procrastinating. Business manager Lorenz Höber requested a delay until their return from their spring tour. He then sent a copy of this correspondence to Pfundtner of the Reich Ministry of the Interior and insisted that "a *Gleichschaltung* with consideration for the preservation of the high artistic quality of the orchestra naturally requires more time."[50]

The presence of Jews in the orchestra immediately led to more problems. On the 1933 spring tour, the Mannheim orchestra attempted to prevent Simon Goldberg, the Jewish concertmaster of the Philharmonic, from leading the two orchestras in a joint concert. Furtwängler protested and was reportedly reproached afterward in his dressing room for his lack of national sentiment.[51] He expressed his anger over this incident in a letter to Goebbels:

> my impressions from the hinterlands, as far as the indigenous concert life is concerned, are especially unfavorable, and I fear that the most subjective and perhaps the "most German" art of our people—I refer mainly to pure, "absolute" music—will, because of its special nature, suffer more from the present-day upheaval than any other artistic field. Unless free competition be restored immediately, and thereby the public once again be in a position to make its judgments count, the uprising of mediocrity which is proliferating in musical life today will succeed and Germany's position in the world as a land of music will be gone.[52]

In the spring and summer of 1933, the orchestra resumed its negotiations with the three administrations and the state broadcasting concerns, this time with decisive, if delayed, results. The first signs of progress came in May 1933 when the orchestra secured a contribution from the new Reich of 100,000 RM.[53] This set into motion a series of meetings and correspondences on the reorganization of the orchestra. A meeting on 31 May included representatives from the Propaganda Ministry, the Reich Ministry of Finance, the Prussian ministries of Finance and of Science, Art and Popular Education, the city government, two radio broadcasting companies, and Furtwängler and Höber from the orchestra. It was not a very productive session, but instead was dominated by a tendency to pass the buck. The city and the Reich representatives each tried to saddle the other with the responsibility of subsidies, while the Prussian and broadcasting representatives claimed the issue was beyond their jurisdiction.[54]

After this meeting, the participants slowly and reluctantly gave in as the propaganda minister exerted behind-the-scenes pressure on all parties concerned. A letter of 2 June from the office of Goebbels to the Prussian finance minister, Popitz, requested that the latter approve a subsidy equal to the Reich's contribution, pointing to Prussia's intransigence of past years.[55] The Prussian government begrudgingly approved a small one-time contribution (12,000 RM of the requested 100,000 RM), only because of the emergency and with the understanding that the orchestra would eventually come to a more comprehensive agreement with the Reich.[56]

The Propaganda Ministry then exerted pressure on the city. The mayor conceded halfheartedly to approve an additional emergency subsidy of 20,000 RM but, aping the Prussians, made it clear that this was no indication that the city would assume more responsibility. This concession came only with the anticipation that the orchestra would reach some agreement with the Reich and Prussia.[57] The third party to succumb to the pressures, the Reich Radio Broadcasting Company, drew up a new contract with the orchestra in August and tried to prevent Furtwängler from contracting Jewish soloists. This condition was totally unacceptable to Furtwängler,[58] who was concurrently involved in a campaign to bring prominent "non-Aryan" soloists and conductors to Berlin for the following season.[59] Nevertheless, by such back-door measures, Goebbels effected indirect pressure on the orchestra from all sides: The city and Prussia pressed the Philharmonic to reach an agreement with the Reich, and the broadcasting concern tried to enforce anti-Semitic practices.

While the orchestra waited for the crucial decisions of outside powers to determine its fate, tensions within its membership mounted. Some friction arose from the dismissal of the former members of the Berlin Symphony Orchestra who had been taken on when the two orchestras merged. These members, released from the Philharmonic on order of Hitler in October 1933, wielded the only influence left to them by refusing to give up their shares of the corporation until their demands were met.[60] Other tensions arose concerning the retention of Jews in the orchestra and how this might jeopardize its reorganization. Furtwängler had, according to the disgruntled former Symphony Orchestra members, secured permission from Goebbels early in 1933 to keep on the Jewish members until further notice, which infuriated the Nazi Party members in the orchestra.[61]

Most of all, members seemed to need constant reassurance that the Philharmonic would survive and that its long-awaited reorganization would soon become a reality. Throughout July and August, the board tried to ease these uncertainties, as echoed in an open letter from Furtwängler to the members:

> Dear Sirs: The Führer and the Reich government have given me the assurance that the Berlin Philharmonic Orchestra will, under all circumstances, be retained. Reichsminister Dr. Goebbels has added to this assurance the condition that absolute leadership of the orchestra in artistic and personnel matters is bestowed upon me. For these reasons I expect that any discontent within the orchestra will cease in the future. No decisions can be reached without me and my approval. My 12-year association with you, dear sirs, should guarantee to you that all of the steps taken by me are only in the interest of the orchestra.[62]

Most striking in this open letter is Furtwängler's promise that the "absolute leadership" ("absolute Führung") of the orchestra would be in his hands, indicating that the orchestra would adopt the *Führerprinzip* (leadership principle). At a Philharmonic press conference in mid-September, the orchestra managers Lorenz Höber and Rudolf von Schmidtseck made this point in even stronger terms. The *Vossische Zeitung* reported: "With praise for Furtwängler, who is the greatest artistic and economic support of the orchestra, [Höber] concluded that in the future he will be more a 'Führer' than ever before," and Schmidtseck proclaimed: "that German art is to be set on a national foundation and that the *Führerprinzip* must also be introduced in the arts."[63] It was Furtwängler's understanding that Goebbels had proposed as a condition of the takeover that Furtwängler be granted "the leadership and authoritative direction of the orchestra," that he be "named Führer," and that the orchestra operate under the *Führerprinzip*.[64]

Goebbels had won the support and confidence of Furtwängler and orchestra members with such assurances of artistic and administrative autonomy, but these promises were not to survive the actual *Gleichschaltung*. On 30 November 1933, the Reich announced its decision to take over the Philharmonic effective 15 January 1934, when each member/shareholder of the orchestra would receive 600 RM for his share of the corporation and become a Reich employee.[65] In a closed meeting on 10 March 1934, without any orchestra representatives present, high officials of the Reich decided on the new structure of the organization. The Philharmonic was to retain the form of a corporation in name only. This corporation would consist of one share, and that share would become the property of the Reich government. An administrative council was to include Walther Funk from the Propaganda Ministry, Pfundtner from the Reich Ministry of the Interior, Manteuffel from the Reich Ministry of Finance, a representative from the Reich Economic Commission, and only one representative from the orchestra. As a symbolic gesture of retaining the corporation "spirit," one member of the Propaganda Ministry would have the authority to call a meeting to seal contracts with orchestra members as employees of the "corporation."[66]

Furtwängler, who had been led to believe that he would retain his absolute authority, would be appointed merely as conductor with a contract committing him to a set number of concerts. Two business managers were to replace Berta Geissmar, the Jewish general manager: one manager for artistic matters who would also serve as second conductor, and one to handle all business affairs and to be the liaison to the Reich ministries.[67] Two days after the closed meeting several officials from the Propaganda Ministry met with Furtwängler to discuss his contract and various personnel changes. The supposed guarantee of absolute leadership that Goebbels had promised him received its final blow at this meeting. The minutes report: "Finally Mr. Furtwängler posed the question of whether he would have a seat and a vote in the administrative council. This was denied, but he was informed that naturally he would be heard at any time in the administrative council."[68]

In this way the orchestra and the government reached their mutual goal. The Reich government had finally taken control of the most famous orchestra in Germany, and the Berlin Philharmonic won financial security as a state-supported institution after years of fruitless negotiation with the various levels of government. In the years that followed, the Philharmonic enjoyed prestige and material benefits as the official Reich orchestra. It was common for Nazi leaders to take a personal interest in protecting and promoting their pet cultural institutions and at times to interfere in artistic matters,[69] and Goebbels assumed such a role in the Philharmonic organization. He referred to it in correspondences as "my orchestra,"[70] enjoyed the title of the orchestra's "guardian,"[71] and paved the way toward securing special privileges for it and circumventing laws regarding wages and contracts for musicians.[72]

Eventually Hitler also took an interest in the orchestra's well-being because of the worldwide reputation of the Philharmonic and its conductor. In accordance with his personal wish, the orchestra members entered a special wage category in consideration of the Philharmonic's "artistic achievements and special cultural-political significance."[73] The orchestra earned this privilege not only with its numerous appearances abroad but also with its participation in the festivities of the 1936 Olympic Games.[74] The special wage classification went into effect in 1938, a season in which the orchestra participated in seven major events per order of the Propaganda Ministry. These included the Reichsparteitag, the film on the Olympic games, and the two major cultural events of the year: the Tag der deutschen Kunst, best known for its parallel exhibit "Degenerate Art," and the Reichsmusiktage, with the corresponding exhibit "Degenerate Music."[75] The "official Reich orchestra" also took part in the first-anniversary celebration of the Reich Music Chamber, various other concerts for the Reich Culture Chamber, and the special celebrations for Hitler's birthday, and it performed at the Paris World's Fair. In addition, it held special concerts for the Hitler Youth and the arms industry. A film on the Berlin Philharmonic, entitled *Philharmoniker* and directed by Paul Verhoeven, was produced with Goebbels' endorsement and premiered in December 1944.[76]

As a Reich orchestra, the Philharmonic also came into closer working relationships with Party organizations. These ties helped to boost the flagging attendance that followed the Depression. The orchestra did not hesitate to invoke its official status to win cooperation from these organizations. In one instance, while urging "Strength through Joy" to settle its accounts, the orchestra management emphasized: "Certainly any business relationships between you as a National Socialist organization and us as a National Socialist Reich orchestra should run smoothly."[77] Although the specific duties of a Reich orchestra had never been spelled out officially, pressures from the government and from within the orchestra's new administration compelled the Philharmonic to be at the Reich's disposal for all major events. Hans von Benda, the artistic manager of the orchestra from 1935 to 1939, complained of Furtwängler's unwillingness to conduct at official functions: "I have always presented Dr. Furtwängler with the view that the Reich orchestra must be available for all of Germany's official occasions, which is also the burning desire of the orchestra itself. . . ."[78]

As the Reich granted more benefits, the orchestra made additional sacrifices that went beyond rearranging its concert schedule to accommodate official duties. The greatest sacrifice in autonomy was the loss of administrative authority to the Propaganda Ministry. According to the final arrangements, the administrative council of the corporation consisted of three representatives from that ministry (one of whom served as the chairman), three others from the Reich government, and only one from the orchestra.[79] The Propaganda Ministry had the authority both to appoint the artistic and business managers and the members of the council and to dictate the use of the orchestra's capital.[80] The orchestra had to report regularly to Walther Funk in his capacity as chairman of the council and consult him on special questions of tours, guest conductors, musicians' contracts, and a variety of business matters.[81] Certainly the most dramatic loss was the sacrifice of the orchestra's Jewish members, who all seem to have emigrated shortly after the transfer of authority, with only a few members married to Jews staying on longer. In 1938, concertmaster Hugo Kolberg left the orchestra and went to England, presumably because of his Jewish wife.[82] By 1939, three members with Jewish wives remained, but the wives were not allowed to attend concerts.[83]

Despite the common notions of *Gleichschaltung*, the Propaganda Ministry seems to have stayed clear of aesthetic issues in the case of the Berlin Philharmonic. If the musical repertoire of concert programs from 1934 through 1945 is any reflection of the ministry's involvement in artistic matters, then it is safe to say that such involvement was very limited. Philharmonic programs after January 1934 were only slightly more conservative than in earlier years. Before the *Gleichschaltung*, the orchestra had occasionally championed some of the less radical avant-garde composers, especially Hindemith and Honegger, but not overwhelmingly so. The Philharmonic was and had been fairly conservative in its programming since the turn of the century.

Authors who have written on the history of the Berlin Philharmonic, including Wolfgang Stresemann (son of the former chancellor and *Intendant* of the orchestra from 1959 to 1978, and again in the early 1980s), have made an exaggerated claim that the orchestra carried on a form of resistance in its concert programs by performing works that had been prohibited. They list Bartók's *Music for Strings, Celesta and Percussion,* Mendelssohn's incidental music to *Midsummer Night's Dream,* and Stravinsky's *Kiss of the Fairy*.[84] In addition, we find Mendelssohn's violin concerto in March of 1935, and several other works by Stravinsky as late as December 1938. Strictly speaking, these were not radical departures from official policy. Bartók's music had been featured even at events sponsored by the Music Chamber[85] and was never formally prohibited, although critics often linked his name with the "Jewish circle" of atonal composers.[86] Bartók was not featured in the "Degenerate Music" exhibit, but after finding out that he had been omitted, he promptly wrote to the authorities insisting that he, too, be on their list of undesirables.[87]

Mendelssohn, although regarded as an important figure in German music history, had been a target of anti-Semitism as early as 1850 in Wagner's anti-Semitic writings and in the arguments of twentieth-century racial theorists who dabbled in music history. The music for *Midsummer Night's Dream* became a center of controversy in 1935 when the Reich Music Chamber offered commissions to composers to write incidental music to replace Mendelssohn's. Theaters stopped performing Shakespeare's play rather than use substitutes that were, even at the admission of some of the most ardent National Socialists, inferior to Mendelssohn's work. Much of his music continued to be performed and was even praised in the press until 9 November 1936, when a grand symbolic gesture of removing his statue in front of the Leipzig Gewandhaus called national attention to his racial background. After that date, individuals who performed his music met with somewhat harsher measures than before, but institutions, especially churches, continued to use his music without reproach simply by omitting his name from the printed program.[88]

Stravinsky's music remained popular in Hitler's Germany and was widely performed, despite the fact that he was featured in the notorious exhibit of "Degenerate Music" in Düsseldorf in 1938.[89] After some initial misgivings about his racial origins in the early years of the new regime, he was rehabilitated in 1936 and enjoyed great successes all over Germany thereafter.[90] There were 18 separate productions of *Firebird* between 1935 and 1940 and a highly successful staging of *Persephone* in Braunschweig in 1937.[91] The German premiere of his *Card Game* was even featured at the Gaukulturwoche in Dresden in 1937.[92] It was not until the first months of the war that the Reich Music Chamber issued an order prohibiting further performance of his works because of his French citizenship.[93]

By featuring Stravinsky as conductor and composer, the Berlin Philharmonic probably helped dispense with any ambiguities over the aesthetic suitability of his music. One Stravinsky performance that attracted particular attention was the Philharmonic's rendition of the *Rite of Spring* under Kleiber's baton in November 1934. While the *Völkischer Beobachter,* the official Nazi Party organ, chastised Kleiber for bringing before the public such "racially alien music of a noise comic promoted in Jewish circles,"[94] the *Frankfurter Zeitung* praised the conductor for finally loosening the bonds of program policy.[95] In 1938, the Berlin Philharmonic promoted Stravinsky even further by making a recording of *Card Game* under the composer's own direction.

The limitations on performing works by particular composers never constituted a set policy, except in the obvious cases of composers such as Schoenberg whose names came to symbolize "Jewish degeneracy." For all other cases, it seems that any bans on musical compositions depended entirely on the political acceptability of the texts, and the period from 1933 to 1945 saw only four published lists of banned music, beginning in 1938.[96] Censors added names of works to the blacklist one by one as foreign policy and social circumstances dictated, but there were few universal controls on actual performances. It is unlikely that the Philharmonic could realistically "resist" any official policy by performing unacceptable works, as Stresemann and others have suggested. The orchestra was in such a prominent position in German musical life and was under such close scrutiny by the Propaganda Ministry that any performance of controversial or blacklisted works would not have gone unnoticed.

The Nazis' assumption of authority over the Berlin Philharmonic signified its salvation from the financial ruin that had threatened it for over a decade. In return, the orchestra had to perform at official functions, submit to the will of interfering Party administrators, make some concessions in its repertoire to fit ideological guidelines, and lose its Jewish members. The idealistic notion of a totally self-sufficient, privately run organization evaporated once and for all. This is not to say, however, that the autonomy it once enjoyed as a private corporation could have persisted had Hitler not appeared. From the time the Philharmonic entered negotiations with government branches in 1912, it was clear that self-administration was a luxury it could no longer afford. As the orchestra's financial situation worsened in the 1920s, the importance of self-government diminished.

An orchestra-as-corporation was an unusual phenomenon for its time and was even the subject of ridicule. In a speech delivered at a conference of the Social Democratic Party in 1929, Ernst Reuter stated: "Although I am a staunch supporter of the corporation form for public firms, I must warn against turning every merely feasible or unfeasible concern into a corporation. In this way one can run an otherwise good principle into the ground. For instance, I am not at all sure why a philharmonic orchestra here in Berlin must be brought into the form of a corporation. (Laughter)."[97] Although city officials struggled to preserve the spirit of the corporation in their reorganization plans and opposed making the orchestra members civil servants,[98] they had already assumed responsibility for the orchestra's financial matters by placing city officials on its board.[99] Even after 1933, Reich administrators paid homage to the corporation concept and gave the appearance of preserving it, albeit in a mocking manner. The problem of sacrificing autonomy for security had been a concern for the orchestra and the Berlin musical public from the time the first negotiations for reorganization began, but financial insecurity left little room for choice. The corporation-orchestra experiment had failed within 30 years of its inception, and the Philharmonic would never regain the independence it once had.

Germany's economic crisis left the Philharmonic at the mercy of any holders of public resources. At the same time, the orchestra had also suffered from a loss of income on its own. Financial failure was due not only to internal mismanagement and external vicissitudes but also to sinking attendance. The decline in box-office sales was certainly a reflection of the hard economic times, but not exclusively. The growth of mass culture in music cannot be underestimated, and the prevailing mood of the times dictated that music be brought back to the *Volk*.

The most effective means to bring music to the *Volk* was to make music an active rather than a passive experience, and the Weimar years witnessed an explosion of amateur music-making. Within the workers' movement alone, the Deutscher Arbeitersängerbund grew from nearly 250,000 members in 1920 to nearly 500,000 in 1928.[100] Bourgeois and right-wing amateur groups appeared as well, in the form of male choirs, mixed choirs, amateur orchestras, and chamber ensembles. In response to these new trends, a large number of music periodicals dedicated to music education, folk music, and amateur performance were created toward the end of the First World War, and the period following the Inflation of 1922/23 saw the emergence of important new multivolume performance editions for choruses and small ensembles.

Informal private music-making, or *Hausmusik*, formed the core of the amateur movement, probably because any individual could pursue it free of commitments and alone or in small gatherings. The Depression had severely reduced normal concert attendance and created a situation in which entertainment had to be sought more at home.[101] As the demands of amateur musicians rose, the *Hausmusik* movement received continuous praise well into the first years of Hitler's Reich for boosting the economy by helping instrument manufacturers, music publishers and retailers, and private music instructors.[102] *Hausmusik* also conveniently fit in with a socialist perception of the history of music. It had flourished in the eighteenth century but suffered a setback in the late nineteenth century that coincided with a bourgeois admiration for virtuosi. Its recent resurgence could be attributed to modern society's growing awareness of the needs of the masses for musical expression.[103] Music historians' depiction of *Hausmusik* as a prebourgeois phenomenon[104] was in harmony with the goals of both the Weimar and the National Socialist state to steer cultural support toward education and mass participation.

Music historians and politicians also agreed on the position of the symphony orchestra in modern society. As scholars rallied behind the revival of amateur music-making, they aimed their criticisms at the concert hall—the hallmark bourgeois musical institution. Musicologist Werner Korte juxtaposed socialist sentiments with the stated goals of Hitler and Rosenberg by recommending music as a means to gain an understanding of the "biological organism of our völkisch structure." He attacked the bourgeois concert hall as a superficial institution and suggested it be exploited for its educational potential by encouraging active rather than passive musical experiences.[105] Meanwhile legislators across the political spectrum waged war on such relics of bourgeois cultural superiority as the Berlin Philharmonic Orchestra.

Symphony orchestras were notably behind the times, holding fast to monumental works written explicitly for the concert hall and disregarding the changes in public taste. Even in Berlin, generally recognized as the center of artistic experimentation, the Philharmonic's programs of the 1920s consisted largely of Romantic works and paid virtually no attention to popular trends. Easily 90 percent of the works presented in concerts from 1927 on were written in the seventeenth, eighteenth, and especially nineteenth centuries. The Philharmonic was not even a forum for new or experimental works. Aside from the late Romanticist Richard Strauss, who was fairly well represented, Stravinsky was the only contemporary composer who fared well. Hindemith's works appeared occasionally, but Schoenberg saw only one of his works premiered and only one performance of his more popular and highly romantic ballet *Verklärte Nacht.*

The symphony orchestra would have been destined to become little more than an obsolete reminder of late nineteenth-century bourgeois musical culture, had shrewd politicians not recognized its propaganda potential abroad. Institutions such as the Philharmonic served a purpose, even if they did not fit comfortably in the scheme of mass culture. Their chief value lay in their appeal outside Germany as symbols of German accomplishments, and this reason alone was enough to make the effort to preserve them worthwhile.

The Berlin government recognized the orchestra's importance for the city's reputation as a world music center. In the campaigns to rally support from Prussia and the Reich in the 1920s, the orchestra and the city consistently emphasized its "cultural-political" and "foreign policy" value as an "ambassador" of German culture, but they failed to convince the Reich and Prussia of the orchestra's international importance. The Nazis, on the other hand, were well aware of its "cultural-political" value from the outset. The new government was far more concerned with establishing itself in the eyes of the outside world as a cultured entity and was determined to hold on to the Philharmonic and to Furtwängler at all costs, even if it meant giving the orchestra a false sense of organizational control. Goebbels tolerated Furtwängler's challenges to racial policies and made promises to him that he had no intention of keeping. He also preserved the label of "corporation" after taking complete control of the orchestra's administration, probably in an effort to deceive the orchestra members into believing that they still had some independence and to secure their loyalty.

The new designation of *Reichsorchester* gave the Philharmonic the symbolic duty of representing the new Reich as an ambassador of German culture to foreign allies and to the occupied territories. Its high level of artistic achievement would serve as a foil to foreigners criticizing the barbarism of the new regime and as positive propaganda for the impending cultural encroachment on occupied territories. The orchestra entertained Germany's troops and allies and wasted no time in promoting German culture by touring regions shortly after their occupation. The Philharmonic toured Denmark in July 1940, Holland, Belgium and France in September 1940, and made frequent appearances in the former Czechoslovakia, Hungary, Romania, Bulgaria, Serbia, Croatia, Italy, Scandinavia, and Poland up through June 1944.[106] Concerts continued even after the bombing of the "Philharmonie" concert hall early in 1944, and the orchestra concluded its last months of wartime activities with a concert for the Wehrmacht in March 1945 and a "concert for Minister Speer" on 11 April.[107]

The Propaganda Ministry preserved and indeed rescued the "Berlin Philharmonic Orchestra, Inc." from total dissolution, but what it managed to save was no longer the model of artistic autonomy and democratic music-making catering to the high-brow tastes of German society. By the 1930s, the Philharmonic was threatened with extinction. It was forced to compete for private support with the growing amateur movement, to compete for government funds with social welfare programs, and to compete for audiences with the radio, the cabaret, and the cinema. The Hitler regime gave priority to its preservation as a symbol of Germany's grand musical tradition and as a public relations vehicle outside the Reich. At home, however, cultural policymakers of both the Weimar Republic and the Third Reich saw it in their best interest to promote instead the music created for and by the *Volk*.

Notes

1. See, for example, Michael Kater, "The Revenge of the Fathers: The Demise of Modern Music at the End of the Weimar Republic," *German Studies Review* 15, No. 2 (May 1992): 295-315.
2. Schoenberg declared his retreat from pleasing the public by proposing the Society for Private Musical Performances in Vienna in 1918. The statement of aims is translated in Piero Weiss and Richard Taruskin, eds., *Music in the Western World* (New York: Schirmer, 1984), pp. 431-32, and in Nicholas Slonimsky, ed., *Music since 1900,* 4th ed. (New York: Scribner, 1971), pp. 1307-8.
3. W. L. Guttsman, *Workers' Culture in Weimar Germany* (New York: Berg, 1990), pp. 158-59.

4. Kim H. Kowalke, "Looking Back: Toward a New Orpheus," in *A New Orpheus: Essays on Kurt Weill,* ed. K. Kowalke (New Haven, CT: Yale University Press, 1986), pp. 5-6.
5. John Willett, *Art and Politics in the Weimar Period: The New Sobriety, 1917-1933* (New York: Pantheon, 1978), p. 211.
6. Peter Muck, *Einhundert Jahre Berliner Philharmonisches Orchester: Darstellung in Dokumenten,* vol. 1, *1882-1922* (Tutzing: Schneider, 1982), pp. 305-14.
7. The orchestra's contract to play at the Scheveningen health resort came to an end in 1912. In order to guarantee the salaries of the orchestra members and to see it through its summer slump, the city promised a yearly subsidy of 60,000 marks that was to continue until 1923. In return, the orchestra agreed to perform 40 popular concerts *(Volkskonzerte)* at reduced admission and six children's concerts with no admission charge—Muck, vol. 1, pp. 393-403.
8. *Stenographische Berichte über die öffentlichen Sitzungen der Stadtverordnetenversammlungen der Stadt Berlin,* published by the Berliner Magistrat, meeting of 1 December 1927, p. 938.
9. As described at a meeting of the city council, "business-minded individuals" took advantage of the orchestra's financial need, and, under the guise of "doing something for the arts," gained a monopoly over the organization. Ibid., meeting of 16 December 1926, p. 1109. A later account explains that the Philharmonic found itself bound by disadvantageous contracts with both the concert agent Wolff & Sachs and the owner of the "Philharmonie" concert hall, the Landecker firm. The latter was particularly reprehensible, since the orchestra was paying huge rents for a hall with inadequate acoustics, and the owner prohibited radio broadcasts for any concerts performed on the premises. Ibid., meeting of 1 December 1927, p. 940.
10. Confidential report, 18 June 1927, Bundesarchiv Koblenz (hereafter cited as BAK): R 55/1144, fol. 25.
11. Report on meeting between Lange (Berlin Stadtsyndikus) and Kestenberg (Preußisches Kultusministerium), 4 July 1927, BAK: R 55/1144, fol. 31.
12. *Stenographische Berichte,* meeting of 1 December 1927, p. 939.
13. Ibid., meeting of 12 September 1929, p. 753.
14. Ibid., meeting of 16 December 1926, p. 1109.
15. The city's subsidy rose from 60,000 RM, sustained from 1911 to 1923 and adjusted during the inflation, to 200,000 RM in 1927. "Bericht über die Entwicklung der wirtschaftlichen Verhältnisse des Philharmonischen Orchesters," (no date), BAK: R 55/1144, fols. 74-75.
16. Magistrat to Reichsminister des Innern, 6 February 1928, BAK: R 55/1144, fol. 57.
17. While the Reich was taking its time in reaching a decision, the city was forced to come through with another 50,000 RM, and the orchestra was forced to

borrow the remaining 45,000 RM. The Reich Finance Ministry refused to cover the 45,000 RM loan. "Betreff: Philharmonisches Orchester" (no date), BAK: R 55/1144, fols. 50-53.

18. *Stenographische Berichte,* meeting of 1 December 1927, p. 941.
19. Preußischer Minister für Wissenschaft, Kunst und Volksbildung to the Reichsminister des Innern, 17 April 1928, BAK: R 55/1144, fol. 60.
20. In 1926, Friedrich C. A. Lange noted in his diary the recommendation of merging the Berlin Philharmonic and the Berlin Symphony Orchestra in order to have to support only one organization, presumably as a municipal orchestra (Lange, *Groß-Berliner Tagebuch 1920-1933* [Berlin: Berlinische Verlagsbuchhandlung, 1951], entry for 21 January 1926, p. 76). A second recommendation for reorganization came in a meeting in the summer of 1927 between Lange and Leo Kestenberg, Prussian administrator of musical affairs, when the two considered solving the budget problems by making the members of the orchestra equivalent to city civil servants (Aktenvermerk, 4 July 1927, BAK: R 55/1144, fols. 31-32).
21. Report on meeting, 13 December 1928, BAK: R 55/1144, fol. 71. Further refinements of the reorganization plan included assigning proportional amounts of the deficit to be covered by the three governments, taking into account the probability that Prussia would not be overly cooperative. Donnevert met with representatives from the city and Prussia and drew up the proposal that the city assume five-eighths of the 400,000 RM deficit, or 250,000 RM, the Reich two-eighths, and Prussia one-eighth, or the city assume three-quarters (the report erroneously states "8/16" but gives the figure 300,000, or three-quarters of the 400,000 RM deficit), the Reich three-sixteenths, and Prussia only one-sixteenth. Report [by Donnevert] dated 23 January 1929, BAK: R 55/1144, fol. 94.
22. Magistrat to Donnevert, 23 January 1929, BAK: R 55/1144, fol. 96.
23. "Städtische verstaatlichte Philharmoniker," *Vossische Zeitung,* 23 September 1929, reprinted in Muck, vol. 2, *1922-1982,* p. 71.
24. "Berliner Philharmoniker G.m.b.H. Der 1/2-Millionen-Zuschuß der Stadt/Furtwänglers Vertrag/Das künstlerische Programm," reprinted in Muck, vol. 2, p. 72.
25. Lange, *Groß-Berliner Tagebuch,* entry for 8 January 1930, p. 132.
26. Wilhelm Furtwängler, "Das Philharmonische Orchester," in Alfred Einstein, *50 Jahre Berliner Philharmonisches Orchester* (Berlin: n.p., 1932), p. 16.
27. Furtwängler to Brüning, 30 August 1930, BAK: R 43 I/828, fol. 174.
28. The city initially reduced its annual subsidy from 360,000 RM to 240,000 and then reduced its promised semiannual subsidy of 120,000 RM by half as part of its emergency program, forcing the Philharmonic musicians and the assistant

conductor to suffer pay cuts, while the less famous Berlin Symphony Orchestra received all of its benefits as promised, unaffected by the emergency cuts. "Musik zwischen Hangen und Bangen," *Nachtausgabe* [name of newspaper omitted in reprint], 2 October 1931, reprinted in Muck, vol. 2, pp. 87-88; and "Soll das Berliner Philharmonische Orchester zerschlagen werden?" *Berliner Zeitung,* 11 November 1931, reprinted in Muck, vol. 2, p. 88.
29. Lange, *Groß-Berliner Tagebuch,* entry for 10 June 1932, p. 170.
30. "Berliner Sinfonie-Orchester endgültig aufgelöst," *Nachtausgabe* [name of newspaper omitted in reprint], 6 June 1932, reprinted in Muck, vol. 2, p. 92.
31. Muck, vol. 2, p. 96.
32. Lange, *Groß-Berliner Tagebuch,* entry for 16 July 1932, pp. 171-72.
33. Donnevert to Finanzamt "Börse" in Berlin, 10 January 1933, BAK: R 55/1146, fol. 85.
34. Donnevert to Finanzministerium, BAK: R 55/1146, fol. 89.
35. *Stenographische Berichte,* meeting of 1 December 1927, pp. 998ff. Hoffmann-Gwinner refers to the fact that the well-known conductors never lead the popular concerts, admission prices are too high, and the "Philharmonie" concert hall does not allow radio broadcasts of the concerts held there.
36. *Stenographische Berichte,* meeting of 9 September 1929, pp. 753ff.
37. Lange, *Groß-Berliner Tagebuch,* p. 164.
38. Opinion expressed by Prussian Kultusminister. Summary report "Betreff: Philharmonisches Orchester," presumably written in June 1927, BAK: R 55/1144, fol. 51.
39. Confidential report on meeting with Kestenberg, dated 18 June 1927, BAK: R 55/1144, fol. 25.
40. Aktenvermerk, 4 July 1927, BAK: R 55/1144, fol. 31; Preußischer Minister für Wissenschaft, Kultur und Volksbildung (signed von Achenbach) to Reichsminister des Innern, 17 April 1928, BAK: R 55/1144, fol. 60.
41. Lorenz Höber, Geschäftsführer of the Berlin Philharmonic, to Dr. Höpker-Aschoff in the Preußisches Finanzministerium, 27 January 1931, Geheimes Staatsarchiv Berlin-Dahlem (hereafter cited as GStA): Rep. 151/1054, fol. 2.
42. Berndt to Reich Ministry of the Interior, 10 October 1927, BAK: R 55/1144, fols. 40-41.
43. Donnevert to Finanzamt "Börse" in Berlin, 10 January 1933, BAK: R 55/1146, fol. 85.
44. A letter dated 6 April 1933, just a few weeks after the establishment of the Propaganda Ministry, reports:
> the director of the ministry, Mr. Greiner, has just informed me over the telephone that the music director Dr. Furtwängler has also turned to Reichsminister Dr. Goebbels on the question of an increase in the

Reich's subsidy for the Philharmonic Orchestra. On the basis of this conversation, Dr. Goebbels has it in mind to claim responsibility for the Philharmonic Orchestra within his ministry and if necessary intends to bring up the matter tomorrow or in one of the next cabinet meetings.

Letter presumably from Donnevert (bears same hand-signed initial as other letters) to "Herrn Staatssekretär," 6 April 1933, BAK: R 55/1146, fol. 112.

45. Draft of minutes of meeting, 12 April 1933, GStA: Rep. 151/1054, fols. 8-9.
46. Berta Geissmar, *The Baton and the Jackboot* (London: Hamish Hamilton, 1944), p. 77.
47. Fred K. Prieberg, *Musik im NS-Staat* (Frankfurt: Fischer, 1982), pp. 43-44.
48. The two letters appear in Joseph Wulf, *Musik im Dritten Reich* (Gütersloh: Mohn, 1963), pp. 86-89, and in English translation in Jeremy Noakes and Geoffrey Pridham, *Documents on Nazism, 1919-1945* (London: Jonathan Cape, 1974), pp. 342-44.
49. Hafemann held the position of "state inspector for the protection of businesses."
50. Hafemann to orchestra, 22 April 1933, BAK: R 55/1146, fol. 141; orchestra to Hafemann, 26 April, ibid., fol. 142; and Höber to Pfundtner, 26 April, ibid., fols. 139-40.
51. Geissmar, pp. 81-82.
52. Furtwängler to Goebbels, 30 April 1933, BAK: R 55/1138, fols. 102-5.
53. Muck, vol. 2, p. 102.
54. Notes from meeting of the same day (31 May 1933), GStA: Rep. 151/1054, fols. 12-13.
55. Office of the Propagandaminister (signature illegible) to Popitz, 2 June 1933, GStA: Rep. 151/1054, fol. 10.
56. Minutes of 28 July meeting, dated 31 July 1933, GStA: Rep. 151/1054, fol. 32.
57. Bürgermeister to Preußisches Finanzministerium, 22 September 1933, GStA: Rep. 151/1054, fol. 36.
58. Höber to von Keudell, 18 August 1933, BAK: R 55/1147, fols. 54-56.
59. Geissmar, pp. 91-97.
60. Fritz Schröder to Hitler [no date], BAK: R 55/1147, fols. 34-35; Schwebel to Finanzministerium, 17 May 1934, BAK: R 55/1147, fol. 102; Walter Neander to NS Kriegsopferversorgung, 10 November 1933, BAK: R 55/1148, fol. 44.
61. "Tatsachenbericht über Vorgänge im Berliner Philharmonischen Orchester" [no date, no earlier than January 1934], BAK: R 55/1147, fols. 43-47.
62. Furtwängler to members of the orchestra, 1 August 1933, BAK: R 55/1147, fol. 25.

63. "Arbeitsplan der Philharmoniker," *Vossische Zeitung,* 18 September 1933, reprinted in Muck, vol. 2, p. 105. Schmidtseck was the orchestra's Nazi Party representative.
64. "Arbeitsgebiet und Arbeitseinteilung der Geschäftsführung des Berliner Philharmonischen Orchesters" [no date], BAK: R 55/1148, fol. 61.
65. Muck, vol. 2, pp. 112-13.
66. Keudell to Funk [minutes of meeting of 10 March 1934], 12 March 1934, Berlin Document Center (hereafter BDC), Furtwängler file.
67. Keudell to Funk [minutes of meeting of 10 March 1934], 12 March 1934, BDC Furtwängler file.
68. Minutes of meeting between "Dir. 1" and Furtwängler, 14 March 1934, BDC Furtwängler file.
69. Göring, for instance, had control over the Prussian state theaters in his capacity as Prussian minister of the interior. He took this role very seriously, exerting his authority in artistic and personnel questions for "his" opera house and "his" theaters.
70. Reichsminister für Volksaufklärung und Propaganda to Preußisches Finanzministerium, 27 October 1936, GStA: Rep. 151/1054, fol. 53; Reichsminister für Volksaufklärung und Propaganda to Generalintendanten in Dresden and Munich, 9 July 1934, GStA: Rep. 151/216.
71. *Berliner Philharmonisches Orchester: 1882-1942* (Berlin: Berliner Philharmonisches Orchester, 1942). The first page of this publication displays a full-page portrait of Goebbels with the caption: "Der Schirmherr des Berliner Philharmonischen Orchesters."
72. Preußischer Finanzminister to Ministerpräsident, 19 February 1935, GStA: Rep. 151/200.
73. Reichsminister für Volksaufklärung und Propaganda to Preußisches Finanzministerium, 27 October 1936, GStA: Rep. 151/1054, fol. 53.
74. Goebbels to Reichsminister der Finanzen, 13 August 1936, GStA: Rep. 151/1054, fols. 59-60.
75. "Bericht des künstlerischen Leiters über die Spielzeit 1938/39," BAK: R 55/197, fol. 94.
76. Muck, vol. 3, *Die Mitglieder des Orchesters. Die Programme. Die Konzertreisen. Erst- und Uraufführungen,* pp. 260-61, 263, 265-68, 273-75, 278-81, 287, 293-94, 297-99, 301-3, 305-7, 309-10, and 312-14. On the film *Philharmoniker,* see Muck, vol. 2, p. 179; and Elke Fröhlich, ed., *Die Tagebücher von Joseph Goebbels: Sämtliche Fragmente* (München: K. G. Saur, 1987), vol. 4, p. 661 (entry for 27 May 1941), where Goebbels claims to have thought out the entire plot outline already.

77. Letter from orchestra to NS Kulturgemeinde in der NS Gemeinschaft "Kraft durch Freude," 18 January 1935, BAK: R 55/1148, fol. 109.
78. Lengthy report by von Benda [no date, no earlier than January 1940], p. 4, BDC Hans von Benda file.
79. Keudell to Funk [minutes of meeting of 10 March 1934], 12 March 1934, BDC Furtwängler file.
80. Gesellschaftsvertrag des Berliner Philharmonischen Orchesters, 19 June 1934, BAK: R 55/951, fols. 228-32.
81. BAK: R 55/192, fol. 25; R 55/197, fol. 186; R 55/1148, fols. 10, 54, and 173.
82. Kohler to Staatssekretär, 17 August 1938, BAK: R 55/197, fol. 33.
83. Stegmann (Berlin Philharmonic Orchestra) to Goebbels, 13 October 1939, BAK: R 55/197, fol. 109.
84. Dieter Blum and Emanuel Eckardt, *Das Orchester: Die Innenwelt der Berliner Philharmoniker* (Stuttgart: Scripta Verlag, 1983), pp. 123-24, and Wolfgang Stresemann, *The Berlin Philharmonic from Bülow to Karajan: Home and History of a World-Famous Orchestra* (Berlin: Stapp Verlag, 1979), pp. 83-84.
85. Prieberg, p. 299.
86. Wulf, p. 372.
87. Wulf, p. 372, n. 1.
88. Prieberg, p. 145.
89. Stravinsky protested his inclusion in the exhibit and received an apology from the foreign affairs office in Paris. Joan Evans, "Stravinsky's Music in Hitler's Germany," paper delivered at the meeting of the American Musicological Society, Chicago, November 1991, pp. 11-12.
90. Ibid., pp. 4-8.
91. Ibid., pp. 10-11.
92. Prieberg, p. 54.
93. Evans, p. 13, and conversation with the author; Heinz Drewes (head of RMVP music department) to NSDAP Reichsleitung, Hauptstelle Musik, 3 January 1940—BAK: NS 15/99: "Above all, performances of works by protected composers from hostile foreign countries, for example Debussy, Ravel, Stravinsky, must cease." According to Evans, p. 13, the Reich Music Chamber issued an official ban on Stravinsky on 1 February 1940.
94. Dr. Fritz Stege, "Ausgerechnet Strawinsky? Zweites Kleiber-Konzert in der Philharmonie," *Völkischer Beobachter*, No. 320 (16 November 1934), p. 6.
95. "Kleiber dirigiert Strawinskij," *Frankfurter Zeitung*, 17 November 1934. Clippings of this review and the review in note 94, above, are in GStA: Rep. 151/1054, fol. 39.
96. Donald W. Ellis, "Music Censorship in the Third Reich," Memphis State University, Tennessee (ms., photocopy in the Wiener Library, Tel Aviv).

97. Ernst Reuter, *Schriften, Reden* II (Berlin: Propyläen, 1973), p. 274.
98. "It is not agreeable to us that the members of the orchestra become so-called civil servants under this reorganization [1929].... The Philharmonic Orchestra had its greatest era as long as the members were free artists. We feel that artistry and civil service will not go well together." *Stenographische Berichte*, meeting of 12 September 1929, p. 755.
99. These officials could review the books and determine how much aid was needed and how it could best be used (Aktenvermerk, 4 July 1927, BAK: R 55/1144, fols. 31-32; and Magistrat-Kunst to Reichsinnenministerium, 11 June 1928, BAK: R 55/1144, fol. 65). Their number rose from one to five in 1929, and in 1932, the new corporation contract drawn up for the merger of the Philharmonic with the Symphony Orchestra allowed two members from the Reich Ministry of the Interior to serve on the board as well (Oberbürgermeister to Reichsinnenministerium, 15 October 1932, BAK: R 55/1146, fol. 77).
100. Guttsman, p. 158.
101. Fritz Jöde, "Jugendmusikbewegung und Hausmusik," *Die Musik* 24 (1932): 564-69.
102. Eugen Schmitz, "Die Zukunft der Hausmusik," *Hochland* 17 (1919-20): 254-56; Georg Schünemann, "Die Lage der Hausmusik," *Die Musik* 24 (1932): 561-64; Peter Raabe, "Wege zur Belebung der Hausmusik," *Allgemeine Musikzeitung* 60 (1933): 353-55.
103. Schünemann, pp. 562-63.
104. Karl Blessinger, "Repertoirebildung und Gebrauchsmusik," *Allgemeine Musikzeitung* 56 (1929): 311; Schünemann, p. 561.
105. Korte, "Bildungs- und Ausbildungsfragen der Musik," *Die Musik* 28 (1936): 348-56.
106. Muck, vol. 3, pp. 296, 300, 308, and 311.
107. Ibid., p. 314.

4

The Foundations of Theater Policy in Nazi Germany

Bogusław Drewniak
Translated from the German by Glenn R. Cuomo

> Whether actor or poet
> now the same applies
> Each is now only a straightforward
> Devotee to the Führer and Reich
> —Dr. Rainer Schlösser, Reich dramaturgist[1]

SOURCES AND STUDIES

Investigators of the state of theater in the "Third Reich" have a relatively large number of sources at their disposal. These consist primarily of the documents of Joseph Goebbels' Reich Ministry for Popular Enlightenment and Propaganda (Reichspropagandaministerium für Volksaufklärung und Propaganda, or RMVP) and other central agencies in the state and the Nazi Party. In addition to these documents, which are located in Germany's main archives,[2] there are documents of "provincial" origin in numerous archives in Germany as well as in the territories occupied by the Germans after 1938. The extant archival material—in part still little known—represents a treasure trove for further research. The handwritten and typed sources are supplemented by many printed materials: newspapers, specialized journals, and documentations,[3] and last but not least by the published memoirs of several contemporaries, artists in particular. Of course these memoirs, which at the same time are more or less defenses, present a world different from the one depicted in the documents.[4]

The techniques of coercion with which the Nazi regime subjugated the arts have been described often. The specialized literature on the subject of theater under National Socialism includes important works of literary scholarship,[5] monographs,[6] and works focusing on selected themes.[7] Furthermore, there are numerous publications available on theatrical life in the individual cities and provinces of the Reich.[8] Nevertheless, the material pertaining to theater policy and the actual theatrical practice in the Nazi state has not yet been completely processed and collected. This fact is noteworthy in that so much else is being published on the Third Reich. But it is in part understandable: Theater scholars and contemporary historians both think that National Socialist theater policy is not entirely their subject.

TRADITION AND THE NAZI PRESENT

In 1933, a political regime came into power in Germany that also wanted to revolutionize the theater, one of its favorite children. The Hitler regime demanded a "reconstruction of the German theater," and, from a scholarly and distanced perspective, we can say in retrospect that of all the public cultural institutions, theater probably was the one shaken the most in the Nazi state. While we can speak of a far-reaching restructuring of the ideological (political and "racial") foundations of this artistic institution, in the last analysis, characteristic structures of the German theater were affected little after the Nazi assumption of power. At first the Nazi Party and the state apparatus emphasized the alternative theater form of the *Thingspiele* (Thing plays, an open-air performance form based on the early Germanic ritual assembly known as the *Thing*); however, they soon retreated from a one-sided preference for the "choral-declamatory mass play."[9] As early as 1936 the *Thingtheater* lost its "importance to the Reich." Although the various early forms of the new "Volk play" were respected, and to a limited extent even promoted, the state endorsed a formal structure in the Aristotelian tradition.

From 1934 on, there was often debate on the dissolution of private theaters, and for political reasons their financial support was cut back significantly. In contrast, the regime deliberately promoted the expansion of various touring theaters (into Nazi enterprises). Having developed in a surprisingly short period of time from relatively modest beginnings, open-air theater temporarily became an essential component of summertime cultural life. Troupes performed in front of medieval fortresses and castles, in market squares, in the woods, on stone ridges, and the like. Whereas in 1932 there were approximately 50 open-air stages, in 1937 Germany had more than 200.

In general, however, the theater was supposed to maintain a tradition of high cultural standards in the employment of its means "for the spiritual struggle." It was bound to forms that had been evolving for generations. As a consequence, the tasks of the transformed theater did not deviate from the existing principles for the makeup of theater programs prior to the National Socialists' assumption of power. Leopold Jessner, for example, the artistic manager and director at the Staatliches Schauspielhaus Berlin, adhered to the following hierarchy: (1) classics, (2) standard works of contemporary literature, (3) attempts by young authors, and (4) entertaining pieces.[10] The outward organization thus remained relatively undisturbed. Yet behind it a "revolution" took place step by step. The politically motivated selection of theatrical pieces and their production, the promotion of desirable authors and themes, the elimination of theatrical material that was "alien to the race" (a very flexible concept), the so-called politics of the day, and numerous other restrictions substantially changed theater in Nazi Germany. The apogee occurred during the war period.

Theater was dependent on people. The German theater scholar Uwe-Karsten Ketelsen asked "What made it possible that most of the 'great names' of Third Reich theater were already great before 1933 and remained so after 1945?"[11] The Nazi regime needed "great names." When it came to power, it was willing to make more than just a few concessions to authors, composers, directors, performers, and stage designers who already had gained a reputation. To be sure, many theater people—including the most prominent names—had to leave their positions, mostly for "racial" reasons. Many went into exile. In the vacuum created, many minor devotees of the art—who were "politically acceptable"—rushed to the vacated positions. Moreover, many of the big names of the theater and screen were all too happy to appear on the stage that Goebbels offered them; these opportunists saw nothing besides their own talent. In isolated cases, the accommodation to propagandistic and political contents was probably a means of deception to protect the artistic institution and politically and racially persecuted individuals. The director of the Deutsches Theater in Berlin, Heinz Hilpert, and the principal conductor of the Berlin Philharmonic, Wilhelm Furtwängler, can be mentioned as examples here.[12] Whether those who remained in Germany and collaborated made the correct decision remains a controversial question to the present day. On the one hand, the great American-born violinist and conductor Yehudi Menuhin speculated how extraordinary political circumstances could have moved artists to demonstrate the courage of their convictions: "I have to admit, if I were living in America and America got a fascist regime I would be the first to leave the country, and I do not find that to be courageous at all. I would have a much higher opinion of myself if I decided to stay and do what I could."[13] Bernhard Minetti, on the other hand, an actor who stayed and continued his career on both the stage and in film under the Hitler regime, describes this period in less noble and "heroic" terms:

> I didn't look. I closed my eyes, knowing what Hitler signified. I did nothing against it. Perhaps I was a coward. These are questions of conscience. I see through the evil of the world. I also saw through National Socialism. I am not stupid and insensitive. But I learned to maintain my distance. I developed the ability to close myself off out of self-protection. My existence is my life in the theater. To be an actor is my drive, my necessity. I had to keep myself alive in the service of literature, as its enacter. Theater was my salvation and has been so up until this day.[14]

The Berlin theater scholar Hennig Rischbieter, too, provides no accounts of courage of one's conviction: "It is fundamentally horrible how quickly even the formerly leftist theater people accommodated the Nazis at a time when no immediate coercion existed."[15]

The Nazi state knew what it had in its artists and concerned itself with their material well-being. It enticed them with money and titles, such as "state performer, general artistic director, professor, member of the Reich cultural senate," and the like, as well as with prizes, medals, and honors. At official state and Party functions, Hitler and his vassals liked to surround themselves with prominent figures from stage and screen. That did not mean, however, that the Nazi potentates loved all these artists.

Germany at that time was the richest site of theatrical activity in Europe. Around 1932/33, the "Old Reich" encompassed approximately 200 competing communal, state, and private theatrical companies. Of the 167 permanent theaters listed in the 1932 *Bühnenjahrbuch,* 120 were run as nonprofit enterprises. The spectrum ranged from highly funded opera houses (15 in number) and drama stages of the highest quality to a large number of medium-level multipurpose municipal auditoriums, down to smaller enterprises. During the 12 years of Nazi rule, the number of permanent theaters increased steadily, mostly through territorial annexations rather than through new construction. (The most important new buildings of the prewar period were in Dessau and Saarbrücken.) For many cities new theaters were planned: mass stages in the large cities but also in smaller locations. "Even in small cities the theaters must be constructed in such a way—Hitler decreed—that they offer space for the broad masses. Theater belongs to the *Volk*. The prices have to be regulated accordingly."[16]

According to the figures calculated by the Reich Office of Statistics, in 1939 Germany, including the "Ostmark" (Austria) and the Sudetenland, possessed 241 state, provincial, and municipal theaters with 211,479 seats; 47 private theaters with 45,264 seats; 44 summer theaters with 24,675; and 129 open-air theaters with 236,800 seats. The number of cities that could claim a permanent theater as their own grew to 303; 182 performing troupes not based at one location set up their "tents" temporarily in theaterless localities. These troupes consisted of 45 provincial and traveling stages, 20 guest performance stages, 74 traveling theatrical enterprises, 30 low-German dialect stages, and 13 peasant theaters. For the season 1942/43, there was in the "Greater German Reich" a total of 322,287 theater seats and 358 theater houses. In addition, there were a few German theaters in the Protectorate of Bohemia and Moravia, Poland (Generalgouvernement), Holland, France, Norway, the Balkans, the Baltic republics, and the Soviet Union. The number of people working in theater grew from 26,119 in the 1934/35 season to 36,441 after the *Anschluß*, and by 1939/40, the German theaters employed 38,400 people. Some 17,700 of them remained obligatory members of the Reichstheaterkammer (RTK, or Reich Theater Chamber) established by the National Socialists. A further 7,240 theater employees were orchestra members who, with the exception of the conductors, were members of the Reichsmusikkammer (Reich Music Chamber). The Deutsche Arbeitsfront (DAF; German Labor Front) comprised 13,400 theater people (the stagehands, administrative personnel, as well as ushers, coat checkers, etc.). The membership of the Theater Chamber can be broken down into the following professional categories: 230 managers and directors, 790 artistic stage managers, 2,730 actors, 1,560 actresses, 1,600 male vocalists, 1,140 female vocalists, 870 stage managers and prompters, 4,260 chorus members, 1,800 dancers, and 1,900 technical staff members. During the last season of 1943/44, some 45,000 people were employed by the theater.

Visiting the theater came to be considered a "national obligation," rather than merely an evening's distraction for the wealthy; no longer the center for magic, elation, and distraction, productions focused on the "struggle." The number of theatergoers tripled from 520,000 in 1932 to 1.6 million in 1936 and grew steadily until 1943. As the Nazi leadership stated, the theater visit was supposed to uplift people—"Aryans," at least—from their daily routine and to aid in the mastering of life in the National Socialist sense. As early as 1933, the

Hitler regime had made plans to prohibit Jews from attending public theaters, cinemas, and the like.[17] This measure was not instituted until after the great pogrom in 1938.[18] During the war, the residents of the occupied areas in the East and foreign forced laborers in the Reich also were subjected to bans on attendance or to extensive restrictions.

The Nazi state's attempt to shift theater from the private sphere more and more into the focal point of a "national cultural policy" culminated in a series of key events, the Reich Theater Festival Weeks. With the Propaganda Ministry and the Reich Chamber of Culture acting as their sponsors, these festival weeks took place in conjunction with programmatic speeches by Goebbels. Very often the "Führer" was present, although he refrained from making any official proclamations. But during these weeks Hitler's favorite composers (first and foremost Richard Wagner) and dramatists he admired (such as Dietrich Eckart) were given major consideration. The first Reich Theater Week took place in Dresden from 27 May to 3 June 1934, opening with Wagner's *Tristan und Isolde* in the State Opera. Both Hitler and Goebbels were in the box of honor. The second Reich Theater Week, which took place in Hamburg from 16 to 23 June 1935, concluded with a gala performance of the *Meistersinger* in the State Opera, with Hitler in attendance. Wilhelm Furtwängler stood at the podium, and the best talents from the entire Reich sang as guest performers. Just as festive in character was the next Reich Theater Week in Munich (10-17 May 1936). Wagner's *Rienzi,* at the State Opera, opened the celebration, and Hitler, Hess, Goebbels, and other prominent Nazis attended as guests of honor. The fourth Reich Theater Festival in 1937 moved to western Germany, opening in Cologne and closing in Worms. The next one, originally planned for Stuttgart, was eventually transferred to "liberated" Vienna (12-19 June 1938). From then on Goebbels wanted Vienna to be the festival's permanent location, yet only the sixth Reich Theater Festival Week in 1939 was held there. As a sign of the "ever-strengthening alliance with Italy" that year, Goebbels invited numerous official guests from the neighboring country. Thereafter, the war prevented these expensive festival weeks from taking place.

The Heidelberg Reich Festival Performances, established in 1926, were significant for and highly esteemed by the entire nation. Whereas the Reich League of German Open-air and Volk Plays in Berlin was considered to be the organizer, in reality these festival plays were under the direct control of the RMVP. As its actual patron, Goebbels in 1939 was made an honorary citizen of Heidelberg. The Propaganda Ministry also promoted several other special events connected with the honoring of the great authors allowed in the Third Reich (Shakespeare, Goethe, Schiller, and Grabbe, among others).

"The theaters must above all things also be accessible to the youth," Hitler proclaimed in 1938. "Not at eighteen is the young person ready for the theater, but from his earliest youth on. One has to train young talent for the theater."[19] The Reich dramaturgist Rainer Schlösser argued along these lines: "The success or failure of our efforts to win over the youth for the theater is tantamount to the life or death of our theater culture."[20] In this vein, the regime carried out the strongly politically oriented Reich Theater Days of the Hitler Youth (in Bochum in 1937, in Hamburg in 1938); the Festival Plays of the German Youth in Weimar (under the patronage of the German Schiller Organization); the Theater Week of the Hitler Youth, also in Weimar; the Theater Week of the Hitler Youth in Heilbronn; as well as the Hitler Youth and Theater events held since 1939 in Erfurt.

Of course, the Bayreuth Festival Performances experienced their greatest blossoming in the Nazi period. Winifred Wagner, the "Mistress of Bayreuth," held the direction firmly in her hand. As sole patron, only the Führer appeared in public, while Goebbels maintained an objective distance from the performances and supported them with Propaganda Ministry funds only out of consideration of Winifred Wagner's influence with Hitler.[21] In order to fill the seats in Richard Wagner's Festival Theater, numerous state and Party agencies—*nolens volens* also Goebbels' ministry—had to make a great effort. After 1939, the aim of festival performances was to further the war effort. The Nazi organization Kraft durch Freude (KdF, or Strength through Joy) transported wounded and decorated soldiers, armaments workers, and others to Bayreuth and treated them as "honored guests." Even in 1943 KdF accommodated some 30,000 guests, and as late as 1944, special trains carried soldiers and armaments workers to Bayreuth for the fifth Wartime Festival Performances.

In 1938, the Reich took over the famous festival plays in Salzburg—now part of the Ostmark—which since 1922 had been a site of artistic pilgrimage in Europe. Bernhard Paumgartner, a "Salzburg cultural institution," was relieved of his office as director of the Mozarteum, and the well-known German conductor Clemens Krauss became *maître de plaisir*. With great propagandistic pomp directed by Goebbels, the Salzburg Festival took place as a Reich event for the first time in the summer of 1938. In 1939, the Salzburg Festspielhaus was remodeled—a project for which Hitler donated 350,000 Reichsmark (RM). However, the festival performances found their true patron and supporter in the person of the Reich propaganda minister. In Salzburg—in stark contrast to Bayreuth—Goebbels felt at home and appeared as the host.

It was not by accident that the festival performances in Salzburg lost some of their luster. By 1938, many artists who had lent the events prestige and character were not allowed or no longer wanted to appear. Yet the festival on the River Salzach did not have to worry about its privileged status. In Salzburg there seemed to be no lack of money. While as before, Mozart remained the mainstay of the festival performances, the Propaganda Ministry was working on a new concept. In the summer of 1942, Clemens Krauss stated that he had received a ten-year contract as director of the festival performances and had been given the task of establishing a prominent art center for Mozart in Salzburg, similar to what had been done for Wagner in Bayreuth. The Reich subsidies were tripled, but the effort never progressed beyond the planning stage. Despite these long-range preparations, in 1943, Hitler decreed that the Salzburg Festival performances no longer take place. In order to avoid showing foreign countries that wartime shortages had caused the cessation of these cultural events known throughout the world, a Salzburg Theater and Music Summer 1943 was put on from 4 to 29 August.

THE STATE AND OFFICIAL PARTY APPARATUS FOR CONTROL

The theater policy of the National Socialist holders of power remained a highly opaque web of overlapping competencies. In the Third Reich theater policy was made by several state and Party organizations and agencies, including Goebbels' Theater Department in the Reich Ministry for Popular Enlightenment and Propaganda together with the Reich Theater Chamber under its control; the Party agencies of Alfred Rosenberg; Robert Ley's German Labor Front; and the Leisure Time Organization KdF and its theater clubs. Not all of them had an organized power base. The Prussian State Theaters (comprising Berlin's two representative stages, the Deutsche Staatsoper and the Preußisches Schauspielhaus, as well as some provincial theaters) were under the control of the Prussian minister president, Hermann Göring. In other provinces, or *Gaue*, the local *Gauleiter* exercised a not inconsiderable influence on theater policy. The influences of diverse Nazi organizations, such as that of the Reich Youth Leadership, also should not be underestimated and should be investigated in more depth. The Gestapo, with its innumerable spies, was an important factor—especially with respect to bans. Although these state, police, and Party power apparatuses functioned each for itself, by necessity also in union, this did not result in chaos. All worked together to the advantage of the system.

Of decisive importance were the regulations introduced by a uniform Theater Law of 15 May 1934 and subsequent executive orders. With the help of this law and the legislation establishing the Reich Chamber of Culture,

Goebbels consolidated into his purview almost all the previous provincial theatrical jurisdictions. This does not mean that the leadership claim of the Propaganda Ministry in all theater questions was uncontested. Due to Göring's efforts in Prussia, for example, a Prussian law was enacted regarding the restructuring and administration of the state theaters.[22]

In the Third Reich, the Theater Department in the Propaganda Ministry oversaw all personnel, subsidy, and program policy. The only exceptions were the theater administrations of the Prussian State Theaters, which were within the purview of the Prussian minister president. Following the various reorganizations of the ministry, the Theater Department, as the ministry's twelfth section, was divided in seven subdivisions with the following charges:[23]

1. Personnel matters. The Theater Department oversaw the hiring and confirmation of managers and artistic directors (first conductors, dramaturgists, heads of production) with the cooperation of the provinces and the cities (when they were legal entities), with the Reich Propaganda Offices,[24] which functioned as the Propaganda Ministry's provincial branches (which also had a culture department with a section for theater and music), and with the cooperation of the RTK as well as the Party offices. The department oversaw support of theatrical employees and of young talent with the collaboration of the RTK, theatrical agencies, agents, and stage directors, under the supervision of the RTK.

2. Reich dramaturgy. The Theater Department screened and supervised the entire production in the area of drama, opera and operetta, with the aid of the stage organization; it examined and influenced the programs of all German stages, and furthered interaction between playwrights, composers, and theater managements.[25]

3. Choreography. The Theater Department supervised artistic, social, stage, and folk dance; and created guidelines for the training of young talent and of dance directors and dance teachers through the "German Dance Stage" and the "German Master Schools for Dance."[26]

4. Theater budget. The Theater Department managed the funds for the Reich theaters; processed subsidy matters of the other theaters; assisted traveling stages; and promoted theater culture.

5. Special performances. The department oversaw preparation and execution of the Reich Festival Performances (held in Heidelberg at first; after 1939 also in Salzburg following the annexation of Austria); preparation for the Reich Theater Festival Weeks, the Grabbe-Days, and the Reich Theater Days of the Hitler Youth; total coordination of all summer festival plays put on in the Reich; supervision of the

festival weeks of individual stages; assisting the youth, open-air, and puppet theaters.

6. Theater law. The Theater Department supervised the execution of the theater law, especially of the granting of licenses to theater operators by the RTK; the processing of special tax matters related to theaters; the pursuit of copyright questions; and assisted in the operation of the lay theater and the supervision of the Reich theaters.

7. Theater matters in foreign countries. This department processed all representative guest performances abroad, as well as of foreign ensembles and artists within the borders;[27] in addition, it assisted German theaters in foreign countries.

Otto Laubinger became head of the Propaganda Ministry's Theater Department in April 1933 and was simultaneously appointed by Goebbels to be president of the RTK. Laubinger, born in 1892, had been affiliated with the Berlin Staatstheater since 1920 and ranked among its most eminent performers. The "highest theater civil servant of the Reich" held these offices only in the first phase of the Nazi Theater Revolution, for Laubinger died in 1935. His successor was Rainer Schlösser, with whom all the most important developments in theatrical life in the Third Reich are linked.

Dr. phil. Schlösser, born in 1899 in Jena, was the son of a university professor and director of the Goethe-and-Schiller Archive in Weimar. Early on he found his way to the National Socialists. A collaborator of the *völkisch* press since 1924, he became Alfred Rosenberg's closest colleague and a member of the National Socialist German Workers' Party (NSDAP) as of 1 October 1931. With the consent of Adolf Hitler, the publisher of the *Völkischer Beobachter,* Schlösser became this Party organ's cultural-political editor in 1931. In the Hitler Youth, he directed the Cultural Office of the Reich Youth Leader, eventually attaining the rank of *Obergebietsführer.* As a journalist, critic, and author of politically oriented poetry, he had extensive cultural-political experience. In October 1933, he transferred to the Reich Propaganda Ministry, where he assumed the office of the Reich dramaturgist. At the same time he became a member of the presiding council of the RTK. As Laubinger's successor after 1935 and Reich dramaturgist, Schlösser simultaneously directed the entire Theater Department in the Propaganda Ministry and also functioned—until 1938—as president of the RTK. Schlösser remained in Goebbels' ministry right up until the end.[28] In 1945, he was captured by Soviet soldiers, taken outside the city, and shot.

According to his official charge as Reich dramaturgist, Schlösser was to promote the application of National Socialist cultural principles and, empowered by the propaganda minister, to relieve the stage managements from "occasionally occurring uncertainties" by issuing "information as to the non-objectionability of dramatic works." Officially, the Reich dramaturgist was thus considered the sole authority for "declarations of objectionability."[29] In this way the office of the Reich dramaturgist represented a central state censoring organ in all questions concerning the makeup of theater programs. The dramaturgist's charge derived from the Theater Law enacted in May 1934, which placed both public and private theaters under the supervision of the Reich propaganda minister and authorized him to prohibit or to demand the performance of certain works.[30] As the Propaganda Ministry's representative, the Reich dramaturgist routinely intervened in program policy; in important cases he consulted with Goebbels. Before the start of every season, the program of every theater in the German Reich had to be presented to the Reich dramaturgist for approval.[31] Moreover, it was compulsory to notify him of special holiday events three weeks in advance.[32]

The Nazi state was willing to invest considerably in theater; since the theaters almost always depended on financial subsidies, the state had special possibilities to make its desired influence and planned manipulation known. The subsidies sometimes had more significance than the censorship machinery. When evaluated in terms of its propagandistic influence, the RMVP Theater Department appeared to be less significant than the departments for film, press, or direct propaganda, for example. However, if we compare the individual budgets, we arrive at quite different measures of importance. In the period from 13 March 1933 to 31 March 1943, the Reich Propaganda Ministry's total expenditures amounted to 1,308,233,707.57 RM. An enormous sum, according to the rate of exchange at the end of 1937, it was the equivalent of more than $520 million US. Among the budget expenditures, theater took first place, receiving 232,945,933 RM (26.4 percent), followed by the so-called active propaganda (21.8 percent) and film (11.5 percent).[33]

The Propaganda Ministry's budget provided direct financing only to stages that could be considered Reich theaters. Up until the war's outbreak, these consisted only of the Theater des Volkes in Berlin (as of 18 January 1934); Theater des Westens in Berlin (as of 22 July 1935); the Municipal Opera in Berlin (as of 1 July 1934), which was renamed Deutsches Opernhaus; the Deutsches Theater in Wiesbaden (as of 1 August 1935); and the Volksbühne in Berlin from 1938 on. Over the course of the war, additional theatrical institutions were added. The most important of these were Vienna's state theaters (the Staatsoper and the Burgtheater together with the Akademietheater), which were highly funded in accordance with the Führer's wish. After special arrangements in the summer of 1941, the Vienna state theaters were considered to be true Reich theaters subordinate to the Reichsstatthalter "only as far as their local cultural direction was concerned." They appeared in the

Propaganda Ministry's budget for the first time that year. In general, however, Goebbels resisted an outright takeover, especially when it came to stages in the occupied territories. It was one thing to take control of the theaters, but another to incorporate them directly into the ministry's budget as Reich undertakings. Consequently, in most cases the financial involvement remained at the subsidy level. Thus, for example, Heinz Hilpert, the director of the "private" Deutsches Theater in Berlin, was de jure a lessee and obligated to remain in continuous contact regarding finances. This fact, of course, forced political concessions from this famous theater and its famous head.

According to the "guidelines for the granting of Reich subsidies to theaters," these subsidies served the purpose of "bringing the theater to the level of performance required for cultural-political reasons or to carry out a specific . . . singular task in the area of theater."[34] In 1933, the Propaganda Ministry subsidies were still very insignificant: around 400,000 RM. In 1934, the subsidies increased substantially, and they continued to grow from year to year. The results can be seen in the following table from a Propaganda Ministry report of 8 February 1943.[35]

Reich Subsidies (in Reichsmark) for German Theaters

	Years	
	1934	1942
Reich theaters	4,000,000	22,200,000
State, municipal, and traveling theaters	5,000,000	14,200,000
Open-air stages	300,000	135,000
Private theaters	300,000	150,000
Festival weeks		1,800,000
Dance schools		370,000
Support for young talent		340,000
Künstlerdank*		250,000
Theaters abroad		1,000,000
Theaters in the Protectorate Bohemia-Moravia		3,300,000
Theater renovations	70,000	1,100,000
TOTAL:	9,670,000	44,845,000

*This was the Goebbels Foundation, which supported needy artists.

With the establishment of the Propaganda Ministry and the Reich Culture Chamber, an institutionalized rivalry between Goebbels and Alfred Rosenberg arose. It was to last until the end of the Third Reich, even though it was hardly visible to the public. Whereas Rosenberg was convinced that he possessed a more profound understanding of art and culture than the propaganda minister, Goebbels viewed his rival as a pure theoretician incapable of organization. Nonetheless, Rosenberg did have some experience in theater matters. Moreover, he had a staff of coworkers at his disposal who had already been dealing with theater issues before the Nazi assumption of power. As early as 1929, one of Rosenberg's closest colleagues and a dedicated adherent to the Nazi cause, Dr. Walter Stang, had set up and assumed the direction of the Dramaturgical Office in the Kampfbund für Deutsche Kultur, founded by Rosenberg in December 1928. In 1933, the Dramaturgical Office evolved into the Theater Department of Rosenberg's National Socialist Cultural Community (Nationalsozialistische-Kulturgemeinde, or NS-KG), which assimilated the Kampfbund in 1934. On 24 January 1934, Rosenberg was appointed the Beauftragter des Führers für die Überwachung der gesamten geistigen und weltanschaulichen Schulung und Erziehung der NSDAP (Führer's Delegate for the Supervision of the Entire Spiritual and Philosophical Schooling and Education of the Party). This pretentious-sounding assignment brought with it a small agency in the Party, which internally carried the rather modest title Dienststelle Rosenberg. Hitler conceived this not only as a consolation for the "old fighter" Rosenberg, but also as a way to keep under surveillance the true cultural dictator, Joseph Goebbels. In order to effect the "systematic education of all *Volksgenossen* (fellow Germans) who regularly partake in cultural life in the spirit of the National Socialist Weltanschauung,"[36] on 6 June 1934 Rosenberg ordered the consolidation of the Kampfbund für Deutsche Kultur with the Reich Organization "German Stage" into the NS-KG. This organization, in turn, later was incorporated into the Party organization Kraft durch Freude (KdF). In 1935, Walter Stang was named head of the NS-KG, which by the end of that year already had 1.5 million members in 2,000 local chapters. The overwhelming majority of the members were unsophisticated, low-income *Volksgenossen*, who up until this point had more or less stayed away from the theater. The NS-KG was integrated into the Office for the Promotion of Art (Amt Kunstpflege) within Rosenberg's "supervision office." The NS-KG constantly attempted to exert a decisive influence on the makeup of theater programs not only as a sui generis censor but also as the organizer of mass performances. Rosenberg's agency examined the plays and also paid close attention to whether the artists fulfilled the National Socialists' ideological expectations. Frequently the list of artists who were "unreliable" from a "cultural-political standpoint" included widely recognized and honored names.

In 1936, Walter Stang reported on the first successes of the Nazi Cultural Community in Berlin:

> Our continuously growing membership made it possible for us to systematically build up a program of events in Berlin. Not only through the number of events does this signify an enormous upturn in the cultural life of the Reich capital, which was formerly dominated by Jews and Marxist asphalt literati ["decadent, metropolitan men of letters"], but this fills us with special pride because we succeeded in demonstrating that our will to cultivate and promote only the most valuable is being understood and acknowledged by all classes and professions of the *Volk*. This year we can now send no less than 750,000 visitors into Berlin's theaters, in particular into the Staatsoper, both state theaters, and into other notable Berlin theaters. And we thus make possible the realization of a program based not only on the consideration of box office success, but primarily on artistic and cultural considerations. . . .[37]

Soon, however, the NS-KG could no longer organize mass events of this type. Through a forced agreement between Alfred Rosenberg and Robert Ley—for technical and financial reasons as well as political factors—in 1937, the NS-KG became part of the Nazi organization "Kraft durch Freude" under the auspices of the DAF. Soon the "idealistic" demands of the organizations under Rosenberg's direction were subjugated to the "materialistic" interests of this influential leisure-time organization. This shift in emphasis occurred with the Führer's approval. With its usual reservations, the Propaganda Ministry was, of course, also in agreement.

To be sure, the KdF adopted Rosenberg's thesis—"The cultural assets of the nation should not be the prerogative of the moneyed class"—but it was altered fundamentally as far as the form and the intrinsic value of theater visits were concerned. This change did not affect the special closed theater performances (which were maintained in order to eliminate the inferiority complexes of working people). Yet now participation in the general theater offerings was fostered, with cheap tickets or other promotional offers at the box office. No longer was it a matter of bringing a broad spectrum of "*Volksgenossen*" to an explicitly propagandistic theater; the goal turned to capitalizing propagandistically on the mass attendance in the bourgeois-traditional theater.[38]

By 1937 the KdF had already taken over the cultural support of the soldiers as the Wehrmacht's equivalent of the USO. At that time the first "soldier stages" came about as touring theaters with professional actors. Some permanent professional theaters also were employed in the support of the Wehrmacht. As early as September 1939, at the war's onset, several existing or newly formed ensembles took on the duties of front-line theaters. In addition, numerous permanent stages traveled to the front to entertain the troops. In October 1939, the Supreme Command of the Wehrmacht (Department Wehrmacht Propaganda) now shared the responsibility for the deployment of front-line theater groups with the KdF and the Propaganda Ministry. The Wehrmacht provided the funds, and the overall planning was done by the Propaganda Ministry.[39] The Supreme Command organized the overall troop support together with the KdF, while the Propaganda Ministry assisted only in special cases when performances of the highest quality were concerned. Furthermore, this ministry was responsible for guest performances in "the European territory undergoing a new ordering" under the Nazi occupation, which were taking on an extraordinary scale. Naturally, these activities differed significantly depending on the region and target audience. Neutral countries and those friendly to the Third Reich were also flooded with German artistic performances. They were not always a matter of glorifying military deeds or celebrating annexational tendencies; often the performances only attempted to gain political sympathies, by the misuse of high traditional values of Europe. Until 1944, entire caravans of German theater people—among them many of the most prominent[40]—were on the road in Europe in order to present what the state and they themselves took to be German culture. Thus the theater served the "cultural-political mission" of demonstrating that Hitler's Germany could dominate Europe both culturally and militarily.[41]

PROGRAM CONTROL AND PROGRAM INFLUENCE

To what extent did those in power succeed in "nazifying" or politicizing the makeup of the theater programs? What determined the nature of German theater in the Hitler era? Scholars of theater, history, and political science are debating these questions today. My findings show that the politicizing of the programs, especially in the area of legitimate theater, proceeded very rapidly.

It is hardly possible to calculate the exact number of theater performances in the Third Reich, just as it is impossible to determine the attendance rates. In the occupied territories, as on the front, where a lot of theater was performed, no statistical records were kept, and even if there are some relevant data in isolated cases, these numbers do not provide the full picture. Similar difficulties arise when attempting to investigate the makeup of the programs. According to estimates for the years 1933 to 1944, there were some 30,000 productions of promoted or tolerated theatrical pieces.[42] But even here such concepts as "promoted" or "tolerated" do not give a clear picture. What was to be promoted was determined by the politics of the day. For example, the promoted infamous drama *Schlageter* by Hanns Johst, a hit in the season 1933/34, soon lost its political desirability. Richard Euringer's mystery play *Deutsche Passion,* honored with the state prize in 1934, was dropped very quickly from repertoires due to its "pacifist tendencies." Even Schiller's *Wilhelm Tell,* one of the Führer's favorite plays and incidentally one of the author's most performed works, was not only removed from stages in 1941 but also taken out of libraries and eliminated from school performances. The ideas contained in the piece stood in opposition to the plans for the "new ordering of Europe": Several principles of the German medieval Imperial Age had suddenly become useful and were not supposed to be challenged. Similar other examples abound.

Already in the first theater seasons of the Nazi era, almost everything had disappeared from the programs that the National Socialists had stigmatized due to the "Jewish" origin of their authors or composers. And the National Socialists' anti-Semitism was "so aggressive that no Reich dramaturgist was needed to enforce it in the theater. And it was so central that its moderation never was considered."[43] In contrast, the Reich dramaturgist exercised much more personal initiative when it came to banishing the "theater of the Left" from German stages: It disappeared entirely. Even shortly before the Nazi assumption of power, the socially critical theater of the Left was already on the decline, especially in the provinces. In comparison, the continuous rise of the "theater of the Right" was breathtaking (whose beginning success could already be seen in the first years of the worldwide depression)—the rise of the entire corpus of *völkisch*-conservative dramatic literature or dramatic works created in the "spirit of National Socialism."

After three years of the "National Socialist rebuilding" of the German theater, a journalist had good reason to observe: ". . . the un-German, sensationalist plays catering to the basest instincts have disappeared together with the Marxist-oriented problem plays and the agitational reportages. In addition to the tribute to the classics and the good old German entertainment play, their place has been taken by the new historical drama, the *völkisch* drama of the day, the creations of the new poetic generation. . . ."[44]

In the first years of the Hitler regime, the situation in the realm of theater remained ideologically ambiguous. Even the Propaganda Ministry was at first in favor of the alternative theater form of the *Thingspiele*. A change of sorts occurred in the years 1936 and 1937, when it became clear that such overtly nationalistic theatrical forms as the *Thingspiele* generally lacked artistic merit and were unpopular with the German public. Hitler, too, was against the all-encompassing politicizing of the traditional theater. In 1938, he stated in private: "The performances must be 'illusion' to the masses. The little man knows all too well life's seriousness. Because life is serious, enjoyment therefore must be pleasant."[45] After the war broke out, the enjoyment had to get more and more pleasant. Accordingly, Goebbels and his Reich dramaturgist attempted to implement their program policy with caution. Only in isolated cases did the Propaganda Ministry exercise pressure toward a bold "Nazification" of the theater programs. Nevertheless, there was no lack of guidelines for a restructuring of the programs that would be "in keeping with the times."

Apart from these guidelines and the influence of the Reich dramaturgist, each theater management, especially that of the leading, world-renowned stages, could draft the programs freely according to their own artistic sense. "Nobody could force Gründgens to perform theater in the manner he did, quite the contrary," writes Uwe-K. Ketelsen.[46] However, Gründgens' situation in the Third Reich was a special case, and it provides no basis for an overall assessment of the political attitude of the theater managements. In any case, the great actor, too, tried both as performer and artistic director to accommodate the new political leadership. Many theater directors were conformists who safeguarded themselves in all respects, above all with the Nazi hierarchy. The requirement for local approval of the theater program must be recalled. Out of fear of confrontations with regional authorities and Party agencies, bans were anticipated that therefore did not even have to be pronounced. Of course, some theaters tried to remain above such political interference, but such attempts were often condemned to failure.

Most requests for either the banning or promotion of works were made by the Rosenberg office. It constantly emphasized the primacy of the Party over the state. Officially those in the "Rosenberg circle" acknowledged that due to considerations of foreign and domestic policy, the state organs frequently had to make decisions that represented a compromise when measured against the principles of the Nazi movement. However, in close contact with the Gestapo, Rosenberg's staff—primarily the main office for the Promotion of Art (Hauptamt für Kunstpflege), with its offices of Theater (headed by Karl Künkler) and Music (headed by Herbert Gerigk)—waged a continuous battle with the Reich dramaturgist for a "National Socialist" makeup of the theater programs. The political problem play was favored, even if it ran counter to the audience's preferences. Yet while adhering to the same basic political orientation, the Reich dramaturgist sought to be flexible: The theater people should cooperate, the public should come into the theaters. If the theatergoers stayed away, the theater could not fulfill its political mission, to say nothing of the financial problems that would arise. The Reich dramaturgist, a virtuoso of the "Goebbels-Rosenberg balance," very often was at a loss on how to handle the attacks on program policy.

Of course, the Reich dramaturgist's "liberalism" had its limits. Similarly, there were comical incidents in the Propaganda Ministry when it came to decisions about which plays could be produced and how. There were even jokes about the "rampant plague of literary adaptations." Personnel in the theater department were wary about making positive recommendations, often due to political caution. Schlösser disapproved of such a "sibyllistic and negative" practice and recommended "always to respond positively in the dramaturgical sector and to provide titles of plays."[47] Yet such a procedure frequently put officials at risk. The Propaganda Ministry had no direct, uniform "blacklist" for dramas, and the confidential lists of proscribed literature contained only relatively few banned dramatic authors.[48]

Even the classics were not exempt from an ideological test before they made it to the stage. This resulted in numerous restrictions and manipulative measures regarding the selection and interpretation of these works.[49] Lessing's *Nathan der Weise*, for example, was now allowed to be performed only by the Theater of the Jewish Cultural Organization, which was in existence until 1941. His *Minna von Barnhelm*, on the other hand, became a hit after 1933. The works of Schiller and Goethe (although at the onset even the latter, the cosmopolitan, also seemed suspect to some "orthodox" National Socialists) were among the most-performed classics. With ceremonies in Weimar and Marbach sponsored by the state, Party and municipal governments, the Hitler regime exploited the occasion of Schiller's 175th birthday on 10 November 1934 to "reclaim" the dramatist for the "National Socialist Revolution." The *Völkischer Beobachter* report on the ceremonies disavowed any connection between the two representatives of Weimar classicism and the political ideals of the Weimar Republic:

> The liberals of past epochs have tried again and again to claim the two Weimar poet Princes Friedrich von Schiller and Wolfgang von Goethe as their own.
>
> In this way the best and most noble part of their works was counterfeited and the nation was shown a distortion of their true essence. Friedrich von Schiller was a revolutionary, and thus the men of the revolts after the World War tried to turn the fervent nationalist Schiller into a Jacobian....[50]

Speaking at the ceremony in Weimar, Goebbels went to the other extreme and transformed the "Jacobian" into a colleague of Horst Wessel and Hanns Johst: "Had Schiller lived in these times, without doubt he would have become the great poetic champion of our revolution. He had the character it takes to devote himself to it with all his might. And he possessed the artistic genius one needs to give it creative form...."[51] Probably hardly an area dealing with classic German literature, from scholarly editions up to film, existed in which Schiller was not assigned a significant role in the "rebirth" of intellectual life in the Third Reich. Having missed the chance to stage a similar "commemoration" of the centennial of Goethe's death in 1932, the National Socialists had to be content with exploiting his oeuvre, an act that Thomas Mann branded as the greatest betrayal of the entire German cultural tradition.

The problem of productions of classic works was an issue for the Reich dramaturgist just as it was for directors. Indeed, even Gründgens agreed with Walter Stang in a conversation: "... if one espoused a Weltanschauung one then really had to carry it out to the last consequence, even if in doing so one would not stop for a Goethe or Kleist."[52] And exiles commenting on Heinrich George's "classic role" as Götz von Berlichingen stated: "He likes to present him as a kind of National Socialist meeting hall brawler...."[53] In the Reich, of course, such criticisms were not allowed to appear. As early as 28 November 1936, the propaganda minister issued a directive banning art criticism as the expression of "Jewish infiltration into art" and "individualistic arbitrariness." The "National Socialist art description" with no free selection of a point of view took its place.[54]

As a matter of course the Reich dramaturgist tried to promote new "dramatic literature" through numerous competitions and the like. The results, in terms of quality, were pitiful. Today we can no longer determine how many new plays were written then—it must have been thousands. An estimated 2,000 premiered during the twelve years of the Hitler regime, but only about 300 were put on more than five times. For many plays no texts are extant today. Several authors did assert themselves: Eberhard Wolfgang Möller, Hans Rehberg, Curt Langenbeck (one of the few pro-regime authors who at least understood his trade), Sigmund Graff, Friedrich Bethge, and the Austrians Richard Billinger and Hermann Heinz Ortner were among the successful representatives of the politically oriented "practical drama." Comedy authors were uncontestedly the most successful. The so-called light practical drama, naturally also determined by the politics of the day, constantly dominated in the program.

After 1933, extensive licensing restrictions affected foreign dramatic literature. In its effort to disseminate as many different trends in world theater as possible, the German theater of the Weimar period had almost always been open to foreign influences. Only rarely did it occur to someone—the *völkisch-*nationalistic circles excepted—to set quotas, for example, regarding the proportion of foreign authors in the programs or even to prescribe that a predetermined percentage of new productions must be reserved for German playwrights. In the Third Reich both the significance of imported works and their influence on German authors and directors declined substantially. According to the opinion in many National Socialist circles, only German art represented the highest values, and "foreignness" had become an outright plague in German theatrical life. To a certain extent this attitude also formed the basis for the Propaganda Ministry's repertoire policy, at least in the sense of a long-term mission. An all-too-rigorous action naturally was not possible. At first only foreign plays whose subject matter or author conflicted directly with Nazi principles were banned from the stage—and even this was done gradually. The current political relations with the respective state was a more decisive criterion. Such a xenophobic policy had a deleterious effect in a period when theater and drama were undergoing an enormous development; German theater people remained cut off from almost all the issues and trends. Indeed—with few exceptions—they hardly were aware of the new styles and views coming from France and the United States, for example. From a purely statistical perspective, the entire matter, at first, did not seem catastrophic: In the 1934/35 season approximately 300 stage pieces by German authors were performed, as compared to 65 foreign works, 13 of which even had their world premieres in Germany.

The National Socialist state pronounced no ban on the drama of antiquity. But even here there were barriers: Plays that praised the Dionysian lifestyle or affirmed the advantage of democratic institutions remained "undesirable." Shakespeare was one of the most performed authors in Germany altogether, both before and after 1933. Yet the choice of which of his plays were produced, in part their productions as well, changed. Many politically rather than artistically motivated controversies arose in the evaluation of some productions, such as *Othello, A Midsummer Night's Dream* (here the controversy focused mainly on the accompanying music), *Hamlet, Julius Caesar, Anthony and Cleopatra,* and above all the *Merchant of Venice.* The Third Reich tried to view the Great Man from Stratford as a "germanicized poet." The more contemporary English writing was represented primarily by Oscar Wilde (his works were also filmed) and especially by George Bernard Shaw, whose *Pygmalion* had its first film adaptation in Nazi Germany, of all places. Furthermore, isolated productions included plays by W. Somerset Maugham, Merton Hodge, and John Galsworthy, to name only the most important authors. Rarely were American authors performed; when they were, the preference was for light plays. Avery Hopwood's popular farce *The Model Husband* (Der Mustergatte) was known far and wide since Wolfgang Liebeneiner's film version of 1937. With Heinz Rühmann in the leading role, this work even was among the Führer's favorite films. Hopwood's hit play *Our Little Wife* (Unsere kleine Frau), also filmed in 1938, enjoyed great popularity as well.[55] As far as French drama was concerned, tested entertainment plays were performed and some were also filmed. Only the "old Russians" were performed. (During the period of the Soviet-German rapprochement there even was a "Russian wave" in German theaters.) Scandinavian drama continually held a privileged position, with some politically motivated restrictions. And the "Berlin–Rome Axis" brought about a special treatment of selected authors from Italy.

In the realm of the musical theater, restrictions existed and gradually increased from the beginning of the Nazi era. As early as 1935, the Propaganda Ministry produced a "list of undesirable non-Aryan composers." While not released to the public, the list was meant as a guideline for German stages. Henceforth works of 108 composers from the German cultural domain were no longer permitted to be performed.[56] Actually this blacklist merely confirmed what had already been practiced: Almost all of these works had not been performed since the Nazis' assumption of power. In the same year, by order of the Reich dramaturgist, German theaters were sent a "German Opera Program," which recommended a total of 118 composers with 275 works in ranked order.[57] The bans increasingly encompassed "non-Aryan" foreign composers, "for the protection of the cultural life of the German people."[58] Yet not until 1939 was there a directive for the "listing of undesirable musical works": "Musical works which contravene the National Socialist cultural will are included in an index compiled by the Reich Music Chamber of undesirable and harmful music."[59] Thereafter, in the "Official Communications of the Reich Music Chamber," a total of only approximately 150 titles or composers was published in the blacklists. However, many other names and works were subjected to bans that the Nazis did not pronounce officially.

The repertories of operetta companies underwent the most serious change as a result of the exclusion of "non-Aryan" composers. But it was not until 1935/36 that the operetta programs were completely "Jew-free." The percentage of operetta composers affected by the National Socialists' anti-Semitism was extraordinarily large compared to that of opera composers. Despite this massive intervention, the offering in operetta performances hardly diminished. Quite the contrary: The proportion of operettas in the programs grew steadily, reaching its peak during the war years. Fewer and fewer works by fewer and fewer composers were being performed more and more. The prime beneficiary of this development was Franz Lehár, although even he, the Führer's favorite composer, was looked upon by the "orthodox" Nazis as having "Jewish blood" and being "contaminated." A number of operettas were revised and thus "reclaimed for German stages."[60]

After the war's outbreak, interference intensified and the bans increased. The theaters' artistic directors reported that as a result of the war, programs had to be completely overhauled. The bans targeted theater pieces from "enemy countries," with only few exceptions. With Hitler's approval the "germanicized" Shakespeare continued to be performed. Now, however, most of the historical dramas were dropped from the programs, and the total number of Shakespeare performances decreased steadily. Many productions of the *Merchant of Venice* were misused for propagandistic purposes. Like Shakespeare, George Bernard Shaw was also permitted, although there were restrictions in the selection of plays, and the productions were supposed to demonstrate a "new spirit." Because many official agencies had repeatedly attacked performances of Shaw's works, Goebbels directed Leopold Gutterer in his ministry "to enlighten the offices concerned that Bernard Shaw is not even an Englishman, but an Irishman and secondly that his plays are so much in accord with our propaganda against England that Shaw's elimination from the German theater programs would be a noticeable propagandistic loss."[61] Fourteen Irish authors, among them Sir Roger Casement, John Millington Synge, and William Butler Yeats, were also spared a ban. In 1942, the Propaganda Ministry circulated a confidential "List of English and North American Authors" that functioned as a blacklist. It covered some 1,500 authors who had been published in Germany after 1900. Purely scientific works were excluded. The named authors were no longer permitted to be published in Germany. By the end of 1942, only 167 names were on the list of "Reich-German" translations from the English that were allowed to be sold or loaned in libraries during the war.[62] American literature (including dramatic works) disappeared almost entirely from public view; only some 30 authors or book titles were on the list of translations from American works allowed to be sold or loaned after 1941.[63]

The bans also affected German theater pieces that in the opinion of the local authorities did not fit the new situation. In 1940, the Reich dramaturgist complained to Goebbels:

> Lately there has been an accumulation of appeals directed to me to stop dramatic works against which political objections allegedly could be raised ... I know that artistic circles are observing with growing concern how few plays can stay absolutely beyond reproach, if one fears that even works that have become classics disturb our present measures.... I see the danger here that agencies outside of our ministry, some of them more, some less competent, are subjecting works of art to a scrutiny that is not compatible with the certain amount of tolerance a victorious nation can afford.[64]

With Goebbels' consent, the office of the Reich dramaturgist attempted to continue the "liberal" program policy it had practiced during the prewar period. However, the attacks became more virulent in the wake of the first German military defeats. At "a time when the ideological opponents" were preparing "for a new assault even behind the front," and "Gestapo reports" drew attention to "increasingly demoralizing influences,"[65] Rosenberg's agency prepared for a new blow against the authority of the Reich dramaturgist. The Propaganda Ministry, it claimed,

> has limited itself essentially to the organizational and financial support of the theater and has now as before pursued a policy of the free play of the forces within the theater world. A uniform cultural-political line could not be detected. Especially in the programs, not only Berlin's, but also throughout the Reich, works have been cropping up again and again which were promoted by the Reich Propaganda Ministry, although, from the perspective of their political attitude, they had to give rise to the most serious reservations precisely with respect to the great popularity that the theater is enjoying today.[66]

The "imposition" of authors from countries friendly to the Reich on German audiences was also challenged.[67] In Rosenberg's view, the consequences of the Reich dramaturgist's policy were clear: The Rosenberg agency should "receive the charge to exercise a precensorship of all works to be performed at German theaters and for all planned publications."[68] This push by the Rosenberg agency went nowhere. The leadership claim of the Propaganda Ministry in all theater questions was, at least in theory, uncontested.

At this time, when the Allies' bombs were destroying one city after the other, Germany still had an astonishingly multifaceted theater life. Where the theater structures were destroyed, troupes performed in provisional spaces. Above all things, the Nazis wanted to prove to themselves and to the world that even in the most severe war conditions, Germany was still capable of keeping theaters, cinemas, and concert halls open day after day. The illusion collapsed on 20 August 1944. As the "plenipotentiary for the total war effort" Goebbels decreed: "all theaters, music halls, cabarets, and drama schools are to close as of 1 September. . . . " Most theater people—with the exception of a small, select group of "indispensable people"—were drafted into military service or sent to work in the war economy. The Deutsches Opernhaus in Berlin, the pride of the propaganda minister, took its leave on 31 August 1944 with *The Marriage of Figaro*. A large number of theaters that were still intact were transformed into cinemas.

Notes

1. Bundesarchiv: Abteilung Potsdam: Bestand Reichsministerium für Volksaufklärung und Propaganda, Bd. 162, fol. 265 (hereafter cited as BA/Potsdam: RMfVP).
2. Here we should mention the Bundesarchiv in Koblenz (hereafter cited as BAK) with its branches, the former Zentralarchiv der DDR in Potsdam (now Bundesarchiv: Abteilung Potsdam), and the Political Archive of the Auswärtiges Amt (Foreign Office) in Bonn.
3. Among them is the well-known five-volume *Dokumentation* by Joseph Wulf, which was first published in the 1960s by the Sigbert Mohn Verlag in Gütersloh.
4. See Barbara Panse, "Die Theatermacher und die Macht: Barbara Panse zur Auswahl der nachfolgenden Eintragungen aus den Goebbels-Tagebüchern," *Theater Heute*, No. 9 (1989): 4-21.
5. First and foremost we have to mention here the seminal studies of the *völkisch*-nationalistic tendencies in German literature and in German theater by Uwe-Karsten Ketelsen. See also the collective review: Konrad Dussel, "Theatergeschichte der NS-Zeit unter sozialgeschichtlichem Aspekt. Ergebnisse und Perspektiven der Forschung," *Neue politische Literatur* 32 (1987): 233-45.
6. Jutta Wardetzky, *Theaterpolitik im faschistischen Deutschland: Studien und Dokumente* (Berlin: Henschel Verlag Kunst und Gesellschaft, 1983); Bogusław Drewniak, *Das Theater im NS-Staat: Szenarium deutscher Zeitgeschichte 1933-1945* (Düsseldorf: Droste Verlag, 1983).
7. Wolf-Eberhard August, "Die Stellung der Schauspieler im Dritten Reich. Versuch einer Darstellung der Kunst- und Gesellschaftspolitik in einem totalitären Staat am Beispiel des Berufsschauspielers" (Ph.D. diss., Universität München 1973). This study's author did not utilize archival sources, which affected his overall findings.
8. Konrad Dussel, "Provinztheater in der NS-Zeit," *Vierteljahrshefte für Zeitgeschichte* 38, No. 1 (1990): 75-111.
9. Ibid., p. 104.
10. Leopold Jessner, *Schriften. Theater der zwanziger Jahre*, ed. Hugo Fetting (Berlin: Henschel Verlag Kunst und Gesellschaft, 1979), p. 34.
11. Uwe-Karsten Ketelsen, "Rezensionen," *Forum Modernes Theater* 1, No. 1 (1986): 105.
12. Numerous works have appeared on Heinz Hilpert and his work in theater, including a recent anthology: Michael Dillmann, *Heinz Hilpert. Leben und Werk* (Berlin: Akademie der Künste-Edition Hentrich, 1990).

13. Quoted from *Kultur-Chronik. Nachrichten und Berichte aus der Bundesrepublik Deutschland,* 4/1991: 21.
14. Bernhard Minetti, "'Ja, nichts sonst.' André Müller spricht mit dem Schauspieler Bernhard Minetti," *Die Zeit,* 9 July 1993, p. 13.
15. *FU-info. Das Magazin der Freien Universität Berlin,* No. 5 (1989): 4.
16. Memorandum of 16 June 1938—BAK: NS 10/44, fol. 3.
17. Until 1941, the Jews were granted the limited opportunity to be active in the Jewish cultural organizations that remained under the strict supervision of Hans Hinkel in the Propaganda Ministry.
18. This resulted in the intensification of the cultural work of the Jewish Cultural League.
19. Memorandum of 16 June 1938—BAK: NS 10/44, fol. 3.
20. Ibid.
21. See the Propaganda Ministry reports of 11 October 1934 and 12 June 1937—BAK: R 55/1251, fols. 129-30, and R 55/264, fols. 63ff.
22. For details see August, pp. 63ff.
23. Until October 1934, the Theater Department was, among other things, also responsible for matters pertaining to music and the visual arts.
24. In 1937, the Reich Propaganda Offices attained the status of Reich agencies, but "in the course of the unification of Party and state" they were run by the *Gau* Propaganda Leaders of the NSDAP, who functioned simultaneously as the provincial cultural administrators.
25. As early as 1933, an "Advisory Office for German Dramatists" was created under the direction of the Reich dramaturgist, "so that these dramatists, in adherence to the new Zeitgeist, can collaborate in the creation of a drama of the present and of the future"—BAK: R 55/1164, fol. 124. This advisory office was, however, unable to handle the flood of practical demands that were made of it, and it was soon dissolved.
26. The "Deutsche Tanzbühne" (Berlin-Dahlem) and the "Deutsche Meisterstätten für Tanz" (Berlin-Grunewald) were administered as of 1 April 1940 as agencies of the Propaganda Ministry.
27. These matters were taken over by the Foreign Office.
28. In September 1944, the Propaganda Ministry dissolved its separate departments for theater, music, and visual arts and consolidated them into a Culture Department headed by Schlösser.
29. Dussel, "Provinztheater," p. 95.
30. "Einheitliches Theaterrecht," *Völkischer Beobachter,* No. 137 (17 May 1934).
31. Some German stages abroad, especially those that depended on financial support from the Reich, also sent their programs to Berlin for scrutiny.

32. These holidays were: Day of the Seizure of Power (30 January), National Day of Mourning for the Dead from the World War (16 March; since 1934 called Heldengedenktag, Heroes' Remembrance Day), Good Friday, the Führer's Birthday (20 April), Tag der Arbeit (1 May; National Labor Day), Erntedanktag (Harvest Thanksgiving Day; the first Sunday in October), the Memorial Day for the Victims in front of the Feldherrnhalle (9 November; this was the most important celebration during the Third Reich, commemorating the "early fighters" who died in the unsuccessful 1923 Munich Beer Hall Putsch), and Bußtag (Repentance Day, the third Wednesday in November).
33. Film—at the time the most important medium—had at its disposal much more funds, which were not recorded directly in the Propaganda Ministry's budget.
34. Note of 20 April 1944—BAK: R 55/648, fols. 5ff.
35. BAK: R 55/648, fol. 20.
36. *Völkischer Beobachter,* No. 165 (14 June 1934).
37. Generalappell 1936 der NS-Kulturgemeinde—BAK: NS 15/90, n.p.
38. Special closed performances were reinstituted during the war years. In 1941, approximately 23 percent of the entire theater performances took place as closed events for soldiers or armaments workers.
39. With a newly created department "*Truppenbetreuung*" (troop entertainment).
40. In this context we should note the discrepancy between the facts and the claim made by Inge von Wangenheim, the daughter-in-law of the famous actor Eduard von Winterstein: "In contrast to Furtwängler, who allowed his Philharmonic Orchestra to celebrate western musical culture in occupied Europe, Gründgens had not permitted the Staatstheater one solitary visiting performance abroad"— see Inge von Wangenheim, *Die tickende Bratpfanne: Kunst und Künstler aus meinem Stundenbuch* (Rudolstadt: Greifenverlag, 1974), pp. 128f. Even during the war, Gründgens and his ensemble traveled as "cultural representatives" to the occupied territories. Wangenheim's statement also contrasts with remarks about Furtwängler made by Herbert Gerigk in Rosenberg's Office for the Promotion of Art. In 1935, Gerigk reported to the Gestapo that the maestro " . . . apparently was only waiting for the moment when he could come out in public for a differently oriented cultural-political line. . . ."—Amt Kunstpflege to Gestapo, 18 December 1935—BAK: NS 15/69, n. p.
41. A prime example of the National Socialists' concept of the theater's role in the "new Europe" is the published text of a lecture Heinz Kindermann gave on 26 January 1944 at the University of Vienna, Heinz Kindermann, *Die europäische Sendung des deutschen Theaters* (Wien: Verlag der Ringbuchhandlung, 1944).
42. *FU-info,* p. 4.

43. Dussel, "Provinztheater," p. 97.
44. Quoted from Joseph Wulf, *Theater und Film im Dritten Reich. Eine Dokumentation* (Gütersloh: Sigbert Mohn, 1964), p. 34.
45. Memorandum of 16 June 1938—BAK: NS 10/44, fol. 3.
46. Ketelsen, p. 105.
47. Memorandum of 23 September 1942—BA/Potsdam: RMfVP, Bd. 235, fol. 167.
48. Already at the beginning of the Third Reich, the first blacklists of undesirable authors and books appeared, although at the time they were not centrally managed. Not until 1935 did the RSK in conjunction with the RMVP release its first list of undesirable authors. The Deutsche Bücherei in Leipzig later expanded and updated the lists until 31 December 1944. These lists were considered extremely confidential.
49. Several studies on this topic have already appeared. One of the most important is Bernhard Zeller, ed., *Klassiker in finsteren Zeiten, 1933-1945. Eine Ausstellung des Deutschen Literaturarchivs im Schiller-Nationalmuseum Marbach am Neckar*, 2 vols. (Marbach: Deutsche Schillergesellschaft, 1983).
50. "Der Führer ehrt Friedrich von Schiller: Staatsakt der Reichsregierung und Thüringischen Staatsregierung im Weimarer Nationaltheater," *Völkischer Beobachter*, No. 317 (13 November 1934), p. 1; excerpted in Joseph Wulf, *Literatur und Dichtung im Dritten Reich. Eine Dokumentation* (Gütersloh: Sigbert Mohn, 1963), p. 340; Wulf mistakenly assigns the date 13 February 1934 to this article.
51. "Die Schiller-Gedenkrede des Reichsministers Dr. Goebbels," *Völkischer Beobachter*, No. 317 (13 November 1934), p. 6.
52. Memorandum for Alfred Rosenberg of 7 April 1943—BAK: NS 8/242, fol. 191.
53. *Die Zeitung* (London), 26 October 1943.
54. As incredible it may sound, Goebbels declared himself to be an opponent of censorship. Even in wartime he stated: "Any censorship by authorities jeopardizes the free development of cultural life. It also contradicts the concept of the Reich Culture Chamber, which wants to lead the people producing culture but not to exercise petty scrutiny of their works"—letter of 19 November 1943 in BAK: R 43 II/1232.
55. Bogusław Drewniak, *Der deutsche Film 1938-1945* (Düsseldorf: Droste, 1987), p. 560.
56. Dussel, "Provinztheater," p. 97.
57. Ibid., p. 96.
58. Joseph Wulf, *Musik im Dritten Reich. Eine Dokumentation* (Gütersloh: Sigbert Mohn, 1963), pp. 328f.
59. Ibid.; see also Fred K. Prieberg, *Musik im NS-Staat* (Frankfurt/Main: Fischer, 1982), passim.

60. These adaptations were supervised by the Reichsstelle für Musikbearbeitungen (Reich Office for Musical Adaptations), in the Propaganda Ministry's Music Department.
61. Willi A. Boelcke, *Kriegspropaganda 1939-1941: Geheime Ministerkonferenzen im Reichspropagandaministerium* (Stuttgart: Deutsche Verlags-Anstalt, 1966), pp. 639-40.
62. Among these authors were: Matthew Arnold, Jane Austen, William Blake, Robert Browning, Samuel Butler, Thomas Carlyle, John Keats, Christopher Marlowe, Samuel Pepys, Daniel Defore, Charles Dickens, Henry Fielding, Sir Walter Scott, Robert Louis Stevenson, Jonathan Swift, Alfred Tennyson, William Makepeace Thackeray, and Pelham Grenville Wodehouse.
63. Spared were all works by James Fenimore Cooper, Ralph Waldo Emerson, Nathaniel Hawthorne, Washington Irving, Henry Wadsworth Longfellow, Herman Melville, Edgar Allan Poe, Henry David Thoreau, Mark Twain, and Walt Whitman, in addition to individual titles by Jack London, John Steinbeck, and a few other publications.
64. Schlösser to Goebbels, 23 January 1940—BA/Potsdam: RMfVP, Nr. 235, fols. 17f.
65. Schreiben des Amts Dramaturgie und Darstellende Kunst (Künkler), 10 March 1943—National Archives Microcopy, T454, Reel 81.
66. Ibid.
67. Ibid. In March 1943, Rosenberg's agency stated: "One must not overlook how Italy and Hungary right now are pushing their cultural agendas for Europe, in order to realize that from a propagandistic standpoint this forceful imposition of Italian and Hungarian plays is not really necessary."
68. Ibid.

5

Nazi Film Policy: Control, Ideology, and Propaganda

David Welch

THE MINISTRY FOR POPULAR ENLIGHTENMENT AND PROPAGANDA

Analyzing the political function of propaganda in the Third Reich is complicated by the fact that it was simultaneously channeled through three different institutions: the Reich Ministry for Popular Enlightenment and Propaganda (Reichsministerium für Volksaufklärung und Propaganda), the Central Propaganda Office of the Party, and the Reich Chamber of Culture. Moreover, the political structure of the Third Reich was based on the twin pillars of the Party and the state. According to Hitler, it was the task of the state to continue the "historical development of the national administration within the framework of the law," while it was the function of the Party to "build its internal organization and establish and develop a stable and self-perpetuating center of the National Socialist doctrine in order to transfer the indoctrinated to the State so that they may become its leaders as well as its disciples."[1] The creation of the Propaganda Ministry in March 1933 was a significant step toward the merging of the Party and the state. Goebbels continued to be head of Party propaganda, but he greatly strengthened both his own position within the Party and the scope of propaganda by setting up this new ministry—the first of its kind in Germany.

Two days after his appointment as propaganda minister, Goebbels outlined his view of the role of the new ministry in a revealing speech to representatives of the German press:

> We have established a Ministry for Popular Enlightenment and Propaganda. These two titles do not convey the same thing. Popular enlightenment is essentially something passive: propaganda, on the other hand, is something active. We cannot be satisfied with just telling the people what we want and enlightening them as to how we are doing it. We must replace this enlightenment with an active government propaganda that aims at winning people over. It is not enough to reconcile people more or less to our regime, to move them toward a position of neutrality toward us; we would rather work on people until they are addicted to us. . . .[2]

With the creation of the Propaganda Ministry, propaganda became primarily the responsibility of the state, although its departments were to be supported and reinforced by the Party's Central Propaganda Office (Reichspropagandaamt), which remained less conspicuous to the general public. Indeed, the two institutions often merged into one apparatus; not only would their respective organizations and responsibilities correspond closely, but many of the leading positions in the ministry and the Reichspropagandaleitung were held by the same officials. Originally Goebbels had planned only five departments for the new ministry to embrace radio, press, active propaganda, film, and theater. The number of departments was later expanded, but by April 1933, the ministry had acquired its basic structure and begun its activities. During the war even Goebbels' staunch antibureaucratic stance could not prevent his ministry from being subjected to the process of expansion and bureaucratization, and the number of departments actually increased to 14.

THE REICH CHAMBER OF CULTURE

Kulturpolitik (cultural policy) was an important element in German life, but the Nazis were the first party to organize the entire cultural life of a nation systematically. As the Propaganda Ministry ominously proclaimed when it announced the Theater Law of 15 May 1934: "The arts are for the National Socialist State a public exercise; they are not only aesthetic but also moral in nature and the public interest demands not only police supervision but also guidance." The Reich Chamber of Culture (Reichskulturkammer, or RKK) was established by a law promulgated on 22 September 1933. It represented a triumph for Goebbels in his bitter struggle with the Nazi "ideologist" Alfred Rosenberg, who before 1933 had claimed responsibility for cultural matters through the establishment of his Combat League for German Culture. The Reich Chamber of Culture allowed the minister of propaganda to organize the various branches of the arts and cultural professions as public corporations. Seven individual areas were organized as separate chambers: literature, theater, music, radio, film, visual arts, and the press. The creation of the RKK is an excellent example of the process of *Gleichschaltung,* the Nazis' term for the obligatory assimilation within the state of all political, economic, and cultural activities following Hitler's assumption of the chancellorship. The RKK acted as an agent of this "coordination" in that it allowed the Propaganda Ministry to exert its control over almost all aspects of German cultural life. As propaganda minister, Goebbels acted as president of the RKK, with the power to appoint the presidents of the subordinate chambers. Through him the chambers' jurisdiction spread down to both the nation's regional administration *(Länder)* and the Party's own political districts *(Gaue).* This not only facilitated the Propaganda Ministry's control over individual chambers, but, equally important, it also allowed the ministry to coordinate its propaganda campaigns.

The chief function of each chamber was to regulate conditions of work in its particular field. This involved the keeping of a register and the issuing of work permits. No one refused such a permit could be employed in his or her profession. To be denied membership in the chamber, therefore, spelled professional ruin. To those sympathetic to the regime, on the other hand, enforced membership in such an immense organization represented financial security and public recognition. The law that established the RKK conferred on Goebbels the power to exclude all those who were considered racially or politically objectionable.

As the Nazi revolution was to bring about a new consciousness that would transcend the political structure, it followed that artists too had a revolutionary role to play. In one of his first speeches as propaganda minister, Goebbels outlined the future role of German art: "Modern German art's task is not to dramatize the Party program, but to give poetic and artistic shape to the huge spiritual impulses within us. . . . The political renaissance must definitely have spiritual and cultural foundations. Therefore it is important to create a new basis for the life of German art."[3]

Under the Nazis, art was seen as an expression of race and would underpin the political renaissance that was taking place. Whereas modernism was associated with "decadent" Jewish-liberal culture, art under National Socialism would be rooted in the people as true expression of the spirit of the People's Community *(Volksgemeinschaft).* At the height of his power, Hitler succinctly summarized his concept of culture and the role of the artist in a speech delivered on 19 July 1937 at the opening of the House of German Art in Munich, which was intended to exhibit officially approved art:

> During the long years in which I planned the formation of a new Reich I gave much thought to the tasks which would await us in the cultural cleansing of the people's life; there was to be a cultural renaissance as well as a political and economic reform. . . . As in politics, so in German art life, we are determined to make a clean sweep of empty phrases. . . .
>
> The artist does not create for the artist. He creates for the people, and we will see to it that the people in future be called to judge his art. No one must say that the people has no understanding for a really valuable enrichment of its cultural life. . . . The people in passing through these galleries will recognize in me its spokesman and counselor. It will draw a sigh of relief and gladly express its agreement with this purification of art. . . . The artist cannot stand aloof from his people. . . .[4]

This speech defined what was and what was not artistically desirable in the Third Reich. Moreover, it was believed that the control mechanism of establishing the seven chambers under the umbrella of the RKK would allow the regime largely to dispense with a formal system of censorship; "objectionable" artists either had been purged or would exercise self-censorship, for fear of losing their livelihood.

In practice, the regime became increasingly sensitive to artistic criticism of any kind, and Goebbels eventually was persuaded that once a work of art had been officially approved, it was not the function of the critics to criticize it. On 13 May 1936, he issued a proclamation that banned the writing of critical reviews on the evening of a performance *(Nachtkritik)*. Justifying his position the propaganda minister declared: "Artistic criticism no longer exists for its own sake. In future one ought not to degrade or criticize a well-meaning or quite respectable artistic achievement for the sake of a witty turn of phrase."[5]

Such measures were clearly intended as a warning to critics not to question the regime by means of hostile reviews of officially approved artistic works (ranging from a piece of sculpture to a feature film). Eventually, on 27 November 1936, Goebbels decided to ban all art criticism by confining critics to writing merely "descriptive" reviews *(Kunstbetrachtungen)*. In future, all critics would need a special license from the RKK, and such licenses would be given only to critics over the age of 30. The day after Goebbels' famous order, his press chief at the ministry, Alfred Ingemar Berndt, informed the Reich Cultural Senate:

> Judgment of the art work in the National Socialist State can be made only on the basis of the National Socialist viewpoint of culture. Only the Party and the State are in the position to determine artistic values from this National Socialist viewpoint of culture. If a value judgment has been issued by those who are appointed to pass judgment, the art editor, may, of course, employ the values thereby established.[6]

Thus under the Nazi regime art criticism was never an aesthetic but always a political question. In practice, art criticism came more and more to resemble publicity material distributed by the state to promote a particular venture. Although the ban met with some hostility (especially abroad), a further manifestation of the Nazis' intolerance occurred as early as 10 May 1933, a few months before the RKK was established, in Berlin's Franz Joseph Platz, with the barbarous ceremony of the "Burning of the Books." There the works of "decadent" writers were thrown on a ceremonial bonfire, and Goebbels made a speech broadcast on German radio in which he referred to such writers as "the evil spirit of the past" and declared that "the age of extreme Jewish intellectualism is over . . . the past is lying in flames . . . the future will rise from the flames within our hearts."[7]

Kulturpolitik in the Third Reich had a "revolutionary" role in a professed attempt to create a "people's culture" that would express the new art forms of the National Socialist revolution. Government statistics regularly purported to show the increasing number of "people's theaters," "people's films," "people's sculpture," "people's radios," and so on, all of which were intended to reflect the manner in which art was being brought to the people and expressing the artistic impulses of the "national community." Objectivity and opinion, however, were eliminated and replaced by a definition of truth as defined by the Nazi regime. Conformity of opinion and action were also secured within the *Kunstwelt* (artistic world) itself. In order that art reflect the ideological precepts of National Socialism, it was imperative that artists themselves be sympathetic toward the aims and ideals of the new regime. Accordingly, a "cleansing" process of *Entjudung* eliminated Jews and other "political undesirables" from working in German cultural life. The result of these measures led inevitably to an overwhelming cultural mediocrity that produced "safe," conventional art rather than the vibrant "people's culture" that the regime purported to encourage. In 1941, Goebbels was forced to admit at a press conference: "The National Socialist State has given up the ambition of trying to produce art itself. It has wisely contented itself with encouraging art and gearing it spiritually and intellectually to its educative function for the people."[8]

THE REORGANIZATION OF
THE GERMAN FILM INDUSTRY

Hitler and Goebbels shared a deep interest in film. Shortly after his appointment as minister for popular enlightenment and propaganda, Joseph Goebbels declared that the German cinema had been given the mission of conquering the world "as the vanguard of the Nazi troops."[9] Film propaganda was Goebbels' special interest, for he believed in the power of film to influence people's thoughts and beliefs, if not their actions.

As early as the 1920s, the National Socialists had infiltrated their members into many spheres of public life.[10] The entire organization of the Party, the division into administrative sectors, and the structure of leadership were built up as a state within a state. The Nazis were therefore well placed to take control of a film industry that had largely prepared itself to be controlled, as will be seen later. The ordinary citizen was largely unaware of the Nazis' behind-the-scenes *Gleichschaltung* (coordination) of the German cinema. To achieve this "coordination," the Hitler regime instituted a plethora of complex laws, decrees, and intricate state machinery to prevent nonconformity. In accordance with a policy that was to become traditional in the Third Reich, the Party organization was kept separate from state administration at both national and regional levels, while at the same time remaining closely linked.

During 1932, the film industry was still recoiling from the continuing effects of the recession in world trade and the advent of sound films, which involved considerable expenditure at a time when total receipts were falling, companies were going bankrupt, and film theaters were changing hands at an alarming rate. The German film industry responded with the so-called SPIO Plan of 1932. The SPIO (Spitzenorganisation der Deutschen Filmindustrie e.V.) was the industry's main professional representative body, and its principal concern was to strike a satisfactory relationship among the production, distribution, and exhibition sectors while at the same time retaining the traditional structure of the industry. Significantly, the SPIO was dominated by the large film companies (particularly Ufa); therefore it did not come as a surprise that these companies should produce a plan that blatantly discriminated against the German Cinema Owners' Association (Reichsverband Deutscher Lichtspieltheater e.V.), whom they accused of flooding the market with too many film theaters, price cutting, and retaining a disproportionate share of total receipts. The Cinema Owners' Association retorted by complaining, quite justifiably, that they were expected to exhibit films they were given regardless of their suitability or box-office appeal.

In the months following Hitler's appointment as chancellor in January 1933, the divisions within the Party that had flared up in 1932 became an issue again. Certain organizations such as the Nazi Trade Union (the Nationalsozialistische Betriebszellen Organisation, or NSBO) and the "Combat League for German Culture" (Kampfbund für deutsche Kultur) put forward radical solutions to the film industry's problems, demanding centralization and the banning of all films that offended the *völkische* Weltanschauung. Goebbels on the other hand was more realistic and appreciated that the *Filmwelt* (film world) did not welcome these forces of Nazi extremism. He was unwilling to undertake an immediate nationalization of the industry not only on ideological grounds but for the pragmatic reasons that Alfred Hugenberg, who owned the largest film company, Ufa, was a member of the new cabinet as minister of economics and that the Party in general depended on big business for its finances.

However, on 9 February 1933, at the Cinema Owners' annual conference, the Nazi elements demanded that their leader, Adolf Engl, should be elected to the association's board. Their argument that the small owners faced bankruptcy in the face of unfair competition from the large companies seemed to be confirmed when the SPIO Plan was published nine days later. On 18 March, the entire board of the Cinema Owners' Association resigned, thus giving Engl and the NSDAP complete control. They responded by demanding that all cinema owners express unconditional loyalty to Engl's leadership within two weeks.[11]

Cinema owners were not the only sector of the industry to be effectively "coordinated" in this manner; throughout March and April the NSBO had been active in all spheres of film production—from cameramen to film actors and composers. When the Nazis banned all trade unions in early May 1933, the industry's "official" trade union DACHO (Dach-Organisation der Filmschaffenden Deutschlands e.V.) was dissolved and absorbed into the NSBO,[12] which was itself transferred automatically to the German Labor Front (Deutsche Arbeitsfront), the only permissible trade union. The DACHO therefore had little chance to prevent its own dissolution, though there is no evidence that any united stand was organized.

The film industry presented a number of structural, economic, and artistic problems for the builders of the new German society. Indicative of the high estimation of the cinema in the Third Reich is the fact that a "provisional Reich Film Chamber" (*vorläufige* Reichsfilmkammer) was founded by Goebbels over two months before the Reich Chamber of Culture, of which it became a part. The creation of the Reichsfilmkammer (RFK) on 14 July 1933 is an excellent example of the process of coordination in that it allowed the Propaganda

Ministry to exert its control over both film-makers and the film industry as a whole. The structure of the RFK was scarcely changed after it had been incorporated into the Reich Chamber of Culture. Its head and all-responsible president was subordinate only to the president of the RKK, that is, to the propaganda minister. The first president of the Film Chamber was Dr. Fritz Scheuermann, a financial expert who had been involved in secret plans to implement the recommendations of the SPIO Plan, which had been merged with the RFK in July. Scheuermann was assisted by a vicepresident, Arnold Räther, who also was head of the Film Office of the National Socialist German Workers' Party Propaganda Office. There was an Advisory Council *(Präsidialrat)* consisting of financial experts from Goebbels' ministry and the banks; and the specialist advisory councils taken from the individual *Fachgruppen,* as the former SPIO elements were now called. The various sections of the industry were grouped together into ten departments, which controlled all film activities in Germany. The centralization, however, did not lead to what the propaganda minister claimed—the harmonization of all branches of the industry—but rather it harmed the substance of the German film industry by limiting personal and economic initiative and artistic freedom.

The *Filmwelt* greeted the Nazis with some misgivings. The industry was not entirely convinced that it could expect much constructive assistance from the new regime. To offset these fears and to gain control over film finance, the Nazis established a Filmkreditbank (FKB). Announced on 1 June 1933, it would provide credit for a crisis-ridden film economy that had been badly hit by the costs of installing equipment for the new "talking movies" and by the effects of the Depression on film audiences. The idea of the Filmkreditbank had originally been proposed in the SPIO Plan to encourage independent production by lending money to approved filmmakers at highly competitive rates. In practice, the FKB began the National Socialists' disastrous film policy and resulted in the dependence of private film producers on the Nazi state. However, at the time of its inauguration, the FKB was greeted with great enthusiasm from all sides of the film industry. By 1936, the FKB was financing over 73 percent of all German feature films and dealing almost exclusively with distributors who could guarantee that a film would be shown nationwide.[13] As a result, the smaller companies' share of the market continued to decline as the process of concentration increased. This proved a further step toward creating dependence and establishing a state monopoly that would destroy independent initiative.

The Filmkreditbank functioned to all intents and purposes as a normal commercial undertaking except that it was not expected to make large profits. The FKB took the form of a private limited liability company formed out of the Reichskreditgesellschaft, the SPIO (acting as a cover for the Reichsfilmkammer), and a number of the main banks. However, within a year the banks transferred their shares to the Film Chamber, and on Goebbels' personal initiative the RFK president became the Filmkreditbank's chairman. To secure financing from the bank, a producer had to show he could raise 30 percent of the production costs as well as convince the FKB that the film stood a good chance of making a profit. Until the loan was repaid, the film became the property of the bank. Thus, private financing lost all freedom and any opportunity for making a profit. Within a short time the Filmkreditbank also became an important means of securing both economic and political conformity. The FKB, acting on behalf of the government, could refuse all credit at the preproduction stage until a film reflected the wishes of the regime. Significantly, there is no evidence to suggest that the film industry was unwilling to accept this form of self-censorship.

Apart from regulating the financing of films, one of the main purposes of establishing the Reichsfilmkammer was the removal of Jews and other "*entartete Künstler*" ("degenerate artists") from German cultural life, since only racially "pure" Germans could become members. Whoever wished to participate in any aspect of film production was forced to become a member of the RFK. Goebbels, however, was given the power to issue exemptions from these conditions, should he need to do so. By 1936, the *Kulturpolitische Abteilung* of the NSDAP Film Department had begun publishing a new illustrated film magazine, *Der deutsche Film,* to disseminate Party policy relating to the film industry through consciously anti-Semitic propaganda. Statistics were published in film magazines and books that purported to expose an overwhelmingly Jewish influence in film production. The standard Nazi work on the German film industry claimed to show the situation on the eve of the Nazi seizure of power, 70 percent of all scripts were written by Jews, 50 percent of all directors were Jewish, and 70 percent of all production companies were owned by Jews.[14] Although the industry had been heavily dependent on Jewish artists and executives, these figures were a gross exaggeration. Nevertheless, because Nazi propaganda identified Jewish influence with the downfall of German culture, it was only to be expected that the Hitler regime would use the struggle in the film industry to stir up racial hatred. The man entrusted by Goebbels with the *Entjudung* (removal of Jews) was Hans Hinkel, who in May 1935 was given overall responsibility for all matters relating to RKK personnel policy. Hinkel brought about a radicalization of that policy. By arranging for the Jews to have their own separate cultural organization (a sham organization called Der Jüdische Kulturbund, the showpiece for which was a theater in Berlin), Hinkel justified the total elimination of Jews from German cultural life.[15] Not surprisingly, these policies resulted in the emigration of all those who either could not or would not submit to such conditions. The loss of talent was severe, but the Nazis were able to retain a veritable reservoir of talented actors, technicians, and artistic staff.

On 28 March 1933, Goebbels introduced himself to the *Filmwelt* at a SPIO-Dach-Organisation der Filmschaffenden Deutschlands function at the Kaiserhof. He presented himself as an inveterate film addict (which he was) and showed considerable ingenuity in mitigating many of the industry's fears caused by the already extensive exodus. Films, he said, were to have an important place in the culture of the new Germany. But he warned that filmmakers must, in the future, learn to regard their profession as a service, not merely as a source of profit. Goebbels went on to mention four films that had made a lasting impression on him: Sergei Eisenstein's *Battleship Potemkin,* the American film with Greta Garbo *Anna Karenina,* Fritz Lang's *Die Nibelungen,* and Luis Trenker's *Der Rebell.* According to Goebbels, the German cinema was in a state of spiritual crisis that "will continue until we are courageous enough to radically reform German films." National Socialist filmmakers, he argued, "should capture the spirit of the time." What was not required in these films was "parade-ground marching and the blowing of trumpets." In calling for the industry's cooperation in this new venture, Goebbels concluded by declaring that with this new conviction "a new moral ethos will arise," allowing it "to be said of German films, as in other fields, 'Germany leads the world!'"[16]

To consolidate his position, Goebbels still desired more power than he had hitherto secured through the Reichskulturkammer legislation. He also needed some form of legal confirmation to be able to supervise films in the early stages of production. Goebbels settled both these issues by creating a revised version of the Reich Cinema Law (Reichslichtspielgesetz). Enacted on 16 February 1934, this new legislation attempted to create a "positive" censorship by which the state encouraged "good" National Socialist films instead of merely discouraging "bad" ones. The new Cinema Law anticipated three different channels through which this positive censorship could be achieved: a compulsory script censorship, an increase in the number of provisions under which the Censorship Office (Filmprüfstelle) might ban a film, and an expanded system of distinction marks *(Prädikate)* awarded by the regime to worthy films.

The most significant innovation of the new Cinema Law was the institution of a precensor *(Vorzensor),* a role assumed by a Propaganda Ministry official called the Reich film dramaturgist *(Reichsfilmdramaturg).* If a producer wished to make a film, he had first to submit a "treatment" to the film dramaturgist, who was appointed directly by Goebbels. If this synopsis was passed, the full scenario could be written, and it would have to be approved before shooting could begin. In most cases, the film dramaturgist could supervise every stage of production. The orders he issued and the changes he suggested were binding. As the representative of the Propaganda Ministry, he could even interfere with the censorship exercised by the Censorship Office in Berlin. Later on compulsory script censorship meant that before work on a film could begin, a 12-page synopsis had to be seen and approved by the ministry. A complete shooting script had to be submitted at least four weeks before filming was due to start. In order that the film dramaturgist not be inundated at the last minute with scripts that were not seriously intended to be shot, production chiefs were required to sign a declaration stating that they had every intention of filming the submitted synopsis.

The new film legislation greatly extended the powers of censorship, which it prescribed in some detail. It replaced the original law of 12 May 1920, which had regulated films during the Weimar Republic. Although Weimar censorship was initially a democratic one—"films may not be withheld out of political, social, religious, ethical, or ideological tendencies"—the intervention of the censor was permitted when "a film endanger[ed] public order or safety . . . or endanger[ed] the German image or the country's relationship with foreign states. . . ."[17] The examination of films was delegated to two Censorship Offices *(Prüfstellen)* in Berlin and Munich. Each office had two chairmen who examined films with the aid of four assessors drawn from the teaching and legal professions and from the film industry itself. The revised law of 1934 joined the two *Prüfstellen* together and incorporated them as a subsidiary office of the Propaganda Ministry. The procedure by which the Censorship Office reached its decisions was also revised. Under the 1920 law, decisions were arrived at by means of a majority vote, and if a film was banned, its producer could appeal to the Supreme Censorship Office (Oberprüfstelle). After 1934, the power to decide whether a film should be exhibited rested entirely with the chairman.[18]

According to Paragraph 4 of the 1934 Cinema Law, all films were to be submitted to the censor. Public and private screenings were made equal in law. Even film advertising in the cinemas was censored. For each print of a film, a censorship card had to be issued, which contained the official report on the film together with an embossed stamp of the German Eagle. In all matters concerning censorship, the propaganda minister had the right of intervention. Either he could appeal to the Oberprüfstelle or, by circumventing the Prüfstelle, he could forbid the release of various films directly. In the Second Amendment to the Cinema Law of 28 June 1935, Goebbels was given extra powers to ban any film without reference to the Prüfstelle, if he felt it was in the public's interest. Not only was the entire censorship apparatus centralized in Berlin, but the previous rights of local governments to request the reexamination of films was now the exclusive prerogative of the Propaganda Ministry.

In addition to direct censorship, the film industry depended on a system of distinction marks *(Prädikate)*, which was really a form of negative taxation. During the Weimar Republic, these distinction marks were considered an honor and an opportunity to gain tax reductions. Under the Nazis, however, a film had to obtain a *Prädikat* not only to benefit from tax reductions but to be allowed to be exhibited at all. Films without these distinction marks needed special permission to be shown. A further incentive was that producers whose works earned a *Prädikat* now received an extra share of the film's profits. By 1939, there were 11 distinctions ranging from "politically and artistically especially valuable" to "culturally valuable." "Film of the Nation" *(Film der Nation)* and "valuable for youth" *(Jugendwert)* differed from the others in that they carried no tax relief. Nevertheless, these special awards greatly enhanced a film's status. Furthermore, they were decisive for selection in schools and Nazi youth organizations. After 1938, no cinema owner was allowed to refuse to exhibit a film with a political distinction mark if a distributor offered one.

The *Prädikate* system not only produced certain financial advantages. As a key to the film's political and propagandistic content, these distinction marks also helped to establish the appropriate expectations and responses on the part of cinema audiences. "Politically valuable" clearly reflected a political message completely acceptable to the Party, whereas "artistically valuable" was understood in the sense of cultural propaganda and was given only to prestige films and those reserved for export.

Secure in the knowledge that film censorship had been reorganized according to the principles of the NSDAP, Goebbels now embarked on his next project, the nationalization of the film industry. In fact this would be carried out in two stages, largely through a process that escaped the notice of the ordinary citizen. When the Nazis came to power, there were four major film companies operating in Germany. To have nationalized them immediately would have damaged their contacts with foreign distributors, which in turn would have reduced the not inconsiderable revenue and foreign currency earned from Germany's film exports. It seemed advisable therefore to proceed warily with the nationalization of the cinema industry and not alarm the outside world unnecessarily. Yet as German film exports continued to decline under the Nazis and production costs continued to increase, the Propaganda Ministry decided secretly to buy out the major shares in the film companies and to refer to them as *staatsmittelbar* (indirectly state controlled), rather than state owned. Germany's military victories in 1939/40 had created a German-dominated film monopoly in Europe, which Goebbels' ministry believed it could exploit only if the film industry produced 100 films per year. Toward the end of 1941, it became increasingly clear that this target was not being reached. The only solution, it was decided, lay in a complete takeover by the state. To this end, the nationalization of the film industry was completed in 1942. On 10 January 1942, a giant holding company, Ufa-Film GmbH (called Ufi to distinguish it from its predecessor) assumed control of the entire German film industry and its foreign subsidiaries. Every aspect of filmmaking was now the immediate responsibility of Ufa-Film GmbH. The Reichsfilmkammer had become merely a bureaucratic administrative machine, and Ufi, thanks to its vertical organization, was a mere receiver of orders from the Propaganda Ministry. This represented an enormous concentration of a mass medium in the hands of the National Socialist State and, more specifically, the minister for popular enlightenment and propaganda. With his task completed, Goebbels could sit back and reflect on the wisdom of his actions: "Movie production is flourishing almost unbelievably despite the war. What a good idea of mine it was to have taken possession of the films on behalf of the Reich several years ago! It would be terrible if the high profits now being earned by the motion-picture industry were to flow into private hands."[19]

FILM POLICY: IDEOLOGY AND PROPAGANDA

An analysis of the different types of film produced during the Third Reich reveals a good deal about Goebbels' *Filmpolitik*. Of the 1,100 feature films produced between 1933 and 1945, only about one-fifth were overtly propagandistic with a direct political content. Less than half of these films (96 out of 229) were "state-commissioned films" *(Staatsauftragsfilme)*, which included the most important films from a political standpoint and were given disproportionate funding and publicity.

Of the entire production of feature films, virtually 50 percent were either love stories or comedies, and 25 percent dramatic films, such as crime thrillers or musicals. Regardless of the genre, all went through the precensorship process and all were associated with the National Socialist ideology in that they were produced and performed in accordance with the propagandistic aims of the period.

It can be seen from the figures presented in the table that there was no clearly formulated policy regarding the percentage of films that were to be allocated to each particular category. However, it is discernible that as the war dragged on, particularly after Stalingrad, when disillusionment set in, the number of political films declined and the Nazi cinema served increasingly to facilitate escapism, or *Wirklichkeitsflucht*. These figures reflect both the diversi-

Percentage of Films Exhibited, 1934-1944

YEAR	Comedies	Dramas	Political Films
1934	55	21	24
1935	50	27	23
1936	46	31	23
1937	38	34	28
1938	49	41	10
1939	42	40	18
1940	52	28	20
1941	40	20	40
1942	36	37	27
1943	62	30	8
1944	53	39	8

The compilation is taken from the Propaganda Ministry's directives on how films should be reviewed plus the *Prädikate* that were awarded to each film. For analyses of Nazi films see also: Gerd Albrecht, *Nationalsozialistische Filmpolitik*; Francis Courtade and Pierre Cadars, *Le Cinéma Nazi* (Paris: Losfeld, 1972); Erwin Leiser, *Nazi Cinema* (New York: Collier Books, 1975); Bogusław Drewniak, *Der deutsche Film 1938-1945. Ein Gesamtüberblick* (Düsseldorf: Droste, 1987); Hilmar Hoffmann, *Es ist noch nicht zu Ende: Sollen Nazikunst und Nazifilme wieder öffentlich gezeigt werden?* (Badenweiler: Oase, 1988), and H. Hoffmann, *"Und die Fahne führt uns in die Ewigkeit." Propaganda im NS-Film* (Frankfurt/Main: Fischer, 1988).

fication of the Nazi cinema and its inherent escapism, although they can be misleading and should not be misinterpreted.

Some writers have talked about the relative "normality" of a German (as opposed to "Nazi") cinema that remained largely unaffected by state ideology, producing a variety of genre films and performing essentially the same emotional and aesthetic function that the cinema performed both before and after the Third Reich.[20] It is true that when you take some of the "entertainment" films *individually,* their ideological content may appear, *prima facie,* flimsy and indeed innocuous. One of the most popular films during the Third Reich was director Rolf Hansen's 1942 love story *Die große Liebe* (The great love), whose themes, stereotypes, and filmic elements have parallels to many American films of that era, as well as to films before and after the Third Reich. The film is about a celebrated Scandinavian singer who, through her love for a German air force officer, experiences what it is like to be a soldier's wife on the German home front, feeling the threat of war. The woman (played by Zarah Leander) is initially depicted as a selfish prima donna who feels superior to other people. But after she meets the fighter pilot, she begins to take an active part in the war effort. Even after spending the night with the famous singer, the pilot still places his sense of duty above his love for her. He is contrasted favorably with a composer (with the un-German name of Ruchnitzky) who makes no contribution to the war effort and continues to dream only of his love for the singer. Some of the songs in the film with uplifting titles such as "I Know There'll Be a Miracle" and "The World's Not Going to End Because of This" became hit tunes.

It might be claimed that such a film could easily have been produced in Hollywood with a similar moral that in time of war, no woman, regardless of her wealth and fame, can expect to make demands of the fighting men or place her desire for personal happiness above a sense of duty and the common good. It is for this reason, for their seeming normality within film conventions, that such "entertainment" films are still shown on German television today (albeit with subtle cuts). The fact that the Allied Control Commission did not ban *Die große Liebe* after the war but allowed it to be shown in Germany indicates that it was not perceived as a political film. And yet the film was a *Staatsauftragsfilm* commissioned by the Propaganda Ministry and carried the distinction marks "politically and artistically especially valuable" and "valuable to the nation."

With its charismatic female star, catchy songs, and intense love story against the background of war, *Die große Liebe* is a good example of Goebbels' policy of injecting propaganda into popular entertainment. The film's specific propagandistic purpose was to uplift morale and strengthen the home front at a time when Germany's military situation was taking a turn for the worse and beginning to look hopeless to many. It presented the holding-out message of the regime in an especially appealing way:

> [W]hen Zarah Leander sang "The World Is Not Going to End Because of This" and, in her husky and powerful-masculine voice, offered unbroken optimism to those who did not quite believe in their own luck any more and even less in a "final victory": "I Know There'll Be a Miracle," then the audience was simply fascinated. It heard and saw what it wanted to believe. To be sure, that was not much different from what the propaganda slogans promised. But it was much more attractive, beguiled the eye and ear.[21]

Besides the film's other overt propagandistic strategies, such as, for example, the downplaying of the effects of the bombing raids on German cities and the emphasis on solidarity among the civilian population, recent research has identified subtler ideological as well as specifically filmic mechanisms as instrumental in its propagandistic manipulation; these are beyond the scope of the present analysis.[22]

Two points must be borne in mind when discussing Nazi *Filmpolitik*. First of all, Goebbels often allowed an important message to be concealed in a scenario that appeared to advance quite unexpected, even contrary views. He could do this safe in the knowledge that during the Third Reich, films would not have been viewed in isolation or as part of an open flow of information and ideas that are commonly associated with pluralistic societies. Second, feature films were **not** shown in isolation but as part of a carefully structured film program. The normal program would consist of a trailer, newsreel, and feature film invariably accompanied by a carefully selected short film. Goebbels wanted the overt, aggressive propaganda confined to the newsreels; in one speech he declared: "The task of modern art is not to dramatize the Party program but to give poetic and artistic shape to the huge spiritual impulses within us."[23] In pursuit of this, he encouraged the production of films that promoted nationalism, militarism, elitism, and racism—feelings that could be utilized to fuel the Nazi impulse.

In this context it is important to make a general distinction between the political intention of a film and its actual content. In a highly politicized and "closed" society such as the Third Reich, even the apolitical becomes significant in that so-called entertainment films tend to promote the official worldview of things and to reinforce the existing social and economic order. Propaganda is as important in reinforcing existing beliefs as it is in changing them, and even the most escapist entertainment can, as Goebbels noted, be of value to the national struggle, "providing [the German nation] with the edification, diversion, and relaxation needed to see it through the drama of everyday life." Stephen Lowry has pointed out "the legitimizing function of the private sphere" in Nazi ideology. By helping to maintain the illusion that a "private sphere free of politics" existed, the seemingly nonpolitical film, which "tended to completely confirm petit-bourgeois values," strengthened a passive consensus and thus represented an important propagandistic tool.[24] Rather than disseminating too many overt propaganda films, the entire organizational, artistic, and technical resources were concentrated upon a limited number of carefully selected and meticulously produced large-scale *Staatsauftragsfilme*. Their lavish budgets, choice of big-name stars, awarding of official prizes, and support of the government-controlled press helped to lift these films above all competing productions. The comparatively small number of overtly political films were supplemented by documentary films, short "cultural" films, and newsreels, which became increasingly important during the war.[25]

The themes that recur in the cinema of the Third Reich are central to the National Socialist *Weltanschauung*, and these ideas were repeated at carefully chosen intervals. Goebbels kept prestigious film propaganda at its maximum effectiveness by spacing out the films concerned—except, that is, for the newsreels *(Deutsche Wochenschau)*, which depended on their ability to capture the immediacy of events. The full-length documentaries were all the more effective for their comparative rarity. Perhaps the two best-known documentaries of the Nazi period are Leni Riefenstahl's *Triumph des Willens* (Triumph of the Will, 1935) about the 1934 Party rally in Nuremberg, and *Olympiade* (Olympia, 1938), a four-hour record of the 1936 Olympic Games held in Berlin, which proved to be an ideal vehicle for Nazi propaganda to foreign countries. Susan Sontag, in an excellent piece on "fascinating fascism," referred to these films' "stunning symmetry and choreography, their mass human celebrations of surrender and death."[26] Similarly impressive for the manner in which they demonstrated the physical and military strength of Nazism and reflected the nation's mood of elation and triumph were the so-called *Blitzkrieg* documentaries: *Feldzug in Polen* (Campaign in Poland, 1939), *Feuertaufe* (Baptism of fire, 1940), and *Sieg im Westen* (Victory in the West, 1941). These campaign films invoked almost every aspect of the Nazi mythology of war and generally set the tone for a whole series of military education films *(Wehrerziehungsfilme)* directed specifically at the youth audience. During the first half of the war, such films would include *Jakko* (1941), *Kadetten* (Cadets, 1941), *Kampfgeschwader Lutzow* (Battle squadron Lutzow, 1941), *Kopf hoch, Johannes!* (Chin-up, John!, 1941), *Blutsbruderschaft* (Blood brotherhood, 1941), and *Himmelhunde* (Skydogs, 1942). Interestingly, these early war films were the only film genre that the Nazis felt confident enough to present in a contemporary context.

It is surprising to find few indications of an overall pattern or strategy of film propaganda. To be sure, a trilogy of films eulogized the *Kampfzeit* (time of struggle) and glorified the movement and its martyrs in 1933 *(SA-Mann Brand, Hitlerjunge Quex, Hans Westmar)*. Similarly, three films were produced in 1940 that were intended to prepare the German people for the final solution to the "Jewish problem" *(Die Rothschilds, Jud Süss, Der ewige Jude)*. And likewise, 1941 marked the highest concentration of *Staatsauftragsfilme* commissioned by the Propaganda Ministry. But Goebbels' main concern was to keep the important themes of Nazi ideology constantly before the public by releasing an optimum number of state-commissioned films.

In accordance with Hitler's dictum of orienting the masses toward specific topics, a number of these *Staatsauftragsfilme,* together with carefully coordinated campaigns in the press and radio, attempted to dramatize central tenets of the National Socialist program. Such films were invariably classified at the time as *Tendenzfilme.* This was a term employed during the Third Reich to describe a certain type of film that exhibited "strong National Socialist tendencies." Without necessarily mentioning National Socialism, these propaganda films advocated various principles and themes identifiable with Nazism that the Propaganda Ministry wished to disseminate periodically. The importance of these *Tendenzfilme,* according to a film critic writing in 1938, "was that from the very beginning they attempt to lead the audience in the direction of certain ideas, not by the use of crude symbols, but by the strength and conviction of the artists' inner experiences that find expression through the medium of film."[27] That the references to Hitler's regime and National Socialist ideology could be unmistakable, however, is obvious in Veit Harlan's successful film *Der Herrscher* (1937). The protagonist, Clausen, head of an industrial dynasty modeled after the Krupps family, becomes a powerful contemporary Führer figure who helps to rebuild Germany by bequeathing his factory to the community. Again and again his words are blatantly reminiscent of Hitler's rhetoric. Clausen's closing speech sounds like a threatening justification for the regime's existence:

> Gentlemen, we are here to provide work and bread for millions of people. We are here to work for the community of the nation. The aim of every industrial leader conscious of his responsibility must be to serve this community. This will of mine is the supreme law which governs my work. All else must be subordinated to this will, without opposition, even if in doing this I lead the firm into ruin. He who does not submit himself to this supreme law has no place in the Clausen factories!

Other *Tendenzfilme* were: *Das alte Recht* (The old right, 1934), the justification of the State Hereditary Farm Law; *Ich für Dich—Du für mich* (I for you—you for me, 1934), emphasizing the importance of *Blut und Boden* (Blood and soil), which defined the source of strength of the "master race" in terms of peasant virtues and the sacredness of German soil; *Der Ewige Wald* (The eternal forest, 1936), an attempt to create national solidarity and demonstrate the need for "living space" *(Lebensraum); Sensationsprozeß Casilla* (The sensational trial of Casilla, 1939), anti-American propaganda designed to ridicule the American way of life; *Heimkehr* (Homecoming, 1941), the sad fate of German nationals living abroad; *Ich klage an* (I accuse, 1941), an exposition of the Nazis' euthanasia campaign.

These films illustrate Goebbels' desire to mix entertainment with propaganda. Unlike Hitler, Goebbels believed that propaganda was most effective when it was insidious, when its message was concealed within the framework of popular entertainment. Goebbels therefore encouraged the production of feature films that reflected the ambience of National Socialism rather than of those that loudly proclaimed its ideology. He believed that such a policy would not prevent him from creating an ideologically committed cinema that was essentially German in character. Goebbels was considerably influenced by the Soviet example and even ordered that film education be extended to the schools and youth organizations in an effort to make German youth more conscious of film culture. The ultimate failure of the Third Reich to create a revolutionary "people's" culture that would reflect the experiences of the much-heralded *Volksgemeinschaft* can be attributed more to the inherent contradictions of National Socialism than to Goebbels' film policy.

Goebbels' *Filmpolitik* resulted in a monopolistic system of control and organization that maintained profits and managed to quadruple the annual number of cinemagoers between 1933 and 1942. For both political and economic reasons the Propaganda Ministry made intensive efforts to increase the number of cinemagoers. By means of Popular Film Days and campaigns such as The Cinema Goes to the Village, the regime attempted to entice sections of the rural population (comprising some 25 percent of the entire population) into the mobile cinemas. In addition, collective cinema visits were organized for schools, youth organizations, garrisons, and factories, where a carefully selected film program would be screened.

Particularly important were the *Jugendfilmstunden* (youth film hours), film performances organized jointly by the Hitler Youth and the Propaganda Ministry. The first *Jugendfilmstunden* began on a monthly basis in 1934. With reports of their effectiveness, the authorities decided that even more emphasis should be placed on film propaganda. Thus by 1936, these events were being organized nationwide every Sunday. In 1939, a special distinction mark "valuable for youth" *(Jugendwert)* was specifically introduced for these occasions. As already mentioned, although not strictly a *Prädikat,* the award greatly enhanced a film's status and was decisive in the selection of films to be shown in schools and youth organizations.[28]

Film was only one factor in creating an uncritical audience, but it had an important function because when people read newspapers or listened to the radio, they were more conscious of the propaganda content. The cinema, in contrast, was associated with relaxation and entertainment and was therefore all the more dangerous, particularly as the *Gleichschaltung* of the German cinema had been carried out behind the scenes. It is clear that when the Nazis assumed power, they thought highly of film as a propaganda weapon. The need for conformity in a totalitarian state meant that the film industry had to be reorganized according to the ideas of the NSDAP. Like all forms of mass communication, film had to correspond with the political *Weltanschauung* and the propaganda principles of the Party. The communications media—the press, radio, and film—had a circular interrelationship in that they supplied each other with themes in the manner prescribed by the state, and supported each other in their effect by a simultaneous and graduated release of information, which was disseminated, controlled, and modulated by the state.

When Goebbels came to office as minister for popular enlightenment and propaganda, he asked the studios to "capture the spirit of the new Germany" by making the nation conscious of its *völkisch* identity. Only when this was achieved, he announced, "would immortal Germany march once more over the cinema screens of the world."[29] (It is supremely ironic that the cinematic image of Goebbels that would survive the collapse of the Third Reich was his depiction in a succession of Hollywood films [*Confessions of a Nazi Spy, The Hitler Gang*] as a slimy, reptilian schemer.) By striving to produce films that would satisfy its fascist masters, the Nazi dream factory recycled *völkisch* themes that aimed to achieve the desired conformity. The recurring features that can be identified immediately include the use of stereotypes and repetitious demonstrations of patterns of conduct and visual images approved by the regime and accentuated by nationalistic music. In this way—often with the help of historical examples—the audience's desirable emotions were evoked while undesirable rational thought was eliminated. What made these films so effective and apparently seductive was their banality; by visiting the cinema, people could pretend that fascist ideology or principles, as disseminated in films, did not meaningfully impinge on everyday life or force them to restructure their system of values radically. Film, then, could provide a comforting continuity with the past. There is nothing new in this, other that in the Third Reich totalitarian solutions were being implemented amid widespread political indifference. Although it is difficult to assess precisely the success of the films produced under National Socialism—and there is evidence that a number of films did not have the desired effect—in general, film, the medium of the first half of the twentieth century, helped to destroy rational thought and human feeling and create apathy and indifference to suffering. The vicious, anti-Semitic films that were to prepare the nation for the Holocaust are the most conspicuous examples. The result of the Nazi ideology, disseminated by an ideologically committed cinema, was the monster that had been predicted by Heinrich Mann, "ein Herrenvolk aus Untertanen"—a master race of obedient subjects.[30]

FILM PROPAGANDA FOR "TOTAL WAR"

Goebbels' principal cinematic objective had been the production of a major Nazi work of art. During the war, he pinned his hopes on the gigantic historical epic *Kolberg* (1945), which has been called "the apotheosis of the Nazi film"[31] and as such bears testimony to Goebbels' control over the film industry until the end as well as to his almost obsessive personal involvement with film production. On 5 June 1943, at a time of heavy civilian casualties from Allied bombing raids and widespread defeatism, Goebbels mentioned reading Veit Harlan's manuscript for the new *Kolberg* film until late at night. He anticipated its propagandistic usefulness for the military situation in the winter 1943/44: "Then we will have to have at our disposal films that promote and praise tough resistance."[32] However, as was so often the case before, Goebbels deemed it necessary to modify the screenplay to accommodate his own ideas.

This last *Film der Nation,* premiering on 30 January 1945, the twelfth anniversary of Hitler's assumption of power, dramatizes the struggle of a small Prussian town during the Napoleonic War. In the film, Kolberg's civilian population insists on making a courageous attempt at resisting the invading French forces against the will of the local military commander, who plans to surrender to the superior enemy force. Goebbels allocated a budget of 8.5 million Reichsmark to the colossal production. And at a time when the Red Army had already crossed the East Prussian frontier, he pulled whole units of troops out of the front lines to act as extras in the battle scenes. Veit Harlan's account of *Kolberg*'s production, of the enormous expenditure of resources in particular, attests to the high priority Goebbels and Hitler assigned to cinema's propagandistic instrumentalization even at a time of imminent defeat.[33] According to Harlan, both the Führer and his chief propagandist thought the film would be more important than a military victory. When Goebbels had commissioned Harlan in 1943 to make the film, he wrote that it was the film's task to show "that a nation unified at home and at the front could overcome any enemy."[34]

As one of the last efforts of National Socialist film propaganda aimed at manipulating the German population with myths about the *Führerprinzip,* national idealism, sacrifice, and the indomitable spirit of the German people, *Kolberg* stands out as a propaganda vehicle that blatantly recycles Nazi slogans, songs and parts of Goebbels' speeches. To a large extent, the film is a dramatization of Goebbels' Total War speech at the Berlin Sportpalast on 18 February 1943, in which the minister prepared the civilian population for greater sacrifices, demanding more solidarity with the military in the war effort. But there are also parallels to other Goebbels speeches of that time, including speeches he made at *Volkssturm* rallies. These striking affinities—at times verbatim quotations—corroborate Harlan's claim that Goebbels wrote many of the film's dialogues and speeches himself. When Captain Schill addresses the people of Kolberg in order to show the French emissary that the citizens are determined not to surrender but to become a "people of soldiers" and emphasizes the civilians' importance for the "salvation of the Fatherland," both the situation and Schill's words echo the final part of Goebbels' Total War speech. There—just like Schill—the propaganda minister turned to the crowd in order to elicit a clear signal: ". . . [The German people] does not want total war, say the English, but capitulation. . . . Do you want total war? . . . The mightiest ally there is in this world, the people themselves, stand behind us and are determined, together with the Führer—regardless of the cost and with the acceptance of the gravest sacrifices—to fight for victory. . . ."[35] Goebbels' famous closing words: "People arise, and storm break loose!" which he borrowed from the nineteenth-century nationalist poet Theodor Körner, play an important role in the film's framing story. This slogan is not only sung by marching "mobilized" civilians in the opening and closing scenes but is also repeated verbatim at the film's beginning and end in Gneisenau's appeal to the Prussian king to enlist the aid of the people in the cause of the war.

Whereas Goebbels gave a realistic picture of Germany's military situation in his speeches during the later war years, his policy with respect to film was to reduce the number of films treating political and military subjects in favor of love stories and operettas that would provide relaxation and escapism for the population and thus help maintain morale. *Münchhausen* (1943), a lavish two-year color production that preceded the *Kolberg* production at the Ufa studios, was an entertaining, fantastic movie spectacle completely different in character from *Kolberg*, which offered very little distraction from a harsh reality. All of *Kolberg*'s positive main characters sounded like the propaganda minister in his public appeals to the German civilian population at that time. And the enormous sacrifices of the town's citizens for nationalistic ideals in a desperate situation left the audience with only the bleakest outlook for their own future. In essence, *Kolberg*'s message reflected Goebbels' radical stance on the question of total war and capitulation. This becomes especially clear in a key scene where Kolberg's mayor, Nettelbeck, implores the new military commandant Gneisenau not to surrender, despite the fact that the Prussian troops are hopelessly outnumbered and outgunned by the French besiegers:

NETTELBECK: But we haven't fired our last bullet yet! . . . We are not letting [Kolberg] go even if we have to claw into the ground with our bare hands. In our town we do not give up. No, they will have to cut off our hands to slay us one by one.... I even promised our King that we would rather be buried under the rubble than capitulate. I have never pleaded to anyone, but I get down on my knees, Gneisenau. Kolberg must not be surrendered.

GNEISENAU: That's what I wanted to hear from you, Nettelbeck. Now we can die together.

Kolberg shows that Goebbels remained the propagandist to the very end. Whether, at the time the Third Reich was facing its *Götterdämmerung,* Hitler's minister for popular enlightenment and propaganda truly believed that he could carry the manipulation and deception of the masses to even further extremes with the help of the film medium or whether he had begun to live in a cinematic world of his own imagination is a question that cannot be answered here. An incident at the Propaganda Ministry on 17 April 1945, the day Soviet troops crossed the Oder River in their massive final assault on the Reich's capital, is open to either interpretation. There, after a screening of *Kolberg,* the propaganda minister extolled the virtues of holding out to his incredulous staff and promised them a part in another splendid film, which would be shown in 100 years—a film of the "Twilight of the Gods" in Berlin in 1945:

> Gentlemen, in a hundred years' time they will be showing another fine color film describing the terrible days we are living through. Don't you want to play a part in this film, to be brought back to life in a hundred years' time? Everybody now has the chance to choose the part which he will play in the film a hundred years hence. I can assure you it will be a fine and elevating picture. And for the sake of this prospect it is worth standing fast. Hold out now, so that a hundred years hence the audience does not hoot and whistle when you appear on the screen.[36]

Clearly, Goebbels was happy to accept *Kolberg* as his testament to future generations, whom he entrusted with the task of immortalizing on celluloid his own "heroic" role during the Red Army's siege of Berlin. As a propagandistic vehicle for his fanatical total war and holding-out policies, *Kolberg* is indeed the ultimate Goebbels film, but ironically it is also the "dramatized Party program" Goebbels had once claimed the regime did not want to see.[37] From a cinematic point of view, *Kolberg,* together with the other color films *Münchhausen* and *Die goldene Stadt* (1942), indicated that the Germans had achieved considerable success in approximating the technical advances and level of artistic accomplishment Hollywood had achieved years earlier. However, the main legacy of this effectively produced propaganda film, which was never put to the full test since it was released when Germany's total defeat was imminent and Berlin did not even have an intact theater for its premiere, is the awareness *Kolberg* gives us of how the film medium can be manipulated to serve the opportunistic purposes of its masters.

Notes

1. See Hitler's final address to the Nuremberg Party Congress of September 1935 in Norman H. Baynes, ed., *The Speeches of Adolf Hitler*, 2 vols. (London: Oxford University Press, 1942), vol. 1, pp. 438-49.
2. Speech to representatives of the press 15 March 1933 taken from WTB (*Wolffs Telegraphisches Büro*) press agency report of 16 March 1933 deposited in the Bundesarchiv in Koblenz (hereafter cited as BAK).
3. Quoted in Oskar Kalbus, *Vom Werden deutscher Filmkunst, Teil 2: Der Tonfilm* (Altona-Bahrenfeld: Cigarettenbilderdienst, 1935), p. 101.
4. Baynes, ed., vol. 1, pp. 584-92.
5. *Film-Kurier*, 13 May 1936.
6. "Vortrag zu einem brennenden Problem. Ministerialrat Berndt sprach vor dem Reichskultursenat über Kunstrichter und Kunstdiener," *Völkischer Beobachter*, No. 334 (29 November 1936).
7. Cf. Helmut Heiber, ed., *Goebbels-Reden: Band 1: 1932-1939* (Düsseldorf: Droste, 1971), pp. 108-11.
8. Elke Fröhlich, "Die Kulturpolitische Pressekonferenz des Reichspropagandaministeriums," in *Vierteljahrshefte für Zeitgeschichte* 22, No. 4 (1974): 358-59; quoted in *Nazism 1919-1945: Vol. 2: State, Economy and Society 1933-1939*, eds. Jeremy Noakes and Geoffrey Pridham (Exeter: University of Exeter, 1984), p. 409.
9. *Völkischer Beobachter*, 20 May 1933.
10. The process is described in Dietrich Orlow, *The History of the Nazi Party, Vol. 1: 1919-1933* (Pittsburgh: University of Pittsburgh Press, 1969).
11. For further details of the organization of the Nazi cinema, see David Welch, *Propaganda and the German Cinema 1933-1945* (Oxford: Clarendon Press, 1983), pp. 2-38.
12. "Auflösung der 'Dacho,'" *Völkischer Beobachter*, Münchener Ausgabe, No. 131 (11 May 1933).
13. BAK: R 55/484, Filmkreditbankbilanz, 1943.
14. Curt Belling, *Der Film in Staat und Partei* (Berlin: "Der Film" Verlag, 1936), pp. 15-16.

15. For further information on the Jüdischer Kulturbund, see Herbert Freeden, *Jüdisches Theater in Nazideutschland* (Tübingen: Mohr, 1964).
16. The full text of Goebbels' speech of 28 March 1933 is reproduced in Gerd Albrecht, *Nationalsozialistische Filmpolitik: Eine soziologische Untersuchung über die Spielfilme des Dritten Reichs* (Stuttgart: Ferdinand Enke Verlag, 1969), pp. 439-42.
17. Albrecht, p. 512.
18. For a brief discussion of censorship and film during the Weimar Republic and the manner in which it favored extreme right-wing groups, see David Welch, "The Proletarian Cinema and the Weimar Republic," *Historical Journal of Film, Radio and Television* 1, No. 1 (1981): 3-18.
19. Quoted in Louis P. Lochner, ed., *The Goebbels Diaries 1942-1943* (Garden City, NY: Doubleday & Co., 1948), p. 38, entry for 22 January 1942.
20. For further discussion of this viewpoint, see Hans Dieter Schäfer, *Das gespaltene Bewußtsein: Über deutsche Kultur und Lebenswirklichkeit 1933-1945* (München: Hanser, 1981).
21. Peter Reichel, *Der schöne Schein des Dritten Reiches: Faszination und Gewalt des Faschismus* (München: Carl Hanser, 1991), p. 194.
22. For an in-depth analysis of *Die große Liebe,* see Stephen Lowry, *Pathos und Politik: Ideologie in Spielfilmen des Nationalsozialismus* (Tübingen: Niemeyer, 1991), pp. 116-201.
23. Quoted in Kalbus, p. 101.
24. Lowry, p. 27.
25. For an analysis of the role of newsreels, see David Welch, "Nazi Wartime Newsreel Propaganda," in *Film and Radio Propaganda in World War II: A Global Perspective,* ed. Kenneth R. M. Short (Knoxville: University of Tennessee Press, 1983), pp. 201-19; and Welch, "Goebbels, Götterdämmerung, and the Deutsche Wochenschauen," in *Hitler's Fall: The Newsreel Witness,* eds. Kenneth R. M. Short and Stephan Dolezel (London: Croom Helm, 1988), pp. 80-99.
26. Susan Sontag, "Fascinating Fascism," in *Under the Sign of Saturn* (New York: Farrar, Straus & Giroux, 1980), pp. 87-91. For a discussion of short feature films that have been largely ignored, see Günter Knorr, *Deutscher Kurzspielfilm 1929-1940* (Wien: Verlag des Dokumentationszentrums ACTION, 1977).
27. G. Eckert, "Filmintendenz und Tendenzfilm," *Wille und Macht, Führerorgan der nationalsozialistischen Jugend* 4 (15 November 1938): 19-25.
28. For a more detailed discussion of the Youth Film Hours and educational film propaganda in general, see David Welch, "Educational Film Propaganda and the Nazi Youth," in *Nazi Propaganda: The Power and the Limitations,* ed. Welch (Totowa, NJ: Barnes & Noble, 1983), pp. 65-87.

29. "Dr. Goebbels vor den Filmschaffenden. Erste Versammlung der 'Reichsfachschaft Film,'" *Völkischer Beobachter*, No. 42/43 (11/12 February 1934).
30. I am grateful to Gerhard Schoenberner for drawing this point to my attention.
31. David Stewart Hull, *Film in the Third Reich: A Study of the German Cinema 1933-1945* (Berkeley: University of California Press, 1969), p. 261.
32. Cf. Joseph Goebbels, *Tagebücher 1924-1945*, ed. Ralf Georg Reuth (München: Piper, 1992), vol. 5, p. 1937.
33. See Veit Harlan, *Im Schatten meiner Filme. Selbstbiographie* (Gütersloh: Sigbert Mohn, 1966), pp. 184-89.
34. Goebbels' letter of 1 June 1943 is reproduced in ibid., p. 183.
35. Helmut Heiber, ed., *Goebbels-Reden: Band 2: 1939-1945* (Düsseldorf: Droste, 1972), pp. 204-6.
36. Rudolf Semmler, *Goebbels—The Man Next to Hitler* (London: Westhouse, 1947), p. 194, entry for 17 April 1945.
37. Cf. Goebbels' speech at the opening of the Reich Chamber of Culture on 15 November 1933, in Helmut Heiber, ed., *Goebbels-Reden: Band 1: 1932-1939* (Düsseldorf: Droste, 1972), p. 137. See also the speech's earliest published version, where his statement: "Was wir wollen ist mehr als dramatisiertes Parteiprogramm" received special emphasis in the text—"Die Öffnung der Reichskulturkammer: Minister Dr. Goebbels Eröffnungsrede," *Völkischer Beobachter*, No. 320 (16 November 1933), p. 2.

6

A Guide through the Visual Arts Administration of the Third Reich

Jonathan Petropoulos

In the year 1937, the artistic policy of the National Socialist regime finally crystallized: Modernism or, more specifically, expressionistic and nonrepresentational art, was conclusively proscribed, and Nazi art, with its stilted, monumental figures, was thrust before the public with all the propagandistic energy that the government could muster. During the four years of National Socialist rule prior to this grandiose attempt at clarification, the arts administration was characterized by vigorous debates, conflicting policies, and confusing alliances among the leaders. Hitler had declined to impose his own antimodernist views upon the nation, and the subleaders attempted to fill the vacuum by determining and enforcing policy. The public resolution of this divisive debate in 1937 was symbolized by two exhibitions organized by the government; both were in Munich and opened on successive days in mid-July. The officially sanctioned works were placed in the first annual Große Deutsche Kunstausstellung (GDK), thus inaugurating the museum commissioned by Hitler, the Haus der Deutschen Kunst. The rejected modernist art confiscated from German museums was assembled for the infamous *Entartete Kunst* ("Degenerate Art") exhibition. Opened by Hitler's proxy Adolf Ziegler, the president of the Reich Chamber for the Visual Arts, the highly ideological show sought to defame modern art, while simultaneously attacking other declared enemies, most notably Jews, Communists, and supporters of the Weimar Republic. Both exhibitions attracted extraordinary crowds—especially *Entartete Kunst,* which evolved into a traveling exhibition and appeared throughout the Reich over the next three years.[1] Over 3 million people eventually saw the show, and extensive newsreel and press coverage further amplified the message sent by the leaders to the public. A pamphlet called *Ein Führer durch die Ausstellung Entartete Kunst* was produced once it was evident that there was tremendous popular interest in the subject. The pamphlet explained the rationale behind the regime's proscription of modernist art, and did so in a manner that illuminated the National Socialist ideology.[2]

In a broader sense, the Nazi leaders' administration of the arts expressed fundamental characteristics of the regime. Its bureaucratic organization was dynamic to the point of appearing improvisational; hierarchical and yet at the same time uncoordinated; responsive to Hitler's policies, while still subject to the whims of the subleaders. This bureaucracy expanded steadily over time, becoming more oppressive and totalitarian; clearly it reflected the increasingly radical and violent course of the regime. From a point of departure during the *Kampfzeit* (the "period of struggle") and early years after the "seizure of power," when no coherent policy existed and various pressure groups vied with one another to represent the Party's cultural aspirations, a network of offices evolved that provided the leaders with an effective tool to implement their totalitarian designs. Whether this entailed stifling unacceptable artists, expropriating the art owned by Jews, or plundering the cultural patrimony of neighboring lands, a host of agencies that made up the visual arts bureaucracy carried out the Nazis' oppressive and hegemonic policies. The following guide through this complicated maze of state and Party offices concerned with art aims to aid those who wish to explore the Third Reich and its culture.

On 13 March 1933, Hitler took the crucial first step in the formation of the Nazi cultural bureaucracy when he overcame the opposition of President Hindenburg and appointed Joseph Goebbels to the newly created post Reichsminister für Volksaufklärung und Propaganda. Goebbels rapidly emerged as the "czar of Nazi culture," due not only to his dual positions in the Party and state apparatuses (besides his serving as a minister, he was *Gauleiter* of Berlin and the head of the National Socialist Party's propaganda office), but also due to the shrewd and aggressive manner in which he discharged these offices. During the spring and summer of 1933, he expanded his Propaganda Ministry by encroaching upon his colleagues' administrative turf. He took over the press office from the Reich Chancellery, the supervision of advertising from the Economics Ministry, broadcasting from the Postal Ministry, and censorship powers from the Ministry of the Interior.[3] His skillful empire-building, what his chief rival Alfred Rosenberg called "Organisationskunst" (art of organization), took on new proportions in the autumn of 1933, when he created the Reichskulturkammer (Reich Chamber of Culture, or RKK), with seven arts-specific chambers.[4] Assuming the presidency of the entire complex, Goebbels moved beyond the governmental sphere (where he supervised hundreds of employees) to the public realm, as every practicing artist and "cultural worker"—from bookseller to landscape architect—came under his purview.[5] The Reichskulturkammer embraced many features of the Italian Fascist corporatist counterpart.[6] Yet this was an entirely new administrative structure in Germany. And as Goebbels managed the RKK in concert with the Propaganda Ministry, he now possessed unprecedented means with which to shape the cultural life of the nation.[7]

Goebbels' outlook on the arts had another affinity with that of the Italian Fascists: a toleration and even a sympathy for modernist artistic styles. The cosmopolitan and educated Dr. Goebbels sincerely admired the work of many German expressionist painters and sculptors. Beyond placing the watercolors of Emil Nolde on the walls of his first official residence, and exhibiting a sculpture by Ernst Barlach in his office, Goebbels declared in early speeches that expressionism harkened back to the medieval gothic, and conveyed the profundity of the German soul.[8] In 1933 and 1934, Goebbels became the key figure for the NSDAP's more socialistic and idealistic wing, many of whose members believed that modern art had a place in the new Reich.[9] Goebbels, however, was not so much a pro-modernist as he was an ultranationalist. He aimed at a cultural policy that would bring prestige to the nation and the Nazi government and, as propaganda minister, was inclined to tolerate modern artists if they reflected positively upon Germany and were not Communists. Goebbels therefore actively recruited talented artists and cultural figures, hoping that they would collaborate with the regime. He sought to give the poet Stefan George the top post in the Reichsschrifttumskammer (Literature Chamber), Fritz Lang the same post in the Filmkammer (Film Chamber), and tried to lure Marlene Dietrich back from Hollywood to bolster the German film industry, which he increasingly controlled.[10] Despite eliciting only rebuffs from these figures, Goebbels achieved partial success as he persuaded Richard Strauss and Wilhelm Furtwängler to serve in the Reichsmusikkammer (Reich Music Chamber). The overall effect of his early efforts to reorganize the arts administration was mixed. Although the wide-ranging attack on those with leftist political views and the regimentation of the new order sent many artists into exile, a considerable number remained. And of those who stayed, many held out in the hope that they could continue with their careers.

The fortunes of the progressive artists rested upon the failure of Alfred Rosenberg, the fiercely antimodernist Party philosopher who aspired to Goebbels' leading position. Rosenberg emerged from amid the multitudinous cultural critics and conservative groups as the leading advocate of a *völkisch* aesthetic policy, the central tenets of which were an insistence upon traditional artistic styles, a penchant for glorifying Germanic themes and rural, premodern lifestyles, and a racialistic (pro-"Aryan") agenda. During the "period of struggle," Rosenberg played a key role in the NSDAP's cultural propaganda. His Kampfbund für deutsche Kultur (Combat League for German Culture) was the movement's most prominent cultural organization, and his position as editor of the *Völkischer Beobachter* provided him with an important forum.[11] However, throughout 1933 Rosenberg's ambitious plans were stymied. As Goebbels expanded his offices, Rosenberg remained on the periphery of the burgeoning Nazi bureaucracy. His sole appointment in 1933 consisted of being named the head of the Party's Foreign Affairs Department *(Außenpolitisches Amt)*, a position of marginal importance. The frustrated ideologue tried in vain to find a role for his Kampfbund; he eventually scrapped much of the organization as he transformed it into the Nationalsozialistische-Kulturgemeinde (NS Cultural Community, or the NS-KG) with a focus on theater.[12] Rosenberg's organization therefore remained outside the state and Party structures, which forced him, when he wished to pronounce on cultural matters, to turn to pamphlets and other low-yield propagandistic devices. It was not a propitious situation for the leader of the *völkisch* camp.

Hitler finally granted Rosenberg his much-desired foothold in the cultural bureaucracy in January of 1934, giving him a Party appointment with the pompous title Beauftragter des Führers für die Überwachung der gesamten geistigen und weltanschaulichen Schulung und Erziehung der Partei und gleichgeschalteten Verbände (Führer's Delegate for the Supervision of the Entire Spiritual and Philosophical Education and Instruction of the Party and Incorporated Associations). The appointment appeared to be an effort to counterbalance the growing power of Goebbels: Hitler's divide-and-rule philosophy could not brook the monopoly then held by the propaganda minister in the cultural sphere.[13] Hitler's views on modern art also ran contrary to those of Goebbels.[14] While he had refrained from imposing his own views regarding abstract art on the nation, he had nonetheless forced the propaganda minister to remove the Nolde watercolors from the walls of the remodeled official residence. As was often his style, Hitler waited and observed the course of the debate over modern art then being led by Goebbels and Rosenberg before rendering his verdict. Rosenberg's appointment served to counterbalance Goebbels' power. It also clearly signaled Hitler's reservations about the regime's present cultural program.

In Hitler's September 1934 "cultural address" at the annual Nuremberg Party Congress, he spoke equally harshly of both Goebbels' and Rosenberg's artistic views, giving neither camp the opportunity to claim his favor. Hitler attacked modern art, decrying abstraction and other forms of "cultural Bolshevism," but he still fell short of launching a full-fledged campaign or issuing a legal ban. And while criticizing modern art, Hitler simultaneously ridiculed Alfred Rosenberg's revivalist ideas. He called the *völkisch* ideologues "teutomaniacs" and "backward-lookers" and mockingly queried, "perhaps they would like us to defend ourselves with shields and crossbows?"[15] The net effect of this twofold attack was to weaken the positions of both Goebbels and Rosenberg in the cultural bureaucracy, and hence encourage the involvement and efforts of other figures.

The key rivals to Goebbels and Rosenberg all possessed significant bureaucratic bases from which to begin. Hermann Göring held posts as a *Reichsminister,* the minister president of Prussia, the chief of the Luftwaffe, and the head of the Four-Year Plan; Bernhard Rust served as Reich minister of science, education and popular instruction; Baldur von Schirach headed the Hitler Youth; and Robert Ley oversaw the German Labor Front. The architect Albert Speer emerged as another powerful figure in the cultural bureaucracy. He received commissions from other leaders or held subsidiary positions until gaining the important and independent post of General Building Inspector for Berlin in January 1937. Heinrich Himmler, the *Reichsführer-SS* and chief of the German Police, and Martin Bormann, who held a leading position within the Party apparatus, also gradually became more involved with art and cultural policy, wielding their greatest influence during the war.

The overlapping purviews of state, police, and Party agencies that involved themselves in cultural affairs afforded these subleaders a greater opportunity for independent initiative and encouraged the formation of interministerial alliances. Robert Ley, for example, launched the workers' leisure-time organization, the Kraft durch Freude (KdF), within the German Labor Front (DAF). At this early stage, Ley relied on the assistance of both Goebbels and Rosenberg: The propaganda minister provided the name of the KdF, many ideas for programs, and placed employees from his ministry in prominent staff positions. Rosenberg, on the other hand, merged the Kampfbund für deutsche Kultur with a theatergoers' association under Ley's auspices called the Reichsverband "Deutsche Bühne," and together they formed the NS Cultural Community (NS-KG). This new organization (formed in June 1934), which both men hoped would rival and eventually replace the Reichskulturkammer, was, in one historian's words, "bodily incorporated into the DAF."[16] Ley therefore had both the KdF and the NS-KG as bureaucratic platforms from which to launch his initiatives.[17] Within the KdF, Ley hired Hans Weidemann and Otto Andreas Schreiber, both pro-modernist cultural bureaucrats formerly in Goebbels' employ, to organize art exhibitions for workers. In staging shows in factories and at the local community centers, they reached a relatively large audience.[18] Weidemann and Schreiber were able to express their aesthetic views in this way for approximately two years, and among other tactics, they employed on their juries individuals such as Erich Heckel (an expressionist painter formerly of the group known as *Die Brücke* [the bridge]), the modernist architect Mies van der Rohe, and the composer of atonal music Paul Hindemith. In operating what was effectively the cultural office of the KdF they served as one of the focal points of the pro-modern movement.[19] Ley never expressed a clear position on the debate over modernism. Parallel to this balancing act between Goebbels and Rosenberg, he simultaneously offset the more liberal KdF office by employing the more conservative Albert Speer to head the office Schönheit der Arbeit (Beauty of Labor), which also arranged exhibitions and published pamphlets on architectural and industrial design.[20] For Ley, the creation of Speer's office, like the KdF agency of Weidemann and Schreiber, proved important because it allowed him a voice in the administration of culture. It also helped him establish contacts with other leaders and often caused them to curry favor with him. Ley's behavior was not unlike that of Göring, Rust, Himmler, and Schirach: They were responsible for a flurry of initiatives that often enacted self-serving and even contradictory policies. Therefore the Reich's cultural policies were highly confused during the years 1934 to 1936.

This confusion, marked by rhetorical and bureaucratic conflict, found clearest expression in the ongoing debate over modernism, as the issue remained unresolved until 1937. The years 1934 to 1937 were, to be sure, difficult for proponents and practitioners of modern art. A number of subleaders interpreted Hitler's 1934 cultural address at Nuremberg as marching orders and exerted themselves to the utmost to undermine the position of the new art. In early 1935, the pro-modernist journal *Kunst der Nation,* which had been published for two years by an exhibition group with a similar orientation called *Der Norden,* was forced out of existence by government officials. (Alfred Rosenberg played a leading role here.)[21] Bernhard Rust, who administrated the state museums through his Reich Ministry, realized that joining the antimodern forces would allow him to be more active in the Nazi state. While previously ambivalent about the modern collections under his jurisdiction, Rust became increasingly involved with the disposition of the works—especially once the Olympic Games had concluded and the veneer of moderation was peeled away. On 30 October 1936, he ordered the closing of the Berlin National Gallery's modern art section and the sequestration of the modern art then housed therein on the top floor of the former Kronprinzenpalais. The modern collection had twice been weeded of those works perceived as scandalous, as the directors Alois Schardt and Eberhard Hanfstaengl had tried to placate the antimodern faction.²² These measures paled in comparison to the purging process that began in early 1937. Works by Max Beckmann, Emil Nolde, Ernst Ludwig Kirchner, Ernst Barlach, and others were confiscated and removed to a Berlin depot.²³ Modernism, then, was clearly under attack, although a decisive defeat was yet to come.

The absence of a "positive" or National Socialist program for art—such a program really only emerged in 1937—as well as the continued existence of certain pro-modernist bastions helped lull some observers into a state of continued hopefulness. The scholar Reinhard Merker noted of Kirchner that "for years [he] had no idea that the days of the Avant-Garde were numbered and he believed until 1935 that the Nazis viciously attacked him out of error."²⁴ Emil Nolde continued to paint in his studio in Schleswig-Holstein, periodically appealing to Nazi officials to recognize his commitment to the NSDAP and sponsor his art.²⁵ Exhibitions of modern art also took place during this transitional period. The Galerie Ferdinand Möller in Berlin, for example, organized the show *Dreißig deutsche Maler* during the summer of 1936, which included works by Ernst Barlach, Lyonel Feininger, and Karl Schmidt-Rottluff.²⁶ In April of 1937, the gallery managed to show works by Emil Nolde—a remarkable feat considering that 27 pieces by him were included in the *Entartete Kunst* exhibition opening three months later.²⁷ Yet one must not form an overly positive impression of the atmosphere in 1936 and 1937. The *Dreißig deutsche Maler* exhibition took place during the Olympic Games, at a time when the regime sought to give foreign visitors a false impression of the country. (Along these lines, the National Socialists removed the virulently anti-Semitic newspaper *Der Stürmer* from newsstands.) For the Nolde show, Möller thought it unwise to produce a catalog, suspecting that it would provoke the regime and be confiscated. Later, in May and June 1937, the Galerie Ferdinand Möller exhibited watercolors and woodcuts by the modernist artist Christian Rohlfs. It was to be the gallery's last show during the Third Reich.²⁸

With the departure of the foreign visitors, Nazi officials felt less constrained about imposing a more repressive cultural program. In November 1936, Goebbels also grew more radical. First, he announced new restrictions on art criticism, limiting the writing of reviews to a few reliable editors *(Schriftleiter)* and forbidding the *Nachtkritik* (the appearance of a review the day following an opening).²⁹ This afforded the propaganda minister greater control over the commerce of ideas concerning art, as the censors were guaranteed time to act. In keeping with his move to a more intrusive role for his ministry, Goebbels metamorphosed into an antimodernist. Consistent with his character, he became one of the most strident and active members of the camp. The motivation underlying Goebbels' volte-face on expressionist and abstract art is complex. Whether he was sincerely brought around by Hitler's vision or cynically exploited the opportunity to increase his own power is difficult to determine. Regardless, Goebbels personally took the lead combatting modern art. To facilitate this aggressive stance, he replaced the pliable and even moderate first president of the Chamber for the Visual Arts, Eugen Hönig, with the more doctrinaire Nazi painter Professor Adolf Ziegler (whose sobriquet was "master of the German pubic hair" because of the "artistic realism" of his nudes).[30] Hönig's departure was but one of many signals Goebbels sent to alert the nation to the shift in cultural policy.

Certainly the most dramatic aspect of the more aggressive antimodernist campaign was the purging of modern art from the state museums. The origins of this project are complex and still not entirely clear. As mentioned earlier, the modern art section of the Kronprinzenpalais was closed by Rust in October 1936, although Goebbels and representatives from his ministry had a hand in this measure as well, since the question of jurisdiction remained unresolved.[31] A few months later, in early 1937, Goebbels engaged the artist and vitriolic antimodern activist Wolfgang Willrich—who had created a sensation with his book *Die Säuberung des Kunsttempels* (subtitled a *Kampfschrift*, or "fighting manifesto")—and charged him with forming a purging commission.[32] Willrich worked primarily with members of the Propaganda Ministry, in particular with the head of the visual arts department, Walter Hansen, but his commission made little progress due to the lack of a formal or public order. Most of the state museums' modern art remained in place until the spring of 1937, when Goebbels made Ziegler responsible for the operation. The propaganda minister demonstrated his seriousness about the project by providing Ziegler with the necessary authorization and by trying to reform the purging commission so as to include representatives of other offices (most notably those under the purview of Rosenberg and Rust).[33] Ziegler's marching orders were made public only in July 1937. Yet even in their clandestine form they empowered him and his colleagues to remove systematically all artworks from the period 1910 to 1933 which were deemed "degenerate" (with stylistic considerations—abstraction and "unrealistic" colors—being paramount). The commission eventually purged some 17,000 artworks from museums (of which approximately 5,000 were paintings) and transported them to storage facilities in Berlin; the process lasted six months.[34] The purging action affected more than 100 museums in all.[35] In a post-facto law of 31 May 1938, signed by both Hitler and Goebbels, the state museums were promised some future compensation from the revenue generated by the disposal of the proscribed art. Indeed, after a considerable amount of squabbling among Goebbels, Rust, Göring, and Walther Funk (by then the minister of economics), certain museums were given funds to replace the works they had lost. The payments involved were, however, quite small, as the Nazi regime sold the modern art at bargain prices and did not direct all of the proceeds to the museums.[36]

The campaign against modern art alienated certain segments of the German population, to whom it appeared barbaric and unnecessarily intolerant, but it nonetheless served the Nazis' propaganda purposes by vividly expressing key tenets of their ideology. Hitler and the other leaders who formulated cultural policy developed an interlinked set of assumptions. The salient features were the notion of unifying the nation against a common enemy, rejecting elitist or unintelligible art, disliking internationalism (or "cultural Bolshevism," as they termed it), associating modernism with the Weimar Republic, and recognizing the supposedly conspiratorial involvement of the Jewish-controlled press and art dealers. Despite the opprobrium that the degenerate art campaign elicited in foreign lands (and within Germany after the war), its propagandistic efficacy was considerable.[37] As noted, the record attendance of the traveling exhibition (in part due to free admission) and its widespread coverage in the press and media brought this exercise in cultural politics to the masses in an unprecedented manner. The organization of subsequent exhibitions in this vein—including "The Eternal Jew," which opened in November 1937, the "Degenerate Music" show of 1938, and "The Soviet Paradise" exhibition of 1942—attests to the Nazi leaders' satisfaction with the results.[38] That a few of the leaders personally profited financially from the disposal of the modernist artworks was a fringe benefit.[39] The propaganda value of the negative campaign was of paramount importance.

In comparison with this effort at vilification, the task of creating a new, representative artistic style proved much more challenging to the ruling elite. Indeed, the struggle even to identify a characteristic "Nazi art" proved difficult, as a process of experimentation took place during the first years of the Third Reich. Artists such as Arno Breker, Joseph Thorak, and Adolf Ziegler gradually did find their mature (and infamous) idioms. But it is revealing that Hitler expressed extreme displeasure with the artworks submitted in 1937 for the first annual "Great German Art Exhibition" at the Haus der Deutschen Kunst. He initially nullified the jury's selections for the show—claiming the works they had approved were not of a sufficiently high standard and therefore did the regime a disservice. After contemplating canceling the exhibition, he decided to put the project in the hands of his photographer and artistic advisor Heinrich Hoffmann, which enabled Hitler to supervise the new selection process more closely.[40] Despite these difficulties in finding suitable artworks to represent the new epoch, the first annual "Great German Art Exhibition" (and the simultaneous unveiling of "the temple of German art," as Hitler referred to the museum he had commissioned in 1933) marked the "coming out" of Nazi art. The 884 works that were selected from the over 15,000 submissions reflected the "Nazi style": the representational, "blood and soil" oriented art that came to be associated with the regime. It is difficult to perceive any significant changes or developments in the officially sanctioned art during the following eight years, other than a moderate increase in the number of works with military themes during the war years.[41] Similarly, Hitler's pronouncement on art on 18 June 1937—the highlight of the contemporaneous festival known as the Day of German Art—expressed views that did not change during the course of his rule. In his diaries, Joseph Goebbels expressed his opinions about the annual GDK, noting on occasion that progress was being made in terms of contemporary artistic production. He commented that the show of a given year was better than the previous ones.[42] Yet this represented only wishful thinking on his part.

While 1937 stands as one of the turning points in the history of art during the Third Reich as a result of the unequivocal rejection of modern art and the emergence of the official art, the year 1938 deserves equal recognition because it marked the introduction of violence into the administration of culture. This year marked the beginning of the program to confiscate Jewish-owned artworks, which often entailed imprisonment or other measures against the owners. At this point Himmler's police also began to enforce restrictions placed upon artists with greater assiduousness. This more aggressive policy paralleled the radicalization in other spheres in 1938. The forced *Anschluß* with Austria in March and the annexation of the Sudetenland in September highlighted the foreign adventurism, while the anti-Jewish pogrom of the "Night of Broken Glass" (Kristallnacht) in November signaled changes on the domestic front.

The first confiscations of artworks undertaken by the National Socialists occurred immediately after the "*Einmarsch*" into Austria in mid-March 1938. This coincided with the spontaneous attacks on Jews by Austrian Nazis, who reacted to the lifting of the ban on their political activities. The historian Bruce Pauley has described this initial outburst: "The first few days following the German annexation witnessed a veritable orgy of plundering and brutality perpetrated against the Jews. Only rarely were these acts committed by German Nazis, and less still by German soldiers; rather it was Austrian Nazis and even non-Nazis who now released the hatred they had pent up against the Jews. . . ."[43] The state authorities were not too far behind the mob in moving against the Jews. Himmler's forces (mostly the Gestapo, with some assistance from the Sicherheitsdienst, or SD) led the way. But clearly they were not alone. To quote Bruce Pauley again: "Aryanization . . . transpired so precipitously—being delayed only by administrative and legal technicalities—that on 4 April Josef Bürckel, the Reich commissioner for the reunification of the Ostmark with the

Reich . . . halted further arbitrary confiscations of Jewish property in order to prevent any more damage to the Austrian economy. . . ."[44] The Nazi leaders quickly developed a more orderly process of seizing Jewish assets, with those Jews wishing to emigrate and those labeled political enemies being immediately stripped of their property. These confiscations took place before any formal legal basis existed; the relevant laws were passed only in November 1938.[45] Illustrative of the "supralegal" behavior of the Nazi authorities was the experience of Louis de Rothschild, who was captured at the Viennese airport trying to flee the country in March 1938, and imprisoned in the Hotel Metropol until May 1939, when he and family members abroad negotiated his release. The cost of his freedom was virtually all of his property in Austria: Under the guise of collecting "Reich emigration taxes," the Nazis assumed control of the family's bank assets, as well as his and his brother Alphonse's residences, personal property, and art collections.[46] The impressive holdings of other prominent Viennese Jewish families—the Guttmanns, the Thorsches, and the Goldmanns—contributed to the formation of an extraordinary accumulation of plundered art. Additionally, families designated *staatsfeindlich* (enemies of the state) such as the extraordinarily wealthy Bondy family from Czechoslovakia, and later the Lanckoronskis from Poland—lost their Austrian property when they fled or when their countries entered into a state of war with Germany.[47] This impressive haul induced Hitler to order that the treasures be handled in an organized fashion. In June 1938, he wrote to Himmler and other authorities that the confiscated works were not to end up in the hands of top officials.[48] Later, he empowered the Berlin art dealer Karl Haberstock to compile an inventory and file a report.[49] Hitler initially refrained from dictating the fate of the plunder. While he intimated that the works would perhaps be distributed to Austria's provincial museums, he took care to keep his options open. Above all, he explicitly stated his authority to determine the fate of the artworks, a policy that came to be known as the "Führervorbehalt," or "Führer's prerogative."[50] By the autumn of 1938, the works were being removed to storage facilities, the first of which was the Rothschilds' confiscated hunting lodge in Waidhofen outside Vienna. By October, the first floor of the Neue Hofburg palace in the heart of the city had become the key depot.[51]

In the *Altreich*—that part of Germany existing prior to Nazi expansion— the first confiscations of art owned by Jews took place following Kristallnacht ("crystal night"). The attacks and looting on 10 and 11 November were followed in early December by decrees issued by Göring (as head of the Four-Year Plan), as well as Funk (minister of economics) and Frick (minister of the interior). All of these measures aimed at excluding Jews from the country's economic life and expropriating their property. The two main decrees, dated

20 November and 3 December, provided for the "Aryanization" of Jewish businesses and required the declaration of all assets in excess of 5,000 Reichsmark (RM).[52] Clearly then, the "Aryanization" process, which began in early 1938, accelerated in the autumn of that year and hence led to the transfer of many art dealerships to trustees appointed by the state.[53] One of the reasons for the Nazis' efficient confiscation program lay in the step-by-step way in which the action unfolded. Whether this came about due to effective planning or was just the natural course of radicalization (or most likely, a combination of both), the Nazis repeatedly built upon existing measures in this assault against German Jewry. For example, the decree of 26 April 1938 requiring Jews to declare assets in excess of 5,000 RM proved invaluable in locating important artworks.

The markedly increased repression in 1937 and 1938 became noticeable in the cultural realm, as practicing artists also experienced diminished freedom and less official toleration. The primary devices used by Goebbels to prevent unwanted artistic production were the *Ausstellungsverbot* (ban on exhibiting) and the *Malverbot* (ban on painting). Prior to 1937, formal restrictions of this nature were seldom invoked against artists.[54] But after this point, stringent measures became quite common. Examples include Gerhard Marcks receiving an *Ausstellungsverbot* in 1937, Otto Dix being arrested in early 1939 during the "action against unreliable intellectuals" (which followed the attempted assassination of Hitler in the Munich Bürgerbräukeller), and Emil Nolde, Willi Baumeister, and Karl Schmidt-Rottluff all experiencing *Malverbote* in 1941.[55] A renewed round of purges of the Prussian Academy of the Arts also took place in 1937. (The first had taken place in 1933.)[56] Among those forced to resign their appointments were Ernst Barlach, Ludwig Mies van der Rohe, Rudolf Belling, Max Pechstein, and Ernst Ludwig Kirchner.[57]

After 1938, the National Socialist leaders continued to work vigorously at their dual program of stifling modern art while promoting the work carried out in the approved forms. The art historian Berthold Hinz has argued that "never before National Socialism had comparable financial means and political power been at the service of aesthetic activity."[58] Cultural patronage was a high priority for the Nazis; more specifically, they developed a variety of ways to sponsor the production of art. The huge "Great German Art Exhibition" in Munich, mentioned earlier, was but one example. Nearly all works exhibited at the show were for sale, and the Nazi leaders were the best customers, as Hitler, Goebbels, Himmler, and Ley, among others, bought in bulk.[59] Additionally, there were government-funded shows in venues ranging from factories to town halls. In most instances, the exhibited works were offered for sale. Even on this more local level, it was not uncommon for the *Gauleiter* or *Kreisleiter* to buy works. Such gestures of support for local artists afforded good publicity, and the common existence of "slush" funds or accounts for patronage facilitated the generosity. The large-scale building programs undertaken by the Nazi regime also created an opportunity for patronage. In 1934, Walther Funk signed a decree stipulating that the budgets of state construction projects must have at least 2 percent devoted to artistic embellishment (mosaics, frescos, sculptures, etc.).[60] While this decree was eventually suspended in the latter part of the decade due to the country's full employment and the shrinking ratio of artists to building projects, it conveys the regime's concern for patronage.[61] Beyond the welfare of the common artist, there was the desire to create artistic superstars; and to this end, successful sculptors such as Arno Breker and Josef Thorak were provided with remarkable resources and extravagant commissions. Eventually these leading figures were in such demand that they were able to accept commissions from only the highest leaders and the most prominent architects, such as Albert Speer and Hermann Giesler. Records documenting Speer's payments to Arno Breker for sculptures that adorned the architect's buildings, for example, convey the scale of their projects: 27,396,000 RM was paid out between 1938 and 1945.[62] Additionally, Breker was provided with a huge studio at Jackelsbrüch, outside of Berlin, where he engaged more than 100 assistants.[63] One document in the Bundesarchiv recorded Speer's gift of 60,000 RM to the sculptor; and, in 1942, Hitler awarded Breker a tax-free "*Dotation*" (grant) of 250,000 RM.[64] (The average worker earned 150 RM per month.)[65] As recorded in Picker's *Tischgespräche* (Table conversations), Hitler mentioned he had arranged that Breker's annual income of 1 million RM would not be reduced by more than 15 percent through taxes.[66] In Thorak's case, the sculptor's income increased tenfold between 1932 and 1943; and when his huge studio in Munich was bombed during the war, he was able to move to Schloß Prielau bei Zell am See, which had been confiscated from the widow of Hugo von Hofmannsthal.[67] Clearly the approbation of the Nazi leaders could be very profitable for artists during the Third Reich.

The legacy of the National Socialists' artistic endeavors is unquestionably far more negative than positive, with their brutal and arrogant policies affecting not only the Reich but also neighboring lands. In 1939, they began to export the violence and repression that had emerged so visibly in the cultural sphere during the previous year. The areas affected that year were, in chronological order, Czechoslovakia, the South Tyrol, Poland, and the Baltic states. The expropriation of art and the restrictions placed on the inhabitants of these regions formed part of a broader geopolitical plan. With the exception of the South Tyrol, which was ceded to Italy for the sake of firming up the Axis alliance (and arguably as compensation for the Italians not opposing the *Anschluß* of Austria), the cultural policies of the National Socialists aimed at an extension of the Reich territories.

The Nazi worldview contained a cultural element: German hegemony was to be realized both in the appropriation of artworks and in the determination of the annexed (or subordinate) regions' cultural and propaganda policies.

The Nazis' plundering campaign or, in their minds, the quest to control the material expression of Europe's artistic heritage, combined a loosely formulated plan with an opportunistic outlook. With their imperialistic ideology as the chief motivation, they exploited the possibilities that arise only during wartime to set up looting agencies in virtually every part of the continent. Although the dynamic character of this bureaucracy makes it difficult to identify any master planner, Hitler and the increasingly powerful Martin Bormann (who became head of the Party chancellery after Rudolf Hess's departure in May 1941, and Hitler's private secretary in 1943) stand out as the coordinators of the overall program. Himmler and Heydrich, however, maintained considerable autonomy as their SS empire expanded and they were able to initiate numerous operations. The army also tried to maintain its independence, and to this end an office for the "protection of art," the Amt Kunstschutz (Art Protection Office) was formed under the leadership of Franz Graf Wolff-Metternich with the aim of protecting collections and monuments threatened by the fighting. The Kunstschutz office proved incapable of resisting encroachments by the less conscionable Party agencies; and the relieving of Wolff-Metternich from his post in October 1943 signaled the total defeat of the forces of restraint.[68] Joachim von Ribbentrop, the foreign minister, tried to direct confiscation actions in France through the German ambassador, Otto Abetz, but he lost the bureaucratic battle to Rosenberg and had to be content with overseeing a *Sonderkommando* (special detachment) which bore his name and operated in the Soviet Union. Even the most successful plunderer, Alfred Rosenberg, who had his special staff, the Einsatzstab Reichsleiter Rosenberg (ERR), search out Jewish-owned art on both the Western and Eastern fronts, came more and more under the thumb of Bormann.

Hitler was apprised of the activities of the numerous plundering agencies, although he had a genuine interest in only one aspect of the program: the acquisition of artistic masterpieces—works that were to be placed in a museum in his honor. On 26 June 1939, Hitler granted a secret commission (a *Geheime Reichssache*) to Dr. Hans Posse, the director of the Dresden Gemäldegalerie, to oversee the creation of a Führermuseum in Linz, Austria.[69] Hitler envisioned the museum as forming the centerpiece of a cultural complex in his childhood hometown. There would be an opera, a symphony, theaters and cinemas, as well as Kraft durch Freude (Strength through Joy) hotels. The idea was to transform the provincial Austrian city into the cultural mecca of Europe by the early 1950s. The preeminent architects of the Third Reich—Hermann Giesler,

Roderich Fick, and Albert Speer—were charged with designing the complex, and the latter was awarded the prize assignment of creating the plans for the Führermuseum.[70]

Hitler provided Posse with almost unlimited resources in order to obtain the finest art available. Posse and his successor, Dr. Hermann Voss, spent an estimated 163 million RM on paintings and, to a lesser extent, tapestries and sculptures.[71] Buying into a Faustian bargain, the two directors proved notably unscrupulous in their quest to create the world's greatest museum. Besides engineering forced sales, they acquired for Hitler the finest works confiscated from Jews and other declared enemies, and they appropriated the best of the foreign plunder. As Posse, Voss, and their staff on the Sonderauftrag Linz were small in number, they relied on other agencies to secure the plunder. This meant that they traveled incessantly during the war, as they inspected potential additions to the collection. They might go to the Neue Hofburg in Vienna to survey the works taken from Austrian Jews, travel to the Netherlands to view the depots there, or attend auctions at the Hôtel Drouôt in Paris. It was a competitive enterprise that required great energy and a fair amount of cunning, for Göring and his agents, as well as a host of other leaders, also pursued art. Posse wrote to his immediate superior, Martin Bormann, in the autumn of 1940 about a planned trip to Belgium, "I wish to arrive earlier than certain other people and catch them napping."[72] Göring, for his part, was said to have remarked about the competition for artworks (with disingenuous bravado), "as collectors, we are, the Führer and I, private persons: first come, first serve."[73]

Next to Hitler and Göring, Himmler proved the most assiduous collector. The *Reichsführer-SS* had numerous personal projects involving artworks. A pseudointellectual and dreamer, Himmler also possessed the resources to pursue his malevolent programs. Crucial to his cultural aspirations was his organization Das Ahnenerbe (translated at the Nuremberg trials as Ancestral Heritage Research Organization), a Berlin-based research foundation that employed scholars and scientists to investigate topics pertaining to the "Germanic race."[74] Himmler began his affiliation with the Ahnenerbe in 1936 and then assumed its presidency in 1939. Under his leadership the organization undertook, among numerous other projects, the program to help ethnic Germans transport their cultural goods to the Reich as they migrated from the South Tyrol and the Baltic states.[75] This operation involved the transfer of artworks from churches, museums, and monuments, as well as that of private property. Often there was overlap between the staff of the Ahnenerbe and the SD/Gestapo forces: a professor of prehistory at the University of Rostock, Peter Paulsen, provides one example, as he worked for the research foundation while holding the rank of *Untersturmführer* (lieutenant) in the Gestapo.[76] Himmler's various projects involving art—including museums execrating the culture of the Jews and that of Freemasons, as well as an SS museum in Berlin—motivated him to seek control of the works themselves. However, as most of the museums under his purview did not concern art of the highest quality, and as he remained dedicated to Hitler, Himmler's agents usually were not in direct competition with those working on behalf of the other top leaders.

In heading the most rapacious plundering agency, Alfred Rosenberg also found himself constantly engaged in political feuds and jurisdictional disputes. His ERR made its most noticeable mark in occupied France, as over 21,000 artworks belonging to French Jews were sent first to the Jeu de Paume in Paris for cataloging and packing and then on to the storybook castle of Neuschwanstein in Bavaria.[77] Charged with securing the cultural artifacts (art, archives, and libraries) of the "opponents of National Socialism," Rosenberg himself conceived his mission as collecting objects that would further postwar educational programs in the National Socialist vein. This "ideal," however, was quickly undermined for two reasons: First, because Göring managed to infiltrate and co-opt the ERR—which enabled the *Reichsmarschall* to commandeer over 700 works for his own collection (including Boucher's *Diana,* Watteau's *Galante Scène,* and Velázquez' *Portrait of the Infanta Margarita Teresa*);[78] second, because Bormann and the representatives from the Sonderauftrag Linz steadily encroached on Rosenberg's independence—to the point where Bormann pushed for the elimination of the ERR in 1943 (with responsibilities to be transferred to those more pliable than the *Reichsleiter*).[79] In principle, Göring's order of 5 November 1940 established the policy for dividing the plunder: Hitler (or his Linz agents) had priority in selecting works from the ERR's cache, with Göring and then Rosenberg (as the representative of his Hohe Schule—or Nazi university system) having subsequent prerogatives.[80] But as Göring's agents often circumvented the normal review process and directed works to their master before the ERR staff or Hitler's agents could see or lay claim to them, all parties involved adopted a more competitive bearing. This naturally translated into more vicious bureaucratic infighting.

In the areas where the plundering campaigns yielded rich harvests, heated rivalries developed among the Nazi perpetrators. In Belgium and the Netherlands, as in France, the ERR, not surprisingly, faced stiff competition. The Dienststelle Mühlmann, named after the Austrian *SS-Oberführer* (major general) and notorious plunderer Kajetan Mühlmann, actually emerged as the dominant agency in the Low Countries. Mühlmann had close ties not only to Himmler but also to other key leaders, including Göring, Arthur Seyß-Inquart (the *Reichskommissar* of the Netherlands), governor-general of Occupied Poland Hans Frank, and Martin Bormann. Mühlmann had previously led looting squads in Austria and

Poland, and he used this experience to cultivate powerful benefactors. The Dienststelle Mühlmann offices in the Hague and in Brussels ultimately processed more plunder in the Netherlands and Belgium than the ERR or any other Nazi agency, and the art that they did not hand over to Hitler or Göring was sold to other officials or directed to auction houses for public sale.[81]

The plundering administration on the Eastern Front was as internally competitive as that in the West, but its structure remained even more confused due to the continued fighting and the relative lawlessness of the region. Clearly the dominant forces belonged to Himmler and Heydrich, as the SS and SD terrorized all regions from the Baltic to the Black Sea. Himmler in particular collected tremendous quantities of treasure through his various agencies. Alongside the grisly business of processing gold teeth and family heirlooms, the SS plundered artworks and cultural artifacts. The castles and museums of the Soviet Union were hit especially hard. At the International Military Tribunal in Nuremberg, the Soviet prosecutor claimed that 427 of the 992 museums that fell into German hands were plundered and/or destroyed.[82] Himmler's forces oversaw the storage of what remained of the plunder, and he went so far as to create an office to peddle some of the higher-quality art. Called the Vugesta, an acronym for Verwaltungsstelle für jüdisches Umzugsgut der Geheimen Staatspolizei (Office for the Administration of Jewish Property Removed by the Gestapo), this SS agency sold paintings to a number of top leaders during the war, including Baldur von Schirach, who acquired Lucas Cranach's *Madonna and Child* in 1943.[83] The other Nazi agencies that spearheaded the despoilment of the region were the Sonderkommando Ribbentrop, the Einsatzstab Reichsleiter Rosenberg-Ost, and the staff attached to Rosenberg's Reich Ministry for the Occupied Eastern Territories. The Sonderkommando Ribbentrop proved especially notorious in its destructiveness, as its field commander, SS-Standartenführer (colonel) Freiherr Eberhard von Künsberg, combined a heartless disposition with an undeniable expertise. (He had cut his teeth as plunderer in France in 1940 while working on behalf of Ribbentrop and Abetz.)[84] His Sonderkommando on the Eastern Front advanced behind the three invading German army groups to collect their booty. Both the advancing and retreating armies practiced a type of scorched earth policy; neither side yielded territory to the other with much left intact.[85] The Soviets, of course, tried to evacuate many movable objects, including artworks, during their retreats. But the rapidity of the German advances, and the Soviets' policy of not evacuating works until the last moment—political authorities frequently prevented curators and conservation experts from taking precautions because of the defeatist implications—meant that a number of cultural treasures remained in the combat zones.[86]

Despite the demands of war, the Nazi government continued to organize cultural events and patronize certain favored practitioners. The "Great German Art Exhibition" remained a fixture in Munich through 1944, with special catalogs being produced in mass quantities for the troops. Local officials still found ways to stage cultural events in their cities and towns, though these came increasingly under the supervision of the central government. Martin Bormann, Alfred Rosenberg, and a number of the more zealous Party members exerted steady pressure to nazify all sectors of civic life. This entailed, among other things, changing traditional ceremonies and celebrations, creating new forms of communal associations, and organizing more propagandistic exhibitions—all with the aim of furthering indoctrination.[87] Independent cultural events— those not cleared by Berlin—became more difficult to stage. Baldur von Schirach, for example, tried to implement his own moderately modern cultural views in Vienna. His sponsorship of the *Junge Kunst in Deutschland* exhibition reflected his lack of success here, as this show, which included works with expressionistic elements, was closed on Hitler's orders three days after its opening. The decision to cancel the *Junge Kunst* exhibition in February of 1943 was not due to any violation of the "total war" measures that had been proclaimed earlier in that month in the wake of the German defeat at Stalingrad. Rather it stemmed from stylistic issues, as Hitler was convinced—after being lobbied by such conservatives as Rosenberg and Ziegler—that the show represented a subversion of the state and Reich.[88]

The Nazi officials expended considerable energy in implementing a cultural policy in the occupied lands that reflected their ideological tenets. In Poland, this entailed repressing the indigenous Polish culture and promoting the Germanic. The closing of the universities and the attacks against faculty members are well documented.[89] The art plunderer Kajetan Mühlmann, who answered to Göring, Himmler, and Frank, organized commandos that confiscated nearly all the works belonging to the state, the church, and the aristocracy. Other SS troops pursued less precious artworks.

Concomitantly, art exhibitions for the occupation troops were part of a program to maintain the Germans' supposedly high level of cultural accomplishment. In France, Arno Breker was the only Nazi artist to have a solo exhibition, a retrospective housed in the Orangerie of the Louvre in the summer of 1942. The reception at the opening on 15 May represented a stunning display of collaboration as Ambassador Otto Abetz and Vichy Education Minister Abel Bonnard were joined by officials from their respective governments as well as a number of prominent French artists, including Aristide Maillol, André Derain and Jean Cocteau.[90] An exhibition on National Socialist architecture entitled *Neue Deutsche Baukunst,* which featured models and designs by Speer, also traveled throughout Europe and to Turkey during the war.[91] The Nazis continued to organize thematic and explicitly propagandistic shows. *Das Sowjet-Paradies,* mentioned earlier, toured Western Europe, and *Le Juif et la France, Franc-maçonnerie Devoilée* (Freemasonry unveiled) and *Warschau klagt an* (Warsaw accuses) serve as further examples of this genre.[92] Like their precursor, the "Degenerate Art Exhibition," these exhibitions were supposed to shock and titillate audiences. The message conveyed by the Nazis' cultural events expressed their worldview. They believed that they were creating a "new order" where German superiority, a natural outgrowth of their biological endowment, would find expression. The cultural events they organized aimed at proving that the "Aryan" was a bearer of culture, both historically (which necessitated the revaluation of artworks in favor of German artists) and at present (hence, the glorification of Nazi artists).

The Germans' defeat at Stalingrad in early 1943 initiated a turning point in the government's cultural policies, although the full implementation of the new measures took over a year. The "total war" program eliminated most activities not directly contributing to the fighting effort. There were fewer art exhibitions; many periodicals ceased publication (however, not the official art journal *Kunst im Deutschen Reich);* and artists found it more difficult to obtain exemption from military service *(UK-Stellung),* with, for example, only 19 figures making Goebbels' list of the chosen.[93] The cultural bureaucracy thus contracted from 1943 to 1945. Joseph Goebbels, named by Hitler to the post of plenipotentiary for total war, oversaw the cutbacks. He closed down the Kraft durch Freude program completely and organized staff cuts throughout the government and the Party.[94] Goebbels ordered art academies to be shut down and museums to be closed (having earlier begun the process of evacuating artistic treasures to rural storage sites).[95] Art galleries and auction houses were also supposed to cease their activities—though few did so completely, with discreet deals being more common than public auctions.[96] Some artists, such as Emil Nolde and Arno Breker, were able to continue to work in their rural ateliers (the first clandestinely in "inner emigration," the second by virtue of his connections with influential officials).[97] The military drafted many other artists. Otto Dix, for example, who had been harassed and even arrested during the war while living in isolation in Hemmenhofen near Lake Constance, was compelled to join the *Volkssturm* (civil militia). There he fought the invading French army, and after the ensuing collapse and surrender, faced a term of internment at Colmar, where he painted landscapes and portraits of French officers.[98]

A number of conclusions can be drawn from a study of the administration of the visual arts in National Socialist Germany. For one, it is striking how nearly all of the top leaders participated in the formation and implementation of policy. Jurisdictional boundaries existed, but often overlapped or were not clearly defined. Thus, alongside Goebbels, Rosenberg, and Rust—the three officials whose job description entailed making cultural policy—Göring, Himmler, Speer, Ley, Frick, Bormann, and a host of independent-minded officials such as Reichsstatthalter Schirach and Reichskommissar Seyß-Inquart asserted themselves in this sphere.[99] The governing elite comprised, to use Martin Broszat's phrase, the "*Polykratie*" of the Third Reich—the web of multiple and intertwined offices that characterized the governmental structure.[100] Hannah Arendt has described this bureaucratic redundancy in other fields: Jewish policy, the supervision of students, legal affairs and foreign policy.[101] The visual arts administration was consistent with this pattern of competitive, overlapping offices. In fact, with the exception of the persecution of the Jews, in no other sphere did so many top leaders engage themselves.

Their attraction to artistic matters was heightened because of Hitler's personal interest. The visual arts bureaucracy attests to the personalized and charismatic quality of his leadership. That which interested Hitler elicited the attention of his subordinates.[102] It is clear that Hitler possessed a sincere and even passionate interest in art—an interest that extended back to his youth, when he had attempted to become a painter.[103] This artistic proclivity continued after Hitler came to power: Albert Speer noted in his memoirs that he amassed a collection of 125 drawings and sketches by Hitler during the course of their collaboration, which began in 1934.[104] With respect to Hitler's mature worldview, Edward Peterson has observed: "The singular ability to remember ships and libretto is significant in that it indicates what interested him: power-war and art-music. . . . It is precisely these interests which dominate Hitler's role as government head. . . ."[105] Peterson's conception of Hitler as an assertive leader in the cultural sphere certainly holds true for the latter half of the Third Reich.[106] But it must be remembered that Hitler assumed an inconclusive stance with respect to many aesthetic issues in the years immediately after the seizure of power, as most notably exemplified by his choosing not to impose his own private antimodernist views on the nation and resolve the dispute about expressionism until late 1936. In the years 1933 to 1937, the combination of Hitler's interest in the arts and his reluctance to dictate cultural policy induced the subleaders to become active in this realm of the government. The final result, in an administrative sense, might be best described in terms of Martin Broszat's observation that the Third Reich was governed by means of a tension between a "Führer absolutism" and the "departmental polycracy."[107] A dialectic or a complicated interplay between the two existed, as neither in itself determined the evolution or course of the National Socialist state.

Because the visual arts administration involved Hitler and so many of the highest-ranking leaders, it offers revealing insights into the Nazis' goals and ideology. This is the second main conclusion that can be derived from examining the arts bureaucracy. A complete exploration of these connections is not feasible here, but in its broadest outline, it must be noted that the National Socialist leaders viewed themselves as cultured men for racial reasons (as "Aryans" they were supposedly de facto creators and promoters of culture) and that they were radically chauvinistic about their Germanness. As ultranationalists, their imperialistic aspirations were not merely political and economic but also cultural. They sought both domestic and foreign recognition of the superiority of German culture, whether in literature, music, painting, or the other arts. As stated earlier, Hitler undertook plans to construct the world's largest and most important art museum in Linz, and in doing so, he claimed the entirety of European culture as a buildup to the Third Reich. (Of the 6,755 paintings he collected, 5,350 were Old Masters.)[108] Beyond any thoughts of personal glory, this enterprise reflected Hitler's effort to take physical possession of Europe's artistic tradition. His plans to organize the Führermuseum so that German paintings of the nineteenth and early twentieth centuries (Spitzweg, Waldmüller, and Thoma, for example) were placed alongside the work of Vermeer, Rembrandt, Titian, and other Old Masters represented an effort to revaluate the art and reinterpret the European artistic tradition. The Germans would be portrayed as the successors to the Old Masters, and thus gain the respect Hitler and his cohorts thought they deserved.

Despite their interest in the visual arts, and their investment of time and money into patronage and support, the Nazi leaders were clearly unable to foster a meritorious or lasting art in their own time. In regulating the production, exhibition, and, to a lesser extent, commerce of artworks, they sapped the vitality and individuality from the artists' creations. The leaders themselves suspected their failure as patrons. As noted earlier, Hitler rejected the jury's selection of paintings for the first "Great German Art Exhibition" in 1937 because the submissions were of such obviously poor quality, and Goebbels, despite an almost unflagging optimism about the regime, repeatedly grumbled about the quality of artistic production.[109] In regarding themselves as the new elite in German society, the Nazi leaders felt a sense of commitment to the nation's culture in a way that had undertones of *noblesse oblige*. Art was something for which they, as members of a "new aristocracy," bore responsibility. To some, such concern for the arts might seem incongruous with the Nazi leaders' personalities and ideological agendas, which were in opposition to the enlightened and humane values commonly associated with the arts. A closer examination, however, reveals that the Nazis' active participation in the administration of culture was consonant with their malevolent worldviews. In discussing the leaders' artistic policies, one must therefore make sure not to equate interest with accomplishment, as they had much of the former and little of the latter.

Notes

1. See Christoph Zuschlag, "An 'Educational Exhibition': The Precursors of *Entartete Kunst* and Its Individual Venues," in *"Degenerate Art": The Fate of the Avant-Garde in Nazi Germany,* ed. Stephanie Barron (New York: Abrams, 1991), pp. 83-103.
2. It is not clear who wrote the pamphlet. *Entartete Kunst* was organized by a 24-year-old Austrian named Hartmut Pistauer, who was employed by the Institut für Deutsche Kultur- und Wirtschaftspropaganda. This agency ultimately answered to Goebbels as head of the Propaganda Ministry.
3. See Michael Balfour, *Propaganda in War, 1939-1945. Organizations, Politics and Publics in Britain and Germany* (London: Routledge & Kegan, 1979), p. 14. Other valuable works on Goebbels and the creation of his ministry include: Ralf Georg Reuth, *Goebbels* (Munich: Piper, 1990); Helmut Heiber, *Goebbels: A Biography* (New York: Da Capo, 1972); Robert Edwin Herzstein, *The War That Hitler Won: The Most Infamous Propaganda Campaign in History* (New York: Putnam, 1978); and Z. A. B. Zemon, *Nazi Propaganda* (London: Oxford, 1973). See also Joseph Goebbels, *Die Tagebücher von Joseph Goebbels: Sämtliche Fragmente, 1923-1940,* ed. Elke Fröhlich (Munich: K. G. Saur, 1987), 4 vols.
4. For Rosenberg's use of the term, see his letter to Martin Bormann, 30 July 1941, in the Bundesarchiv Koblenz (hereafter cited as BAK), NS 18/530.
5. Note that the Visual Arts Chamber of the RKK contained 42,000 members by 1936: 14,300 painters, 4,200 graphic artists, and 2,900 sculptors. See Hellmut Lehmann-Haupt, *Art Under Dictatorship* (New York: Oxford University Press, 1954), p. 68.
6. For the similarities between the RKK and the Italian Fascist corporatist organ for culture, see Edward Tannenbaum, *The Fascist Experience: Italian Society and Culture, 1922-1945* (New York: Basic Books, 1972), pp. 243-44, 281-82, 293-95. See also Martin Jürgens, "Faschismus und Moderne: Anmerkungen zum politischen Charakter des italienischen Faschismus," in *Die Dekoration der Gewalt: Kunst und Medien im Faschismus,* eds. Berthold Hinz et al. (Gießen: Anabas, 1979), pp. 205-12.

7. For a consideration of the impact of the RKK on the public at large see Volker Dahm, "Die Reichskulturkammer als Instrument kulturpolitischer Steuerung und sozialer Reglementierung," *Vierteljahrshefte für Zeitgeschichte* 34 (January 1986): 53-84.
8. For the Nolde watercolors, see Albert Speer, *Inside the Third Reich* (New York: Macmillan, 1970), pp. 57-59. For the Barlach sculpture, *Mann im Sturm*, in Goebbels' office on the Wilhelmplatz, see Heinrich Hoffmann, *Hitler: Wie Ich Ihn Sah* (Munich: Herbig, 1974), p. 149. For Goebbels' pro-modernist sentiments, see his "*Rede vor den Theaterleitern*, 8 May 1933," in *Dokumente der Deutschen Politik* (Berlin: E.S. Mittler, 1939).
9. See Hildegard Brenner, "Art in the Political Power Struggle, 1933-1934," in *Republic to Reich: The Making of the Nazi Revolution*, ed. Hajo Holborn (New York: Vintage Books, 1972), pp. 395-434. Goebbels' patronage of pro-modern groups, such as *Der Norden*, is discussed by Stefen Germer, "Kunst der Nation: Zu einem Versuch, die Avantgarde zu nationalisieren," in *Kunst auf Befehl? Dreiunddreißig bis Fünfundvierzig*, eds. Bazon Brock and Achim Preiß (Munich: Klinkhardt und Biermann, 1990), pp. 21-40.
10. Reinhard Merker, *Die bildenden Künste im Nationalsozialismus: Kulturideologie, Kulturpolitik, Kulturproduktion* (Cologne: DuMont, 1983), p. 131. Merker adds that Goebbels also wished to lure Thomas Mann back from exile.
11. See Alan Steinweis, "Weimar Culture and the Rise of National Socialism: The Kampfbund für deutsche Kultur," *Central European History* 24, No. 4 (1991): 402-23.
12. See Reinhard Bollmus, *Das Amt Rosenberg und seine Gegner: Studien zum Machtkampf im nationalsozialistischen Herrschaftssystem* (Stuttgart: Deutsche Verlags-Anstalt, 1970), pp. 71-85.
13. On Hitler's philosophy of organizing subleaders, see Martin Broszat, *The Hitler State: The Foundation and Development of the Internal Structure of the Third Reich* (London: Longman, Eng. ed., 1981), p. xiii.
14. For Hitler's long-standing antipathy toward modern art, see the passages in *Mein Kampf: Eine Abrechnung* (Boston: Houghton Mifflin, 1971), pp. 258-63. See also the account of a dinner party conversation in 1932 in Otto Wagener, *Hitler: Memoirs of a Confidant*, ed. Henry Turner (New Haven, CT: Yale University Press, 1985), pp. 308-11.
15. For extensive quotations from the speech, see Klaus Backes, "Adolf Hitlers Einfluss auf die Kulturpolitik des Dritten Reiches" (Ph.D. diss. Rupricht-Karl Universität, 1984), p. 112. This study was revised and published as *Hitler und die Bildenden Künste: Kulturverständnis und Kunstpolitik im Dritten Reich* (Düsseldorf: DuMont, 1988). See also Hildegard Brenner, *Die Kunstpolitik im Nationalsozialismus* (Reinbek: Rowohlt, 1963), p. 82.

16. See Herbert Rothfeder, "A Study of Alfred Rosenberg's Organization for National Socialist Ideology" (Ph.D. diss., University of Michigan, 1963), pp. 82, 94-95.
17. Note that the initial plan was to have the two organizations work together: The NS-KG was to be responsible for the *Kulturpropaganda* of the KdF. Personnel problems and other rivalries prevented this cooperation. See Bollmus, *Das Amt Rosenberg und seine Gegner*, pp. 71-72.
18. See Brenner, in Holborn, ed., pp. 410-11. See also Elaine S. Hochman, *Architects of Fortune: Mies van der Rohe and the Third Reich* (New York: Fromm International, 1990), pp. 172-210.
19. See Brenner, in Holborn, ed., p. 411. In 1935, Schreiber even managed to obtain the post of curator for the German art entry to the Chicago World's Fair. He sent a selection of paintings to America that scandalized the conservative camp back in Germany.
20. Reinhard Merker called Robert Ley "one of the most ideologically indifferent men at the top of the NSDAP." See Merker, p. 136. Note that Ley admired modern architecture. See Bazon Brock, "Kunst auf Befehl?" in Brock and Preiß, eds., p. 18. For more on the Amt Schönheit der Arbeit, see Anson Rabinbach, "Beauty of Labour—The Aesthetics of Production in the Third Reich," *Journal of Contemporary History* 11, No. 4 (December 1976): 43-74.
21. For more information, see Germer.
22. These two directors of the Nationalgalerie succeeded Ludwig Justi, who had played a pivotal role in the state's collecting of modern art. Schardt had scaled back the section on expressionist art in the Kronprinzenpalais, but apparently not sufficiently enough for Rust and the conservatives, as they arranged for him to be replaced by Hanfstaengl. See Annegret Janda, "The Fight for Modern Art: The Berlin *Nationalgalerie* after 1933," in Barron, ed., pp. 105-19.
23. See ibid., p. 112.
24. See Merker, p. 133.
25. There are many works on Nolde's experiences in the Third Reich. See, for example, Christa Rudloff, *Materialien zur Kunst- und Kulturpolitik im "3. Reich" am Beispiel Emil Nolde* (Nuremberg: Germanisches Museum, 1982), and Ernst Schürer, *Emil Nolde: Works From American Collections* (University Park, PA: Penn State, 1988). Other modernist artists continued to make appeals for tolerance to the government. Max Pechstein, for example, wrote to Goebbels with this purpose in mind and noted that his eldest son was an "*SA-Mann*." See Reuth, p. 368.
26. See Eberhard Roters, *Galerie Ferdinand Möller: die Geschichte einer Galerie für Moderne Kunst in Deutschland 1917-1956* (Berlin: Gebrüder Mann, 1984),

pp. 123-41. Note that the Galerie Ferdinand Möller later became one of the four main dealers that sold "degenerate art" abroad for the regime. See Andreas Hüneke, "On the Trail of Missing Masterpieces" in Barron, ed., pp. 121-33.
27. The show was entitled *"Emil Nolde: späte und frühe Gemälde, Aquarelle, Zeichnungen"* and ran during April and May of 1937. See Roters, p. 133. For the number of works by Nolde in the *Entartete Kunst* Exhibition, see Barron, ed., p. 319.
28. See Roters, p. 140.
29. For the official announcement of the restrictions on art criticism, see the *Mitteilungsblatt der Reichskammer der bildenden Kunst* (December 1936). This periodical can be found in the Institut für Zeitgeschichte in Munich (hereafter cited as IfZG). Note also that the prohibition against *Nachtkritik* in theater had been issued by Goebbels at an earlier date (13 May 1936). See David Welch, *Propaganda and the German Cinema: 1933-1945* (New York: Oxford University Press), p. 21.
30. For more on Ziegler, see Robert Wistrich, *Who's Who in Nazi Germany* (New York: Bonanza Books, 1982), p. 347.
31. The conflict between Goebbels and Rust concerned the distinction between art produced by *lebendige* (living) and *tote* (dead) creators. Goebbels had control over the former, and Rust the latter. See BAK: R 21/209 for the negotiations during the autumn of 1936.
32. See Wolfgang Willrich, *Die Säuberung des Kunsttempels: Eine kunstpolitische Kampfschrift zur Gesundung deutscher Kunst im Geiste nordischer Art* (Munich: Lehmann, 1937). For more on Willrich, see Glenn Cuomo, "Purging an 'Art-Bolshevist': The Persecution of Gottfried Benn in the Years 1933-1938," *German Studies Review* 9, No. 1 (February 1986): 95-105.
33. See Mario-Andreas Lüttichau, "'Deutsche Kunst' und 'entartete Kunst,'" in *Nationalsozialismus und "Entartete Kunst,"* ed. Peter-Klaus Schuster (Munich: Prestel, 1987), p. 96.
34. See Günther Dünkel, "Die Liquidierung der Kunst," *tendenzen* 157 (January-March 1987): 51.
35. For lists of works lost by specific museums, see Franz Roh, *"Entartete" Kunst. Kunstbarbarei im Dritten Reich* (Hannover: Fackelträger Verlag, 1962), pp. 123-248.
36. The issue of compensation paid to museums has been debated by scholars. See, for example, Wilhelm Arntz, "Bildersturm in Deutschland: Das Schicksal der Bilder," *Das Schönste* 8, No. 6 (June 1962): 33. Arntz argues that no payments were made. Archival sources indicate otherwise. See the Geheimes Staatsarchiv Preußischer Kulturbesitz, Rep. 90, 2464, for receipts and letters of acknowledgment from museum personnel.

37. For an argument along these lines, see Georg Bussmann, "Degenerate Art—A Look at a Useful Myth," in *German Art of the 20th Century* (Munich: Prestel, 1985).
38. The *Entartete Musik* Exhibition opened in Düsseldorf in May 1938 and was organized by Hans Severus Ziegler, with a related catalog, *Entartete Kunst: Eine Abrechnung* (Düsseldorf: Völkischer Verlag, 1938). See Albrecht Dümling and Peter Girth, eds., *Entartete Musik: Zur Düsseldorfer Ausstellung von 1938: Eine kommentierte Rekonstruktion* (Düsseldorf: Kleinherne, 1988); and Fred Prieberg, *Musik im NS-Staat* (Frankfurt: Fischer Taschenbuch, 1982). *Das Sowjet-Paradies* opened in the Lustgarten gallery in Berlin in 1942. A resistance group with a Communist orientation tried to set it afire. While they did considerable damage to the exhibit, they did not destroy it. The attack resulted in the arrest of many of the group's members. See Allan Merson, *Communist Resistance in Nazi Germany* (London: Lawrence & Wishart, 1985), pp. 240-43.
39. See Jonathan Petropoulos, *Art As Politics in the Third Reich* (Chapel Hill: University of North Carolina Press, forthcoming 1996). Göring, Goebbels, and other leaders involved themselves directly in the selling of art, and this contributed to the formation of their personal collections.
40. Hoffmann's account of this episode, where he describes the 8,000 submissions, the first selections of the 12-person jury, and Hitler's subsequent involvement is in his memoirs, *Hitler Was My Friend* (London: L. Burke, 1955), pp. 169-70.
41. For studies of themes in Nazi art, see Berthold Hinz, *Art in the Third Reich* (New York: Random House, 1979); Otto Thomae, *Die Propaganda-Maschinerie: Bildende Kunst und Öffentlichkeitsarbeit im Dritten Reich* (Berlin: Gebrüder Mann, 1978); Frankfurter Kunstverein, eds., *Kunst im 3. Reich: Dokumente der Unterwerfung* (Frankfurt: Frankfurter Kunstverein, 1974); Peter Adam, *Art of the Third Reich* (New York: Abrams, 1992); and Joachim Petsch, *Kunst im Dritten Reich: Architektur, Plastik, Malerei* (Cologne: Vista Point, 1983).
42. Compare Goebbels' evaluation of the 1937 show (e.g., his entry for 6 June, where he notes "Bei der Plastik geht es noch, aber bei der Malerei ist es z. T. direkt katastrophal") and that of the 1938 GDK (e.g., the 9 July entry, ". . . Plastik sehr gut. Bilder teils ganz hervorragend, teils etwas kitschig"). See Goebbels, vol. 3, pp. 167 and 476.
43. Bruce Pauley, *From Prejudice to Persecution: A History of Austrian Anti-Semitism* (Chapel Hill: University of North Carolina Press, 1992), p. 280.
44. Ibid., p. 284.
45. The formal law was called *Die Verordnung über die Einziehung volks- und staatsfeindlichen Vermögens im Lande Österreich*, 18 November 1938. See the *Gesetzblatt für das Land Österreich* 167, No. 589 (1938).

46. See Ernst Kubin, *Sonderauftrag Linz: Die Kunstsammlung Adolf Hitler. Aufbau, Vernichtungsplan, Rettung. Ein Thriller der Kulturgeschichte* (Vienna: Orac, 1989), pp. 21-23. See also Jakob Kurz, *Kunstraub in Europa, 1938-1945* (Hamburg: Facta Oblita, 1989), pp. 18-24; and the less scholarly treatment in David Roxan and Kenneth Wanstall, *The Rape of Art: Hitler's Plundering of the Great Masterpieces of Europe* (New York: McCann, 1965), pp. 26-27.
47. For the Bondys' fate and the initiative taken by local museum officials to confiscate their collections, see Kurz, pp. 21-22. For the expropriation of the Lanckoronski family property in Vienna, which occurred in October 1939, see BAK: R 43/1270a.
48. See BAK: R 43 II/1269a, fol. 5: Lammers (within the Reich Chancellery) to Himmler, 18 June 1938.
49. For Haberstock's assignment, see BAK: R 43 II/1269a, fols. 166-67, *Vermerk* from the Reich Chancellery, 25 February 1939.
50. The term is first used in the 18 June 1938 letter from Lammers to Himmler, BAK: R 43 II/1269a, fol. 5.
51. In September of 1938, the Kunsthistorisches Museum assumed responsibility for overseeing the artworks; by October 1938, the *Reichsstatthalter* of Vienna, Seyss-Inquart, reported that the works were now in the Neue Burg under guard by Himmler's forces. See Kurz, pp. 18-22.
52. The full titles of the decrees are *Die Verordnung über die Einziehung volks- und staatsfeindlichen Vermögens*, and *Die Verordnung über den Einsatz des jüdischen Vermögens*. Note that efforts to ascertain Jewish holdings began earlier than the post-*Kristallnacht* decrees: for example, in April 1938, both the Four Year Plan Office and the Reich Ministry for Economics issued overlapping decrees that required "the reporting of all Jewish assets and property." See Avraham Barkai, *From Boycott to Annihilation* (Hannover: University Press of New England, 1989), pp. 113-18.
53. See Lucy Dawidowicz, *The War Against the Jews* (New York: Holt, Rinehart and Winston, 1975), p. 97. She notes that prior to the autumn of 1938, approximately 50 Jewish businesses per month were being transferred to state trustees, but that the number of cases increased to 235 per month by November.
54. There were some exceptions to this rule: for example, Ludwig Gies suffered the *Ausstellungsverbot* in 1934 as did Oskar Moll in 1935; but these cases were rare.
55. For Dix's experience, see Fritz Löffler, *Otto Dix: Life and Work,* trans. R. J. Hollingdale (New York: Holmes and Meier, 1982), p. 96. For Nolde's experience, which led him to work in less easily detected watercolors, see Rudloff, Schürer, as well as William Bradley, *Emil Nolde and German Expressionism* (Ann Arbor, MI: UMI Research Press, 1986), pp. 114-24. A brief sketch of Karl Schmidt-Rottluff's career appears in Barron, ed., pp. 340-47.

56. See Hildegard Brenner, *Ende einer bürgerlichen Kunst-Institution: Die politische Formierung der Preußischen Akademie der Künste ab 1933* (Stuttgart: Deutsche Verlags-Anstalt, 1972).
57. See Merker, p. 157. In 1933 the Preußische Akademie der Künste had asked a number of left-wing artists to withdraw, including Otto Dix and Käthe Kollwitz, as they were the most politically active of their profession who remained in Germany.
58. See Hinz, *Art in the Third Reich,* p. 159.
59. Hitler would typically purchase 200 to 300 works from the GDK (out of 1,100 to 1,500 that were exhibited). See the figures in Thomae, pp. 42-43. Goebbels discusses his annual purchasing trips in his *Tagebücher,* and photographic albums assembled by the curatorial staff that document his acquisitions are in the Adolf Hitler Collection in the Library of Congress. (Albums for Robert Ley are also located there.) For Himmler's visit to the GDK and the purchases he made in August 1942, see BAK: NS 19/3165.
60. See the 22 May 1934 *Erlaß* concerning the artistic embellishment of public construction projects, signed by Walther Funk (then of the Propaganda Ministry) in BAK: R 2/26722, fol. 5-6. This file also contains later amendments to this decree.
61. The repeal of the 1934 ordinance took place in 1937 and is noted in BAK: R 2/26723, fol. 98, 5 April 1938.
62. The figure of 27,396,00 RM is given by Magdalena Bushart, "Überraschende Begegnung mit alten Bekannten," in *NS-Kunst: 50 Jahre danach,* ed. Berthold Hinz (Marburg: Jonas Verlag, 1989), p. 35.
63. See Michéle Cone, *Artists Under Vichy: A Case of Prejudice and Persecution* (Princeton, NJ: Princeton University Press, 1992), p. 160. Albert Speer designed Josef Thorak's impressive atelier. For pictures and architectural drawings, see Leon Krier, *Albert Speer. Architecture: 1932-1942* (Brussels: Archives Architecture Moderne, 1985), pp. 207-10.
64. For the "Gift of *Reichsminister* Speer," see BAK: R 120/3460a, fol. 13, dated March 1945. For Hitler's award, see BAK: R 43 II/986, fol. 51: a "Dotation" signed by Bormann and dated April 1942. Breker's close cooperation with the regime was also reflected by his position as vicepresident of the Reich Chamber of the Visual Arts (and having Helena Rubenstein's "Aryanized" home in Paris put at his disposal during the war). In his de-Nazification trial in 1948, he claimed to have been an unpolitical artist and stated that he had no money. He was fined 100 DM and permitted to work again. (He enjoyed renewed success in the postwar period.) See the collection of newspaper clippings concerning Breker in the Institut für Zeitgeschichte in Munich.

65. Jackson Spielvogel, *Hitler and Nazi Germany* (Englewood Cliffs, NJ: Prentice-Hall, 1988), p. 183.
66. Henry Picker, ed., *Hitlers Tischgespräche im Führerhauptquartier, 1941-1942* (Bonn: Athenäum Verlag, 1951), p. 391.
67. Gert Kerschbaumer and Karl Müller, eds., *Begnadet für das Schöne. Der weiß-rote Kulturkampf gegen die Moderne* (Vienna: Verlag für Gesellschaftskritik, 1992), pp. 103-4.
68. For an overview of the activities of the *Kunstschutz*, see the biased but still useful report of Franz Graf Wolff-Metternich, "Exposé du Comte F. Wolff-Metternich," in Jean Cassou, *Le Pillage par les Allemands des Oeuvres d'Art et des Bibliothèques Appartenant à des Juives en France* (Paris: CDJC, 1947), pp. 149-77. See also Kurz, pp. 138-51, 188-89.
69. Note that Posse had been rehabilitated by Hitler in 1938, after having been fired from the directorship of the Dresden museum by the local *Gauleiter*, Martin Mutschmann. See Kubin, pp. 17-18. The project evidently remained secret until 1942: At Posse's funeral in December, Goebbels made brief mention of the project. See the file of newspaper clippings concerning Posse at the IfZG. The first concerted effort at publicity occurred in the wake of the defeat at Stalingrad, as Hitler permitted Heinrich Hoffmann to publish an illustrated article on the Führermuseum in the periodical *Kunst dem Volk*. Hitler evidently thought that such ambitious plans for the future would boost morale.
70. See Hermann Giesler, *Ein anderer Hitler. Bericht seines Architekten. Erlebnisse, Gespräche, Reflexionen* (Leoni am Starnberger See: Druffel Verlag, 1977), p. 352.
71. See Matila Simon, *The Battle of the Louvre: The Struggle to Save French Art in World War II* (New York: Hawthorne, 1971), p. 77. This figure is difficult to verify, as is the claim made by Janet Flanner that Hitler's collection was worth $400 million. See Janet Flanner, *Men and Monuments* (New York: Harper, 1957), p. 226.
72. See S. L. Faison, *Consolidated Interrogation Report No. 4, Linz: Hitler's Museum and Library* (OSS Report, 15 December 1945), Attachment 60: a letter from Posse to Bormann, 14 October 1940.
73. See Jean Vlug, *Report on Objects Removed to Germany from Holland, Belgium and France during the German Occupation on* [sic] *the Countries* (Amsterdam: Stichting Nederlands Kunstbesit, 25 December 1945), p. 49.
74. For the best study on the organization, see Michael Kater, "Das Ahnenerbe: Die Forschungs- und Lehrgemeinschaft in der SS" (Ph.D. diss., Karl Ruprecht Universität, Heidelberg, 1966), later published as *Das "Ahnenerbe" der SS, 1935-1945* (Stuttgart: Deutsche Verlags-Anstalt, 1974).
75. Note that Himmler was also named to the post of Reich commissioner for the strengthening of Germandom (*Reichskommissar für die Festigung deutschen*

Volkstums) on 7 October 1939: The repatriation program thus was undertaken under his aegis. A sense of the range of the programs undertaken by the Ahnenerbe can be gained by examining the career of its business manager, Wolfram Sievers: He was one of the great art plunderers working on behalf of the regime, and he was executed in 1948 after a trial before the International Military Tribunal. The main reason for the death sentence was his order sending 115 Jews and political prisoners to the gas chambers in order to help build a skeleton collection of "*Untermenschen.*"

76. For Paulsen's Gestapo affiliation, see the Polish Information Ministry, *The nazi kultur in Poland* (London: His Majesty's Stationery Office, 1945), p. 100. See also the files on Paulsen in the *Sammlung Kater* in the IfZG, as well as documents No. 367 and No. 369 from the International Military Tribunal at Nuremberg. Note that the professor led the infamous *Sonderkommando Paulsen,* which looted throughout Poland; the commando's most illustrious trophy was the Veit Stoß Altar from the Church of Mary in Cracow.

77. The best studies of the ERR include Bollmus, Cassou, and Simon.

78. See *L'Exposé du Ministre Public: Le Pillage des Oeuvres d'Art dans les Pays Occupés de l'Europe Occidentale* (January 1946), in the Centre Documentation Juive Contemporaine, Paris (hereafter cited as CDJC), XIII-51. Theodore Rousseau, *Consolidated Interrogation Report No. 2: The Göring Collection* (OSS Report, 15 September 1945), pp. 23-24 and Attachment 5. Rousseau notes "it can be fairly estimated that they [the ERR pictures commandeered by Göring] constitute almost 50 percent of [the collection's] total, the ERR alone supplying in the neighborhood of seven hundred objects." Key employees of the ERR who worked for Göring included the Staff Leader Gerhard Utikal, the plunderer Kurt von Behr, and the art historian-cataloger Hermann Bunjes.

79. See Bormann to Rosenberg, 26 January 1943, in BAK, NS 8/242, fols. 162-64.

80. Göring issued an order of 5 November 1940 establishing a hierarchy for the control of the confiscated art: Hitler, Göring, Rosenberg's Hohe Schule, and then German museums. See BAK: NS 8/59, fols. 25-27. See also the photographic reproduction of the order in Göring's hand in Cassou, pp. 48-49. Rosenberg received the commission for the Hohe Schule from Hitler in January 1940: ten institutions were envisioned, which were to be realized after the war. A representative branch was the Institut für Judenforschung in Frankfurt, which focused on the Jews with typical Nazi biases. For an overview of the Hohe Schule, see BAK, NS 8/264. See also Reinhard Bollmus, "Zum Projekt einer nationalsozialistischen Alternativuniversität: Alfred Rosenbergs 'Hohe Schule,'" in *Erziehung und Schulung im Dritten Reich,* ed. Manfred Heinemann (Stuttgart: Klett-Cotta, 1980), pp. 125-52.

81. The best sources on the *Dienststelle Mühlmann* are Vlug, and A. J. van der Leeuw, *Die Bestimmung der vom deutschen Reich entzogenen und von der Dienststelle Dr. Mühlmann übernommenen Kunstgegenstände* (Amsterdam: Rijkinstitut voor Oorlogsdocumentatie, 1962). For more on the auction houses that thrived due to Nazi business (both purchasing and consigning works), including Lange's (Berlin), Dorotheum (Vienna), Weinmüller's (Munich and Vienna), and the Hôtel Drouôt (Paris), see James Plaut, *Consolidated Interrogation Report No. 1: Activity of the Einsatzstab Reichsleiter Rosenberg in France* (OSS Report of 15 August 1945), and Faison.
82. International Military Tribunal, *Trial of the Major War Criminals* (Nuremberg: IMT, 1947), vol. 8, pp. 74-88.
83. See the Allied interrogation of Schirach in OMGUS (Office of the Military Governor of the United States) 5/347-3/3.
84. For Künsberg's looting in France, see Wolff-Metternich's account in Cassou, pp. 166-71. There is minimal literature on the Sonderkommando Ribbentrop; see Ruth and Max Seydewitz, *Der Raub der Mona Lisa* (Moscow: Militärverlag der UdSSR, 1965); and Roxan and Wanstall, pp. 115-17.
85. For a description of the brutality of the fighting and confiscations, see Paul Enke, *Der Bernsteinzimmer Report* (Berlin: Verlag der Wirtschaft, 1986); and Sergei Varshavsky and Boris Rest, *Saved for Humanity: The Hermitage During the Siege of Leningrad, 1941-1944* (Leningrad: Aurora Art Publishers, 1985).
86. For the tribulations of Soviet art experts, see Konstantin Akinsha and Grigorii, "Spoils of War: The Soviet Union's Hidden Art Treasures," in *ARTnews* 90, No. 4 (April 1991): 130-41; and the second part, "The Soviets' War Treasures: A Growing Controversy," in *ARTnews* 90, No. 9 (September 1991): 112-19.
87. See Richard Grunberger, *The 12-Year Reich: A Social History of Nazi Germany, 1933-1945* (New York: Holt, Rinehart and Winston, 1971): see the chapter "Ritual and Führer Worship."
88. See the catalog *Junge Kunst in Deutschland. Veranstaltet vom Reichsstatthalter in Wien Reichsleiter Baldur von Schirach* (Vienna: Künstlerhaus Wien, 1943). See also Baldur von Schirach's memoirs, *Ich glaubte an Hitler* (Hamburg: Mosaik Verlag, 1967); and Oliver Rathkolb, "Nationalsozialistische (Un-) Kulturpolitik in Wien, 1938-1945," in *Im Reich der Kunst: die Wiener Akademie der bildenden Künste und die faschistische Kunstpolitik,* eds. Hans Seiger, Michael Lunardi, and Peter-Josef Populorum (Vienna: Verlag für Gesellschaftskritik, 1990), pp. 247-71.
89. See Charles Estreicher, *Cultural Losses in Poland* (London: Author, 1944); and the Polish Information Ministry. For the deportation of the Cracow faculty, the so-called *AB-Aktion,* see Werner Rings, *Life with the Enemy, 1939-1945* (New York: Doubleday, 1982), p. 36.

90. See Sarah Wilson, "Collaboration and the Fine Arts, 1940-1944," in *Collaboration in France: Politics and Culture during the Nazi Occupation*, eds. Gerhard Hirschfeld and Patrick Marsh (Oxford: Berg, 1989), p. 119; and Cone, pp. 155, 235. See also Arno Breker, *Paris, Hitler et Moi* (Paris: Plon, 1972), pp. 133-36.

91. See BAK: R 3/1735 and 1736 for the *Speer Chronik* compiled by Rudolf Wollters. See, for example, the entry of 20 September 1941 for the opening of the exhibition in Budapest and 15 March 1942 entry, when it opened in Madrid.

92. See, for example, the poster for the Brussels venue of *"Das Soujet-Paradies"* from March-April 1943 in Frankfurter Kunstverein, eds., p. 213. For the Paris exhibitions Freemasonry Unveiled, which opened at the Petit Palais in October 1940, and France and the Jew, which began its run at the Palais Berlitz in September 1941, see Gilles Perrault and Pierre Azema, *Paris Under the Occupation* (Paris: Vendome Press, 1989), pp. 83-85, and Simon, p. 95. For *Warsaw Accuses,* see Charles de Jaeger, *The Linz File* (Exeter: Webb and Bower, 1981), p. 115.

93. While Goebbels in theory determined war exemptions for all artists, other leaders would occasionally use their influence to obtain the *Unersetzliche Künstler-Stellung* and save their favorites from being drafted by General Walter von Unruh, who oversaw conscription. See Jan Tabor, "Die Gaben der Ostmark: Österreichische Kunst und Künstler in der Nationalsozialistischen Zeit," in Seiger, et al., eds., p. 282.

94. See Heiber, pp. 307-11.

95. Among the many studies of the storage and safeguarding of artworks by the National Socialists, see Cay Friemuth, *Die geraubte Kunst: der dramatische Wettlauf um die Rettung der Kulturschätze nach dem Zweiten Weltkrieg* (Braunschweig: Westermann, 1989); Irene Kühnel-Kunze, *Bergung—Evakuierung—Rückführung: Die Berliner Museen in den Jahren 1939-1959* (Berlin: Gebrüder Mann, 1984); Jeanpaul Goergen, "'X' heißt Vernichtung: Als die Nazis moderne Kunst verbrannten," in *Zitty,* 26 (1 July 1986): 42-52; Thomas Howe, *Salt Mines and Castles: The Discovery and Restitution of Looted European Art* (Indianapolis: Bobbs-Merrill, 1946); and James Rorimer, *Survival: The Salvage and Protection of Art in War* (New York: Abelard Press, 1950).

96. See Hans Boberach, ed., *Meldungen aus dem Reich, 1938-1945: die geheimen Lageberichte des Sicherheitsdienstes der SS* (Herrsching: Pawlak, 1984). These once-secret reports of the SD contain numerous observations about exhibitions, artists, and the art market.

97. The wartime experience of the two artists are described in their memoirs: Emil Nolde, *Reisen, Achtung, Befreiung, 1919-1946* (Cologne: DuMont, 1967); and

Arno Breker, *Im Strahlungsfeld der Ereignisse, 1925-1965: Leben und Wirken eines Künstlers. Porträts, Begegnungen, Schicksale* (Preußisch Oldendorf: Schütz, 1972).

98. See Andrea Hollmann and Ralph Keuning, "Berühmt und berüchtigt: Otto Dix 1891-1969," in *Dix,* eds. Galerie der Stadt Stuttgart (Stuttgart: Verlag Gerd Hatje, 1991), p. 26.
99. See Karl Höffkes, *Hitlers politische Generale: die Gauleiter des Dritten Reiches* (Tübingen: Grabert Verlag, 1986).
100. See Broszat, p. 294.
101. Hannah Arendt, *The Origins of Totalitarianism* (San Diego: Harcourt Brace Jovanovich, 1973 ed.), pp. 396-403.
102. It should be noted that Hitler actively tried to cultivate an awareness of culture among his subleaders. See, for example, Goebbels' remark of 16 June 1938: "Der Führer bedauert sehr, daß einige unserer Gauleiter so wenig Verständnis für die Kunst haben," in *Die Tagebücher von Joseph Goebbels,* vol. 3, p. 457.
103. Hitler's repeated inability to gain admission to the Vienna Akademie der bildenden Künste has been discussed in many studies. See, for example, William Jenks, *Vienna and the Young Hitler* (New York: Columbia University Press, 1960). See also Billy Price, ed., *Adolf Hitler als Maler und Zeichner: ein Werkkatalog der Ölgemälde, Aquarelle, Zeichnungen und Architekturskizzen* (Zug: Gallant Verlag, 1983).
104. Speer, p. 200.
105. Edward Peterson, *The Limits of Hitler's Power* (Princeton, NJ: Princeton University Press, 1969), p. 9.
106. For more on this issue see Ian Kershaw, *The Nazi Dictatorship: Problems and Perspectives of Interpretation* (London: Edward Arnold, 1989), specifically, the chapter entitled "Hitler: 'Master' of the Third Reich or 'Weak' Dictator."
107. See Broszat, pp. 294-327.
108. See Faison, p. 78.
109. For one of many examples, see Joseph Goebbels' diary entry for the 1938 GDK, "Das Niveau der Ausstellung ist ganz unterschiedlich . . . teils etwas kitschig." Entry for 9 July 1938, in *Die Tagebücher von Joseph Goebbels,* vol. 3, p. 476.

7

Literary Policy in the Third Reich*

Jan-Pieter Barbian
Translated from the German by Glenn R. Cuomo

ORIENTATION: THE SOURCES AND THE STATE OF RESEARCH ON THE TOPIC

Whoever embarks on the search for extant documents on Third Reich literary policy will have to travel extensively. Several factors have contributed to the dispersal of the seminal materials over several German archives: the confiscation of the documents of the top Reich agencies by the American, Soviet, and British occupation forces; the differing manners in which West and East Germany administered the return of these documents; and finally the decentralization of the relevant agencies at the provincial level. In addition, the destruction of numerous archival holdings as a result of war significantly impedes a complete reconstruction of the events and interactions between people and agencies.

The two largest collections of holdings today are in Coblenz and Berlin. The holdings at the Bundesarchiv Koblenz—Reichsministerium für Volksaufklärung und Propaganda (holdings catalog number: R 55), Reichskulturkammer-Zentrale (R 56 I), Reichsschrifttumskammer (R 56 V), Reichsministerium für Wissenschaft, Erziehung und Volksbildung (R 21), Reichskanzlei (R 43 II), Reichsfinanzministerium (R 2), and Reichssicherheitshauptamt (R 58)—provide information on the state's supervision, regimentation, and support of authors, publishers, the book trade, research libraries, and public libraries. The files' completeness and informational value differ considerably. The same holds true for the official agencies operating within the Party: Whereas we can discern relatively well the activities of the Schrifttumsstelle (Literature Office) within Alfred Rosenberg's sphere of influence through the holdings Kanzlei Rosenberg (NS 8) and Der Beauftragte des Führers für die Überwachung der gesamten geistigen und weltanschaulichen Schulung und Erziehung der NSDAP (NS 15), only disconnected file remnants have survived for the "Parteiamtliche Prüfungskommission zum Schutze des NS-Schrifttums" headed by Philipp Bouhler (NS 11), due to the destruction of this agency's office building in 1943. Likewise only rudimentary holdings exist for the Stab Stellvertreter des Führers. After Rudolf Hess's flight to England, this became the Partei-Kanzlei der NSDAP (NS 6) as of May 1941, and then, under Martin Bormann's direction, it evolved into one of the most important decision-making entities in the Nazi state's power structure. However, the Institut für Zeitgeschichte in Munich published a reconstruction of the Chancellory's correspondence based on the recipients' documents, which makes it possible to reconstruct the interventions by Hess's staff or the Party Chancellory into literary policy.[1] And finally, the holdings Reichspropagandaleitung (NS 18) and Hauptamt für Erzieher/Reichswaltung des Nationalsozialistischen Lehrerbunds (NS 12) contain a multitude of important details on the organization as well as the purport of official Party and state literary policy.

The Berlin Document Center houses the largest holdings of personnel files from the state agencies, as well as of files for "people in cultural professions," who were registered in the seven individual chambers of the Reichskulturkammer. But even here, unfortunately, the records are by no means complete. For example, the personnel files of the staff members of the official Party literary agencies are sporadic, and due to the destruction of Leipzig's book trade center in December 1943, the personnel files of publishers and book dealers are virtually nonexistent. A further obstacle for users is that the holdings are not freely accessible through systematic guide books and that the files that served as evidence for de-Nazification trials in the postwar period were taken out of their original contexts and refiled with no consideration for basic archival principles.

The body of extant documents in the two archives can be supplemented and expanded by the holdings of several provincial archives. The Landesarchiv Berlin preserves an extensive collection of documents from the largest and most important provincial branch of the Reich Literature Chamber in Berlin. The Nordrhein-Westfälisches Hauptstaatsarchiv in Düsseldorf and the Staatsarchiv Würzburg provide detailed insights into the Gestapo's surveillance activity at the regional level. Moreover, Würzburg has the archive of the former Reich Student Leadership, which was responsible for the *Aktion wider den undeutschen Geist* (action against the un-German spirit) and the book burnings of 10 May 1933. With the help of the Staatsarchiv Leipzig, the history of the Börsenverein der Deutschen Buchhändler (the Stock Exchange Association of German Book Traders) and its successor organization, the Bund Reichsdeutscher Buchhändler (League of Reich-German Book Dealers), renamed the Gruppe Buchhandel in the Reich Literature Chamber as of 1936, can be reconstructed at least partially. The Deutsche Bücherei in Leipzig, a part of the Deutsche Bibliothek as of October 1990, holds essential archival materials on governmental censorship policy, together with a unique collection of books from the years 1933 to 1945 on the subject of National Socialist literary policy. In the case of Thuringia, the sparse holdings in Coblenz of documents on the library policy of the Reich Education Ministry can be supplemented with a very informative collection of source material at the Staatsarchiv Weimar. The document holding National Sozialistische Deutsche Arbeiter Partei Gau Baden in the Generallandesarchiv Karlsruhe contains a considerable number of files on persons and official matters of the *Gau* literary commissioner and the district literary commissioners of Rosenberg's Literature Office from the years 1936 to 1943. And finally, the Deutsches Literaturarchiv in Marbach am Neckar holds numerous writers' legacies of correspondence and other unpublished materials that illustrate literary policy in the Third Reich from the perspective of the actors, the conspirators, and the victims.

If we evaluate the quality of work published up to now on the subject, we quickly recognize that while essays and monographs on literature and literary policy of the Nazi period are legion, very few are based on a thorough knowledge and utilization of the source materials. This is especially the case with what has been taken to be the standard work to this day, Dietrich Strothmann's study from 1960,[2] which is full of errors due to his failure to review the agencies' documents and for which not even the published sources were correctly utilized. Joseph Wulf's document anthology, *Literatur und Dichtung im Dritten Reich*,[3] also cannot be used as a source without reservations: In the first place, the selection is incomplete and methodologically flawed, since omissions were not correctly noted. Moreover, Wulf did not intend to provide an objective documentation but rather a political accusation.

As far as the different areas of literary policy in the Third Reich are concerned, the numerous examinations on specialized topics—aside from their problems—do not provide a complete picture. To this day the political as well as the professional and social situation of authors under the National Socialist dictatorship has not been investigated coherently. For a long time the prevalent opinion, which publications have reinforced again and again, has been that writers were either National Socialists or had retreated into "inner emigration." However, as Hans Dieter Schäfer was the first to demonstrate, this view does not hold true for the complex reality of the years 1933 to 1945.[4]

The situation is even worse with respect to publishers and the book trade. To this day the Börsenverein des Deutschen Buchhandels has made just as little effort to come to terms with its past in the Third Reich as most publishing houses.[5] We can only speculate on the reasons for this; but it is likely that in the course of the rebuilding of the West and East German book trade after 1945, there was no interest in unveiling the publishers' and book dealers' less than laudable conduct between 1933 and 1945. Thus here, too, there exist only specialized investigations of different value. In 1971, Dietrich Aigner published an overview of the "indexing" of the so-called harmful and undesirable literature;[6] however, his study does not represent a complete history of book censorship under the Nazi dictatorship. The Salman Schocken Verlag, together with the fate of Jewish books under National Socialist persecution, was the focus of a well-researched study by Volker Dahm.[7] With his investigation of the Hanseatische Verlagsanstalt, which was owned by the German Labor Front since 1933, Siegfried Lokatis made an important contribution to our knowledge of the National Socialists' formation of trusts in the book trade.[8] And for his dissertation on the history of lending libraries in the twentieth century, Michael Kast utilized for the first time sources on the situation during the Nazi period.[9] In contrast, comparable studies on other sectors of the book trade (commission business, export book trade, used book sales, and book clubs) are lacking. Furthermore, no history has been written of the professional and social changes in the German book trade from the worldwide Depression up until the end of the Second World War.

Only lately have scholars begun to show interest in the history of libraries, and so far it is merely sporadic. In 1989, an anthology appeared on *Bibliotheken während des Nationalsozialismus,* a topic on which the Wolfenbüttel research group for library history focused at its fifth annual conference.[10] Whereas Engelbrecht Boese's well-researched and differentiated studies have subjected the institution of public libraries to a relatively detailed scrutiny,[11] Hans-Gerd Happel's dissertation on research libraries provides, at best, a sketchy overview.[12] In both areas many specialized investigations still are needed to provide more accurate knowledge of the mechanisms of the Reich Education Ministry's library policy and to take into account regional peculiarities.[13]

THE BEGINNING: THE SEIZURE OF THE PROFESSIONAL ASSOCIATIONS FOR WRITERS AND THE BOOK TRADE

The culture of the Weimar Republic—the central domain of the outsiders, as Peter Gay aptly phrased it[14]—was already shaken by attacks from the Right at the beginning of the 1930s, just as was its political system.[15] Not only in Berlin, but in the entire Reich, the republic's modernist culture was ridiculed, and the political Right was building up its own "countermodels."[16] There were many actors in this right-wing campaign: Alfred Rosenberg with his Kampfbund für deutsche Kultur (KfdK, or Combat League for German Culture) set up in 1927/28[17]; Joseph Goebbels in his multiple functions as the *Gauleiter* of Berlin, a hardworking journalist of the Nazi press *(Der Angriff)*, and the NSDAP's Reich propaganda leader as of 1932; Wilhelm Frick in his capacity as the minister of the interior and popular education minister in Thüringia (1930/31), and the increasingly influential Nazi contingent in the Reichstag he headed; Alfred Hugenberg, the leader of the DNVP (German National People's Party), with his widely ramified media combine (consisting of August Scherl Verlag, Vera Verlagsanstalt, Ufa, Ala Anzeigen GmbH, Telegraphen-Union);[18] and Max Amann, director of the Nazis' own publishing house, Franz Eher Verlag (with its best-seller *Mein Kampf)*. Furthermore, the possibilities for development of the cultural avant-garde and democratically oriented journalism were seriously limited by: politically motivated rulings by a justice system hostile to the republic; politically influenced censorship authorities, such as the supreme film censorship office in Berlin; and the emergency decree policy of the presiding governments of Brüning, von Papen, and von Schleicher, which was in effect since 1930.[19]

One has to keep this roughly outlined point of departure in mind to understand better the development that started following Adolf Hitler's appointment as Reich Chancellor on 30 January 1933. The *Gleichschaltung* (coordination) completed in the course of the next half year was a stratified process, in which the personnel of public institutions and organizations were changed and their organizational and legal independence was done away with.[20] To a large part, these changes took place under pressure from National Socialist functionaries, who utilized their new executive powers to abolish the basic right guaranteed under the Weimar Constitution to free expression in word, writing, print, image, and related forms (Section 118). The Reich president's "Emergency Decrees" of 4 and 28 February 1933 already rescinded essential elements of the democratic constitutional state before the *Ermächtigungsgesetz* (enabling act) of 24 March 1933 eliminated any kind of parliamentary control and cleared Hitler's way to the unrestricted exercise of his authority.[21]

Through a series of further laws, the structure of cultural life also was permanently changed. The so-called Law for the Re-establishment of the Professional Civil Service of 7 April 1933 affected social-democratic and liberal representatives of the cultural bureaucracy at the provincial and municipal level (especially in Prussia), just as it affected politically undesirable teachers at universities and art academies; employees at museums, musical conservatories, and theaters; librarians; and even members of the Prussian Academy of the Arts, who were not civil servants at all.[22] With the Law for the Seizure of Communist Assets of 26 May and the so-called Law for the Seizure of Assets Hostile to the Nation and the State of 14 July, the major book, newspaper, and periodical presses, as well as the distribution companies of the Kommunistische Partei Deutschlands (German Communist Party, or KPD) and the Sozialdemokratische Partei Deutschlands (German Social Democratic Party, or SPD), were totally wiped out.[23] Their substance had already been weakened since February of that year through book and newspaper bans, as well as through the flight of numerous leftist intellectuals into exile. This flight constituted a part of the emigration wave induced by the National Socialists' persecution measures; in all, approximately 5,500 important figures from the arts, sciences, and journalism fled.[24]

What appears at first to have been the astonishingly rapid restructuring and reformation of cultural life was, however, not solely the result of the power positions the NSDAP had achieved or created after 30 January. Karl Dietrich Bracher has talked about a "process of 'empathizing' with power" and in doing so characterized the attitude of numerous intellectuals who actively supported the *Gleichschaltung* of the arts and sciences.[25] Similarly, many institutions and organizations also accepted the National Socialist intrusions without any noteworthy resistance, in part even expediting them. This lamentable finding can be explained only in the light of the profound insecurity and disorientation induced in intellectuals as well as the general population by the obvious failure of the Weimar Republic's political parties and institutions. In addition, the harsh polarization of political life since the beginning of the 1930s also affected cultural life.

In the realm of literature, essentially four institutions were of political interest to the National Socialists. As the first in line, the Section for Literature in the Prussian Academy of the Arts, founded in 1926, was purged of crucial members and its membership newly "formed."[26] In the brief period between 15 February and 7 June 1933, Heinrich Mann was replaced as president by Hanns Johst, the Reich head of the "Literature Group" in the Combat League for German Culture and since mid-February 1933 the First Dramaturgist at the Preußisches Staatstheater.[27] The nationalistic bard Hans Friedrich Blunck advanced to the position of Johst's deputy; the section's secretary Oskar Loerke was ousted by Werner Beumelburg, an author of books glorifying war. By applying the Law for the Re-establishment of the Professional Civil Service of 7 April 1933, the academy's leadership expelled the section's Jewish authors, although membership in the academy had absolutely nothing to do with the civil service. To replace the members who had either fled into exile or been expelled on political or racial grounds, the section's truncated membership conducted a "by-election" of authors with nationalistic-conservative and National Socialist leanings. Indeed, because the Literature Section was institutionally and financially dependent on the Prussian Culture Ministry, whose provisional head since 4 February 1933 was the National Socialist Bernhard Rust, this restructuring and purging process was pursued energetically. But had the prestigious academy itself been less willing to cooperate with the Reich, its demise would have been more noticeable.

It was the academy president, Max von Schillings, who considered Heinrich Mann to be "unacceptable" and urged him to resign, because the latter had been a signatory to a proclamation for the formation of a unified democratic front against the National Socialist dictatorship. And it was Gottfried Benn—with the assistance of the politically naive Oskar Loerke—who had the remaining section members sign the following declaration in mid-March 1933:

> Are you prepared, in recognition of the altered historical situation, to continue to place yourself at the disposal of the Prussian Academy of the Arts? An affirmative reply to this question precludes political activity in public against the Reich Government and obliges you to loyal collaboration in the spirit of the altered historical situation on the national cultural tasks incumbent upon the Academy according to the statutes.[28]

This was one of the many documents of submission typical for the year 1933. Eighteen of the 27 section members agreed to sign, among them Gerhart Hauptmann, Georg Kaiser, Walter von Molo, and Franz Werfel. Despite a personnel structure to the liking of the new rulers, an ambitious work program, and repeated addresses in praise of the Reich government, the section, which now called itself the Deutsche Akademie für Dichtung, quickly became the object of contention for the conflicting interests of the Prussian minister president Göring, his culture minister Rust, and the intriguer Goebbels. Authors such as Hans Grimm, Rudolf G. Binding, Werner Beumelburg, Gottfried Benn, and Erwin Guido Kolbenheyer, who had looked quite favorably upon National Socialism's ascendancy, had to acknowledge that from a political standpoint, the academy had been totally left out in the cold after the *Gleichschaltung*.

The German section of the PEN Club, which had been in existence since 1921, experienced a similar loss of importance. The new appointments to its executive board and the replacement of its membership started three days after the Reichstag elections of 5 March 1933 and were already completed by the end of April.[29] At the head of this writers' association, hitherto directed by Alfred Kerr, predominantly National Socialist protagonists emerged: the state commissioner in the Prussian Culture Ministry Hans Hinkel, who simultaneously was the Reich organizational head of Alfred Rosenberg's Combat League for German Culture[30]; once again Hanns Johst; Erich Kochanowski, the manager and organizational head of the Berlin Provincial Leadership of the Combat League for German Culture; as well as Rainer Schlösser, who was responsible for the culture section of the *Völkischer Beobachter*. It is therefore no surprise that the general membership meeting of the German PEN Club on 23 April 1933 expressed "the unanimous will henceforth to work in harmony [!] with the national uprising."[31]

In the end, however, the National Socialists' effort to convert the internationally recognized German PEN Section into an instrument for their foreign policy goals failed, due to the specific organizational structure and the political steadfastness of the association's English leadership. In London, at the beginning of November 1933, the executive committee passed a resolution against the oppression of dissenting writers in Germany. Edgar von Schmidt-Pauli, the German delegate present at the meeting, thereupon felt compelled to declare the German section's withdrawal from the international PEN Club. As a countermove a Union nationaler Schriftsteller was started, with Hanns Johst and Gottfried Benn at its head. The union made its appearance to a national and international public in March 1934 with a pompous "appeal" for the salvation of Western culture,[32] but it soon ceased to exist.

In the restructuring of the most significant advocacy group for writers in the Weimar Republic, the Schutzverband deutscher Schriftsteller (SDS),[33] one of its founding members from 1909 played a decisive role. Hanns Heinz Ewers, who—similar to Johst and Benn—had switched over from expressionism to National Socialism, forced his way with a group of nationalist-oriented writers into a meeting of the SDS executive committee on 11 March 1933 and demanded ". . . that the majority of the executive committee should immediately announce its resignation."[34] In a self-glorifying presentation of the events, which Ewers found necessary to write in 1940 when faced with a ban of all his works published before 1933, he continued: ". . . the rest of them should remain in order to elect on their part new executive committee members named by me. I then left with my people and gave the executive committee a quarter of an hour to decide. What I had anticipated happened: these gentlemen's fear and cowardice were so great that they immediately did everything that was demanded of them."[35] Assuming the organization's top position—officially as of 4 May 1933—was Götz Otto Stoffregen, a former Freikorps member, journalist for diverse nationalist press organs, and an NSDAP member since 1932.[36] Hans Richter, the president of the League of German Prose Authors (VDE, Verband Deutscher Erzähler), became Stoffregen's deputy.

But not until after the consolidation of the SDS with the VDE, the Deutscher Schriftstellerverein (German Writers' Club), and the cartel of lyric authors into the Reichsverband Deutscher Schriftsteller (RDS, or Reich Association of German Authors) on 9 June 1933 were the goals and membership structure of the hitherto voluntary advocacy association changed fundamentally. The *Führerprinzip* (leadership principle) was stipulated in the new statutes. Acceptance into the association no longer depended solely on activity as a professional writer; people also had to demonstrate "German racial heritage" as well as "irreproachable political" conduct. However, this barb directed against Jewish and leftist-liberal authors acquired its significance only through the designation of the RDS as a "compulsory organization, the membership in which will determine in the future whether a literary work can or cannot be published in Germany."[37]

In the writers' associations we can at least discern that there had been massive political pressure to reinforce the latent readiness on the part of many of their members to reject writer colleagues from the political left who had been successful up until 1933. But no outside pressure was necessary with the Börsenverein der Deutschen Buchhändler (Stock Exchange Association of German Book Traders), which reacted to the new power structure with an unprecedented series of opportunistic acts of accommodation. The general executive committee of the Börsenverein published in the *Börsenblatt für den Deutschen Buchhandel* of 3 May 1933 an "immediate program for the German book trade," which had already been passed on 12 April in Leipzig.[38] Following introductory declarations of willingness to cooperate with the "national uprising," the president, Dr. Friedrich Oldenbourg, and his seven colleagues in the executive committee formulated demands that were supposed to bring about with the state's support the solution to the economic crisis in the book trade. The market was supposed to be cleansed and the private economic initiative of the traditional book trade enterprises strengthened through the following means:

1. The elevation of the Börsenverein to a "compulsory organization for all book dealers."

2. "State licensing of businesses in the book trade."
3. The pushing back of activities in the book trade undertaken by government institutions, unions, organizations, and political parties.
4. The "reduction" of book clubs.
5. The "immediate and total elimination of book publishing and distribution by department stores."
6. Legal "measures against the unhealthy and nationally damaging dissemination of the so-called modern lending libraries."

In return for the fulfillment of these economic wishes, the Börsenverein promised the National Socialist rulers that: "With respect to the Jewish question, the executive committee relies on the leadership of the Reich government. Its regulations will be carried out unconditionally within the committee's sphere of influence."[39]

In order to follow up with appropriate actions, on 13 May 1933 the *Börsenblatt* published a list with 12 authors—among them Lion Feuchtwanger, Alfred Kerr, Emil Ludwig, Heinrich Mann, Erich Maria Remarque, Kurt Tucholsky, and Arnold Zweig—who "are to be considered harmful for Germany's esteem" and whose works therefore should no longer be disseminated by the book trade.[40] In doing so, the Börsenverein essentially adopted the same value judgment that the Deutsche Studentenschaft had pronounced with its "Aktion wider den undeutschen Geist" and the book burnings of 10 May 1933 in almost all university cities in the German Reich.[41]

On 14 May, the propaganda minister, together with his state secretary and economic expert Walther Funk, announced that he would attend the traditional *Kantate-Treffen* (annual publishers' meeting) in Leipzig's Buchhändlerhaus. In his speech before the assembled membership, Goebbels skillfully emphasized that it was the function of the new "government of the national uprising" to maintain and renew the state:

> This government knows how necessary the spirit is to it; this government knows what the nation's soul needs, and this government is also convinced that the book that reflects the spirit of the time will also make its way in the future. And thus we believe that we are showing the German nation not only the political and economic way to the top, but also the cultural and spiritual way—though under one condition: as generous as we are in the methods and as humane as we are in dealing with our opponents [sic], as narrow, as hard and as relentless are we in [our] principles, must we be in [our] principles. For if principles are supposed to support a state, they then must be of a pitiless strictness. Only on hard ground can a state be built; these ideas, which made their breakthrough on 30 January 1933,

are in their nature anti-international, antipacifist, and antidemocratic. Their nature has been hardened in the thoughts of the struggle, for the purpose of leading the German nation and its thinking back again to race, religion and nationalism, and by their nature to implement the idea of the authoritative personality in all sectors of public life.[42]

The speech's transcript notes "stormy applause." Yet despite the shameless pandering and the establishment of an "action committee" that was supposed to force the "adaptation" of the "Reich-German book trade's professional, district, and local associations" to the "changed historical circumstances,"[43] the leadership of the Börsenverein itself did not escape thorough reorganizational measures. At the end of May 1934, the Reich Literature Chamber (RSK) exerted pressure for the dismissal of Friedrich Oldenbourg, who had served since 1930 as the organization's presiding officer, after Oldenbourg had had an altercation with chamber president Blunck and his deputy Wismann over the plans for the new structuring of German book exports.[44] After the brief interregnum by Kurt Vowinckel, a Berlin publisher of geopolitical works, Wilhelm Baur, who at the time was only 29 years old, assumed the organization's top position in September 1934.[45] Baur was not only an NSDAP member since 1920,[46] he had also worked his way up in the Party's own publishing house, Franz Eher Nachfolger, from unpaid assistant to manager of the NSDAP's Berlin book publishing house. Within very few years he then advanced—under the protection of the press's director Max Amann—through his leading positions in the Börsenverein and in the RSK to be a key figure in the German book trade.[47]

THE ESTABLISHMENT OF THE PROPAGANDA MINISTRY AND THE REICH CHAMBER OF CULTURE

In the *Gleichschaltung* process of cultural life, the Combat League for German Culture had played an essential role. Although since its founding in 1928, the league's leadership had succeeded in building up from its base in Munich an extensive network of local and professional groups and in increasing its membership to approximately 6,000 by 1933,[48] on the whole its political successes had stayed rather modest. Furthermore, due to mismanagement by executive officer Gotthard Urban, the Combat League was on the verge of bankruptcy at the end of 1932.[49] Only the National Socialist seizure of power brought the league back into play. The Berlin provincial leadership, under the direction of Hans Hinkel, "commissioner for special purposes" in the Prussian Culture

Ministry, now intervened vigorously in the personnel restructuring of the writers' associations as well as that of several other cultural institutions and organizations. At the same time, the executive committees of associations for cultural professions throughout Germany turned to the Combat League's leadership in order to carry out the *Gleichschaltung*.

Despite these manifold activities, the Combat League quickly lost any impact on cultural policy in the Third Reich. Even in 1933 it still had no official Party recognition, and consequently it acted without official NSDAP mandate and financial support. Also, Rosenberg distanced himself from Hans Hinkel, in effect paralyzing the league's largest and most important provincial leadership. Joseph Goebbels was the beneficiary of the political incompetence of Rosenberg and his Combat League troops. The Reich propaganda head of the NSDAP and *Gauleiter* of Berlin realized immediately that only a state office with executive powers could guarantee the effective implementation of political interests. After Hitler's nomination, Goebbels was appointed Reich minister for popular enlightenment and propaganda on 13 March 1933. By order of the Reich chancellor, the traditional Reich departments had to turn over many jurisdictions to the new ministry at the end of June, among them those for radio, press, theater, film, music, and literature.[50] On this legal foundation and with the income from the government's radio monopoly, Goebbels could gradually build up a ministry that over the years employed more than 500 staff members and in 1939 had a budget of 97 million Reichsmark (RM) at its disposal.[51] In addition, beginning in July 1933, the ministry oversaw 13 "provincial branches" (as of September, Reich Propaganda Offices), which were responsible for the implementation of ministry policy in their respective areas of jurisdiction and for the surveillance of the population's morale.

A further institution relevant to cultural politics that was connected with Goebbels' name was the Reich Chamber of Culture (RKK; Reichskulturkammer). This "public corporation" was established as a reaction to the efforts of the German Labor Front (DAF; Deutsche Arbeitsfront)—founded on 10 May 1933 after the smashing of the Free Trade Unions—to take over the cultural professions as well in its all-inclusive organization of employers and employees.[52] During August, Goebbels won Hitler over to his plan to consolidate all cultural professions under the roof of one professional institution, which was to manage artists' interests in allegedly "free self-governance," whose direction, however, Goebbels reserved for himself.[53] A Reich law passed on 22 September then established the Reich Chamber of Culture, consisting of chambers for literature, press, radio, theater, music, film, and visual arts.[54]

A comprehensive "Directive for the Execution of the Reich Culture Chamber Law"[55] enacted on 1 November 1933 made membership in one of the seven individual chambers compulsory for all of those individuals involved "in the creation, the reproduction, the intellectual or technical adaptation, the dissemination, the maintenance, the sale or the mediation of the sale of cultural assets" (section 4). The determining criterion for the "obligation to join the Chamber of Culture" was thus the close connection of cultural activity and the public. Here it was supposed to be inconsequential whether this activity occurred in a commercial or charitable context, or whether it was performed by individuals or groups of people, by citizens of the Reich or foreigners working in Germany, by self-employed individuals or employees (section 6). The presidents of the individual chambers had to admit or reject an applicant or expell a member on the basis of "reliability and suitability" (section 10). Above and beyond this, with the aid of "official announcements" and "directives," the presidents could set conditions for the licensing and direction of businesses, as well as for the conclusion of contractual agreements regarding work and entitlement laws (section 25). They could also impose "penalties" and authorize the involvement of police agencies (sections 28-29). An appeal against the decisions of the individual chambers could be filed with Goebbels, the president of the Reich Chamber of Culture. Since the arrangements for the Chamber of Culture law had prohibited any financial burden for the Reich, provinces, and municipalities, all the administrative costs arising in the individual chambers had to be financed through membership fees. Their payment was made compulsory, and their collection was administered as "public taxes" (sections 24 and 30).

In section 1 of the executive order of 1 November 1933, the Reichsverband der deutschen Schriftsteller e.V. had been declared to be a "public corporation" with the title Reich Literature Chamber.[56] Hans Friedrich Blunck assumed its presidency, and Dr. Heinz Wismann was appointed vicepresident. As a member of the Propaganda Ministry, Wismann was supposed to guarantee the close coordination of chamber and ministry policy. In the course of the RDS's transformation into the Gruppe Schriftsteller (Authors' Group) in the RSK on 1 October 1935 and as the result of the assignment of additional jurisdictions in literary policy during the 1930s, what initially was a rather modest staff grew into a swollen bureaucratic apparatus, financed essentially by the chamber members' compulsory contributions.[57] The Börsenverein was chiefly responsible for publishers and book dealers. However, because of its international involvement, it was again separated in October 1934 from the RSK and limited to dealing with purely economic tasks. The Börsenverein's place within the chamber's administration was taken by the newly founded League of Reich-German Book Dealers, which in turn dissolved on 1 October 1936 into the RSK's Gruppe Buchhandel (Book Trade Group) located in Leipzig.

RULE BY BUREAUCRACIES IN COMPETITION WITH ONE ANOTHER

Although the Propaganda Ministry and the Reich Chamber of Culture both fell within Goebbels' purview, by no means were they two harmoniously cooperating institutions. The main reason for this was that the overhasty establishment of the RKK presented the individual chambers with serious organizational problems. Most of the professional associations had been integrated into the individual chambers in 1933; not until the mid-1930s could they be dissolved and a uniform administrative structure set up. The chamber administrations, in which to some extent former association functionaries were now active as state employees, continued to advocate their members' interests, which led to frequent political conflicts with the ministry bureaucracy. Moreover, in the individual chambers, special interests prevailed that contravened the ministry's official policy.[58] The points of friction could be reduced but not entirely eliminated through an extensive reshuffling of jurisdictions; in April 1938, Goebbels restricted the chambers to looking after their "corporate" tasks, such as assisting authors in contract negotiations with publishers, while in future all cultural-political tasks were to be handled by the ministerial departments.

Such friction is especially clear concerning the agencies responsible for state literary policy. Although before he entered into politics Goebbels had plans to become a writer, neither in the Reich Propaganda leadership nor in the first plan for the division of responsibilities within the Propaganda Ministry was there a special department for literature. An auxiliary section in the "Propaganda" Department was responsible for the tasks involving literary policy that had been assumed from the Reich Interior Ministry. This section's head, Dr. Heinz Wismann, who had proved to be an active but discreet functionary during the phase of the *Gleichschaltung* of writers' and book dealers' advocacy associations, significantly expanded his range of activity for the first time with the establishment of the RSK. As vicepresident he supervised and determined the chamber's policy to a decisive degree.

At the beginning of 1934, Wismann attempted—with the minister's backing—to incorporate into the Propaganda Ministry the Reich Office for the Promotion of German Literature (Reichsstelle zur Förderung des deutschen Schrifttums), established in June 1933 by the staff of the KfdK. This plan, according to which the ministry would have acquired both the staff and the groundwork already accomplished in the KfdK office, was thwarted by Rosenberg's bitter opposition. But with the establishment of the Reich Literature Office (Reichsschrifttumsstelle) in June 1934 as an agency subordinate to the ministry, Wismann could lay claim to a stronger presence of the state executive in literary policy. In essence, the Reich Literature Office had the same charge as Rosenberg's office: the promotion of the "new" literature of the National Socialist state. Later, and as of April 1939 with the new name Werbe- und Beratungsamt für das deutsche Schrifttum (Promotion and Advisory Office for German Literature), Wismann's office often assisted the new ministerial department for literature, which was short on staff. Such work involved censorship, evaluations for paper allocations, book propaganda in Germany and abroad, and support of translations of German books in foreign languages. An additional leadership instrument under Wismann's direction was the Reichsarbeitsgemeinschaft für deutsche Buchwerbung (Reich Working Group for German Book Promotion), also formed in 1934, whose task was to prepare the Week of the German Book held since 1934 in the fall. Eventually, on 1 October 1934, Wismann also advanced to be head of the newly installed Literature Department (Schrifttumsabteilung) in the Propaganda Ministry.

Only three staff members handled the extensive field of operations that Wismann had reserved for this new Literature Department: the department head and only two official experts, who were responsible for all domestic and foreign literature questions as well as for libraries. The institutional expansion in 1934 created the foundation for the centralized state control and formation of literary policy—a foundation that could have been consolidated and extended through increased staffing and an expansion of responsibilities. Many factors explain why this goal was not realized by the end of the Third Reich.

For one thing, in May 1934, with the establishment of the Reich Ministry for Science, Education, and Popular Instruction, which Hitler himself had promoted, Goebbels lost responsibility for research libraries, the technical supervision of public libraries, and schoolbooks. Bernhard Rust proved to be a decidedly weak minister, but he had at his disposal a competent and assertive staff, which was able to ward off Goebbels' attempts to regain influence. Furthermore, the Reich Literature Chamber was subject to interventions by three *Reichsleiter*. Max Amann, director of the Eher Verlag, Reich leader for the NSDAP Press and president of the Reich Press Chamber, participated to quite a decisive degree in the determination of book trade policy through Wilhelm Baur, his protégé officiating in Leipzig. With support from Hanns Johst, who assumed the RSK presidency in October 1935 after Hans Friedrich Blunck had resigned under political pressure, Reichsführer-SS Heinrich Himmler channeled SD (Security Service) staff into the chamber administration.[59] And, initially as chief of staff in the Staff of the Führer's Deputy and then as the powerful head of the Party Chancellory of the NSDAP (as of May 1941), Martin Bormann intervened again and again in chamber policy.

The two most important official Party literature agencies also pursued special interests that contravened the state literary policy. The previously mentioned Reich Office for the Promotion of German Literature had evolved from the "book advisory office" established in 1932 in the KfdK's provincial directorate in Franconia. The establishment and development of the Reich Office had been possible only with the financial support of the Reich Propaganda and Interior ministries, the Börsenverein, as well as the support of the Langen-Müller Verlag in Munich. In order to represent the interests of the state ministries contributing to the Reich Office, Dr. Heinz Wismann from the Propaganda Ministry joined the longtime Combat League staff members Hans Hagemeyer, Dr. Rainer Schlösser, and Dr. Hellmuth Langenbucher in this agency's Reich directorate.[60] The declared goals of the Reich Office for the Promotion of German Literature were the purging of the book market of "decadent" literature from the "system period" and the propagation of "native" *(arteigen)* German literature. In principle, nothing changed in this set of tasks when the Reich Office had to be granted autonomy after Wismann's takeover attempt. In June 1934, it was integrated into Alfred Rosenberg's newly created agency Führer's Commissioner for the Entire Spiritual and Ideological Schooling and Education of the NSDAP. United with the Department for the Promotion of Literature (later the Office/Main Office Literature) within Rosenberg's agency, the Reich Office for the Promotion of German Literature was directed by Hans Hagemeyer.[61]

Until 1945, with an enormous staff consisting of Party employees at the *Reich, Gau,* and district level, honorary chief lectors, and regular lectors, Rosenberg's agency undertook a comprehensive examination of all German literature.[62] Yet its activities were not as binding as those of the RSK or the Propaganda Ministry. Rosenberg's literature office never achieved major influence over licensing of professional groups active in the area of literature or book censorship. However, by practicing an ideologically much more radical literary policy than that of Goebbels' ministry, Rosenberg's office could cause the state agencies difficulties with the authorities, which made concessions necessary. Furthermore, the evaluations by the Cultural-Political Archive affiliated with the Rosenberg agency could prevent public readings by certain authors in the leisure and educational institutions operated by the DAF or could incite the Gestapo and SD to act against politically "conspicuous" writers and book dealers.[63]

A "decree" by the Führer's deputy, Rudolf Hess, had established the Official Party Examination Commission for the Protection of National Socialist Literature (PPK, Parteiamtliche Prüfungskommission zum Schutze des NS-Schrifttums) in April 1934.[64] It was charged to keep track of and evaluate the

Konjunkturschrifttum (trend literature) about National Socialism that had been flooding the market since 1933. In order to reactivate the Reich executive manager of the NSDAP, who had become largely functionless in the central Party headquarters in Munich, the shrewd businessman Max Amann suggested that Philipp Bouhler be appointed the commission's "president." Amann's goal here was to stem the flood of publications on the Nazi movement and to have his own publishing house issue all important new publications.[65] This plan did not work out, and the PPK instead began to follow an autonomous course in literary policy. Reasons for this have to do with a way of reacting that is typical for bureaucracies in general but especially characteristic for the decision makers in the National Socialist ruling system: Once jurisdictions and administrative apparatuses had been acquired, they were not only defended against all opposition, but also plans were made to expand them step by step. Like Rosenberg, who at best could have laid claim to the examination of literature with respect to its applicability for the philosophical education of NSDAP members but in fact had his agency watch over the development of all German literature, Bouhler also extended his purview to all writings in National Socialist Germany. Here the PPK, in contrast to the Rosenberg Literature Office, had the advantage of having censorship authority, which Hitler recognized and repeatedly confirmed. Furthermore, Bouhler understood well how to secure and broaden his influence over the formation of literary policy through "working agreements" with other powerholders at the state and Party levels. The inevitable consequence of this development was that until the start of the war, the PPK's main as well as its subsidiary staff proceeded to grow without disruption, so that a fourth comprehensive literature bureaucracy came about.

Those offices acting on the state side—the Literature Chamber and the Literature Department within the Propaganda Ministry—had to deal with a long list of Party agencies. Among others, the Nazi Teachers' Organization, Reich Youth Leadership, Reich Women's Leadership, Reich Organizational Leadership of the NSDAP, the staff of the Führer's Deputy (later the Party Chancellory of the NSDAP), Reich Legal Office, Reich Food Authority, and the Office for Racial Policy all maintained their own respective departments or lector offices for literature.[66] The fact that the Propaganda Ministry's claim to the central direction of literary policy could be realized only partially was, however, not due just to the existence of competing powerholders and offices. Goebbels himself repeatedly gave his enemies the opportunity to criticize and settle open accounts. Thus the minister revealed considerable "deficits" in personnel policy. His department head, Wismann, who had held together and pulled the strings of the state literary policy since 1933, had to leave the ministry in August 1937, because he had remained married to a Jew until as late as 1934.

From his successor Karl Heinz Hederich, who in a merger of two offices in one person remained the acting head of the PPK, Goebbels expected the operations of the state and official Party literature bureaucracies to be unified. Yet once again, as early as October 1938, Goebbels had to part ways with Hederich, since through his claim to omnipotence the latter had gotten into disputes with Amann and Rosenberg as well as with the other departments within the Propaganda Ministry. Hederich's successor, Alfred-Ingemar Berndt, continued the expansion of the personnel and purview of the ministry's Literature Department. However, Berndt, who early on had recognized the department's bleak prospects, transferred back to the radio department in the fall of 1939. Only under Wilhelm Haegert, the former chief of staff of the Reich Propaganda Leadership and until 1937 the head of the ministry's propaganda department, a personnel consolidation set in as of the new year 1939/40.

Goebbels' regaining of power within the NSDAP's ruling circle enabled Haegert to strengthen the Literature Department's position over the course of the war. Due to his assertiveness in 1933, his intellect, and his ability to place himself in the limelight, the propaganda minister had gained many enemies. His affair with the film actress Lida Baarová, which had become public knowledge, the anti-Semitic pogroms in the night of 9 November 1938, which Goebbels had initiated, and the shifting of National Socialist policy to outward expansion had brought the minister, who had been so strong at the onset, to the political sidelines. Not until the juncture in the war of 1941/42, when the Führer again backed and was dependent on his chief propagandist, did Goebbels regain his old ability to succeed.

POLICY TOWARD WRITERS

When delineating the literary policy of state and Party agencies toward writers who had remained in Germany, two levels must be considered. In the first place, we have to consider the political goals and purposes of the different bureaucracies; in the second place, we must look at the writers' living and working conditions under the dictatorship. During the years 1933 to 1945, there was constant tension and interplay between these two levels.

Obviously the political control of authors affected their style of life. Writers were legally obligated to become RSK members. Whoever wanted to become a member of the RDS or, after its dissolution, of the "Authors Group" in the RSK, had to go through a bureaucratic admission process that required from each individual exact information about his or her political past, "racial extraction," publishing activity, and income. In addition, two references were required to attest to the applicant's personal integrity and professional suitability. The chamber administration subsequently increased the stringency of the conditions for RSK membership, and as of April 1938, the obtaining of a "certificate of political good conduct" from the local NSDAP *Gau* directorate became a permanent feature of the admission formalities. If any doubts arose in the process as to the applicant's political reliability, a supplemental evaluation was requested from the Gestapo. In fact, writers living in the jurisdiction of the Gestapo and SD offices, as well as the NSDAP's *Gau,* district, and local branch headquarters, were routinely placed under surveillance. But numerous case studies demonstrate that the evaluations did not always reflect the writer's actual attitude toward the Nazi regime. Moreover, often the chamber administration refused to follow up on negative evaluations from the police or Party agencies with an expulsion from the chamber—which repeatedly led to heated controversies between the state and Party bureaucracies involved.

Alongside the examination of the individual, which could lead to expulsion from the chamber and the concomitant prohibition on practice in the profession—in extreme cases even to confinement in prison or a concentration camp—came the surveillance of publications. The censorship process, which was developed in the 1930s (and will be covered in detail later), proved to be anything but consistent in practice: First, there were no personnel and organizational prerequisites for the introduction of precensorship of the German Reich's immense book production,[67] and second, in many cases the state literature bureaucracy practiced censorship after publication less strictly than the Party agencies wished it to be done.[68] An analysis of authors with indexed works demonstrates that the ban of one or several books by an author living in the German Reich did not necessarily entail expulsion from the RSK. Nevertheless, the book bans by the RSK or Propaganda Ministry and the Gestapo's regular confiscations, combined with many obvious attempts by Party groups and advocacy groups to influence the ban or the revision of individual books, created a climate of latent insecurity.

On the other hand, the state literature bureaucracy tried to put writers loyal to the regime in the service of the Nazi state's propagandist goals. In the course of 1934, the organization of domestic lectures was standardized by an Arbeitsgemeinschaft der literarischen Gesellschaften und Vortragsveranstalter (working group of literary societies and organizers of lectures) within the RSK. Following a series of restructurings, the Reich Literature Office (as of 1939 the Promotion and Advisory Office for German Literature) subordinate to the Propaganda Ministry was responsible for planning and carrying out authors' readings as of 1937. With "suggestion lists" issued annually between 1937 and

1943, "connection tables" to reading trips, free lecture and publishing house brochures, in part even with travel expenses and honoraria covered, the ministry tried to promote public readings by a carefully chosen group of authors. The Propaganda Ministry's selection of authors was, however, still too "liberal" for Rosenberg's Literature Office and for the German Adult Education Organization (Deutsches Volksbildungswerk), which was within Ley's sphere of influence. With a circle of authors selected according to much more stringent political criteria, in the mid-1930s, they therefore started to build up an extensive lecture network, which competed with the state-sponsored readings.

The deployment of German authors abroad, in contrast, remained the undisputed domain of the state literature bureaucracy. Since 1935, author readings regularly accompanied the Week of the German Book Abroad. Here the selection of the readers followed stricter political criteria than within the Reich borders. Between 1940 and 1943, "Literature Propaganda" was once more intensified by means of author readings and book exhibitions in friendly countries and occupied territories. Having arrived at the zenith of its power, National Socialist Germany made an effort in this period to establish itself as the leading cultural state in Europe. That authors, like all the other Muses, were to be used in the end as nothing more than hacks of the political rulers becomes obvious with the European Writers Association. It was founded in the fall of 1941—in the course of the Weimar Authors' Meeting, which since 1938 had been an annual supporting program for the opening of the Week of the German Book. Financed out of the Propaganda Ministry's budget, the association, presided over by Hans Carossa, was supposed to supersede the International PEN Club. Although several renowned authors, among them Felix Timmermans, Robert Brasillach, Pierre Drieu la Rochelle, John Knittel, and Ernesto Giménez Caballero, placed themselves at the association's disposal, with hardly more than 30 members it could not establish an independent existence and disappeared from sight in 1943.

The question remains whether National Socialist literary policy led to any positive results. If at all, they would, at best, be found in what was designated "corporate support" through the RSK. The RDS, which in 1933 had formed the germ cell of the RSK, brought to the chamber numerous demands for the improvement of its members' legal, economic, and social situations—demands that to a large extent had already been made by the organization that had preceded the RDS, the SDS. Among the few successes the corporate advocacy of the writers was able to claim is the standardized publishing contract put into effect by the RSK at the beginning of June 1935, after tough negotiations between the authors' and publishers' sides. On the other hand, the efforts to effect a fundamental reform of copyright and publishing rights fell short of their goal during the war. And in the case of the "standard contract for the acquisition of worldwide filming rights to a previously published work of literature" introduced in November 1943, the economic interests of the film lobby in the Propaganda Ministry prevailed over the RSK's demands for a stronger consideration of the authors' legal and financial claims.

Things did not seem much better with respect to the efforts to improve authors' incomes. The RSK's annual contribution lists, calculated on the basis of a member's gross earnings,[69] indicate that the majority had to be content with a living wage. That writers also were hardly better off economically under National Socialism than they were in the Weimar Republic was at first mainly the result of cutbacks in the cultural sector that went into effect in September 1936 after Hitler's announcement of the second four-year plan.[70] During the war, authors increasingly became the victims of the drastically limited production and distribution of books, due to the shortage of paper, reductions in personnel, and the closing and destruction of publishing houses.

The chamber delegated the time-honored Deutsche Schillerstiftung (German Schiller Foundation) in Weimar to handle the economic distress of many writers; the organization already existed in peacetime and then grew during the war. In order to reduce the burden on the foundation's budget to only such authors who could be utilized for the "spiritual fortification of the home front," starting in 1941, the draft exemptions for a considerable number of RSK members who were active writers were canceled, and they were sent to military service or work in armaments factories.[71] Whereas the welfare payments never rose above the level of alms provided by the state, with political criteria also determining the disposition, the project for old age pensions got bogged down in the bureaucratic mills. In early 1934, the RDS had proposed that the chamber act on the pension plan, and at the opening ceremony for the Week of the German Book in the fall of 1938, Goebbels personally assumed the role of advocate for state-regulated social security for writers in their old age.[72] But this lofty plan never progressed beyond official memoranda and discussions.

The ways in which writers behaved with respect to state and official Party literary policy varied greatly. Hanns Johst and Hans Friedrich Blunck, for instance, used their prominent positions to increase their book sales.[73] Alongside of them stood a guard of devout Nazi apologists, who in and with their works gave eloquent expression to the powerholders' political goals: These writers included Heinrich Anacker, Bruno Brehm, Edwin Erich Dwinger, Kurt Eggers, Herybert Menzel, Agnes Miegel, Wilhelm Pleyer, Gerhard Schumann, and Hans Zöberlein.[74] Membership in the NSDAP alone, however, by no means guaranteed state and official Party support, as shown by Will Vesper's example. After a polemical confrontation in 1934, the author was persona non grata with the

Rosenberg office.[75] And because of the paper shortage, in 1943 Vesper's National Socialist journal *Die neue Literatur* was abruptly merged with the *Europäische Literatur,* published by the Deutscher Verlag, with Vesper, its founder and editor, receiving no further consideration.[76] Other authors, such as Gottfried Benn, Arnolt Bronnen, and Hanns Heinz Ewers, who had served the National Socialists in the beginning phase fell into disfavor in the mid-1930s.[77]

Another group of writers, who had been close to the right of the Party spectrum during the Weimar Republic, suddenly wound up at odds with Nazi cultural policy. Led by Hans Grimm, the author of the colonial novel *Volk ohne Raum* (1926), the "elite" of the nationalistic-conservative authors had been meeting annually in Lippoldsberg since 1934. As of 1936 they constituted a demonstrative counterweight to the band of authors convened in Weimar by the RSK and the Propaganda Ministry. Among the participants at these Lippoldsberger Authors' Meetings were Paul Alverdes, Rudolf G. Binding, Friedrich Bischoff, Hans Carossa, Joachim von der Goltz, Benno von Mechow, Ernst von Salomon, Rudolf Alexander Schröder, and August Winnig.[78] The meetings came to a sudden end after the propaganda minister, who was worried about his leadership role in German literature, threatened Grimm with Ernst Wiechert's fate in the event that Grimm continued his "sectarian" engagement.[79] Because he had openly declared his solidarity with Pastor Martin Niemöller, who had been arrested for speaking out against Hitler's policies in his sermons, Wiechert, too, had been arrested by the Gestapo in 1938. After two months of prison confinement, he was held in Buchenwald Concentration Camp from the beginning of July until the end of August.[80] If one lacked the appropriate protection, as say Gottfried Benn and Ernst Jünger possessed,[81] the limits of one's rejection of National Socialism and simultaneous retreat to a safe private niche could be reached very quickly. The ruling system's ambivalence becomes obvious in the fact that Wiechert's exemplary "punishment" for his "disobedience" had no effect on the publication of his books, the old ones as well as the new.[82]

It is especially difficult to assess the authors who are considered part of the so-called inner emigration, because the range of forms of conduct in opposition to state and official Party policy was extraordinarily varied.[83] Oskar Loerke, lector at the S. Fischer Verlag, or the religiously oriented authors Theodor Haecker and Reinhold Schneider, resolutely withdrew from public life, without, however, giving up their publishing activity.[84] Frank Thiess, who after the war portrayed himself in a dispute with Thomas Mann as one of the protagonists of "inner emigration,"[85] understood quite well from the beginning how to adapt his book publications to the altered political conditions and how to mobilize state authorities against demands for bans from official Party literature agencies.[86]

At first most Jewish writers were still accepted into the RSK, since the propaganda minister had omitted an "Aryan paragraph" in the RKK law for reasons of foreign policy and in consideration of the artists of international stature who had assumed the presidencies of the individual chambers in November 1933. However, after Goebbels had expressed the view at the Chamber of Culture meeting of 7 February 1934 that "a Jewish contemporary in general [was] unsuitable to administer Germany's cultural assets,"[87] by the end of 1935 all "non-Aryan" authors were expelled from the RSK and new applications were uniformly refused. Since from 1935/36 on the RSK demanded from its members and their spouses a "certification of Aryan heritage" going back to 1800, this "problem group" rapidly widened. The "Jewish-related" author Stefan Andres took refuge in the remote Italian town Positano as of 1938,[88] whereas Jochen Klepper remained in Berlin in spite of his Jewish wife. On the basis of his successful novel *Der Vater* (1937), which even National Socialist newspapers had reviewed positively, he obtained a "special permit" from the RSK for his continued work.[89] Werner Bergengruen, too, who was married to a "three-quarter Jewess," was issued such a permit, for which the consent of the RKK president—Goebbels—was required.[90] Elisabeth Langgässer and Mascha Kaléko, on the other hand, lost the possibility to publish their works in 1936 as a result of a chamber directive.[91]

While as of 1933 Erich Kästner could sell his former best-sellers only abroad and otherwise—with the exception of the screenplay for the Ufa film *Münchhausen* (1943)—had to write for the drawer,[92] the "*Asphaltliterat*" (decadent, metropolitan man of letters) Hans Fallada retained unrestricted opportunities for work, despite constant objections by Vesper and Rosenberg.[93] Ernst Glaeser, Gerhard Pohl, and Walter Bauer, who until the early 1930s had been close to the KPD, the Bund proletarisch-revolutionärer Schriftsteller (League of Proletarian-Revolutionary Authors), and the League for Human Rights and whose works consequently had been indexed after 1933 on the "List of Harmful and Undesirable Literature," were not expelled from the RSK, in spite of serious "scruples" in the National Socialist administrative apparatus.[94] For Axel Eggebrecht, who had even been sent to a concentration camp in 1933 for his involvement with the *Weltbühne,* for Erich Ebermayer and numerous other leftist intellectuals from the Weimar Republic, film and the screenplays necessary for it became the "place of refuge."[95] Günter Weisenborn, who belonged to the resistance circle Rote Kapelle and therefore had already been arrested by the Gestapo in 1942 "on suspicion," was even permitted to write dramas during his imprisonment.[96]

The young generation of authors, whose emergence on the scene is normally associated with the early phase of literature in the Federal Republic and the former German Democratic Republic, already had their first publication opportunities in the Third Reich. These authors included Alfred Andersch, Johannes Bobrowski, Günter Eich, Peter Huchel, Marie-Luise Kaschnitz, Wolfgang Koeppen, Hans-Erich Nossack, Herbert Reinecker, Luise Rinser, Ernst Schnabel, Wolfdietrich Schnurre, and Wolfgang Weyrauch, among others.[97] Karl Krolow, who had just turned 27, informed the RSK on 8 March 1942: "The start of my work with large-circulation German newspapers is to be expected. In addition, I have entered into negotiations with a publishing house for a book publication. I therefore consider my application with the request for acceptance to be absolutely necessary."[98]

POLICY IN THE AREA OF BOOK TRADE

In the first two years of National Socialist rule, Germany's publishing industry and book trade institutions had been fundamentally transformed. The Communist and Social Democratic publishing houses had either fled into exile in time or had been expropriated for the benefit of National Socialist enterprises. The large-scale publishing empire of the Deutscher Handlungsgehilfen Verband (German Clerks' Union), which comprised among others the Langen-Müller Verlag in Munich and the Hanseatische Verlagsanstalt in Hamburg, was snatched up by the DAF as the new unified trade union.[99] The "purging" of the book market and libraries, carried out by diverse authorities, and by no means limited to the students' "Aktion wider den undeutschen Geist" (action against the un-German spirit) of spring 1933, endangered the economic substance of many publishing houses and bookstores. Max Amann booted out the owners of the Ullstein combine and for a ridiculously low price assimilated the economically strongest publishing enterprise in the German Reich into the Eher Verlag in 1934.[100] At the same time, Amann embarked on a policy of concentration and monopolization, showing just as little restraint when the Party's own publishing houses were concerned as he did with Jewish and religious ones. Lending libraries, declared by the Börsenverein to be one of the main enemies of the traditional book trade, were subjected by the RSK to strict licensing, regimentation, and continual surveillance by the SD and Gestapo. Starting in 1934, the chamber gradually forced dealers of travel books and publishers of popular literature, books on astrology, graphology, the occult, of technical literature, and of directories and advertising books to submit their books currently in production to state "advisory offices."[101]

Notwithstanding these rigid interventions, the policy of the state literature bureaucracy toward the book trade remained ambivalent. Compared with the treatment of authors, the RSK initially applied the instrument of professional licensing much more prudently and in a more differentiated manner. Even publishers such as Ernst Rowohlt and Gustav Kiepenheuer, whose production from the Weimar period had been almost completely banned in 1933, obtained through the membership in the League of Reich-German Book Dealers the possibility for continued work. Like Rowohlt and Kiepenheuer, former members of the "leftist fringe," Wilhelm Goldmann, a publisher of popular literature, could survive by adapting his publishing program to the altered political circumstances. Whereas Jewish book salespeople and lectors had already been expelled from the RSK by 1935, "non-Aryan" publishers and book dealers were not finally excluded until 1938.[102] Aided by the Propaganda Ministry's Literature Department, Gottfried Bermann-Fischer could sell his father-in-law's publishing house at the end of 1936 under relatively favorable terms, transfer to Vienna the publications that had been banned in Germany, and take a part of his authors' rights to his newly established publishing enterprise there.[103] At the head of the S. Fischer Verlag KG remaining in Germany came Peter Suhrkamp, who attempted to carry on the firm's literary tradition and was not sympathetic to National Socialism.

Humanitarian motives were not the reason for surprising decisions made in particular cases. Rather the Propaganda Ministry aimed to maintain the semblance of a cultural diversity that could be exhibited both at home and abroad; and in conjunction with the Reich Ministry of Economics, the ministry also had a special interest in not endangering the economic basis of the German book trade, which included maintaining jobs and securing book exports. The economic consolidation of the German book trade, which had been shaken by the worldwide Depression, thus is one of the greatest successes of the state literary policy after 1933. From 1938 on and then especially during the Second World War, most German publishing and book trade enterprises recorded rapidly increasing returns, due to a boom aided not only by the immense rearmament program, together with the population's increased buying power, but also by massive state advertising campaigns and subsidies for the book economy.

Thus the Day of the Book, which the Reich Interior Ministry had sponsored since 1929, was expanded into the Week of the German Book after the Propaganda Ministry took over jurisdiction for literary policy. Held annually in the fall starting 1934, this week-long event represented a clever synthesis of economic and political propaganda, which was hidden behind Goebbels' often-repeated motto "Mit dem Buch ins Volk" (with the book to the people). Increased book sales and an enhanced reader interest guaranteed, of course, not only an improved cash flow for publishing, retail, and book trade companies, but likewise the dissemination of the National Socialist ideology contained in the promoted books. The same ambivalent mechanism was operating in the "Promotion of Technical Books," which was intensified by the state literature agencies every spring since 1935. Besides the technical book publishing houses, the technical professional sectors, the main target of this advertising, profited from further training by means of literature. Their increase in productivity, in turn, was supposed to benefit rearmament policy directly and indirectly. The long-term effect of these two national promotion campaigns was reinforced by extensive reporting in the daily press, radio, and specialized journals, as well as by the publication of lists of literature "worth recommending," which had been compiled in the Propaganda Ministry's Reich Literature Office. From 1935 until 1943, through the newly established economic office for the German book trade,[104] a considerable amount of state funding went to the stimulation of book exports, to book exhibitions at home and abroad, the expansion of public, school libraries, and research libraries, and to the establishment of front-line book dealerships, translation agencies, and German book dealerships in occupied foreign countries.

Yet the state continued to intervene in the production and sale of books. To be sure, it never succeeded in setting up universal preventive censorship according to the Soviet Union's model. But by 1936, the Propaganda Ministry had managed to centralize within its jurisdiction post-publication censorship. The *Liste des schädlichen und unerwünschten Schrifttums* (List of Harmful and Undesirable Literature), which as of 1935 was initially administered in the RSK and then as of 1 April 1938 in the Propaganda Ministry's Literature Department, was compiled in the Deutsche Bücherei in Leipzig from 1938 until February 1945. Since a directive of 20 September 1935 signed by Goebbels made it compulsory to provide the Deutsche Bücherei a copy of every newly printed work "within one week of its publication," the state literature bureaucracy could—when necessary—conduct a relatively complete examination of German-language publications, including the literature published in exile.

Independent of the Propaganda Ministry, the Gestapo, the SD, Rosenberg's Literature Office, and the PPK also undertook the routine surveillance of the book market. In particular, the PPK, which under the pretext of protecting National Socialist ideas included more and more types of literature in its purview, made frequent use of its censorship authority. The staff of Bouhler's agency even went so far as to write articles on the topic of National Socialism for lexical reference works such as the Brockhaus encyclopedia and *Meyers Lexikon*. And finally, in several individual cases Hitler himself also intervened in the area of censorship with directives for book bans, disregarding the official channels Goebbels had established.[105]

Although the marketing laws for the book trade were adhered to in principle even under National Socialism, again and again the primacy of politics showed through. In 1934/35, the head of the Propaganda Ministry's Literature Department achieved the regulation of the export matters against opposition from the executive board of the Börsenverein. That Wismann's mistrust of book traders was still deep-seated in 1937 can be seen in the "special assignment" he gave to the former RSK executive manager Gunther Haupt. Haupt was to examine the inventory and the catalogs of the most important German retail companies. As a result of his extensive investigations in Leipzig and Stuttgart, the "special commissioner" proposed that the wholesale bookstores Koehler & Volckmar and Koch & Neff & Oettinger be put under direct state control.[106] Wismann's downfall in June 1937 was one reason this situation never occurred. Another reason was that the Koehler & Volckmar combine's legal position was so unassailable and presumably its backing in influential circles in the economy so strong that, at the end of 1937, its head, Theodor Volckmar-Frentzel, could even ward off the attempt by RSK president Johst to expel him from the Literature Chamber.[107]

The Eher combine would have profited especially from Volckmar-Frentzel's expulsion.[108] Because of Max Amann's excellent relationship to Hitler, his double function as president of the Reich Press Chamber and *Reichsleiter* for the NSDAP Press, and because of the power position of his protégé Wilhelm Baur in the chief office for the book trade in Leipzig, the Central Party Publishing House could, over the course of the 1930s, carry out a process of monopolization that was unprecedented in the history of the German book trade. The purchase of the Ullstein Verlag, which with its approximately 8,000 employees and a business turnover of approximately 50 million RM surpassed the Eher Verlag many times over,[109] had been only a prelude to a spectacular series of acquisitions. A confidential list from April 1943 names no less than 37 publishing houses.[110] Alongside a series of Nazi *Gau* publishing houses are included such respected names as the Deutsche Verlagsanstalt, Frankfurter Societätsdruckerei GmbH, Rowohlt Verlag GmbH, Knorr & Hirth KG, and Albert Langen-Georg Müller Verlag GmbH. During the war the Amann Trust succeeded in establishing a monopoly on the book, periodical, and newspaper market in the occupied territories as well.[111] Eventually, in early September 1944, it purchased Hugenberg's August Scherl GmbH. Already in 1939 the Central Party Publishing House had advanced to be the German Reich's largest economic enterprise.[112] However, Amann never eliminated the Koehler & Volckmar combine and gained control of the intermediate book trade. In any case, despite an enormous amount of favoritism through Wilhelm Baur's chamber policy, the company Lühe & Co., set up in Leipzig, was not able to force these venerable wholesale book dealers out of the market.

In spite of paper rationing, introduced at the beginning of war and administered by the economic office of the German book trade in the area of book production,[113] publishing houses and retail bookstores could largely satisfy the significantly increased demand for books up until 1941. But a clearly perceptible strain on internal resources set in with the invasion of the Soviet Union on 22 June. At first work in the publishing and book trade sectors was impaired by transfer of personnel to the military and armaments production fields. Then the scarcity of paper and binding materials, which was becoming noticeable as of 1942, led to serious bottlenecks. Bitter battles were waged in the economic office of the German book trade over the remaining rationed resources. Next to scholarly production, it was primarily political literature, for which the state authorities, the military, and Party agencies knew how to procure the paper that had become scarce.[114]

Nevertheless, up until 1944, a continually abundant cultural life even in the middle of the war remained a popular topos in the National Socialist propaganda that was supposed to maintain faith in the political leadership and to strengthen the public fighting morale. While the Rosenberg agency already had been organizing the NSDAP's book collection for the Wehrmacht every winter since 1939,[115] the state literature bureaucracy claimed the fulfillment of the German population's reading needs as its contribution to the strengthening of the "inner front." "Rest and relaxation" after "this year's colossal accomplishments" and after "a strenuous day's work" were the slogans issued by the literature functionaries Wilhelm Haegert and Wilhelm Baur for the winter 1941/42.[116] They appealed to German book dealers to open their reduced book stocks "above all" to the "German soldier," to the "German armaments worker," and to the "German women working in the factories," because they "today can make a claim before others to the values and powers of German culture."[117]

These demands might have looked good on paper, but in practice they presented the RSK with enormous organizational problems. In many cases, as victims of bombings, the companies in the book trade and publishing branch themselves needed support from the chamber before they could provide the population with reading material. For this purpose, approximately 300 book reserves were being set up in Leipzig as of 1943 through a 10 percent contribution from the publishers' production. Each reserve contained a maximum of 1,800 volumes, upon which bombed-out retail bookstores and lending libraries could draw without cost to rebuild their sales and lending distribution. From these same reserves the RSK pumped numerous books into book trade centers and areas of industrial concentration that had been destroyed by aerial warfare.[118]

The consequence of continually decreasing production and delivery capacities was a concentration of enterprises, which was accelerated by the destruction of the book trade centers Leipzig, Berlin, and Stuttgart. Moreover, because of Goebbels' proclamation of the "total war effort" in his speech of 30 January 1943 at the Berlin Sport Palace, he was forced to take appropriate steps.[119] In order to release reserves for the military and provide workers for the armaments industry, his Propaganda Ministry now considered extensive plant shutdowns. Due to objections raised by the RSK, as well as the involvement of Reich Propaganda offices, *Gau* leaderships, and provincial economic offices, the closings that actually took place varied greatly according to region; however, in every case they were much more moderate than originally planned.[120] More extensive shutdowns did not come until Hitler had appointed Goebbels on 20 July 1944 to be Reich Plenipotentiary for the Total War Effort. As of 1 September 1944, the entire travel and mail-order book trade had to be shut down, the wholesale book trade and lending libraries were drastically reduced, at least 50 percent of the workforce in retail book trade had to be cut back, and the publishing enterprises were reduced to a core component of approximately 220 companies.[121]

At a time when the curtain was falling over cultural life in Germany, in the state literature bureaucracy alone more than 100 employees were still carrying out their official duties,[122] and Rosenberg's agency and Bouhler's Examination Commission were waging a bitter struggle in the Party Chancellory over jurisdictions and staff sizes.[123] Those people "producing culture," in contrast, received the following curt notice in October 1944 from the head of the "organization" department in the Reich Chamber of Culture's main executive: "For its part, art is at this time neither absolutely nor relatively necessary. In the present stage of the war there is thus no other duty for the German artist but to work directly for the achievement of final victory, either as a soldier or an aid in the fortification, in the maintenance of our Reich's defensive capability."[124]

Notes

*When not otherwise indicated, the following analysis is based on the findings of my dissertation "Literaturpolitik im 'Dritten Reich.' Institutionen, Kompetenzen, Betätigungsfelder," in *Archiv für Geschichte des Buchwesens* (Frankfurt/Main: Buchhändler-Vereinigung, 1993)(hereafter cited as *AGB*).

1. *Akten der Partei-Kanzlei der NSDAP. Rekonstruktion eines verlorengegangenen Bestandes. Sammlung der in anderen Provenienzen überlieferten Korrespondenzen, Niederschriften von Besprechungen usw. mit dem Stellvertreter*

des Führers und seinem Stab bzw. der Partei-Kanzlei, ihren Ämtern, Referaten und Unterabteilungen sowie mit Heß und Bormann persönlich, ed. Institut für Zeitgeschichte. Teil I: Regesten, Bd. 1/Bd. 2; Register Bd. 1/2, Microfiche-Edition, Bd. 1/2 (München: K. G. Saur, 1983).

2. Dietrich Strothmann, *Nationalsozialistische Literaturpolitik. Ein Beitrag zur Publizistik im Dritten Reich* (Bonn: Bouvier, 1960).
3. Joseph Wulf, *Literatur und Dichtung im Dritten Reich. Eine Dokumentation* (Gütersloh: Sigbert Mohn, 1963).
4. Hans-Dieter Schäfer, *Das gespaltene Bewußtsein. Über deutsche Kultur und Lebenswirklichkeit 1933-1945* (München: Carl Hanser Verlag, 1981).
5. Two exceptions are the memoirs of the former head of the Callwey Verlag, Karl Baur, *Wenn ich so zurückdenke . . . Ein Leben als Verleger in bewegter Zeit* (München: Deutscher Taschenbuch Verlag, 1985), pp. 179-346, and Heinz Sarkowski, *Der Springer Verlag. Stationen seiner Geschichte. Teil I: 1842-1945* (Berlin: Springer Verlag, 1992), pp. 325-83.
6. Dietrich Aigner, "Die Indizierung 'schädlichen und unerwünschten Schrifttums' im Dritten Reich," Frankfurt/Main: Buchhändler-Vereinigung, 1971 (Separate publication from the journal *Archiv für Geschichte des Buchwesens*; hereafter cited as *AGB).*
7. Volker Dahm, *Das jüdische Buch im Dritten Reich,* 2 Bde., (Frankfurt/Main: Buchhändler-Vereinigung, 1979/1982) (Separate publication from the *AGB).*
8. Siegfried Lokatis, "Politisches Buchmarketing im Dritten Reich," *AGB* 38 (1992): 1-189.
9. Michael Kast, "Der deutsche Leihbuchhandel und seine Organisation im 20. Jahrhundert," *AGB* 36 (1991): 165-349.
10. Peter Vodosek and Manfred Komorowski, eds., *Bibliotheken während des Nationalsozialismus,* Teil I (Wiesbaden: O. Harrassowitz, 1989).
11. Engelbrecht Boese, *Das Öffentliche Bibliothekswesen im Dritten Reich* (Bad Honnef: Bock & Herchen, 1987); "Die Säuberung der Leipziger Bücherhallen 1933-1936," *Buch und Bibliothek* 35 (1983): 283-96; "Die Bestandspolitik der Öffentlichen Büchereien im Dritten Reich," *Bibliotheksdienst* 17 (1983): 263-82. Supplementary material can be found in Friedrich Andrae, ed. and comp., *Volksbücherei und Nationalsozialismus. Materialien zu Theorie und Praxis des öffentlichen Büchereiwesens in Deutschland 1933-1945* (Wiesbaden: O. Harrassowitz, 1970).
12. Hans-Gerd Happel, *Das wissenschaftliche Bibliothekswesen im Nationalsozialismus. Unter besonderer Berücksichtigung der Universitätsbibliotheken* (München: K. G. Saur, 1989).
13. The first contributions in this area can be found in the anthology *Bibliotheken während des Nationalsozialismus,* as well as in the study by Ingo Toussaint, *Die*

Universitätsbibliothek Freiburg im Dritten Reich, 2nd corrected and expanded ed. (München: K. G. Saur, 1984).

14. Peter Gay, *Weimar Culture: The Outsiders as Insiders* (New York: Harper & Row, 1968).

15. On this context, see among others Karl Dietrich Bracher, *Die Auflösung der Weimarer Republik. Eine Studie zum Problem des Machtverfalls in der Demokratie* (Villingen: Ring-Verlag, 1971); and Hans Mommsen, *Die verspielte Freiheit. Der Weg der Republik von Weimar in den Untergang 1918-1933* (Berlin: Propyläen, 1989).

16. Cf. Gerhard Paul, *Aufstand der Bilder. Die NS-Propaganda vor 1933* (Bonn: J. H. W. Dietz Nachf., 1990).

17. On the founding and activity of the KfdK, see Hildegard Brenner, *Die Kunstpolitik des Nationalsozialismus* (Reinbek bei Hamburg: Rowohlt, 1963), pp. 7-21, and Reinhard Bollmus, *Das Amt Rosenberg und seine Gegner. Studien zum Machtkampf im nationalsozialistischen Herrschaftssystem* (Stuttgart: Deutsche Verlags-Anstalt, 1970), pp. 27-39.

18. See Heidrun Holzbach, *Das 'System Hugenberg.' Die Organisation bürgerlicher Sammlungspolitik vor dem Aufstieg des Nationalsozialismus* (Stuttgart: Deutsche Verlags-Anstalt, 1981).

19. On this topic, see John Willet, *The New Sobriety, Art and Politics in the Weimar Period, 1917-1933* (New York: Pantheon, 1978); Klaus Petersen, *Literatur und Justiz in der Weimarer Republik* (Stuttgart: Metzler, 1988); and Jan-Pieter Barbian, "Filme mit Lücken. Die Lichtspielzensur in der Weimarer Republik: von der sozialethischen Schutzmaßnahme zum politischen Instrument," in *Der deutsche Film von den Anfängen bis zur Gegenwart,* ed. Uli Jung (Trier: Wissenschaftlicher Verlag Trier, 1993), pp. 51-78.

20. For the details of this, see Karl Dietrich Bracher, Gerhard Schulz and Wolfgang Sauer, *Die nationalsozialistische Machtergreifung. Studien zur Errichtung des totalitären Herrschaftssystems in Deutschland 1933-1934,* 3 vols., 2nd rev. ed. (Köln: Westdeutscher Verlag, 1962); Martin Broszat, *Der Staat Hitlers. Grundlegung und Entwicklung seiner inneren Verfassung* (München: Deutscher Taschenbuch Verlag, 1969); Hans-Ulrich Thamer, *Verführung und Gewalt. Deutschland 1933-1945* (Berlin: Siedler, 1986), pp. 231-336; and Norbert Frei, *Der Führerstaat. Nationalsozialistische Herrschaft 1933-1945* (München: Deutscher Taschenbuch Verlag, 1987), pp. 38-85.

21. *Reichsgesetzblatt* (hereafter cited as *RGBL),* Teil I, No. 8 of 6 February 1933, pp. 35-40, and No. 17 of 28 February 1933, p. 83.

22. On this see Hans Mommsen, *Beamtentum im Dritten Reich. Mit ausgewählten Quellen zur nationalsozialistischen Beamtenpolitik* (Stuttgart: Deutsche Verlags-Anstalt, 1966), pp. 39-61.

23. For the text of the laws, see *RGBL*, Teil I, No. 55 of 27 May 1933, p. 293, and No. 81 of 15 July 1933, pp. 479-80. For the context, see Oron J. Hale, *Presse in der Zwangsjacke 1933-1945*, trans. from the English by W. and M. Pferdekamp (Düsseldorf: Droste, 1965), pp. 68-82.
24. The numbers are from Horst Möller, *Exodus der Kultur. Schriftsteller, Wissenschaftler und Künstler in der Emigration nach 1933* (München: C. H. Beck, 1984), p. 38.
25. Karl Dietrich Bracher, *Die deutsche Diktatur. Entstehung, Struktur, Folgen des Nationalsozialismus* (Köln: Kiepenheuer & Witsch, 1970), p. 272.
26. On the following cf. Hildegard Brenner, *Ende einer bürgerlichen Kunst-Institution. Die politische Formierung der Preußischen Akademie der Künste ab 1933* (Stuttgart: Deutsche Verlags-Anstalt, 1972); Inge Jens, *Dichter zwischen rechts und links. Die Geschichte der Sektion für Dichtkunst an der Preußischen Akademie der Künste, dargestellt nach den Dokumenten* (München: Deutscher Taschenbuch Verlag, 1979), pp. 189-228; and Walter Huder, "Die sogenannte Reinigung. Die 'Gleichschaltung' der Sektion für Dichtkunst der Preußischen Akademie der Künste 1933," *Exilforschung* 4 (1986): 144-59.
27. On Johst's transition from ambitious expressionist author to National Socialist propagandist, see Helmut F. Pfanner, *Hanns Johst. Vom Expressionismus zum Nationalsozialismus* (The Hague: Mouton, 1970).
28. Cited from the version corrected by Max von Schillings, in Brenner, pp. 58-59. The final sentence in Benn's version reads: " . . . and obligates you to loyal collaboration on the tasks of the nation incumbent upon the Academy according to the statues."
29. No detailed account of the German PEN-Zentrum during the Weimar Republic and of its *Gleichschaltung* in 1933 has yet been provided. For further information see the supporting material in Barbian, pp. 32-36.
30. Bollmus, p. 39. On the biography of Hinkel, who starting in 1933 rose to be one of the most influential people in the National Socialist cultural bureaucracy, see Bollmus, p. 264, n. 76; as well as Willi A. Boelcke, ed., *Kriegspropaganda 1939-1941: Geheime Ministerkonferenzen im Reichspropagandaministerium* (Stuttgart: Deutsche Verlags-Anstalt, 1966), pp. 85-88.
31. This press announcement of 24 April 1933 about the resolution of the meeting of the general membership of the German PEN-Zentrum the day before is cited in the exhibition catalog *Der deutsche PEN-Club im Exil 1933-1945. Eine Ausstellung der Deutschen Bibliothek Frankfurt am Main*, eds. Werner Berthold and Brita Eckert (Frankfurt/Main: Buchhändler-Vereinigung, 1980), p. 11.
32. "An die Schriftsteller aller Länder! Aufruf der 'Union nationaler Schriftsteller,'" *Völkischer Beobachter*, Berliner Ausgabe, No. 60 (1 March 1934).

33. On the formation, development, and politics of the SDS see the well-founded study by Ernst Fischer, "Der 'Schutzverband Deutscher Schriftsteller' 1909-1933," *AGB* 21 (1980): 1-666.
34. Letter by Ewers to the RSK 10 June 1940, here enclosure 1 "Betrifft: Mein Verhältnis zur Schrifttumskammer," p. 2, in Ewers' RSK personnel file at the Berlin Document Center (hereafter RSK personnel files will be cited as BDC/RSK followed by the author's name).
35. Ewers, "Mein Verhältnis zur Schrifttumskammer."
36. BDC/RSK/Götz Otto Stoffregen.
37. Quote from the RDS guidelines in Fischer, p. 625.
38. *Börsenblatt für den Deutschen Buchhandel* (hereafter cited as *BBl.*), 100, No. 101 (3 May 1933), Redaktioneller Teil: 321-22. The "immediate program" is signed by Friedrich Oldenbourg, Heinrich Boysen, Hellmut von Hase, Paul Nitschmann, Friedrich Alt, Herbert Hoffmann, Albert Diederich, and Ernst Reinhardt.
39. *BBl.*, p. 322.
40. *BBl.* 100, No. 110 (13 May 1933), Redaktioneller Teil.
41. For details see: StA Würzburg/Reichsstudentenführung, Aktenfaszikel I*21 C14/1-4 und IV*1*60/1-4; as well as Hans-Wolfgang Strätz, "Die geistige SA rückt ein. Die studentische 'Aktion wider den undeutschen Geist' im Frühjahr 1933," *Vierteljahrshefte für Zeitgeschichte* 16 (1968): 347-72 (hereafter cited as *VfZG*); Gerhard Sauder, ed., *Die Bücherverbrennung. Zum 10. Mai 1933* (München: Hanser, 1983); and Horst Denkler and Eberhard Lämmert, eds., *"Das war ein Vorspiel nur . . ." Berliner Colloquium zur Literaturpolitik im "Dritten Reich"* (Berlin: Akademie der Künste, 1985).
42. *BBl.* 100, No. 112 (16 May 1933): 355.
43. Ibid., No. 114 (18 May 1933): 361. The Action Committee confirmed on 15 May 1933 by the general meeting of the Börsenverein consisted of Friedrich Oldenbourg together with the National Socialist book dealers and publishers Martin Riegel, Karl Baur, Theodor Fritsch Junior, in addition to Dr. Heinz Wismann from the Propaganda Ministry.
44. For the details of these events, see Staatsarchiv Leipzig (hereafter cited as StA Leipzig)/Börsenverein der deutschen Buchhändler (BV) F 6884.
45. For the details, see *BBl.* 101, No. 224 (25 September 1934): 833-38.
46. BDC/NSDAP Master file/Wilhelm Baur: He was first admitted into the Party on 22 November 1920 (No. 2430) and readmitted after the ban of the NSDAP on 21 March 1925 (No. 51).
47. In mid-October 1934, Wilhelm Baur became—while maintaining his office as director in the Börsenverein—the president of the newly founded League of Reich-German Book Dealers, which replaced the Börsenverein as the professional representation within the RSK. As of 1 October 1936, this league

was dissolved and its membership integrated into the RSK's Group Book Trade. In August 1937, Goebbels appointed Baur vicepresident of the RSK. In addition, Baur worked for the Reich Press Chamber and in Max Amann's office as *Reichsleiter* for the Press of the NSDAP.

48. The numbers are from Bollmus, p. 29.
49. On this see the letter of 9 November 1932 from the publisher Hugo Bruckmann to Alfred Rosenberg, Bundesarchiv Koblenz (hereafter cited as BAK): NS 8/123, fols. 207-8.
50. The text of Hitler's directive is in *RGBL,* Teil I, No. 75 of 5 July 1933, p. 449.
51. The data on the number of staff are from Peter Diehl-Thiele, *Partei und Staat im Dritten Reich* (München: Beck, 1969), p. 219, n. 47; the budget figure is from Helmut Heiber, *Joseph Goebbels* (München: Deutscher Taschenbuch Verlag, 1965), p. 130. Supplementary information from Ernest K. Bramstedt, *Goebbels and National Socialist Propaganda, 1925-1945* (East Lansing: Michigan State University Press, 1965).
52. Letter of 23 August 1933 from State Secretary Walther Funk to the Führer's Deputy, Rudolf Hess, Bundesarchiv/ Potsdam: 50.01/162, fols. 3-4.
53. On this see the "Fundamental ideas on the establishment of a Reich Culture Chamber" presented in August 1933 by the Propaganda Ministry to the Reich Chancellory, BAK: R 43 II/1241 fols. 4-7; as well as the entry about Hitler's consent in Goebbels' diary of 25 August 1933, in *Die Tagebücher von Joseph Goebbels. Sämtliche Fragmente,* ed. Elke Fröhlich, Teil I: Aufzeichnungen 1924 bis 1941 (München: K. G. Saur, 1987), Bd. 2, p. 461.
54. *RGBL,* Teil I, No. 105 of 26 September 1933, pp. 661-62. On the context, see Volker Dahm, "Anfänge und Ideologie der Reichskulturkammer. Die 'Berufsgemeinschaft' als Instrument kulturpolitischer Steuerung und sozialer Reglementierung," *VfZG* 34 (1986): 53-84.
55. *RGBL,* Teil I, No. 123 of 3 November 1933, pp. 797-800.
56. A process that—Dr. Hans Schmidt-Leonhardt, the ministry staff member entrusted with the legal preparations, had to admit in a commentary—was "unusual and daring, when viewed with the eyes of a formal lawyer from the liberal system," since with it hitherto private and autonomous associations were raised to the status of state agencies. Hans Schmidt-Leonhardt, "Die Reichskulturkammer," in *Grundlagen, Aufbau und Wirtschaftsordnung des nationalsozialistischen Staates,* eds. Hans-Heinrich Lammers and Hans Pfundtner, Bd. I/Gruppe 2/Beitrag 20 (Berlin: Spaeth & Linde, 1936), p. 11.
57. Paragraph 30 of the First Executive Directive on the RKK Law of 1 November 1933 had stipulated: "Contributions to the chambers will be collected as public taxes." On the financing of the RSK's administrative expenses, see the estimated budget costs for the years 1934 to 1945 in BAK: R 2/4873-85.

58. On this see Hale, pp. 97-100 and pp. 136-47; Karl-Dietrich Abel, *Presselenkung im NS-Staat. Eine Studie zur Geschichte der Publizistik in der nationalsozialistischen Zeit* (Berlin: Colloquium Verlag, 1968), pp. 2-26; and Barbian, pp. 73-81.

59. Besides Hanns Johst, the following members of the RSK administration belonged to the SS: the vicepresident and head of the Gruppe Buchhandel Wilhelm Baur, the managing director Wilhelm Ihde, the justiciary Günther Gentz, the official advisor responsible for questions on book bans Herbert Menz, and the head of Department III (Book Trade) in Leipzig Karl Thulke. Menz and Thulke's activity for the SD is documented in their SS personnel files at the Berlin Document Center.

60. A detailed description from 1933 of the development, the charges, and the personnel of the Reich Office for the Promotion of German Literature is located in the Deutsche Bücherei Leipzig (Sign. 1933 B 3809).

61. See Bernhard Payr, *Das Amt Schrifttumspflege. Seine Entwicklungsgeschichte und seine Organisation* (Berlin: Juncker & Dünnhaupt, 1941). On the exact circumstances of the establishment of the Rosenberg agency, see Bollmus, pp. 54-85.

62. The evaluations by Rosenberg's Literature Office(s) were published in part in the journal *Bücherkunde,* which came out from 1934 to 1944. In contrast, the *Gutachtenanzeiger* published monthly and annually, which contained positive or negative evaluations of authors, books, and journals, were "strictly confidential" and only for the purpose of internal official use. BAK: NSD 16/27: *Jahres-Gutachtenanzeiger 1936-1940.*

63. An extensive collection of such politico-cultural evaluations, which were produced on request, especially for the Deutsches Volksbildungswerk, can be found in BAK: NS 15/27-33, 253-54, 256.

64. The "decree" is published together with other documents on the PPK in "Verleger-Mitteilungen der Parteiamtlichen Prüfungskommission, Rundschreiben 3," Berlin (7 December) 1938 (ms.). Only to be used for internal communication with the Official Party Examining Commission— BAK: NSD 2/14.

65. See Amann's six-page letter to Bouhler of 10 December 1938, BAK: NS 11/9.

66. For an overview, see Barbian, pp. 138-56.

67. On this see the report of 8 May 1943 by Bernhard Payr, the head of Rosenberg's Literature Office, about a meeting that took place the previous day in the Propaganda Ministry, at which they had discussed the "Führer directive" regarding the supervision of exports of books and periodicals— BAK: NS 8/248, fols. 80-83.

68. This is the only way we can explain why a series of works, such as Horst Lange's novel *Schwarze Weide,* Ernst Jünger's *Marmorklippen,* Ernst Wiechert's legend

Der weiße Büffel oder Von der großen Gerechtigkeit and his novel *Das einfache Leben*, Frank Thiess's *Das Reich der Dämonen*, and Werner Bergengruen's Berlin novel *Am Himmel wie auf Erden* could appear, although they contained encoded criticism of the Nazi system or suggested countermodels to a National Socialist society. On criticism by official Party agencies, see among others the "Jahresbericht 1940" published by the Hauptlektorat Schöngeistiges Schrifttum in the Rosenberg Agency, *Lektoren-Brief* 4, H. 5/6 (1941): 4-8, BAK: NSD 16/59.

69. The RSK's budget estimates for 1934 to 1945 are collected in BAK: R 2/4873-85.
70. On this see the complaints with which a number of authors turned to the RSK in the spring of 1937, in BAK: R 56 V/81.
71. The settling of welfare payments by the Schillerstiftung, which was subordinate to the RSK, in exchange for writers' contributions to the "spiritual fortification" is documented in a letter of 2 February 1940 from the RSK staff member Metzner to the Lord Mayor of Weimar, BAK: R 56 V/76, fol. 406. See also the "file memoranda" of the chamber advisors Alfred Richard Meyer and Loth of 23 May 1941, concerning "Arbeitsbeschaffung und Arbeitsvermittlung," BAK: R 56 V/12, fols. 16, 17.
72. Goebbels' speech is published in the *BBl.* 106, No. 255 (2 November 1938): 853.
73. For documentation of this, see Johst's correspondence in his SS personnel file in the BDC, as well as Blunck's RSK personnel file there.
74. On this see Ernst Loewy, *Literatur unterm Hakenkreuz. Das Dritte Reich und seine Dichtung. Eine Dokumentation* (Frankfurt/Main: Fischer Taschenbuch Verlag, 1983 (1st ed.: Frankfurt/Main: Europäische Verlagsanstalt, 1966); Horst Denkler and Karl Prümm, eds., *Die deutsche Literatur im Dritten Reich. Themen - Traditionen - Wirkungen* (Stuttgart: Reclam, 1976); Uwe-Karsten Ketelsen, *Völkisch-nationale und nationalsozialistische Literatur in Deutschland 1890-1945* (Stuttgart: Metzler, 1976), pp. 79-105; Ralf Schnell, ed., *Kunst und Kultur im deutschen Faschismus* (Stuttgart: Metzler, 1978); Jörg Thunecke, ed., *Leid der Worte. Panorama des literarischen Nationalsozialismus* (Bonn: Bouvier, 1987).
75. See the Party Chancellory telex of 29 May 1942 to Party Comrade Tießler, betr. Beurteilung des Dichters Will Vesper, BAK: NS 18/307.
76. Notification of 5 February 1943 by the Reich Association of German Periodical Publishers to Langen-Müller Verlag, Deutsches Literaturarchiv/Nachlaß Will Vesper: Korrespondenz Langen-Müller Verlag, Mappe 9: 1942-1943 (hereafter the Deutsches Literaturarchiv will be cited as DLA). On Vesper's editorial activity, see Gisela Berglund, *Der Kampf um den Leser im Dritten Reich. Die Literaturpolitik der "Neuen Literatur" (Will Vesper) und der "Nationalsozialistischen Monatshefte"* (Worms: Heintz, 1980).

77. While after an attack in the SS-organ *Das Schwarze Korps*, 2. Jg./Folge 19 (7 May 1936), p. 7 ("Der Selbsterreger!"), Benn had been expelled from the RSK on 18 March 1938, Bronnen and Ewers' publications prior to 1933 were indexed with virtually no exceptions on the RSK's blacklist. For details see these authors' RSK personnel files in the BDC, as well as Glenn R. Cuomo, "Purging an 'Art Bolshevist': The Persecution of Gottfried Benn in the Years 1933-1938," *German Studies Review* 9 (1986): 85-105; and Harald Kaas, "Der faschistische Piccolo: Arnolt Bronnen," in *Intellektuelle im Bann des Nationalsozialismus*, ed. Karl Corino (Hamburg: Hoffmann und Campe, 1980), pp. 136-49.
78. Ernst von Salomon, *Der Fragebogen* (Reinbek bei Hamburg: Rowohlt, 1961) (1st ed. 1951), pp. 193-98; Hans Carossa, *Ungleiche Welten* (Wiesbaden: Insel Verlag, 1951); August Winnig, *Aus zwanzig Jahren 1925-1945* (Hamburg: F. Wittig, 1951), pp. 142-45; on the context, see Hans Sarkowicz, "Zwischen Sympathie und Apologie: Der Schriftsteller Hans Grimm und sein Verhältnis zum Nationalsozialismus," in *Intellektuelle im Bann des Nationalsozialismus*, pp. 120-35.
79. DLA/Nachlaß Hans Grimm: "Korrespondenz mit NS-Partei- und Regierungsstellen, F-G: Gedächtnisprotokoll über die Besprechung am 2.12.[1938] 12.30 h mit Reichsminister Dr. G. in Gegenwart des Reichspressechefs Dr. Dietrich," pp. 1-7. Cf. also *Goebbels-Tagebücher*, Teil I, vol. 3, p. 500: "The author Hans Grimm is holding authors' meetings with a somewhat negative tendency. I will now subject this meeting to some close scrutiny. I will not tolerate any confessional front among the authors. I will drive off these eternal troublemakers" (5 August 1938); on his meeting with Grimm, ibid., pp. 541-42 (3 December 1938).
80. Ernst Wiechert, *Der Totenwald. Ein Bericht* (München: K. Desch, 1946) (= Ernst Wiechert, *Sämtliche Werke*, vol. 9; Wien: K. Desch). For Goebbels' position on the "Wiechert case," see *Goebbels-Tagebücher*, Teil I, vol. 3, p. 499 (entry for 4 August 1938) and p. 522 (entry for 30 August 1938).
81. On this aspect, see Glenn R. Cuomo, "Hanns Johst und die Reichsschrifttumskammer. Ihr Einfluß auf die Situation des Schriftstellers im Dritten Reich," in *Leid der Worte*, ed. Thunecke, pp. 108-32; and Peter de Mendelssohn, "Über die Linie des geringsten Widerstandes. Versuch über Ernst Jünger," in P.d.M., *Der Geist in der Despotie. Versuche über die moralischen Möglichkeiten des Intellektuellen in der totalitären Gesellschaft* (Frankfurt/Main 1987) (1st ed.: Berlin-Grunewald: F. A. Herbig, 1953), pp. 173-235.
82. On this we have the following "information" about Wiechert, which Wilhelm Haegert, the head of the Literature Department in the Propaganda Ministry,

submitted on 13 January 1940 to the state secretary in the Reich Interior Ministry Hans Pfundtner:

> After his release the author was given the opportunity through the Herr Reich Minister [Goebbels] to revise his attitude. Thus at that time his expulsion from the Reich Literature Chamber made necessary by his incarceration was put off as an act of grace, and he was even invited to the first 'Greater German Authors Meeting' in Weimar arranged by the Reich Propaganda Ministry. When he was received by the Herr Minister, Wiechert stated that he looked upon this concession as a special demonstration of clemency and would make an effort in the future to prove himself worthy of it. For this reason we refrained from banning Wiechert's books, which as before can be sold in the book trade. He has merely been required to submit every new work for scrutiny before its publication. (BAK: R 18/5645, fol. 99)

Among the extensive scholarship on Wiechert after 1945, see above all Hildegard Chatellier, "Ernst Wiechert im Urteil der deutschen Zeitschriftenpresse 1933-1945. Ein Beitrag zur nationalsozialistischen Literatur- und Pressepolitik," *Recherches Germaniques* 3 (1973): 153-95; Guido Reiner, *Ernst Wiechert im Dritten Reich. Eine Dokumentation* (Paris: Privately printed, 1974) (= Ernst-Wiechert-Bibliographie 2. Teil); and Jörg Hattwig, *Das Dritte Reich im Werk Ernst Wiecherts. Geschichtsdenken, Selbstverständnis und literarische Praxis* (Frankfurt/Main: Peter Lang, 1984).

83. For a critical view on this, see Eberhard Lämmert, "Beherrschte Prosa. Poetische Lizenzen in Deutschland zwischen 1933 und 1945," *Neue Rundschau* 86 (1975): 404-21; and Klaus Thoenelt, "Innere Emigration: Fiktion oder Wirklichkeit? Literarische Tradition und Nationalsozialismus in den Werken Ernst Wiecherts, Hans Carossas und Hans Falladas (1933-1945)," in *Leid der Worte,* ed. Thunecke, pp. 321-47.

84. See the RSK personnel files in the BDC. Further information can be found in Oskar Loerke, *Tagebücher 1903-1939,* ed. Hermann Kasack (Darmstadt: Lambert Schneider, 1955), here pp. 259-346; Theodor Haecker, *Tag- und Nachtbücher 1939-1945* (München: Josef Kösel, 1947); and Reinhold Schneider, *Verhüllter Tag* (Köln: J. Hegner, 1954).

85. *Die große Kontroverse. Ein Briefwechsel um Deutschland,* ed. and compiled by Johannes Franz Gottlieb Grosser (Hamburg: Nagel, 1963).

86. See, in BDC/RSK/Frank Thiess, the author's correspondence with Hans Hinkel from the years 1934/35, as well as Hinkel's interventions with the Führer's deputy and in the Propaganda Ministry; and the events from September 1935 until March 1936 surrounding Thiess's romantic play *Der ewige Taugenichts* (correspondence between the Staatstheater Stuttgart and the Propaganda Ministry with

interdepartmental communications between the Theater- and the Literature departments) in BA/Potsdam: 50.01/Bd. 200, fols. 50-69. Further details in Gerhard Renner, "Frank Thiess: Ein 'freier Schriftsteller' im Nationalsozialismus," *Buchhandelsgeschichte* 2 (1990): B41-B50.

87. Goebbels' speech on the "corporate structure of the cultural professions" is reproduced in the *Erste Früh-Ausgabe des Deutschen Nachrichtenbüros,* 1, No. 288 (8 February 1934), BAK: R 43 II/1241, fols. 18-19.

88. BDC/RSK/Stefan Andres. On the basis of a "special permit," the author remained a member of the RSK until 1940. He was eliminated from the membership card file because of his permanent residence abroad, which in accordance with the general legal statutes precluded membership in the RKK. See also "St. Andres, Jahrgang 1906. Ein Junge vom Lande," in *Stefan Andres. Ein Reader zu Person und Werk,* ed. Wilhelm Große (Trier: Spee-Verlag, 1980), pp. 13-47.

89. Details in Ernst G. Riemschneider, *Der Fall Klepper. Eine Dokumentation* (Stuttgart: Deutsche Verlags-Anstalt, 1975); and Hellmut Seier, "Kollaborative und oppositionelle Momente der inneren Emigration Jochen Kleppers," *Jahrbuch für die Geschichte Mittel- und Ostdeutschlands* 8 (1959): 319-47; Jochen Klepper, *Unter dem Schatten deiner Flügel. Aus den Tagebüchern der Jahre 1932-1942,* ed. Hildegard Klepper (Stuttgart: Deutsche Verlags-Anstalt, 1955).

90. BDC/RSK/Werner Bergengruen. The master file card for Bergengruen made out by the RKK central administration contains the remark: "Ministerial Advisor Dr. Wismann has intervened on his behalf due to the literary merit of Bergengruen's publications" (n.d., probably 1935/36). In contrast, in an "overall evaluation" issued at the request of the RSK, the NSDAP local branch leadership in München-Salin stated on 14 June 1940: "Bergengruen probably is politically unreliable. Even if he when the occasion requires shows the swastika flag from his window, or always and willingly contributes to collections, his behavior otherwise nevertheless gives reason to view him as politically unreliable" (BDC/RSK/Werner Bergengruen). See also Werner Bergengruen, *Schreibtischerinnerungen* (Zürich: Verlag der Arche, 1961).

91. Elisabeth Langgässer, "Schriftsteller unter der Hitler-Diktatur," *Ost und West* 1, No. 4 (1947): 36-41.

92. BDC/RSK/Erich Kästner. Cf. also Dieter Mank, *Erich Kästner im nationalsozialistischen Deutschland 1933-1945: Zeit ohne Werk?* (Frankfurt/Main: Peter Lang, 1981).

93. BDC/RSK/Rudolf Ditzen (i.e., Hans Fallada).

94. See the RSK personnel files of Bauer, Gläser, and Pohl in the BDC, which contain file entries by the staff of the chamber and the Propaganda Ministry

regarding political evaluations as well as extensive correspondence with the lawyers of these writers who were threatened with expulsion. See also Cuomo, "Hanns Johst und die Reichsschrifttumskammer," pp. 116-19.
95. BDC/RSK/Axel Eggebrecht and Axel Eggebrecht, *Der halbe Weg. Zwischenbilanz einer Epoche* (Reinbek bei Hamburg: Rowohlt, 1975). BDC/RSK/Erich Ebermayer and Erich Ebermayer, *Denn heute gehört uns Deutschland... Persönliches und politisches Tagebuch. Von der Machtergreifung bis zum 31. Dezember 1935* (Hamburg: P. Zsolnay, 1959).
96. Letter of 25 January 1943 from the Chief of the Security Police and the SD (IV A) to the Reichsminister for Popular Enlightenment and Propaganda (z.Hd. des persönlichen Referenten Staatssekretär Gutterer), BA/Potsdam: 50.01/Bd. 210, fol. 578. The letter contains the handwritten remark (from 28 January): "According to information from Dr. Raech, this is a highly confidential matter, in which the guilt of W., who enjoys many privileges in his confinement, has not been proved up to this date."
97. See the respective RSK personnel files in the BDC. On the problem of the transition of literature from the "Drittes Reich" to the Federal Republic or the former GDR, see Schäfer, *Das gespaltene Bewußtsein*, pp. 7-71.
98. Postcard from Kattowitz, Upper Silesia, dated 8 March 1942, BDC/RSK/Karl Krolow. Since his publication activity was only sporadic, Krolow obtained only a "certificate of release" from membership; however, it obligated him to observe the RSK directives just as every regular chamber member did.
99. Andreas Meyer, "Die Verlagsfusion Langen-Müller. Zur Buchmarkt- und Kulturpolitik des Deutschnationalen Handlungsgehilfen-Verbands (DHV) in der Endphase der Weimarer Republik," *AGB* 32 (1989): 1-271.
100. Details in Hale, pp. 136-42.
101. On this in detail, Barbian, pp. 245-54.
102. Details in Dahm, *Das jüdische Buch im Dritten Reich,* Teil 1.
103. The proceedings are documented in BDC/RSK/Gottfried Bermann-Fischer.
104. For details, see Barbian, pp. 95-98 and 282-85.
105. "Führer decisions" that led to book bans can be documented as early as in the 1930s. However, they did not appear in large numbers until 1941, when the Party Chancellory of the NSDAP began to intervene in the literary policy of the Propaganda Ministry and the RSK. See the examples in Barbian, pp. 233-35.
106. "Memorandum about a possible reorganization of the retail book sellers Koehler & Volckmar, Leipzig, and Koch & Neff and Oettinger, Stuttgart [...]" from June 1937, BDC/RSK/Gunther Haupt.
107. The proceedings are documented in StA Leipzig Koehler & Volckmar/122.
108. One of the driving forces behind the expulsion proceedings had been Wilhelm Baur, who here, as in numerous other cases, abused his governmental function

as RSK vicepresident and "head of the German Book Trade" for the business interests of the Central Party Publishing House.

109. The numbers are from Hale, p. 142.
110. BAK: NS 8/213, fols. 255 and reverse. Hale states that in 1943, approximately 150 publishing enterprises with around 35,000 employees belonged to the Eher-Konzern (pp. 25-26).
111. On this see the sketchy overview in Hale, pp. 278-82. No detailed analysis has been done yet either on the Central Party Publishing House's activities in the occupied areas or on the overall issue of the Nazi cultural policy there.
112. Hale, p. 266.
113. On the background to the Economic Office being charged with the distribution of paper, which Wilhelm Baur would have liked to see firmly established in his sphere of influence as director of the Börsenverein, see Baur, pp. 249-52. The distribution of paper for periodical publications went through the Reich Press Chamber headed by Amann.
114. Thus in a letter of 20 February 1942, the RSK managing director Wilhelm Ihde indicated to his president Johst the deplorable situation Hövel brought up at a conference in the Propaganda Ministry that ". . . incredible amounts of paper are being used for political propaganda material and that the men who are granting the paper are well aware in advance of the fact that—with the exception of foreign countries—no person in Germany will even pick up these publications, much less read them," BAK: R 56 V/26, fols. 189 and reverse.
115. On this see the "Report to the Führer on the book donation of the NSDAP for the German Wehrmacht" written by Rosenberg (n.d., December 1939), BAK: NS 8/176, fols. 95-99.
116. "An den deutschen Buchhandel," in: *BBl.* 108, No. 226 (27 September 1941): 329.
117. Ibid.
118. Activity report by the RSK advisor Georg von Kommerstädt for the "Group Book Trade," dated 10 May 1944, BAK: R 56 V/35, fols. 178-81.
119. Helmut Heiber, ed. *Goebbels-Reden, Bd. 2: 1939-1945* (Düsseldorf: Droste, 1972), pp. 158-71.
120. See the report about the joint meeting of the advisory council of the Group Book Trade and of the minor advisory council of the Börsenverein on Tuesday, 5 October 1943 in Leipzig," Pkt. 1 (Report by the director), p. 2, StA Leipzig BV/No. 737.
121. "Merkblatt zur totalen Mobilmachung des Buchhandels," *BBl.* 112 (9 September 1944). On the implementation of these RSK directives, see the report on the joint meeting of the minor advisory council of the Börsenverein and of the advisory council of the Group Book Trade in Rathen a.d. Elbe on 27

September 1944, Pkt. II (Report by the Group Book Trade on the Measures for total Mobilization), p. 3, StA Leipzig BV/No. 738.
122. See the "overview of employees at hand" in the RSK's budget estimate for the fiscal year 1945, Ausgabetitel 4, BAK: R 2/4885, fol. 14.
123. See the correspondence between Bormann and Rosenberg of September 1944 in BAK: NS 8/191, fol. 120, and fols. 149-52.
124. Hans-Peter Meister, "Der Künstler im Krieg," *Die Reichskulturkammer* 2 (1944): 140.

8

The Diaries of Joseph Goebbels as a Source for the Understanding of National Socialist Cultural Politics[*]

Glenn R. Cuomo

> Goebbels's own diaries are lost, so far as can be ascertained.... Goebbels's version of the inner story of the Third Reich would have been beyond serious challenge, a revelation of the deepest historical and personal interest —D. McLachlan, in *Goebbels—The Man Next to Hitler.*[1]

D. McLachlan's 1947 introduction to the memoirs of Joseph Goebbels' press assistant Rudolf Semler are certainly mistaken about the status of the diaries Goebbels had kept from 1923 to 1945. But his assessment of the diaries' value still rings true. Since Louis Lochner's edition of diary fragments from 1942/43, Helmut Heiber's "Early Goebbels Diaries" from 1925/26, and then the "Final Entries" from early 1945,[2] the interest in Goebbels' writings has not diminished. Nor has the controversy subsided over the circumstances of these diaries' production and their reliability as a source for insights into the National Socialist hierarchy.[3] The release from archives in the former Soviet Union of hitherto inaccessible and unknown portions of Goebbels' diaries has intensified rather than quelled the debate that started among scholars in the postwar years. Indeed, when in 1987 Elke Fröhlich compiled the most comprehensive version to date of the diaries from 27 June 1924 to 8 July 1941,[4] the controversy assumed a new dimension in light of her editorial practices and the arrangements that had been made with former East Bloc states and François

Genoud, a Swiss banker and admitted National Socialist sympathizer who had acquired the rights to Goebbels' oeuvre.[5]

The collapse of the Soviet Union brought a happy conclusion to the search for the missing sections of Goebbels' diaries, as Western scholars finally could confirm their long-held suspicion that the bulk of the diaries had fallen into the hands of the Red Army. These speculations proved to be conservative; we now know that the Russian State Archive holds glass-plate microfiche copies of virtually all of Goebbels' handwritten diaries from 1923 to 1941 and of the subsequent typed dictation from 9 July 1941 to 1945.[6]

In the course of the journalistic furor over this discovery, some new diary passages treating major political and wartime developments were published during the summer of 1992.[7] Additional material appeared in Ralf Georg Reuth's five-volume, radically abridged edition of the Goebbels' diaries from 1924 to 1945.[8] In an edition that, oddly enough, is available at present only in Italian translation, David Irving published entries from the period 11 February to 11 November 1938, when he transcribed in its entirety one of Goebbels' 20 notebooks preserved on glass-plate microfiches in Moscow.[9]

All versions of the diaries thus far published will be rendered obsolete by the cooperative efforts of Elke Fröhlich, the Institut für Zeitgeschichte, and the State Archive Service of Russia, which promise to result in definitive editions of Joseph Goebbels' handwritten diaries from 1923 to 8 July 1941 and dictated entries from 9 July 1941 to 1945. Approximately 20 volumes are projected to appear by 1996. At present six volumes of this second part of Fröhlich's edition have appeared: volume 3 (January to March 1942), volumes 7 to 10 (January to December 1943), and volume 11 (January to March 1944).[10] Until the rest of the volumes are published, we have to rely on some past and more recent diary editions—as flawed and fragmentary they might be—to augment Fröhlich's edition. Her two-part edition will serve as the prime source for the present analysis (indicated as *TGB* for the first four volumes from 1987 and *TGB2* for volumes from the second part from 1993/94).[11] David Irving's *Diario 1938* (cited as *Diario 1938*) will supply newly discovered material for 1938. Passages from parts of 1941, 1942, 1944, and 1945 not yet covered by Fröhlich's editions will come from Reuth's five-volume abridged edition, the *Final Entries, 1945,* and from microfilms of the original 7,000 pages of typed manuscript from which Louis Lochner compiled his translation and abridgment of material from 1942/43, as well as from a National Archives microfilm containing fragments of entries from 8 August 1941 to 6 June 1942 and scattered pages from undated entries from August 1941 and what appears to be entries from 1942 and 1943.[12] Although a portion of the microfilmed manuscript of entries from 1942 and 1943 has already been incorporated into *TGB2*, references will be made to the original pages of Goebbels' dictation in order to indicate exactly where the passages occurred in the entries. When possible, cross references will be made both to Fröhlich's *TGB2* and to Lochner's 1948 translation (Lochner), which is still the most widely disseminated edition of Goebbels' diaries.

At this juncture in the consideration of the sources, we must turn to the only version of Goebbels' diaries published in his lifetime, *Vom Kaiserhof zur Reichskanzlei* (1934), an account of the National Socialist German Workers' Party's (NSDAP) final "year of struggle" and the first months of the Third Reich. For this work he utilized entries from 1 January 1932 to 1 May 1933.[13] Goebbels' stylistic enhancements and revisions to the original passages have given rise to much skepticism about these and the rest of the diary entries. With *Vom Kaiserhof* we cannot talk of a "diary in the strictest sense of the word"—totally private notes that were never intended to see the light of day or, as Clifford Geertz put it, "a literary product genre-addressed to an audience of one."[14] Instead we have the product of a master of dissimulation who had previously employed the diaristic form both in his novel *(Michael: Ein deutsches Schicksal in Tagebuchblättern)* and in the weekly "Political Diary" (Politisches Tagebuch) in his newspaper *Der Angriff*,[15] and who now cast himself in the role of the historian of the Nazi Party. In fact, two years later Goebbels entered into a lucrative agreement for the future publication of subsequent diary entries by the central NSDAP press, Franz Eher Verlag in Munich, which had published *Vom Kaiserhof*.

Taking into account these circumstances, coupled with the obvious implications of Goebbels' function as Hitler's propaganda minister, the scholar Bernd Sösemann expresses serious reservations about the documents published as Goebbels' diaries. He views them as a "propagandistic production for posterity," which "misrepresents, distorts and manipulates, often with the intention of putting the protagonist Goebbels on political center stage. . . ."[16] Such extreme skepticism, however, marks a departure from the prevailing attitude of researchers, who, despite doubt about the sincerity of Goebbels' writing, have assigned great source value to his diary entries.[17] Some even found that Goebbels' capacity as historian enhanced rather than diminished the diaries' utility.[18]

Now, in deciding whether to dismiss the diaries outright as a hopelessly biased source, as Richard Taylor does,[19] to hold them suspect, as Sösemann does, or to accept them at face value, as some scholars did when Lochner's edition first appeared,[20] we have to ask whether the prospect of future dissemination would erase all traces of spontaneity and bluntness in the entries. Do we discount entries that came after the publication of *Vom Kaiserhof* demonstrated the texts' commercial value, or those that came after Goebbels negotiated the contract with the Eher Verlag in 1936?

We can answer these questions by examining the diary entries prior to 1932, some of the material excised from *Vom Kaiserhof,* and the entries subsequent to this work. We find a significant degree of veracity and candidness in the entries from all three periods, for Goebbels did not avoid volatile material that would never have found its way into a version of the diaries he would have published in his lifetime. During the period from February to August 1931, for example, he had no compunction about recording his great concern that Ernst Röhm's homosexuality presented the NSDAP with a serious liability. Yet this was the same "S.A. Head and Chief of Staff" who later figured prominently as a dedicated member of the "Old Guard" in the first edition of *Vom Kaiserhof.*[21]

Similarly, Fröhlich's juxtaposition of manuscript entries from 1932/33 available from the Bundesarchiv with their corresponding versions in *Vom Kaiserhof* shows that Goebbels continued to make frank observations on sensitive issues. As we can see in the entry for 23 January 1933, some of Goebbels' remarks were so frank that their publication would have contradicted the very image of the NSDAP and its leadership that his own Propaganda Ministry was projecting. In the unpublished account of a commemoration at Horst Wessel's grave, Goebbels did not conceal his anger at "the unbearable arrogance" of Wessel's mother, who showed up half an hour late for the ceremony (*TGB*-II, 347-48). This entry's version in *Vom Kaiserhof* makes no mention of Frau Wessel and smooths over all critical remarks about the event. Nevertheless, Goebbels' later entries contain nothing but terms of utter contempt for this woman, who had apparently failed to live up to the role he had created for her as the mother of "Germany's best son."[22] However, to announce this "failure" publicly and state, as Goebbels does twice in the diaries, that Frau Wessel "never deserved such a son,"[23] would have undermined the entire martyrdom myth Goebbels had created around the Wessel family.

And finally, we can turn to Goebbels' preface to *Vom Kaiserhof* and his concluding words about the "steadfastness" and "eternal solidarity" that characterized the Nazi "Old Guard": "Let no one believe that among those standing around Hitler there had ever been or in the future there could ever be room for quarreling or feuds."[24] How credible would this statement seem in the face of the later diaries' myriad accounts of power struggles, back-stabbing, and incidents of character assassination among the NSDAP leadership?

Discrepancies between the "sanitized" insider's view of the Third Reich presented in *Vom Kaiserhof* and the more problematical reality represented in the unpublished diaries underscore the latter's status as a preliminary draft. With respect to their content, they are as rough in quality as they are weak stylistically. Frequently laconic and formulaic, the diary entries are simply not up to par with Goebbels' eloquent performances elsewhere. Many passages are so repetitive that they corroborate Lochner's suspicion that Goebbels did not reread his comments from the previous day before writing the next entry.[25] The very spontaneity and unpolished nature of such entries are important, since they lend credence to Viktor Reimann's and Peter Stadelmayer's opinion that these hastily jotted down words record Goebbels' frank opinion at the time, prior to any modification for public consumption.[26] As we shall see, their view is overly optimistic, but not entirely wrong. These texts do seem to constitute the closest example available of "honest writing" by Goebbels.

One guarantee for a substantial degree of candor in the later entries is a key condition in the terms Goebbels had negotiated with Max Amann, the head of the Eher Verlag. Amann did not just provide an exorbitant advance of 250,000 Reichsmark (RM) and subsequent annual payments of 100,000 RM; he also agreed to the stipulation that the diaries be published 20 years after Goebbels' death.[27] This placed the diaries in a radically different context from that of *Vom Kaiserhof zur Reichskanzlei,* which had served to bolster a regime in the process of establishing itself. With himself long gone—and presumably Hitler, who was eight years his senior, and the rest of the Party's Old Guard—Goebbels could have afforded to disseminate the diaries' compromising and unflattering material in unadulterated form.

More likely, however, Goebbels intended to rework the material that would be released posthumously, and this might explain why during the nine years following the publishing agreement he never surrendered any diary manuscripts to the Eher Verlag. In fact, when instead of sending Amann any installments he deposited 20 diary volumes in the Reichsbank's subterranean vault, Goebbels stated his intention to "revise" ("*überarbeiten*") his diaries for posterity, if "fate left me a few years to do it" (30 March 1941; *TGB*-IV, 558). The entries would then have served as an aide-mémoire, as the raw material for the history of the Third Reich he planned to produce at some later date, perhaps after he had left office and retired to his villa at Schwanenwerder.[28] The collapse of the Third Reich denied him the role of an "elder statesman," leaving us only to speculate about the final state of the material he intended to leave to the Eher Verlag. But we do have evidence of some of the revisions he planned. The typed manuscript from the years 1942 and 1943 shows several signs of a "work in progress": blanks left for individuals' names and titles of works that had to be confirmed and notes indicating where supplementary material was to be inserted.[29]

Goebbels never had the opportunity to make these emendations, and when we consider the sheer volume of the diary material, it seems improbable that he ever had the chance to revise any of the earlier preliminary drafts. With the ever-growing burdens of his multiple state and Party functions, Goebbels must have been hard pressed to find time to maintain his prolific rate of production of new entries, to say nothing of going back and editing the thousands of pages he had already written. And we scholars have been the beneficiaries of this omission.

Recent confiscations of diaries kept by U.S. Senator Robert Packwood and Treasury department member Joshua Steiner by investigatory committees have shown that even in the case of politicians, we expect private journals to contain material of a confessional, if not self-incriminating nature. Notwithstanding some reservations due to his role as National Socialism's chief propagandist, Goebbels is no exception.

Here we must consider Goebbels' deviant concept of what constituted "compromising or incriminating material" that should not be recorded for posterity. This was, after all, the man who ordered that the large-scale deportation of Germany's Jews in April 1942 be filmed for "future educational purposes" and who planned to use the gruesome footage of the hangings of conspirators from the failed 20 July 1944 plot for a documentary film *(Verräter vor dem Volksgericht)*.[30] He did not neglect to record the suggestions he provided for a film to justify the "liquidation of the incurably insane."[31] Nor did he refrain from expressing his approbation when he learned of the mass executions of Jews in Poland or from advocating a more rigorous pursuit of the "Final Solution of the Jewish Question" as the war progressed.[32] And precisely the pride Goebbels took both in his virtuosity in deceiving the public and his leading role in the persecution of Jews, "decadent artists," and oppositional clergy would have motivated him to record his official actions in full, if not to exaggerate his role.

This focus on his performance as Reich minister for popular enlightenment and propaganda, *Gauleiter* of Berlin, and president of the Reich Chamber of Culture—to name just his most important functions—came at the cost of the insights a diary often contains about the author's intimate life. If anything, Goebbels' references to his home and family life are stylized to emphasize how little private time he has and how much his work preoccupies him, which probably was the case. He represents himself as a person leading a life of ceaseless activity, a "workaholic" with little opportunity for sleep or relaxation.[33] "Unmenge" ("an enormous number") is his favorite term to denote the quantity of files he has to read, the amount of paperwork he has to finish, and number of issues and problems he has to tackle in conferences with staff.

Just how unique Goebbels' diaries are with regard to his private life can be seen from a comparison with the diaries of his contemporary Thomas Mann. Mann's diaries were of such a private nature that he concealed them from his family and in fact incinerated most of the earlier entries. He later stipulated that the remaining material not be published until 20 years after his death.[34] Among other things, Mann apparently feared the consequences of his open discussion of his homosexuality, which remained a taboo subject during his lifetime. Even though he was writing with a similar delay for posthumous publication, Goebbels never was so honest. He avoided recording the multiple extramarital affairs for which he was infamous. We learn nothing from the entries of how he extorted sexual favors from female staff members and aspiring film stars, earning himself the epitaph "the Stud of Babelsberg" in Germany's Hollywood.[35] No word betrays his serious affair with the Czech actress Lida Baarová, which almost cost him his career in late 1938. On the other hand, we do find the details of his physical breakdown and hospitalization precipitated by the stress of his wife Magda's angry reaction and the ultimatum Hitler issued on her behalf.[36]

Goebbels exercised the same discretion in his treatment of Hitler's "private life," taking care to reinforce the public image of the solitary leader who led a spartan lifestyle in constant service to the nation. The existence of Eva Braun, Hitler's mistress since 1935, would have spoiled this image, and consequently she was ignored for many years. When Goebbels mentioned Eva Braun in June and again August 1943, he left the status of her relationship to Hitler vague (*TGB2*-VIII, 537, and IX, 267, respectively), going so far in a later entry from March 1944 as to create the impression that "Fräulein Eva Braun" just happened to be "visiting Obersalzberg with several girlfriends" (4 March 1944; *TGB2*-XI, 395).[37] With animals, on the other hand, Goebbels had less inhibitions, and he represented Hitler's acquisition of the German shepherd "Blondi" in May 1942 as a welcome addition, since now the "lonely Führer" would have another "living being" around him.[38] In a subsequent entry, it is Blondi, not Eva Braun, whom Goebbels refers to as Hitler's "faithful companion" (25 January 1944; *TGB2*-XI, 171).

Goebbels' choice of reading material reveals another facet of his process of self-fashioning as he constructs the "ideal persona" for himself in the diaries. It does not seem fortuitous that a considerable amount of his diary commentaries should be critical assessments of other people's published diaries, letters, and autobiographies. In maintaining his inflated self-image, Goebbels evidently needed to reassure himself that he was superior to such representatives of the political left as Rosa Luxemburg and August Bebel, whose letters and memoirs he tore apart. As a consequence of his narcissistic tendencies, he also proved to be adept at seeing affinities between his career and the lives of great artists, autocratic rulers, and charismatic figures whom he admired. His models show diverse politics; they range from Machiavelli, Frederick the Great, Thomas

Paine, Napoleon, Hindenburg, Mussolini, Kemal Atatürk, and General Pilsudski, to Rasputin and the Borgias.

With artists, Goebbels' search for "peers" often entered the realm of the ludicrous. When reading in Richard Wagner's *Mein Leben* that a five-year hiatus in Wagner's creativity followed several major compositions, Goebbels could see an analogy to his own "creative slump" after producing the play "Der Wanderer" and *Michael,* two works whose literary merit were in fact negligible to nonexistent (31 July 1924; *TGB*-I, 55).[39] Less than a month later Goebbels fancied himself to be a revolutionary and an "avant-garde artist" in the manner of the young Friedrich Schiller,[40] with whom he believed he shared temperamental as well as facial features (20 August 1924; *TGB*-I, 70-71).

We find the greatest degree of distortion when the entries concern Goebbels' own accomplishments, for the remarks reveal his great vanity and failure at self-scrutiny. Sparing only his "Führer,"[41] Goebbels habitually expounded at length on the incompetency of other members of the Nazi leadership. But he could not accept his style of sarcastic criticism when it was directed at his own person and works.[42] If we were to accept at face value the frequent self-assessments contained in the diaries, then practically every one of Goebbels' speeches had been a smashing success with the audience, which responded with "stormy applause," every piece he had written had been a rhetorical masterpiece, and in ideological confrontations he had bested his opponents.[43]

In short, the diaries have limited value as a document of the efficacy of Goebbels' work as propagandist, but they are all the richer in the insights they provide into his egocentric personality. For one thing, we can note that the degree to which Goebbels would find fault with an artwork or propagandistic strategy appears to have stood in reverse proportion to his involvement in the project's genesis or to the extent he believed the project reflected his directives. As evident from such self-congratulatory comments as "My personal film works are flourishing the best" (25 March 1941; *TGB*-IV, 551), this phenomenon occurs frequently with films in whose production he had intervened rigorously from their initial concept to their final editing.

The best remedy against the distortion caused by Goebbels' hyperbole and more subtle manipulations is not to read the diaries in isolation. The most fruitful analysis will involve the coordination of the entries with the ample documentation available on the activities of Goebbels and his Propaganda Ministry and their interaction with other agencies. Such a comparison yields reassuring results, since no significant discrepancies emerge in Goebbels' version of his official activities. With respect to such controversial items as the statements and suggestions Goebbels had made in the aftermath of the Kristallnacht pogrom he had instigated, the accuracy of his diary account is confirmed by an extant partial transcript of a conference Hermann Göring held on 12 November 1938 with Goebbels, Reinhold Heydrich, Wilhelm Frick, and others.[44] Goebbels' comments on the issues to which he directed his staff's attention correspond to the items of business noted in the transcripts of conferences Goebbels regularly held with the department heads in his ministry.[45] He also recorded quite frankly the praise and criticism contained in the SS Security Service's regular assessments of the effects of his various propaganda strategies. And finally, we can also corroborate certain details of his long conversations with Hitler. For a comment Goebbels had made to Hitler on 26 April 1942 about the film star Emil Jannings' irresponsible political gossiping, we find a direct correspondence between the relevant diary entry and Henry Picker's record of the lunchtime conversation in Hitler's *Tischgespräche* (Table conversations).[46]

In many cases where Goebbels determined cultural policy, the entries are so terse and/or cryptic that we must draw upon outside materials in order to understand them. Often the reverse is also true. The diaries provide the key that unravels a series of complicated policy developments. The case of the eccentric philosopher and founder of the "School of Wisdom" in Darmstadt, Hermann Alexander Graf von Keyserling (1880-1946), illustrates this situation particularly well. If examined in isolation of one another, neither the relevant diary entries nor the extant documents on Keyserling reveal the entire story.

In 1936, Keyserling published *Das Buch vom persönlichen Leben,* a 678-page tome of freewheeling discourses on everything from health, marriage, and liberty to the soul, with occasional remarks on the Weimar Republic, National Socialism, racial matters, and the Führer principle.[47] Alerted to the work by a review in a German-language newspaper from Alsace-Lorraine, the Central Department of the SS Security Service forwarded the suggestion to the Berlin Gestapa *(Geheimes Staatspolizeiamt)* that the book be entered on the "List of Harmful and Undesirable Literature."[48] After receiving two requests from the Gestapa, the Reich Literature Chamber banned the work on 15 February 1937. Less than a week later, it had to report that the Propaganda Ministry had challenged the indexing.[49]

Now, in the atmosphere of gross intolerance that characterized cultural life in Hitler's Germany, official intervention on behalf of a "suspect work" represented the exception rather than the rule. Once the prohibition process was initiated by an influential individual, or by any police, state, or Party agency, normally the work was confiscated and blacklisted. The diaries supply the missing information about this puzzling reversal.

Married to Bismarck's granddaughter, Keyserling had access to highly placed officials in the regime and a powerful intercessor in Field Marshal von Blomberg, the Reich minister of defense and supreme commander of the

Wehrmacht until 1938. According to Goebbels' entries for 27 and 28 February 1937, Blomberg had "put in a good word for Keyserling and his new book," and Goebbels was going to examine it (*TGB*-III, 60-61). Although he considered it "pretentious rubbish" with oppositional tendencies, Goebbels also realized the limited audience this "abstrusely written" work would attract and allowed its dissemination (3 March 1937; *TGB*-III, 64).

His reactive rather than proactive executive manner in Keyserling's case was typical for book bans. In 1935, Goebbels had obtained the exclusive authority to pronounce bans, but he rarely participated himself in indexing procedures unless they involved high-profile foreign authors, such as Sigrid Undset or Sven Hedin, or prominent but "problematical" Germans, such as the late Frank Wedekind. Most cases were handled without his input by the Propaganda Ministry's Literature Department, in conjunction with the Reich Literature Chamber, which managed the list of proscribed authors and titles.

As the diary reports eight months later, Goebbels continued to operate in a reactive mode when Jakob Sprenger, the *Gauleiter* of Hessen-Nassau, persuaded him to reconsider measures against Keyserling, this time against the philosopher's public speaking. On the basis of material Sprenger supplied, Goebbels banned Keyserling from public speaking and placed his writing under precensorship, despite the protest he expected from Blomberg (12 November and 1 December 1937; *TGB*-III, 332 and 352). It now became a contest of wills and influence with Hitler between Blomberg and Goebbels. To forestall further interference from Keyserling's connections in the Nazi hierarchy, on 10 December 1937 Goebbels circulated to the holders of 11 high offices a notice of his edict together with a 13-page negative evaluation of Keyserling's person and work.[50]

Goebbels' comments in the Keyserling case represent an anomaly in one important respect, because in most instances where the diary records his vacillation on a potentially controversial issue, he is weighing the consequences of a more lenient policy versus a ban. In practicing tolerance toward "problematical artists" Goebbels left himself vulnerable to attack from within the Party. His archrival Alfred Rosenberg, for example, advocated a more radical "National Socialist aesthetic" and utilized every opportunity to expose Goebbels' lack of rigor in purging "art Bolshevists." I have analyzed elsewhere in detail the relevance of the diary entries to Goebbels' handling of repeated difficulties that arose between 1933 and 1944 over the continued performance in the Third Reich of works by the Irish dramatist George Bernard Shaw.[51] Goebbels felt a special affinity with Shaw, who wrote many satirical dramas and anti-imperialist political works that lent themselves to propagandistic exploitation and provided Goebbels and his staff with valuable material. But Shaw also did not refrain from making public statements that contradicted Germany's interests, such as his condemnation of Hitler's anti-Semitism and praise for Stalin, which frequently provoked police and Party agencies to call for the banning of Shaw's works from Reich stages. These negative reactions to Shaw precipitated several policy crises for Goebbels, on which he often commented in the diaries. The entries from December 1937 indicate one point when he had become so insecure that he deferred to Hitler, who provided him with the backing for continued tolerance of Shaw's works (cf. 1, 21, and 22 December 1937; *TGB*-III, 352, 376, and 378).

This evidence of Goebbels' willingness to reconsider his measures and of his hesitation to pursue certain courses of action call to mind the reason why one of his principal adversaries, Winston Churchill, never kept a diary. Ironically, Churchill's warning against doing so was recorded in another's diary:

> Sometime during the dinner-table conversation, the question of diaries came up. The Prime Minister [Churchill] said that it was foolish to keep a day-by-day diary because it would simply reflect the change of opinion or decision of the writer, which, when and if published, makes one appear indecisive and foolish. . . . For his part, the Prime Minister said, he would much prefer to wait until the war is over and then write impressions, so that, if necessary, he could correct or bury his mistakes.[52]

With Goebbels' cultural policy, the extant diary entries show he never had the chance to "bury his mistakes." Notwithstanding claims that he misrepresented events to enhance his "historical role" in the Third Reich, he also drew attention over the years to the limitations of his authority by recording many reversals of decisions, failures to implement policy, and unrealized long-term plans. Most notable are the diaries' premature announcements of the fulfillment of certain strategic goals that in reality were never achieved. Among these was his plan in the summer of 1937 to dissolve the Prussian Academy of the Arts. He viewed the academy not just as a relic of the "Weimar system" and symbol of Prussian autonomy that had to be suppressed, but also as a rival cultural institution outside of his control, since, like the Prussian State Theater under Gustav Gründgens' direction, it belonged to the domain of Prussia's minister president Hermann Göring.

The entries delineate a routine procedure that under most circumstances would have culminated in a ban. First Goebbels mentions Hans Hinkel's "devastating report on the new Prussian Academy," where all the "old Bolshevists" have found berths, and Hitler's agreement that the academy "must go" and be replaced by a "German Academy" under Goebbels' direction (24

July 1937; *TGB*-III, 210). Continued references to the academy's elimination during the next days indicate its high priority for Goebbels (*TGB*-II, 212 and 214). At this point he encountered Göring's resistance; and the latter apparently possessed sufficient influence that he could even rescind Hitler's order to dissolve the Prussian Academy (29 July and 5 August 1937; *TGB*-II, 216 and 226). In Goebbels' eyes the issue did not warrant a conflict with Göring, and he abandoned his plan. The Prussian Academy of the Arts would outlast the Hitler regime, albeit in a serious state of atrophy.

Even more frustrating must have been Goebbels' lack of success with a plan to quell his long-standing feud with Rosenberg over the control of cultural affairs by establishing an eighth chamber in the Reich Chamber of Culture for "the Promotion of Art" *(Kunstpflege)*. The new chamber was supposed to incorporate Rosenberg's National Socialist Cultural Community and staff and theoretically would have granted Rosenberg a firmer foothold in the management of cultural policy. Goebbels stated he was willing to make this concession in exchange for "his peace." At the same time, however, he believed he would "maintain the upper hand." As early as 15 July 1936 Goebbels claimed the arrangements were in place for the merger (*TGB*-II, 643; and 1 August 1936: II, 652). But as a result of Rosenberg's intransigence, the process had still not been completed by 1939.

Having reached a dead end with Rosenberg, Goebbels negotiated a merger with German Labor Front leader Dr. Ley, which would bring the labor organization's cultural branch, "Strength Through Joy," into the Reich Chamber of Culture. The two organizations came together in late November 1938 at a joint annual meeting, where both Ley and Goebbels held speeches.[53] Yet once again, Goebbels diary comments proved to be overly optimistic. On 26 January 1939, he claimed to be in "complete agreement with Ley over the question of the Eighth Chamber"; and on 21 March 1939, he stated the merger was "accomplished" and needed only Rudolf Hess's confirmation (*TGB*-III, 562 and 578). Yet nothing transpired in the ensuing two years, and Goebbels' enthusiasm waned, whereas Ley persisted. In the weeks before Germany invaded the Soviet Union, Goebbels' interest revived, and he then described the merger as an ideal "marriage, to which the Propaganda Ministry brings the intelligence and Ley the masses" (21 May 1941; *TGB*-IV, 651). Despite reservations expressed by his own staff members and opposition from within the Party hierarchy, Goebbels pursued the union with Ley's organization and finally, on 2 July 1941, believed they would announce the new "seventh chamber."[54] One more time he came up empty-handed, for, as he recorded, Rosenberg had "torpedoed the introduction of the Seventh Chamber 'Strength Through Joy.'"[55] Thus the plan, which Goebbels believed would have enabled him to "disseminate culture on as large a scale as possible to the broad masses of our nation,"[56] amounted to nothing.

The diary entries prove to be an invaluable source not just with respect to Goebbels' successes and failures in the implementation of his cultural policy, but also with respect to the priorities he set in his oversight of the arts within Hitler's Germany. As fanatical and tireless as he represented himself to be in the execution of his duties, even for Goebbels it was humanly impossible to devote equal attention to each and every task arising from his multiple state and Party functions. Patterns in his entries reveal what policy priorities he set and the extent to which the departments within the Propaganda Ministry monitoring areas of artistic expression operated autonomously. Here it is interesting to note how little the priorities in cultural policy indicated in the entries from 1933 to 1945 differed from the ones Goebbels had outlined in his ministry's original concept, which listed five departments covering radio, press, film, theater, and propaganda. In the *Vom Kaiserhof* version of his diary, he stated that since these areas interested him personally, he would devote his entire energies to them.[57] And even though the Propaganda Ministry later added a department for literature and the establishment of the Reich Chamber of Culture allowed Goebbels to preside over all areas of artistic expression, his statement from March 1933 remained essentially valid.

Aside from the organization of the "decadent art" exhibits and his acquisitions of artworks for his personal collection, gifts to his peers, and the decoration of the Propaganda Ministry, the entries indicate that Goebbels rarely dwelled on the visual arts and showed no interest in monitoring painters, sculptors, or architects. This low priority might not be attributed just to his personal preferences, but also to his location, for as rich as Berlin was in theaters, cinemas, and film studios, under National Socialism it never became the center for the visual arts. The principal national event in these arts continued to be the annual "Great German Art Exhibition" held in Munich's "House of German Art." When Goebbels did attempt to promote Berlin artists during the Berlin Art Weeks established in May 1942, he developed an inferiority complex upon inspection of the exhibition. As he noted in the diary and later in a conversation with Hitler, he quickly realized that the artistic quality of the paintings at his disposal could not compare with that of the works concurrently on display in Munich.[58]

With music, another area not represented by a special department in the Propaganda Ministry, the pattern in the entries indicate that Goebbels' involvement was limited to personnel matters and a few individual cases. When it came to the elimination of "non-Aryans" from the Berlin Philharmonic Orchestra, his duties as Berlin's *Gauleiter* and head of the Reich Chamber of Culture intersected, and for several years he repeatedly mentioned the progress of the purge of Jewish musicians.[59] The entries also record Goebbels' intervention in the periodic feuding between Germany's two preeminent conductors, Wilhelm Furtwängler and the up-and-coming Herbert von Karajan, whom Furtwängler accused of "promoting himself" too much in the press. While taking care not to hurt Furtwängler's pride or challenge his leading position, Goebbels expressed concern that the cultivation of new talents such as Karajan not be neglected.[60] He had such considerations foremost in mind when dealing with the case of the 35-year-old composer Karl Höller. After Hitler had labeled Höller's music "atonal" following a performance under Furtwängler's direction in March 1942, Goebbels went out of his way to prevent the career-stifling consequences this "prejudice" could have had. By working through tape recordings of Höller's music, he assured himself that this first impression was wrong and then passed the material on to Hitler so that he could "get to know another side" of the composer.[61]

Goebbels' comments regarding Höller are consistent both with his policy to promote young artists for the sake of Germany's future cultural life and with his relatively open attitude toward some forms of contemporary music. This attitude was especially evident in the area of music policy he focused on the most, namely music's predominate role in broadcasting. Goebbels was constantly modifying radio programming to accommodate the tastes of the largest contingent of listeners, who preferred light entertainment over serious music. In contrast to more orthodox Party leaders, whose notion of "acceptable German music" was limited to that of the second half of the nineteenth century, Goebbels expressed his belief that musicians in the Reich were capable of producing music that was "modern but not un-German." Whereas he sought to eliminate the last vestiges of "American Jazz" and "Hot Music" from the Reich's air waves, he did foster its German equivalent known as "rhythmic dance music" by establishing a German Dance and Entertainment Orchestra (Deutsches Tanz- und Unterhaltungsorchester) in early 1942.[62]

Although from the time of his Propaganda Ministry's original conception Goebbels had deemed theater worthy of a separate department, the diary entries do not indicate that he participated significantly more in matters of theater policy than in music. To some extent this limited activity might have been due to his Theater Department's efficient operation under the leadership of the Reich dramaturgist Dr. Rainer Schlösser, one of Goebbels' few appointees who remained in his office until the very end of the Reich. As a study of extant Theater Department documents shows, Schlösser and his staff handled most policy-related business independently. Only on rare occasions—for example, when problems arose in 1938 and during the war with Shaw—did the staff believe a matter warranted a "Ministervorlage" (a referral to Goebbels for a decision). Notably, such instances almost always generated comments in the diaries. Besides these difficult cases, the major policy items Goebbels commented on were large-scale budget considerations related to attendance revenues, ticket pricing policy, and subsidies to theaters, which all became increasingly important as wartime contingencies affected the allocation of resources.[63]

Goebbels was, of course, an avid theatergoer and enjoyed the company of actors and actresses. The entries from the 1930s are especially replete with references to the Reich's theatrical elite and his next-day reviews of performances.[64] It was in this context that he recorded his thoughts on contemporary developments in the German drama. He did not mince his words in expressing his condemnation of the *Thingtheater* and other "cultic, Germanic fraud" promoted by Alfred Rosenberg (13 April 1937; *TGB*-III, 109). In 1935, he denounced Rudolf Ahlers' blood-and-soil drama *Erde* as "terrible bullshit" (*TGB*-II, 524); and after attending a performance of Otto Erler's *Thors Gast* in 1938, he despaired about the future of German art if such "Nordic Kitsch," which he labeled "dramatized Rosenberg program," truly represented the new direction (*TGB*-III, 320). But with policy governing the drama's formal aspect and questions of repertoires, Goebbels restricted himself almost entirely to his immediate environment, to the repertoires of the Berlin theaters he patronized, particularly the Deutsches Theater under Heinz Hilpert's direction.[65] As with other areas of artistic expression, Goebbels operated in a reactive mode, intervening only in crisis situations. He did so in April 1942, when he felt compelled to replace Reich Theater Chamber president Ludwig Körner with Paul Hartmann, after Körner had attracted attention by granting state stipends to individuals with "questionable pasts."[66]

The original plan for the Propaganda Ministry did not include a literature department, and despite the addition of one, this area never occupied Goebbels' attention as much as might have been expected given his university education in German literature and his own literary aspirations. Indeed, the entries dispel any notion that Goebbels had cultivated a "love of letters" in his function as propaganda minister and Reich Chamber of Culture president. Just as the mediocrity and derivative nature of both Goebbels' "Stationendrama" *Der Wanderer* and diary novel *Michael* indicate we did not lose a great author to politics, the critical commentaries contained in the diaries on literary matters show the Nazi Party did not rob *Germanistik* of a valuable scholar.[67]

Until wartime developments began to monopolize the entries' content in the early 1940s, Goebbels commented regularly on his reading. These entries, which ranged from laconic evaluative remarks to lengthier criticisms, reflect his lack of cosmopolitan or modernist interests and his adherence instead to a conservative literary aesthetic rooted in nineteenth-century Realism.[68] At the same time, however, Goebbels revealed tastes that occasionally deviated from National Socialist norms for "acceptability," and these personal preferences could affect his policy decisions.

What Goebbels was reading from 1925 to 1945 consisted almost exclusively of nonfiction and fiction prose. During the "years of struggle" before January 1933, he broadened his ideological horizons with the help of numerous historical, political, and socioeconomic analyses of post–First World War Germany written mainly by right-wing nationalists. He learned all he wanted to know about Soviet-style Bolshevism from Trotski's diatribe against the Stalin regime and sensationalist accounts of the "hellish reality" of life under socialism by Iwan Solonewtisch and Alexandra Rachmonova.[69] And in the area of inspirational nonfiction, the entries note the tremendous authority Frederick the Great's writings had for Goebbels, who revered them like the Bible. Over the years he turned to them again and again, read passages aloud at family gatherings, and sought consolation in them during his last days in the Führer bunker.

There is no such discernible pattern in the area of fiction, where we find an eclectic mixture of classics and trivial literature, with a smattering of works from national literatures other than German. To Goebbels, Dostoyevsky was the embodiment of Russian literature. Stendhal apparently was the only notable French author he picked up. British culture fared somewhat better, as Goebbels expressed his appreciation of Shakespeare's works in performance. He read, among other things, a translation of T. E. Lawrence's *Seven Pillars of Wisdom*. As previously mentioned, Goebbels was not only very interested in George Bernard Shaw's plays but also followed closely the Irishman's witty remarks on current developments in British and European politics. Diary entries from 1942 and as late as 1944 indicate that Goebbels used every opportunity to exploit Shaw's commentaries propagandistically (8 January 1944; *TGB2*-XI, 64-65).[70] With certain works, such as W. Somerset Maugham's *Of Human Bondage*, whose German translation *Der Menschen Hörigkeit* he finished reading in April 1939 (*TGB*-III, 592), we can discern a pronounced personal interest, since Maugham's protagonist, Philip Carey, shared Goebbels' artistic pretensions, foot deformity, and troubles coming to terms with his active sex drive.[71]

The fact that American literature was omitted from Goebbels' reading was consistent with his perception that the only useful contributions from that "cultural desert" across the Atlantic were mass-production technology and filmmaking know-how. Thus, while he had ignored the impact made during the Weimar years on the German literary scene by translations of works by Ernest Hemingway, Theodore Dreiser, Thomas Wolfe, Upton Sinclair, and

Jack London, as propaganda minister he later did take the time to study the celluloid images of Clark Gable, Shirley Temple, and Snow White.

Goebbels proved to be a very discriminating reader even with the leading German authors of his time. At one point in 1941, his ministry would confirm he had never read anything by Erwin Guido Kolbenheyer, the much-celebrated author of the *Paracelsus* novel trilogy.[72] Nor did Goebbels show any interest in the blood-and-soil tomes produced by Hans Friedrich Blunck, Gustav Frenssen, Friedrich Griese, Hermann Stehr, Emil Strauß, and Hans Zöberlein. This omission is telling, since these authors occupied important posts in such Third Reich cultural institutions as the Deutsche Dichterakademie (Academy of German Poets) and the Kultursenat (Cultural Senate), and they were the recipients of prestigious literary prizes under the Hitler regime. Moreover, the works of other prominent authors from the period—Agnes Miegel, Ina Seidel, Will Vesper, and Ernst Wiechert—are conspicuously absent from Goebbels' reading material, though they were the very authors recommended in the categories for fiction and poetry in the National Socialist Bibliography of "100 essential books."[73]

In a similar vein, Goebbels recorded on several occasions his rejection of Gerhart Hauptmann, the venerable representative of German naturalism and only holder of the Nobel Prize for Literature who remained in the Third Reich. Although Goebbels honored Hauptmann in public and allowed most of his plays to appear on German stages,[74] he described the septuagenarian dramatist as an "anachronism," whose works he deemed to be of no use to the new regime (*TGB*-II, 719, and III, 336). With Hauptmann we find one of the few instances where Goebbels agreed with Rosenberg on the treatment of an "ideologically suspect" artist. When planning the observance of Hauptmann's eightieth birthday in November 1942, Goebbels complied with Rosenberg's request that neither the state nor the Party be associated with the occasion. He restricted the event to Breslau and limited the number of new productions of Hauptmann's works that theaters throughout the Reich could use to celebrate the author.[75]

It is most telling that in Goebbels' view, the "greatest modern writer alive" and "the only one worth reading" (cf. *TGB*-I, 258; II, 117 and 533; III, 599-600; see also IV, 523) was no German author, but the 1920 Nobel laureate for literature, the Norwegian Knut Hamsun. The sincerity of his praise was evident in the fact that, over the years, Goebbels read with immense satisfaction practically everything written by this antiliberal, reactionary author, who shared the propaganda minister's views on women's biological role.[76] Goebbels got to meet Hamsun in May 1943, and the encounter elicited one of his most enthusiastic diary entries, rivaling his habitual expressions of joy over words of praise from Hitler (19 May 1943; *TGB2*-VIII, 326-27; also in Lochner, 384-86).

In other literary matters there is a degree of latitude in Goebbels' enforcement of National Socialist cultural policy. The opinions contained in the diaries do delineate an independent course from the one set by some of the most influential publications in the Third Reich: the SS organ *Das Schwarze Korps,* the literary journal *Die Neue Literatur* edited by Will Vesper, and Alfred Rosenberg's *Die Bücherkunde.* As the entries indicate, Goebbels intervened against both the "völkisch" faction and *Das Schwarze Korps* when they started to attack the writer Walter von Molo in 1935 because of his "unnationalistic" literary tastes and past support for "undesirable" writers from the Weimar period.[77] After these attacks continued for the next three years, Goebbels summoned Molo, heard him out, examined the "evidence" against him, and decided to help him (*TGB*-III, 407, 426, and 545).[78]

With the prolific author Rudolf Ditzen, who wrote under the pseudonym Hans Fallada, Goebbels' independent course from the leading opinion in Party circles was also clear. There was an ongoing campaign by *Die Neue Literatur* and *Die Bücherkunde* to stifle Fallada's continued success on the Third Reich book market with his treatments of Germany's lower classes during the inflation years *(Kleiner Mann, was nun? Bauern, Bonzen und Bomben,* and *Wir hatten einmal ein Kind).*[79] Despite Vesper's questioning the "moral character" of people to whom Fallada's writing appealed, in early 1938 Goebbels devoured within a week Fallada's most recent novel, the voluminous *Wolf unter Wölfen.* And at precisely the same time *Die Bücherkunde* had condemned the work and placed it on its list of "not-to-be-promoted literature" ("nicht zu fördernde Literatur"),[80] Goebbels was praising the novel and Fallada's talent: "a great, exciting work. . . . That boy certainly knows his stuff" (*TGB*-III, 402 and 422). Such discrepancies are consistent with the postwar claim that Fallada had been caught in the middle of the long-standing feud between Rosenberg and Goebbels over control of Third Reich cultural life and the rumor that had reached Fallada's publisher, Ernst Rowohlt, that Goebbels had supported *Wolf unter Wölfen.*[81] It was clearly to Fallada's advantage that his works found favor with Goebbels, whose control of Reich Chamber of Culture membership and the book indexes gave him the final word on an author's fate. Indeed, Goebbels thought so highly of Fallada's ability to write popular novels that in late May 1943 he wanted to engage him and other "successful authors from the Weimar Period" to write a series of anti-Semitic novels (*TGB2*-VIII, 386).

The consolidation of all *Buchverbote* (book bans) under Goebbels' Propaganda Ministry was a major coup in his contest with Rosenberg and other Party leaders over cultural control. Nominally Goebbels was the principal agent in the pronouncement of all book bans, and he did consider Germany's literary scene his "realm" ("das von mir betreute Gebiet"; *TGB*-III, 522). However, an analysis of his diary commentaries in the light of the copious archival material pertaining to these bans reveals the low priority Goebbels actually had assigned to his role in literary surveillance. Given Goebbels' "hands-on" managerial approach in other sectors of cultural life, it is remarkable that out of the over 1,000 bans processed by the Propaganda Ministry, Goebbels mentions his personal involvement in decisions on the banning of a specific work or an author's oeuvre very rarely. Two of these cases, one involving George Bernard Shaw's plays and the other, the German translation of Sven Hedin's *Tyskland och världsfreden* (Germany and World Peace) had implications for the Reich's foreign policy and ultimately led Goebbels to consult with Hitler.[82] But for the most part, Goebbels commented only on blanket policy decisions, such as the all-out campaign against religious publications or the banning of all works on Russia at the beginning of the war.

In the case of Jochen Klepper, an author who suffered years of persecution because his "non-Aryan" wife disqualified him for membership in the Reich Literature Chamber, Goebbels' disinterest both as a reader and policymaker is puzzling—especially since the author had practically dropped a significant book into his lap. Klepper had written to Goebbels directly on two occasions. Upon his expulsion from the chamber in April 1937, he sent an appropriately obsequious appeal to the minister, together with copies of positive reviews in the press of his moderately successful *Der Vater: Der Roman des Soldatenkönigs*, a historical novel based on the life of Frederick the Great's father, King Friedrich Wilhelm I of Prussia.[83] Nevertheless, Goebbels was not involved in the appeals process that resulted in a special permit allowing Klepper to publish as long as his manuscripts were submitted to the Propaganda Ministry for prior approval. When delays in approval caused Klepper to miss publishers' deadlines, in December 1937 he again turned to Goebbels, this time sending him a copy of *Der Vater*.[84] Although the work was being praised by top circles in the Wehrmacht, had received favorable reviews in the *Völkischer Beobachter* and other Party newspapers,[85] and dealt with historical figures who were of great importance to Goebbels, the diaries contain no record that he had either read the work or taken any personal interest in Klepper's case, which continued to be handled by intermediaries.[86]

Of all the areas of artistic expression under his purview, Goebbels invested the most time and energy and resources of his ministry into the two mass media that had emerged at the beginning of this century: radio broadcasting and the cinema. Especially with broadcasting, he had every reason to do so. When Hindenburg established the Propaganda Ministry, he provided no funding from the state budget. Instead he made the new ministry largely dependent on the revenue generated by the two-mark monthly fees for radio listeners. Thus at the onset of the Hitler regime, when Goebbels had successfully wrested control of broadcasting from the Prussian government and the Interior Ministry, he was obliged to negotiate with the prime controlling agency, the Reich Postal Ministry (Reichspost), which maintained the transmitting stations. They worked out a revenue-sharing agreement, according to which the Postal Ministry received 55 percent of the fees generated by the first 7 million listeners, but only 25 percent of the fees from listeners beyond that number.[87]

The Propaganda Ministry therefore had an excellent incentive to increase the base of 4.2 million radio subscribers that Germany had at the end of 1932. To this end Goebbels immediately promoted broadcasting's equivalent of the "Volkswagen," the *Volksempfänger* (known as the *VE*-301), a mass-produced, moderately priced set with limited reception. When the Reich Radio Chamber president Hans Kriegler later proposed an even cheaper receiver, the 32 RM *Deutscher Kleinempfänger* available on a purchase plan with monthly installments of 1 RM, Goebbels expressed his support for this "good idea for promoting the radio among workers" (28 December 1937; *TGB*-III, 384). Despite the outbreak of war and competing demands for scarce commodities, Goebbels pursued the *Volksempfänger* project, noting in February 1941 the need to intervene and redirect production priorities to *Volksempfänger* instead of brand-name sets in order to replenish the market (5 February 1941; *TGB*-IV, 491).

By 1936, 2.5 million VE-301 units had been produced, and there were 7.2 million radio listeners registered in the Reich.[88] In January 1937, Goebbels expressed his pleasure at this massive expansion and the budget surplus due to income from the radio, which he used to fund other enterprises (*TGB*-III, 15). The sale of 400,000 *Kleinempfänger* after Goebbels had introduced the new set at the Great German Radio Exhibition in early 1938 helped to boost listener numbers over 10 million in the "Old Reich" (Germany excluding Austria and other annexed territories).[89] The Reichspost had never anticipated such immense growth, and in 1941, it sought to renegotiate the original agreement.[90] But when the radio audience reached 12 million by 1942, the opposite situation almost occurred. In April of that year, Goebbels recorded his intention to alter the terms "substantially in the Propaganda Ministry's favor," since in his opinion the Reichspost's share of the fees in no way reflected its contribution.[91] Although he did not carry out this intention, Goebbels could find solace in the 190 million RM his ministry collected when the broadcasting audience reached its peak of 16 million in 1943.[92]

Having attracted millions of new listeners, Goebbels' broadcasting industry had the major task of retaining this audience as loyal subscribers. One consequence was a heightened sensitivity to listener wishes, which was reflected in Goebbels' frequent comments in the diaries on both radio policy and programming practices. Here, in contrast to the cultural sectors of music, theater, literature, and the visual arts, he oversaw the most trivial details of the program planning and intervened routinely in the running of his ministry's radio department.[93] From 1 March 1933, when Goebbels assumed control of the medium, right up through the war years, his diary comments reveal one central consistency in broadcasting policy, a recurring call for *Auflockerung* (relaxation) of the broadcast program (e.g., 14 July 1933; *TGB*-II, 446, 6 December 1935; II, 549, 24 October 1936; II, 706, and 19 April 1940; IV, 118). Mindful of the axiom *docere et delectare,* Goebbels was careful to limit the role of political and ideological material in the broadcasting schedule. Contrary to Leonard Doob's postwar claim that the Nazi authorities had made "a consistent effort to keep entertainment at a minimum,"[94] Goebbels waged an ongoing campaign to make the program more appealing to the largest segment of the audience, the uneducated masses. He constantly modified programming so that light music and other entertaining broadcasts constituted the main fare. From 1935 to 1937, music's dominance in the overall broadcasting program steadily increased from 60 to almost 70 percent.[95] As the diaries indicate, such modifications were necessary, since as early as April 1937, Goebbels was faced with competition from the more attractive musical offerings of foreign broadcasting stations (*TGB*-III, 121).

The main casualty of these programming shifts was broadcasting's verbal component, the *Wortsendungen* (spoken programs): news broadcasts, and literary offerings such as readings from prose works and dramas, as well as radio plays. As his comments indicate, the would-be author Goebbels displayed no bias toward the latter genre in his efforts to cater to popular tastes. Despite the artistic advances the radio play achieved in the 1930s and the demonstration of the genre's propagandistic utility at the onset of the Western campaign in early 1940, the pattern in Goebbels' comments on radio policy show he believed that the fewer radio plays on the air, the greater the audience appeal would be. Other extant documents from his ministry and the broadcasting industry confirm this attitude toward the radio play, which he rejected as "a literary invention" that had no resonance with "the broad masses."[96]

Of course, in his efforts at mass marketing, Goebbels did not altogether relinquish a propagandistic thrust to his radio policy. With such comments as "not so much persuasion. Work in disguise," and "Not so much obtrusive politics. Operate more with the appearance of having no intention" (14 July 1933; *TGB*-II, 446; and 27 November 1935; II, 545), he recorded quite candidly his plan for subtle manipulation of the listening audience. At the Great German Radio Exhibition in 1938, he spoke openly about this strategy: "One will have to take into consideration that political broadcasts will always take up only a small part of the broadcasting time, that they gain any value, however, only through the presence of entertaining and artistic broadcasts, because the latter bring listeners to the radio set."[97]

As Goebbels recorded in subsequent entries, the strategy of combining a minimum of propaganda with a maximum of entertainment continued after the invasion of Poland. If anything, Goebbels focused more attention on radio policy and listener demands in acknowledging the medium's great strategic potential, which was being put to the test for the first time in this century: ". . . the radio is our most potent weapon for sustaining our morale and for wearing down internal opponents" (19 December 1939; *TGB*-III, 670).[98]

The remarks on radio policy show that for Goebbels, ever larger doses of broadcast "entertainment" were necessary to sustain domestic morale. He exercised more latitude in the types of popular music allowed on the air, revoking earlier bans (9 May 1940; *TGB*-IV, 149). Although at the war's outset he had enacted a law prohibiting Germans from listening to foreign broadcasts,[99] many people, including members of the Wehrmacht, defied the ban, in part due to the BBC's superior musical offerings. Thus, as the war effort intensified during the extensive secret preparations for the invasion of the Soviet Union, Goebbels' diary mentions he relaxed the program further to keep his listeners from tuning in to the English (22 May 1941; *TGB*-IV, 653), which corresponds with the directive he issued at the Propaganda Ministry conference on 21 May 1941.[100] He altered the program again in the tense days before the actual attack (11 June 1941; *TGB*-IV, 683); and at this point, Goebbels did not suppress the cynical observation on his intentions: "The radio is singing its cheerful entertainment. That, too, is a means of deception" (16 June 1941; *TGB*-IV, 697-98).

In the entries for early February 1942, Goebbels appears preoccupied with a "fundamental overhaul" of the entertainment segment of the radio program.[101] This culminated in the appointment of three individuals responsible for the three basic categories of "entertainment": light, medium, and elevated music (i.e., classical and "difficult classical music"), which he later subdivided into a total of ten groups that ranged from "light dance and entertainment music" to music that was "more difficult" because it consisted of "unknown classical pieces."[102] In subsequent entries, where the phrase "high spirits are essential to the war" occurs frequently, he defended his broadcasting policy against critics who found the emphasis on popular music too unsophisticated or too "un-German" in its neglect of the classics and allowance for "modern," cosmopolitan musical styles.[103] He had already presented his "justification for the radio's heavy emphasis on entertainment" to the public in his speech "Der

Rundfunk im Kriege" on 15 June 1941 (10 June 1941; *TGB*-IV, 682). He reiterated his position in the speech "Der treue Helfer," broadcast on 1 March 1942.[104]

Goebbels stayed the course of "radio entertainment as warfare" even when the tide turned against Hitler's armies in late 1942. The overwhelming majority of broadcasts in 1943 and 1944 continued to be light music.[105] Even when the Berlin Radio had to sound the alarm as a substitute for air raid sirens destroyed in the Allies' intensified bomber attacks, Goebbels was still "relaxing" the broadcasting program in order to make it more "appropriate to the times" (cf. 1 and 3 February 1944; *TGB2*-XI, 217 and 229). Not until September 1944, when it was impossible to conceal the hopeless military situation, did Goebbels admit in the diaries that he had given up on radio's ability to bolster morale at home on its own.[106]

The diary entries and other relevant material do not just demonstrate that in his cultural policy, Goebbels assigned the mass media much more importance than the traditional forms of cultural expression. The entries also indicate that of the two twentieth-century mass media, film commanded Goebbels' attention the most. He had not been exaggerating when he made this claim before representatives of the film industry in February 1934:

> ... We are of the conviction that film is one of the most modern and economical means that exist for influencing the masses. Therefore a government must not leave the film industry to itself.
>
> We came to film, as to all forms of artistic and cultural activity, with a warm and passionate heart. We not only looked the film industry over from top to bottom and put an end to harmful practices; but also we allowed substantial official support to go to it. I believe there is no government in the entire world whose leader [Führer] and Minister of Culture could say that in the first year of their assumption of power they had viewed virtually all films.[107]

On 4 November 1934 the Reich Film Chamber asserted its authority to scrutinize film subject matter, rough manuscripts, and finished scripts to determine whether their production conformed to the stipulations of the *Reichlichtspielgesetz* (Reich Film Law). Whereas initially the Propaganda Ministry's involvement was restricted to "politically significant" films, its authority soon expanded.[108] Goebbels' diary entry for 13 October 1935 recorded what Hitler's edict of 17 October confirmed: Now Goebbels alone could decide and issue film bans (*TGB*-II, 526).[109] Unlike the situation with book bans, where he routinely delegated his censorship authority to the Propaganda

Ministry's Literature Department, with film he took his function seriously and did not wait to scrutinize the finished product.

From as early as 1935, the entries show Goebbels was poring over synopses, scripts, and first edits of films in progress. While it is not likely that he personally reviewed every one of the over 1,000 films produced within Germany during the Third Reich, the pattern of his remarks indicate that no significant film production escaped his scrutiny and that, at the very least, most other films were subjected to a cursory examination by him. He recorded extensive interaction with Germany's leading film directors, actors, and actresses, as well as his frequent intervention into all phases of the production process. In contrast to the detached ministerial directives that characterized his supervision of other artistic sectors, Goebbels' involvement often took the form of the "friendly advice" he offered to Jenny Jugo, one of his favorite actresses, in order to prevent the ban of what was sure to be "a terrible piece of rubbish" (21 November 1935; *TGB*-II, 542). The entries also show that Goebbels could become quite engaged in a film project, recording almost on a daily basis his preoccupation with the production's progress. He did so when he helped to rework Karl Anton's *Weiße Sklaven* (White Slaves), a treatment of Bolshevism starring Camilla Horn, which Hitler had rejected in its earlier form in October 1936 before accepting the new version in December.[110] Moreover, as Elke Fröhlich has pointed out, Goebbels' comments indicate that people in the film industry cooperated far closer and far more effectively with Goebbels than the "reluctant collaboration" they portrayed in their post-1945 apologias.[111] In fact, according to Goebbels' remarks on the progress of key wartime propaganda films, Veit Harlan, who directed the notoriously anti-Semitic film *Jud Süß*, and Emil Jannings, who wrote the script and starred in the anti-British work *Ohm Krüger*, both demonstrated considerable individual initiative and enthusiasm in developing basic concepts into successful films (15 December 1939; *TGB*-III, 666; 17 December 1940; IV, 436; and 6 April 1941; *TGB*-IV, 565).[112]

When reading Goebbels' comments on the progress of Germany's film industry under his guidance, the frequency with which he referred to Hollywood as the ideal and pursued a policy that sought to emulate the Americans' technical, artistic, and commercial achievements in the film industry is striking. With the exception of a handful of English, French, and Italian works, American films were the only foreign feature films he viewed on a regular basis. His enthusiastic responses to such films as *It Happened One Night* (17 October 1935; *TGB*-II, 527) and *Broadway Melody of 1936* (17 March 1936; *TGB*-II, 588) underscored the value he placed on entertaining cinema with mass appeal. When such appeal was combined with masterful animation and the use of color film, as in Walt Disney's *Snow White and the Seven Dwarfs,* which Goebbels hailed as "a magnificent artistic creation" (*TGB*-IV, 41: 12 February 1940), and in Dave Fleischer's *Gulliver's Travels* (1939), he commented on the necessity to "make every effort to equal the Americans' accomplishments, despite the war" (8 June 1941; *TGB*-IV, 680).

Goebbels' interest in color film technology and in competing with the Americans dates back to 1936, when he attended a demonstration of experimental color films at the Siemens factory and was sufficiently satisfied with the results that he directed Siemens to announce their progress to the public (18 June 1936; *TGB*-II, 628).[113] Yet while the Americans had already demonstrated success in this area with Roy del Ruth's *Garden of Allah* (1936), Goebbels could only state in March 1938 that he was "encouraging energetically research on color film" (*Diario 1938*, 51), and in April 1939 he still had to report that "the preparations for the color film process was proceeding very slowly" (22 April 1939; *TGB*-III, 599). In November 1940, Goebbels reported some progress when he evaluated the first German color film *Frauen sind doch bessere Diplomaten* (Of course, women are better diplomats [*TGB*-IV, 397]), but not until May 1941 did he note that German color films were "almost on par with the Americans" and his plan to "overtake them" (*TGB*-IV, 634-35).

However late, Goebbels did manage to produce some notable color feature films before the war ended (e.g., *Die goldene Stadt* [The Golden City], *Der große König* [The Great King], *Münchhausen, Immensee*, and *Kolberg)*, but he never realized his other goal to develop animated films for the German public. Here, too, Hollywood—or should we say here Walt Disney—set the standard. Goebbels' respect for Disney was evident both in his Christmas gift to Hitler in 1937 of 18 Mickey Mouse films (22 December 1937; *TGB*-III, 378) and his excitement over *Snow White*. In the midst of the secret preparations for Operation Barbarossa, Goebbels scrutinized plans for animated film production in Germany and recorded his support for this "good and useful thing" (15 May 1941; *TGB*-IV, 242), as well as his intention to employ animation for films based on traditional German fairy tales (10 June 1941; *TGB*-IV, 685). The Ufa affiliate, Deutsche Zeichenfilm GmbH (German Animated Film, Inc.), was founded in August 1941 for the purpose of creating "animated features of high quality." Even the increased restrictions on the use of resources after the Stalingrad debacle did not deter Goebbels from promoting domestic animated film production. In September 1943 he still insisted that the development of animated film would best be served by maintaining competition between two companies.[114] Notwithstanding the propaganda minister's encouragement, the Deutsche Zeichenfilm's operations were crippled from the start by the lack of trained artists, the loss of personnel to the draft, and the effects of bombing raids. The handful of short animated films released before the war's end, such as *Der Schneemann* (The Snowman) had been produced either by Deutsche Zeichenfilm's competitor, Fischerkösen-Film-Produktion, or by German subsidiaries outside the Reich.[115]

Hollywood's influence on Goebbels' film policy was not limited to Mickey Mouse and lavish musical revues. From 1940 on, one of the most frequently repeated policy goals in the entries is: "We must dominate the European film industry." The conquest of the European market represented the second stage of Goebbels' long-term strategy to achieve absolute control over both the production and distribution sectors of the film industry and to apply the same monopolistic marketing practices that had made Hollywood so powerful. In the 1920s, Paramount and M-G-M had controlled the lion's share of the German film market through outright ownership of Germany's cinemas,[116] and in the 1930s and 1940s, Hollywood's "Big Five" studios had dictated the terms for the distribution and ticket pricing for their products by owning cinema chains throughout the United States. As an entry from December 1936 reveals, Goebbels believed he soon would accomplish the first stage of his emulation of the Hollywood monopoly by acquiring the entire German film industry (*TGB*-II, 752). After Hitler's victorious Western campaign, a considerable portion of Goebbels' diary comments on cultural matters pertained to the systematic takeover of cinemas in the newly conquered territories, first in France in the fall of 1940 (*TGB*-IV, 365), and then the Balkans in the summer of 1941 (*TGB*-IV, 687).

According to entries from the spring of 1942, Goebbels also targeted France's leading film companies for acquisition. Under German management they would be allowed to continue to produce "kitschy entertainment films" that could satisfy the French viewers without posing any competition for the Germans. As part of this scheme, Goebbels mentioned his directive that "all French actors of more than average talent" be hired for German productions.[117] Such a move represented a reversal of Goebbels' prewar objective to curtail the number of "foreigners" in German films (8 January 1938; *TGB*-III, 394). However, it corresponded to the "pan-European" orientation of the film policy he adopted in June 1941 in preparation for the multinational film market Germany would have to supply "after the war." To achieve this end, Goebbels noted the need "to broaden the range of types and characters" in German film and to gather "stars from all the European countries" in Berlin (*TGB*-IV, 687-88 and 701). With Berlin as Europe's Hollywood, Goebbels hoped to attain the same position of absolute dominance over the European continent that the United States film industry held over the North and South American continents.[118] Much of this policy, such as the suggestion mentioned in April 1942 to establish a "Europa Film Company" that would produce films to replace the

American share of the European market, addressed the postwar situation and never advanced beyond the planning stage.[119]

At the same time Goebbels recorded the progress of his conquest of the European film market and future designs for the medium, he was discussing at length a domestic policy for film and broadcasting that in his opinion played a vital role in the National Socialist war effort. These comments had an essayistic character that set them apart from the main body of his wartime entries, which consisted of prosaic accounts of the military action on the various fronts and summaries of the myriad reports that crossed his desk every day. According to the entry for 26 February 1942, Goebbels saw the need for an intensification of his policy to provide soldiers and civilians ample entertainment because he now realized that the war would not be over soon and that increasingly harsher conditions were inevitable for the civilian population. Evoking the specter of the *Dolchstoß* (stab in the back) theory on Germany's loss in the First World War, he stressed the special need to maintain high spirits on the home front in order to prevent a repeat of the "terrible catastrophe."[120]

The diary entries follow the same line of argumentation that Goebbels presented in what amounted to a three-pronged ideological assault for the cause of "cultural warfare." On 28 February he subjected the leaders of the film industry to a lengthy speech, in which, among many things, he called for increased production of "light, entertaining films" as part of the film industry's contribution to the war.[121] Not fortuitously, this speech came just one day before he justified a similar orientation for the radio in the nationally broadcast piece "*Der treue Helfer*." At the same time, Veit Harlan's Frederick the Great film *Der große König* was screened for the Supreme Command of the Wehrmacht the day before its public premiere at Berlin's Ufa-Palast on 2 March.

The common thrust to all these events was Goebbels' attempt to represent his work in Germany's cultural sector as equal to—if not superior—to that of the front-line generals in the total war effort. The final production stage of *Der große König* had figured prominently in the previous months' entries when Goebbels ordered extensive revisions to the film's treatment of relevant historical material. One key sequence contained a none-too-subtle attack on Hitler's "defeatist" general staff in its depiction of an apparently hopeless military situation in the Seven Years War when Frederick the Great's generals abandoned him after the devastating defeat at Kunersdorf in 1759 had cost him almost half his army. Although Goebbels issued a press directive against drawing any analogies to the present,[122] he did admit in the diary that "individuals with a guilty conscience" would see this and other parallels, which was his original intention.[123]

As he stated repeatedly in the entries, *Der große König* did not just criticize the generals' deficient moral fortitude. By confronting the German nation with the brutal reality of all-out war and the privations at home that accompanied it, the film represented a step toward the "total war" mentality Goebbels would be able to advocate on a large scale after Stalingrad.[124] And in emphasizing the crucial roles of psychological leadership and the bolstering of civilian morale, Goebbels could present himself as a modern-day "Frederick the Great of the Home Front." This was the gist of the following self-congratulatory statement that Goebbels wrote at the time of his film and radio speeches and on the eve of the premiere of *Der große König*. His words were clearly addressed to posterity: "Without doubt the record of history written later will have to state that the political, spiritual and cultural means of national leadership not only did not fail in this war, but that, above all in the area of the home front and of tying the home to the front and vice versa, they have made the most essential contribution to victory."[125]

No less important than Goebbels' representations of his cultural policy as indispensable to the war effort were his frequent assurances in the entries that Hitler endorsed his strategy and was impressed by accomplishments in the various arts under Goebbels' patronage.[126] For film as well as for theater, this led to a curious situation, since, as Hitler claimed elsewhere and Goebbels repeated many times in the entries, Germany's "Führer" would not indulge in theater visits or view any films but official newsreels for the duration of the war.[127] Thus when Hitler was called upon to arbitrate disputes, as occurred with *Der große König*, he acted on the basis of secondhand knowledge of the work. Goebbels always took care to mention this detail when he recorded Hitler's nod of approval for his cultural policy,[128] and he did not forget this reminder even as late as January 1944, when he recorded the directives Hitler issued in reaction to positive hearsay on new films with Henny Porten and Heinz Rühmann (*TGB2*-XI, 169-70). In the latter instance, he might have felt especially obliged to reiterate Hitler's renunciation of cinema in the light of his representation of 23 January 1943 that the Führer had now given up listening to musical recordings. Goebbels' passage closed with an aphoristic remark that was perhaps more appropriate for a street banner in a bombed-out city than a diary: "The Führer's entire life belongs to the war and service to the *Volk*" (*TGB2*-VII, 171).

Goebbels' diaries contain more references to film and other aspects of cultural policy, such as Germany's ongoing competition with Italian film companies and the question of state versus private ownership of cinemas, than can be explored herein. Since Goebbels proved to be especially eloquent when it came to recording the failings of those around him, the diaries are rich with details about the many conflicts he had with rivals in the Party and prominent but "problematical" artists. Thus, we have a decade's worth of critical comments about the "decadent homosexual" Gustav Gründgens, who directed the Prussian State Theater under Hermann Göring's protection. And in the entries from

1942 to 1943, Goebbels referred repeatedly to his efforts to counter Baldur von Schirach's promotion of Vienna as the Third Reich's "cultural capital" to the detriment of Berlin.

Doubtless many new studies on these and related topics will be undertaken once Elke Fröhlich completes the revised diary volumes and makes thousands of pages of unpublished entries available. The material from the prewar years promises to be of great value, in particular the diaries for the critical weeks in early 1933 when Hitler formed his cabinet and established Goebbels' Propaganda Ministry. For much of this period we now have only the entries Goebbels revised for *Vom Kaiserhof zur Reichskanzlei*, and he had every reason to excise any details of his strategic failures and the power struggles among the National Socialist hierarchy from his positive depiction of the newly formed Hitler regime.

Insights into cultural policy might be gained from the supplemental entries for the fall of 1933, when the Reich Culture Chamber was founded and Goebbels made his initial appointments of non–National Socialists, such as Hans Friedrich Blunck and Richard Strauss, the respective presidents of the Reich Literature and Music chambers until 1935. It would be valuable to have Goebbels' comments from this early stage when "racial" and ideological criteria did not dominate cultural policy. In this same context, Goebbels probably recorded his reaction to the massive emigration of Germany's leading artists and his attempts to persuade some individuals to stay.

Perhaps the new diary material will corroborate Fritz Lang's account of a meeting with Goebbels in the early spring of 1933; the propaganda minister allegedly offered the film director the leadership of Germany's film industry, and Lang responded by leaving for Paris the same evening.[129] Scholars who have investigated this legendary encounter should not have been surprised that *Vom Kaiserhof* contains no mention of this meeting or any reference to Lang or his films. In 1934, Goebbels hardly would have drawn attention to a major miscalculation in his personnel plans for the revitalization of the film industry, especially when it concerned a "non-Aryan" who had now become a prominent exile.[130] On the other hand, numerous indications lend credence to Lang's claim of the offer, not the least of which is the diary comment Goebbels made after viewing Lang's *M* in May 1931: ". . . Lang is going to be our director. . . ." (*TGB*-II, 68). From 1929 to May 1933, NSDAP organs such as Goebbels' *Der Angriff* and the *Völkischer Beobachter* had words of praise for Lang's artistic "genius" and contribution to German film's worldwide prestige.[131] We should also not forget Goebbels' speech to representatives of the German film industry on 28 March 1933 at the Kaiserhof Hotel, where he paid tribute to Lang's *Nibelungen* film. The new entries from 1933 on microfiche in Moscow could settle the matter once and for all.

Similarly, the new diary material might shed light on Goebbels' handling of such problem cases as the internationally renowned author Thomas Mann, who did not return from a trip abroad in March 1933 but distanced himself from the anti-Fascist proclamations of the exile community. As with Lang, Goebbels' early entries indicate an interest in Mann's novels and the lasting impression *Buddenbrooks* had made on him. This respect for "Der Buddenbrooksdichter" did not diminish after Mann's transformation in 1930 from German monarchist into an advocate of Weimar democracy and adversary of the NSDAP, although Goebbels did lament the parting of their ways (cf. *TGB*-I, 492 and 504). We know from Mann's sources that his case had found its way to Goebbels when the Bavarian Political Police had tried unsuccessfully to revoke Mann's citizenship in July 1933.[132] At this point, however, we have no documentation on Goebbels' role in the rejection of the Bavarian expatriation attempt. Moreover, with regard to Mann's status in the next three years, we can only speculate that some lingering respect on Goebbels' part might have been behind his considerable delay in sanctions being enacted against Mann's publications in the Reich. Unlike the situation with most of the prominent exile writers, who appeared on the earliest indexes in 1933 and 1934, the blanket ban of Mann's writing did not come until the last possible moment, two days after his German citizenship was finally revoked on 4 December 1936.[133]

In short, many questions on Goebbels' role in National Socialist cultural policy remain open. Even if the new entries from his diaries do not contain the definitive answers, they certainly will help to focus renewed attention to a critical period in European cultural history that we are only beginning to understand fully.

Notes

*Support from the National Endowment for the Humanities Summer Stipend and Travel to Collections Grant Programs, the German Academic Exchange Service, and the University of South Florida Research and Creative Scholarship Grant Program enabled me to conduct research at libraries and archives in the German Federal Republic and the former German Democratic Republic over several summers. With the help of a New College Faculty Development Program grant, I was able to complete the final stages of this project.

1. D. McLachlan's introduction to Rudolf Semmler, *Goebbels—The Man Next to Hitler* (London: Westhouse, 1947), p. 9. In German documents and

Goebbels' diaries his press assistant's name is consistently spelled Semler, not Semmler.

2. Louis P. Lochner, ed. and trans., *The Goebbels Diaries: 1942-1943* (Garden City, NY: Doubleday & Co., 1948); the excerpts in the original German appeared as Lochner, ed. *Goebbels Tagebücher aus den Jahren 1942-43* (Zürich: Atlantis, 1948); Helmut Heiber, ed., *Das Tagebuch von Joseph Goebbels, 1925/26, mit weiteren Dokumenten* (Stuttgart: Deutsche Verlags-Anstalt, 1960); translated as *The Early Goebbels Diaries, 1925-1926* (New York: Praeger, 1963); and Joseph Goebbels, *Tagebücher 1945: Die letzten Aufzeichnungen* (Hamburg: Hoffmann & Campe Verlag, 1977); translated as *Final Entries, 1945: The Diaries of Joseph Goebbels*, edited, introduced, and annotated by Hugh Trevor-Roper (New York: Putnam, 1978).

3. The noted Goebbels scholar Helmut Heiber dismisses the early diaries as "a cheap novel" and believes the wartime entries contain "no final revelations"—H. Heiber, *Goebbels* (New York: Hawthorn Books, 1972), pp. 44 and 253. Ernest Bramsted, in contrast, noted that Goebbels had written the diaries to enhance his reputation with posterity, but Bramsted still made ample use of the diaries for information on Goebbels' role as propaganda minister—E. K. Bramsted, *Goebbels and National Socialist Propaganda 1925-1945* (East Lansing: Michigan State University Press, 1965), p. ix. See also notes 16, 17, 18, 19, and 20 below.

4. Elke Fröhlich, ed., *Die Tagebücher von Joseph Goebbels: Teil I: Aufzeichnungen 1924-1941* (München: K.G. Saur, 1987), 4 vols. See also Elke Fröhlich, "Joseph Goebbels und sein Tagebuch: Zu den handschriftlichen Aufzeichnungen von 1924 bis 1941," *Vierteljahrshefte für Zeitgeschichte* 35, No. 4 (1987): 489-522.

5. Among others, see: Otto B. Roegele, "Lücken, Fehler, Manipulationen: Die Goebbels-Tagebücher sind nachlässig ediert," *Rheinischer Merkur/ Christ und Welt*, No. 1 (1 January 1988): 17; Peter Bucher, "Die Tagebücher von Joseph Goebbels," *1999: Zeitschrift für Sozialgeschichte des 20. und 21. Jahrhunderts* 3, No. 2 (1988): 89-95; the hastily produced and highly polemical work Peter-Ferdinand Koch, ed., *Die Tagebücher des Doktor Joseph Goebbels: Geschichte und Vermarktung* (Hamburg: Facta Oblita, 1988); Claus-E. Bärsch, "Anrüchige Vermarktung: Die ökonomische Re-Nazifizierung des Joseph Goebbels," *Die Zeit*, No. 14 (31 March 1989): 52; Karl-Heinz Janßen, "Der ganze Goebbels: Die unglaubliche Geschichte der Goebbels-Tagebücher," *Die Zeit*, No. 10 (9 March 1990): 19; "Nazi Diaries: Privatising History," *The Economist*, 324, No. 7767 (11 July 1992): 85-86; and Bernd Sösemann, "Die Tagesaufzeichnungen des Joseph Goebbels und ihre unzulänglichen Veröffentlichungen," *Publizistik: Vierteljahreshefte für Kommunikationsforschung* 37, No. 2 (1992): 213-44.

6. According to Dr. Elke Fröhlich at the Institut für Zeitgeschichte in Munich, fax to author on 17 June 1994. See also the preface by Horst Möller, the director of the Institut für Zeitgeschichte, in Elke Fröhlich, ed., *Die Tagebücher von Joseph Goebbels. Teil II: Diktate 1941-1945, Band 11: Januar-März 1944,* Im Auftrag des Instituts für Zeitgeschichte und mit Unterstützung des Staatlichen Archivdienstes Rußlands (München: K.G. Saur, 1994), pp. 7-8; and Bernd Sösemann, "'Die Stunde, da wir über allem stehen...': Kopien, Filme, Mikrofiches: doch Originale fehlen—Zur Quellenlage der Tagebücher," *Die Welt,* No. 159 (10 July 1992): 6.
7. See, for example, the four-part series in *Der Spiegel* from July to August 1992 with hitherto unpublished excerpts from 1934, 1938, 1939, and 1944: *Der Spiegel,* No. 29 (13 July): 104-28; No. 30 (20 July): 100-9; No. 31 (27 July): 102-12; and No. 32 (3 August 1992): 58-75. The citations cover such events as the Reichstag fire, the annexation of Austria and the Sudetenland, the Kristallnacht, Germany's invasion of Poland, the Normandy landing, and the 20 July 1944 plot. None of the passages pertains to cultural policy.
8. Joseph Goebbels, *Tagebücher 1924-1945,* ed. Ralf G. Reuth (München: Piper, 1992), 5 vols. (hereafter cited as *TGB*-Reuth with volume number). The entries in Reuth's volumes follow Fröhlich's edition up to 8 July 1941, with the exception of supplements supplied by David Irving consisting of excerpts from the entries for the following dates: 1 July 1934; 13 and 16 February 1938; 10, 11, 12, and 13 March 1938; 11, 15, 18, 23, 24, 28, and 29 September 1938; 1, 2 and 24 October 1938, and 10 November 1938; 22, 23 August 1939 and 1 September 1939. Reuth does include new material for 9 July to 20 December 1941, and 1942 and 1944, albeit in drastically abridged form. The reduction of the material by 80 percent greatly limits the edition's utility for research purposes. Moreover, Reuth emulates Lochner by eliminating paragraph divisions within the entries and providing no indication of either the content or amount of excised material indicated by ellipsis marks. For an insightful review of Reuth's edition, see Jürgen Michael Schulz, "'Sie werden draußen wohl einiges Interesse finden': Über die Schwierigkeiten, die Goebbels-Tagebücher zu edieren," *Neue Zeit* (Berlin), No. 48 (26 February 1993): 6.
9. Joseph Goebbels, *Diario 1938,* Edizione italiana a cura di Marina Bistolfi; Prefazione di Francesco Bigazzi (Milano: Arnoldo Mondadori Editore, 1993). The Italian edition actually appeared in January 1994. David Irving's German edition, *Der unbekannte Dr. Goebbels. Die geheimgehaltenen Tagebücher des Jahres 1938,* was announced as forthcoming in 1993 by the Grabert Verlag in Tübingen, but it has yet to appear—cf. *TGB*-Reuth: III, 1207, note 31. In his introduction to the Italian edition, Francesco Bigazzi recounts the Russian journalist Elena Rzevskaija's claim that Red Army troops in Hitler's bunker

at the end of the war had recovered ten notebooks of Goebbels' handwritten diaries covering the period 1932 to 8 July 1941. However, the existence of these original materials has not been confirmed—*Diario 1938*, p. xi.

10. Elke Fröhlich, ed., *Die Tagebücher von Joseph Goebbels. Teil II: Diktate 1941-1945,* Im Auftrag des Instituts für Zeitgeschichte und mit Unterstützung des Staatlichen Archivdienstes Rußlands (München: K.G. Saur, 1993-94).

11. Roman numerals will indicate the volumes and Arabic numbers the pages in Fröhlich's two-part edition: e.g., *TGB*-II, 635, or *TGB2*-VII, 41. Notably absent from the sources is Fred Taylor's translation and edition of passages from 1939 to 1941, *The Goebbels Diaries 1939-1941* (London: Hamish Hamilton, 1982). Although Taylor's text corresponds in part to material in volumes 3 and 4 of the Fröhlich edition from 1987, grievous errors in names and mistranslations render it unreliable for scholarly purposes. On the circumstances of Taylor's "pirated" source material and further shortcomings, see Koch, ed., *Die Tagebücher des Doktor Joseph Goebbels,* pp. 221-26; and Michael Kater, "Inside Nazis: The Goebbels Diaries, 1924-1941," *Canadian Journal of History* 25, No. 2 (August 1990): 235.

12. The original diary pages still show Lochner's marginal comments and pencil marks indicating the passages he intended to publish. They are held at the Hoover Institution at Stanford University and available on six microfilms with consecutively numbered frames. The same material, minus frame numbers, was microfilmed by the American Historical Association Committee for the Study of War Documents and is available at the National Archives in Washington, D. C. (Microcopy No. T-84, Rolls 260-66). Roll 267 in this series contains diary material Lochner did not utilize, including complete and partial entries for 8 to 20 August 1941; 25 to 31 May 1942; and 2 to 6 June 1942. This microfilmed material is of vital importance to the present study, since in condensing the 7,000 manuscript pages into a volume that would be appropriate for the "Book of the Month Club," Lochner eliminated the major portion of Goebbels' passages on cultural affairs.

13. Dr. Joseph Goebbels, *Vom Kaiserhof zur Reichskanzlei: Eine historische Darstellung in Tagebuchblättern* (München: Zentralverlag der N.S.D.A.P. Franz Eher Nachf., 1934); translated as *My Part in Germany's Fight* (London: Hurst & Blackett, 1940); reprinted, New York: H. Fertig, 1979.

14. Bronislaw Malinowski's widow, Valetta Malinowska, chose the title *A Diary in the Strict Sense of the Term* when she published her husband's diaries posthumously, because she believed he had not intended to share these writings with anyone—see her preface to Bronislaw Malinowski, *A Diary in the Strict Sense of the Term* (New York: Harcourt Brace & World, 1967), p. ix. The citation by

Geertz is from his discussion of Malinowski's diary, in Clifford Geertz, *Works and Lives: The Anthropologist as Author* (Stanford, CA: Stanford University Press, 1988), p. 78.

15. This was essentially a chronicle of domestic and foreign political and economic developments. Auctorial commentary was absent, and the entries bear no semblance to Goebbels' diary passages that correspond to the dates.

16. Bernd Sösemann, *Inszenierungen für die Nachwelt: Editionswissenschaftliche und textkritische Untersuchungen zu Joseph Goebbels' Erinnerungen, diaristischen Notizen und täglichen Diktaten, Historische Zeitschrift*, Sonderheft 16 (München: Oldenbourg, 1992).

17. Bramsted, for example, distinguishes between the early diaries from 1925/26, "which had not been written with a view to possible publication," and the later diaries (in this case Lochner's edition of the fragments from 1942 and 1943), when he draws upon the early entries for insights into Goebbels' biography— Bramsted, p. 15. He nevertheless relies on the later entries for information on Goebbels' wartime propaganda strategies and agrees with Leonard W. Doob's view that "the manuscript more or less faithfully reflects Goebbels' propaganda strategy and tactics"—cf. Doob, "Goebbels' Principles of Propaganda," in *Public Opinion and Propaganda*, eds. D. Katz, et al. (New York: H. Holt, 1954), p. 509.

18. Heinrich Fraenkel and Roger Manvell, *Goebbels. Eine Biographie* (Köln: Kiepenheuer & Witsch, 1960), p. 252. Gerd Albrecht seconds this opinion in his discussion of Goebbels' diaries as a source for his study—G. Albrecht, *Nationalsozialistische Filmpolitik: Eine soziologische Untersuchung über die Spielfilme des Dritten Reichs* (Stuttgart: Ferdinand Enke, 1969), p. 52.

19. Taylor discounts the diaries as "a public rather than a personal testament" and utilizes the early speeches Goebbels made as propaganda minister as a source for insights into Goebbels' theory of propaganda—R. Taylor, "Goebbels and the Function of Propaganda," in *Nazi Propaganda: The Power and the Limitations,* ed. David Welch (London-Totowa, NJ: Croon Helm-Barnes & Noble, 1983), p. 31.

20. See, for example, the reviews of Louis P. Lochner, ed., *The Goebbels Diaries, 1942-1943* by Allen W. Dulles in *The New York Times Book Review*, 25 April 1948, pp. 1 and 25; and by Carl E. Schorske in *American Historical Review* 54, No. 2 (January 1949): 358-60.

21. In the first of many revisions that would occur in the course of the 44 editions *Vom Kaiserhof* underwent between 1934 and 1944, Goebbels excised all references to Ernst Röhm and other victims of the 30 July 1934 purge. For further details, see Sösemann, *Inszenierungen für die Nachwelt*, pp. 27-28.

22. Jay W. Baird, *To Die for Germany: Heroes in the Nazi Pantheon* (Bloomington: Indiana University Press, 1990), p. 73. Despite its middle-class background,

the Wessel family seemed to provide a model of "sacrifice in service to the nation." Frau Wessel's late husband had been Hindenburg's field chaplain in the First World War, and her younger son Werner, who also was in the Berlin S.A., suffered a tragic death during a skiing excursion a few months before Horst's murder. For further details on the propagandistic exploitation of Horst Wessel's death, see Baird, pp. 73-107.

23. Frau Wessel provoked the first such outburst after a confrontation with Goebbels over her intention to copyright the "Horst Wessel Lied" (i.e., "Die Fahne hoch"), which at the time was functioning as the Third Reich's "second national anthem"—see the entry for 10 June 1933; *TGB*-II, 431. The second incident came three years later, when Frau Wessel christened the schooling vessel *Horst Wessel*—14 June 1936; *TGB*-II, 625-26.

24. *Vom Kaiserhof zur Reichskanzlei*, p. 14. This statement has been translated from the original German of Goebbels' preface to the first edition. The corresponding passage in the English translation from 1940 differs considerably.

25. Lochner, p. 4. Discussing the earlier, handwritten diaries, Irving also comes to the conclusion that Goebbels had neither the time nor the opportunity to go back and revise his entries—Irving, "Introduzione," *Diario 1938*, p. xiii.

26. See Viktor Reimann, *Goebbels*, trans. Stephen Wendt (Garden City, NY: Doubleday & Co., 1976), p. 62; and Peter Stadelmayer's comments on Goebbels' "rough drafts," in "The Story of the 1945 Goebbels Diaries," in *Final Entries, 1945*, pp. xxxv-vi.

27. Cf. 22 October 1936; *TGB*-II, 704: "I am selling Amann my diaries. To be published 20 years after my death. 250,000 Marks immediately and every year thereafter 100,000 Marks. That is very generous. Magda and I are happy. With this Amann has a good investment."

28. Cf. Heiber, *The Early Goebbels Diaries*, p. 15.

29. Page 18 of the entry for 28 April 1943 shows two gaps in the text where the name of the Party official in charge of Lothringen (most likely Josef Bürckel, the *Gauleiter* of Saarpfalz and *Reichsstatthalter* of Lothringen as of August 1940) was to be added later to a report that Horst Slesina, who headed the Reichspropaganda Office of the Westmark, had managed to achieve a "more humane treatment of the population" (Hoover Institution: Reel 4, frame 4293; also in *TGB2*-VIII, 177). The manuscript for the dictations contains several instances where the summary of the military situation ("militärische Lage") that started every entry was to be added later. Since this summary regularly filled six pages, the rest of the entry would start at page seven to accommodate the insertion. The entry for 27 November 1943, in which Goebbels recounted the aftermath of a heavy bombing raid on Berlin, is particularly interesting in this respect. Not only does it start with the note:

"Militärische Lage (Bl. 1-6) nachtragen!" Page 30 of the manuscript consists solely of a reminder to enhance the account of structures and factories destroyed in the raid with "further details about the damages" (Hoover Institution: Reel 6, frame 6566). Since these "gaps" also appear on the glass-plate microfiches that are serving as the basis for the second part of Fröhlich's edition, it appears that in his lifetime Goebbels never had the opportunity to undertake his planned revisions—cf. "Zur Einrichtung der Edition" in *Die Tagebücher von Joseph Goebbels. Teil II: Diktate 1941-1945, Band 11: Januar-März 1944*, ed. Fröhlich, p. 19.

30. See page 23 of the entry for 27 April 1942 (Hoover Institution: Reel 2, frame 2317). On Goebbels' directive for a documentary film on the 20 July plot, see Reuth, *Goebbels*, pp. 559-60.

31. See page 27 of the entry for 30 January 1942 (Hoover Institution: Reel 1, frame 272; also in *TGB2*-III, 220).

32. Cf. the entry for 27 March 1942—*TGB2*-III, 561; also in *TGB*-Reuth: IV, 1776-77. For additional examples of Goebbels' agreement with the "Final Solution" and urging for more rigorous actions against Jews in Germany and Hungary, see Elke Fröhlich, "Hitler und Goebbels im Krisenjahr 1944: Aus den Tagebüchern des Reichspropagandaministers," *Vierteljahrshefte für Zeitgeschichte* 38 (1990): 210-11.

33. Cf. Jürgen Michael Schulz, "Zur Edition der 'Goebbels-Tagebücher': Vortrag auf der German Studies Association Conference 1992," *German Studies Association Newsletter* 17, No. 2 (Winter 1992): 41; and Bernd Sösemann, "'Ein tieferer geschichtlicher Sinn aus dem Wahnsinn': Die Goebbels-Tagebücher als Quelle für das Verständnis des nationalsozialistischen Herrschaftssystems und seiner Propaganda," in *Weltbürgerkrieg der Ideologien: Antworten an Ernst Nolte, Festschrift zum 70. Geburtstag*, eds. Thomas Nipperday, Anselm Doering-Manteuffel, and Hans-Ulrich Thamer (Berlin: Propyläen, 1993), pp. 148-49.

34. According to Peter de Mendelssohn, Mann had already destroyed the earliest sections of his diaries at age 21. In May 1945 Mann then burned the bulk of the entries pertaining to the period prior to 1933. He also had initially wanted a 25-year delay in the diaries' publication before changing it to 20 years— Thomas Mann, *Tagebücher 1933-1934*, ed. Peter de Mendelssohn (Frankfurt/Main: S. Fischer, 1977), pp. xiii-xiv.

35. Cf. Ralf Georg Reuth, *Goebbels* (München: Piper, 1990), pp. 402-3; and Arthur Maria Rabenalt, *Joseph Goebbels und der "Großdeutsche" Film* (München: Herbig, 1985), pp. 130-55.

36. Cf. the entries from 30 December 1938 to 3 January 1939—*TGB*-III, 551-53; and Reuth, *Goebbels*, pp. 403-4.

37. The full passage is as follows: ". . . Fräulein Eva Braun is also visiting Obersalzberg with several girlfriends. I am happy that the Führer finds some distraction through *her/them*." Here Goebbels uses the German pronoun "sie" in a completely ambiguous context and could be referring either to the singular, Eva Braun, or to the plural, the "girlfriends," which would obscure Eva Braun's special status. This passage is also included in Reuth's abridged edition—*TGB*-Reuth: V, 2001.
38. Cf. pages 60-62 of Goebbels' entry for 30 May 1942 (National Archives, T-84 Roll 267). The relevant passage is also included in *TGB*-Reuth: IV, 1807.
39. In his discussion of the performance history of Goebbels' "Der Wanderer," Bruno Fischli notes that the play, which was performed only under the auspices of the National Socialist Theater Organization, did not truly generate any audience interest until after Goebbels had joined the Reichstag in 1928 and gained notoriety—"Zur Herausbildung von Formen faschistischer Öffentlichkeit in der Weimarer Republik," *Weimarer Republik,* hrsg. vom Kunstamt Kreuzberg Berlin und dem Institut für Theaterwissenschaft der Universität Köln (Berlin: Elefanten Press, 1977), pp. 906-8. Similarly, the only publisher Goebbels could find for his "Michael" was the NSDAP Zentralverlag Franz Eher. The Ullstein publishing house had rejected the manuscript earlier. For a blatantly partisan overview of the reception of "Der Wanderer" in Berlin's "bourgeois" and "Jewish" newspapers, many of which either ignored or summarily condemned the play, see the account in Goebbels' own newspaper: Dr. L., "'Der Wanderer' im Wallnertheater," *Der Angriff,* No. 20 (14 November 1927). For a discussion of Goebbels' dependence on models from the German literary tradition in this novel, see Marianne Bonwit, "Michael, ein Roman von Joseph Goebbels, im Licht der deutschen literarischen Tradition," *Monatshefte* 49 (1957): 193-200.
40. See Goebbels' speech in 1934 on the occasion of Schiller's 175th birthday, "Die Schiller-Gedenkrede des Reichsministers Dr. Goebbels," *Völkischer Beobachter,* Norddeutsche Ausgabe, No. 317 (13 November 1934): 6.
41. A telling exception was the occasion when Goebbels was (re-?)reading *Mein Kampf* in 1931 and could not refrain from pointing out its stylistic weakness (*TGB*-II, 62).
42. A good example is the diary entry for 27 January 1931 (*TGB*-II, 13), with Goebbels' outraged reaction to Heinz Pol's scathing review of *Michael*—Heinz Pol, "Goebbels als Dichter," *Die Weltbühne* 27, No. 4 (27 January 1931): 129-34.
43. Cf. Peter Bucher, "Die Tagebücher von Joseph Goebbels," *1999: Zeitschrift für Sozialgeschichte des 20. und 21. Jahrhunderts* 3, No. 2 (1988): 94.
44. See Goebbels' entry for 13 November 1938 (*TGB*-III, 533) and Document 1816-PS, Stenographische Niederschrift (Partial transcript of conference

chaired by Göring on the Jewish Question), *Trial of the Major War Criminals before the International Military Tribunal* (Nuremberg: IMT, 1948), vol. 28, pp. 499-520.

45. Cf. Willi A. Boelcke, ed., *Kriegspropaganda 1939-1941: Geheime Ministerkonferenzen im Reichspropagandaministerium* (Stuttgart: Deutsche Verlags-Anstalt, 1966).

46. See page 29 of Goebbels' entry for 27 April 1942 (Hoover Institution: Reel 2, frame 2323), and the corresponding account of a lunchtime conversation with Hitler in Dr. Henry Picker, *Hitlers Tischgespräche im Führerhauptquartier 1941-1942* (Stuttgart: Seewald, 1965), p. 296. The difference in dates stems from Goebbels' practice of recording the previous day's events.

47. See Hermann Graf von Keyserling, *Das Buch vom persönlichen Leben* (Stuttgart: Deutsche Verlags-Anstalt, 1936), passim, especially pp. 203, 260-305, 343, 414-16, and 470-73.

48. SS-Hauptsturmführer Six to Geheimes Staatspolizeiamt Berlin, undated by sender but stamped by recipient "received 19 September 1936," Bundesarchiv Koblenz: R 58/914, fol. 84 (hereafter cited as BAK).

49. Cf. Geheimes Staatspolizeiamt Berlin to RSK, 5 October and 7 November 1936, BAK: R 58/914, fols. 87-88. RSK (Dr. Heinl) to Geheimes Staatspolizeiamt Berlin, 15 February and 13 March 1937, BAK: R 58/914, fols. 93 and 102; copies of this correspondence are also found in Keyserling's Reich Chamber of Culture file in the Berlin Document Center (hereafter cited as BDC/RKK followed by the individual's name). In addition, see the Gestapa note of 24 February 1937 regarding a telephone conversation two days earlier with Menz from the Reich Literature Chamber, BAK: R 58/914, fol. 96.

50. Cf. the entry for 9 December 1937; *TGB*-III, 352; and Goebbels to Dr. Lammers, Head of the Reich Chancellory; Reich Minister Rudolf Hess, the Führer's deputy; Field Marshal von Blomberg; Reich Foreign Minister von Neurath; Reich Minister of the Interior, Dr. Frick; Bernhard Rust, the Reich Minister for Science, Education and Popular Instruction; Minister President Hermann Göring; Reichsleiter Alfred Rosenberg, the Führer's Delegate for the Entire Spiritual and Ideological Education of the NSDAP; Reichsleiter Philip Bouhler, Head of the Official Party Commission for the Protection of Nazi Literature; Gauleiter Bohle of the NSDAP Foreign Organization; and Reichsstatthalter Sprenger, 10 December 1937, BAK: NS 10/43, fols. 164-78.

51. See Glenn R. Cuomo, "'Saint Joan before the Cannibals': George Bernard Shaw in the Third Reich," *German Studies Review* 16, No. 3 (October 1993): 435-61.

52. Harry C. Butcher, *My Three Years with Eisenhower: The Personal Diary of Captain Harry C. Butcher, USNR, Naval Aide to General Eisenhower, 1942-1945* (New York: Simon and Schuster, 1946), p. 319, entry for 31 May 1943.

53. For an account of the ceremony and the texts of the speeches, see "Gemeinsame Jahrestagung der Reichskulturkammer und der NS.-Gemeinschaft Kraft durch Freude: Festsitzung im Deutschen Opernhaus, Berlin—Dr. Goebbels und Dr. Ley über Arbeitserfolge und Arbeitsaufgaben," *Völkischer Beobachter* (Berliner Ausgabe), No. 330 (26 November 1938).
54. *TGB*-IV, 730. This additional chamber's number changed from eight to seven because the number of original chambers was reduced by one when Goebbels dissolved the Reich Radio Chamber on 28 October 1939 to eliminate administrative redundancy—cf. Ansgar Diller, *Rundfunkpolitik im Dritten Reich* (München: Deutscher Taschenbuch Verlag, 1980), p. 159; and Joseph Wulf, *Presse und Funk im Dritten Reich* (Frankfurt/Main: Ullstein, 1983), pp. 315-16.
55. See page 25 of an undated entry from August 1941; and pages 23 and 11 respectively of two incomplete entries from the late summer of 1941 (National Archives, T-84 Roll 267).
56. See page 23 of an undated and incomplete entry from the late summer (August?) of 1941 (National Archives, T-84 Roll 267).
57. Cf. Goebbels, *Vom Kaiserhof zur Reichskanzlei* (1934), p. 277, entry for 8 March 1933: "I have finished the rough structure of my ministry. It will be divided into five departments, which encompass the areas of radio, press, film, propaganda and theater. These are all areas that interest me personally very much, and if for that reason alone I will commit myself to them with my entire zeal and entire inner devotion."
58. See pages 23-24 of Goebbels' diary entry for 4 May 1942 (Hoover Institution: Reel 3, frames 2528-29); and pages 19 and 30-31 of the entry for 2 June 1942 (National Archives, T-84 Roll 267).
59. The issue of Jews and "half-Jews" in the Berlin Philharmonic first came up in July 1933 and continued to appear until August 1937, *TGB*-II, 443, and III, 223.
60. See, for example, Goebbels' comments on Furtwängler's complaints about Karajan, to which Goebbels reacted by reducing the younger conductor's press coverage (14 and 22 December 1940; *TGB*-IV, 432 and 441). Goebbels later expressed his "pleasure at the positive transformation" Furtwängler had undergone after a foreign tour, since he was no longer engaging in "public disputes" with Karajan, pages 15-16 of the entry for 28 February 1942 (Hoover Institution: Reel 1, frames 948-49; also in *TGB2*-III, 387). However, Furtwängler's jealousy took the upper hand again at the end of 1942, and this time Goebbels sided with the "great future talent" Karajan—see pages 22-23 of the entry for 16 December 1942 (Hoover Institution: Reel 3, frames 3165-66).

61. Cf. page 64 of the entry for 20 March 1942 and page 31 of the entry for 30 April 1942 (Hoover Institution: Reel 2, frame 4744; also in *TGB2*-III, 513; and Reel 3, frame 2428).
62. See, for example, Goebbels' remark that he was "eliminating the last remains of Jazz music from the radio" (2 February 1941; *TGB*-IV, 488); and page 25 of the entry for 18 May 1943, where Goebbels defends the German Dance and Entertainment Orchestra's music against less tolerant critics in the Party (Hoover Institution: Reel 4, frame 4744; also in *TGB2*-VIII, 320-21). For details on this band's establishment, music and its members, see Michael Kater, *Different Drummers: Jazz in the Culture of Nazi Germany* (New York: Oxford University Press, 1992), pp. 127-31.
63. In February 1942, Goebbels recounted the increasing difficulty of subsidizing the theaters to the extent that they could function adequately. At this point he claimed he and his "Führer" wanted to maintain cultural life at the "high level" it had in prewar times—pages 18-19 of the entry for 6 February 1942 (Hoover Institution: Reel 1, frames 432-33; also in *TGB2*-III, 262).
64. For a good overview of Goebbels' comments, see the compilation Barbara Panse based on Fröhlich's 1987 edition of the *Tagebücher*—B. Panse, "Die Theatermacher und die Macht: Barbara Panse zur Auswahl der nachfolgenden Eintragungen aus den Goebbels-Tagebüchern," *Theater Heute*, No. 9 (1989): 4-21.
65. See, for example, the entries for 21 November 1936 and 1 September 1937 (*TGB*-II, 733, and III, 251). For a discussion of Hilpert's relationship to Goebbels and citations of diary entries from 1935 to 1940, in which Goebbels comments on Hilpert's productions, interactions with actors, and programs for the Deutsches Theater and the Kammerspiele, see Panse, pp. 12-14.
66. See pages 13-14 of Goebbels' entry for 17 February 1942, page 11 of the entry for 21 March 1942, and page 20 of the one for 11 April 1942 (Hoover Institution: Reel 1, frames 710-11; also in *TGB2*-III, 330; Reel 2, frame 1488; also in *TGB2*-III, 518; and Reel 2, frame 1901, respectively). Goebbels' warning to Körner on 11 March 1942 about remarks he had made about Max Reinhardt and his acceptance of Körner's letter of resignation from the Reich Theater Chamber presidency are published in Joseph Wulf, *Theater und Film im Dritten Reich: Eine Dokumentation* (Frankfurt/Main: Ullstein, 1983), pp. 108-9.
67. In their examination of Goebbels' university studies, Helmut Neuhaus and Gerhard Sauder have not only corrected the common misconception that Goebbels had been a doctoral student of the Jewish professor Friedrich Gundolf and through him had been introduced to Stefan George's circle of adherents. They also demonstrated the pedestrian character and questionable

methodology of the dissertation Goebbels had written under the supervision of Professor Max Freiherr von Waldberg on the hitherto unexamined Romantic dramatist Wilhelm von Schütz—Helmut Neuhaus, "Der Germanist Dr. Phil. Joseph Goebbels: Bemerkungen zur Sprache des Joseph Goebbels in seiner Dissertation aus dem Jahre 1922," *Zeitschrift für deutsche Philologie* 93 (1974): 398-416; and Gerhard Sauder, "Der Germanist Joseph Goebbels," in *"Das war ein Vorspiel nur. . ." Berliner Colloquium zur Literaturpolitik im "Dritten Reich,"* eds. Horst Denkler and Eberhard Lämmert (Berlin: Akademie der Künste, 1983), pp. 56-81.

68. This preference can be traced to Goebbels' university days, when he held a ceremonial speech, "Wilhelm Raabe und wir," for the Catholic fraternity Unitas Sigfridia—cf. Hans-Jürgen Schrader, "Goebbels als Raabe-Redner," *Jahrbuch der Raabe-Gesellschaft* (1974): 112-15.

69. Cf. Leo Trotzki, *Die wirkliche Lage in Rußland* (1928); Iwan Solonewtisch's two-part account published in Germany under the title *Die Verlorenen: Eine Chronik namenlosen Leidens*: Part I: *Flucht aus dem Sowjetparadies* (1934); and Part II: *Rußland im Zwangsarbeitslager 1933* (1937), (Essen: Essener Verlags-Anstalt); and Alexandra Rachmanova's novel *Die Fabrik des neuen Menschen* (Salzburg: Pustet, 1935).

70. See pp. 15-16 of the entry for 20 May and p. 19 of 21 May 1942 (Hoover Institution: Reel 3, frames 2285-86 and 2910), where Goebbels discusses a Shaw piece that he later cites in his article "Wofür?" which he published in *Das Reich*, No. 22 (31 May 1942), and the next year in the collection *Das eherne Herz*, pp. 330-36.

71. One wonders how Goebbels would have reacted to the caustic commentary by Will Vesper on the translation of Maugham's work. There Vesper rejects the novel as "the embarrassing story of a poor cripple" and wonders who could be interested in "this boring, drawn-out and tedious stuff"—Will Vesper, "Review of W. Somerset Maugham, *Der Menschen Hörigkeit* [Of Human Bondage]. Roman. Aus dem Englischen von Renate Seiller. Zürich: Rascher & Cie 1938," *Die Neue Literatur* 40, Heft 5 (May 1939): 254.

72. Cf. Boelcke, *Kriegspropaganda 1939-1941*, p. 684.

73. Cf. "Die nationalsozialistische Bücherei: Die ersten hundert Empfehlungen," *Der Deutsche*, No. 206 (5 September 1934); and "Die nationalsozialistische Bücherei," *Völkischer Beobachter* (Berliner Ausgabe), No. 254 (11 September 1934): 11.

74. For an informed discussion of Hauptmann's role in Third Reich cultural life, see Eberhard Hilscher's revised edition of his monograph *Gerhart Hauptmann: Leben und Werk* (Berlin: Verlag der Nation, 1987), pp. 403-21. Among other things, Hilscher refutes earlier claims that the National Socialist regime

drastically curtailed productions of Hauptmann's plays and editions of his works.

75. See page 20 of Goebbels' entry of 10 March 1942 (Hoover Institution: Reel 1, frame 1196; also in *TGB2*-III, 447-48); Goebbels' response of 24 June 1942 to Rosenberg's letter of 13 June 1942 (Bundesarchiv, Abteilung Potsdam: Bestand Reichsministerium für Volksaufklärung und Propaganda, Bd. 235, fol. 106); the response Rosenberg sent to Goebbels on 2 July 1942 (BAK: NS 8/172, fol. 78 and reverse); and Rosenberg to Martin Bormann, 7 September 1942 (Paris: Centre de Documentation Juive Contemporaine, CXLII-215, fols. 88ff.).

76. Needless to say, Goebbels' view of Hamsun was not universally held. Liberals and leftists, most of whom were in exile, were no more enthused by Hamsun's archaic style and themes than they were by his pro-Fascist politics—see Franz Schönberner, "Hamsun und die Folgen," *Die Sammlung* (Amsterdam), 1, Heft 2 (1934): 106-8; and Leo Löwenthal, "Knut Hamsun. Zur Vorgeschichte der autoritären Ideologie," *Zeitschrift für Sozialforschung* (Paris), 6, No. 2 (1937): 295-345.

77. See, for example, Gieserich, "Herr Holle, Walter von Molo und wir," *Das Schwarze Korps*, Folge 18 (3 July 1935), p. 13. Walter von Molo's Reich Chamber of Culture file contains a portion of his correspondence with authorities in the radio and the Reich Chamber of Literature regarding these attacks from 1935 to 1937 (BDC: RKK/Walter von Molo).

78. For Walter von Molo's account of his meeting with Goebbels, see Walter von Molo, *So wunderbar ist das Leben: Erinnerungen und Begegnungen* (Stuttgart: Verlag Deutsche Volksbücher, 1957), pp. 362-65.

79. Cf. the rather negative reviews of Fallada's *Wer einmal aus dem Blechnapf frißt* (1934), *Die Bücherkunde* 1, No. 1-4 (July 1934): 10-11; of *Wir hatten einmal ein Kind*, Hellmuth Langenbucher, "Wir hatten mal . . . Grundsätzliches zu einem neuem Buch," *Völkischer Beobachter*, No. 332 (28 November 1934): 6; of *Bauern, Bonzen und Bomben, Kleiner Mann, was nun?* and *Wer einmal aus dem Blechnapf frißt* in *Die Bücherkunde* 1, No. 8-10 (1935): 153-56; as well as Will Vesper's review of *Wer einmal aus dem Blechnapf frißt, Die Neue Literatur* 35, Heft 7 (July 1934): 444, and Vesper's earlier attacks against *Kleiner Mann, was nun?* in *Die Neue Literatur* 33, Heft 11 (November 1932): 537, and 34, Heft 4 (April 1933): 209-10. See also Adolf Kriener, "Dirnen, Zuhälter und Spelunken. Zu Falladas 'eisernem Gustav,'" *Die Bücherkunde* 6, Heft 3 (March 1939): 136-39; and Eberhard Ter-Nedden, "Ein Wort über Fallada," *Die Bücherkunde* 8, Heft 11 (November 1941): 326-31.

80. *Gutachtenanzeiger, Beilage zur Bücherkunde* (February 1938); see also Gisela Berglund, *Der Kampf um den Leser im Dritten Reich: Die Literaturpolitik der*

'Neuen Literatur' (Will Vesper) und der 'Nationalsozialistischen Monatshefte' (Worms: Verlag Georg Heintz, 1980), pp. 103-6.
81. Cf. Günter Casper's afterword in Hans Fallada, *Wolf unter Wölfen,* ed. G. Casper (Berlin and Weimar: Aufbau-Verlag, 1985), vol. 2, pp. 679-80.
82. When Hedin's book about the "new" Germany appeared in Stockholm on 5 May 1937, the press was first directed to ignore it until an evaluation had been completed, according to Press Directive No. 590 of 5 May 1937—cited in Joseph Wulf, *Presse und Funk im Dritten Reich: Eine Dokumentation* (Frankfurt/Main: Ullstein, 1983), p. 101. Hitler subsequently allowed it, and Goebbels expressed his agreement with the decision. Goebbels then suddenly reversed his position after learning that only 2,000 copies had appeared in Swedish and 100,000 would come out in German. He prevented the Brockhaus publishing house from releasing its German translation, and no more than five copies were ever produced—cf. the entries from 23 April to July 1937; *TGB*-III, 121, 134, 138-44; 199 and 378). See also Detlef Brennecke, *Sven Hedin* (Reinbek b. Hamburg: Rowohlt, 1986), pp. 103-4. For Hedin's correspondence with Hitler and Walther Funk regarding the book, see Sven Hedin, *Ohne Auftrag in Berlin* (Tübingen: Internationaler Universitätsverlag, 1949), pp. 15-31. Hedin's original letter of 5 May 1937, which accompanied the copy of *Tyskland och världsfreden* he presented to Hitler, is preserved in the Berlin Document Center (BDC: Parteikanzlei-Korrespondenz/Sven Hedin).
83. Cf. Jochen Klepper to the President of the Reich Culture Chamber [Goebbels], 24 April 1937:
> On 25 March 1937 I was informed of my expulsion from the Reich Literature Chamber. If I now bring up the matter of allowing me the continued practice of my profession in Germany, I ask to be allowed to base my case on my book, which appeared this spring, "Der Vater. Der Roman des Soldatenkönigs." I also take the liberty of referring to the earliest press reviews of the work, which are enclosed. With the most respectful request that you not deny my book your consideration. Jochen Klepper, BDC: RKK/Jochen Klepper.
84. Jochen Klepper to Herr Reichsminister Goebbels, 12 December 1937:
> After in March of this year I was expelled from the Reich Literature Chamber on account of my non-Aryan marriage, on 24 April I directed my plea to you, Herr Minister, as the President of the Reich Culture Chamber, to allow me the possibility of work as a writer in Germany. On 2 September 1937, I obtained the Special Permit I asked for. This obligated me to submit before publication every manuscript, even small newspaper and works on a deadline, to the Reich Literature Chamber for examination.

Since I have held the Special Permit I have been following these stipulations. However it has not been possible for me to get the submitted manuscripts back for publication or to obtain a response to inquiries. The difficulties that have arisen because of this can no longer be bridged over and dealt with. May I ask you, very esteemed Herr Reich Minister, for your intervention so that the Special Permit that was generously granted me can serve its purpose and I again will be able to work as a writer?

Since I hardly can assume that the type of work I do is familiar to you, Herr Reich Minister, I am taking the liberty of having my publisher—the Deutsche Verlags-Anstalt in Stuttgart, Berlin—send you my book "Der Vater. Der Roman des Soldatenkönigs." It is clear to me, esteemed Herr Reich Minister, that you will not be able to devote your time to such a voluminous book. My cordial request is that you pass on my book and my case to the gentleman in your ministry, whom you believe is responsible for handling my affair, and to determine the measure of good will that I may be granted.

Once again with the most respectful request not to deny me your interest.
Heil Hitler!
Very respectfully, Jochen Klepper
(The handwritten original is in the Berlin Document Center; Klepper's copy is preserved at the Deutsches Literaturarchiv: Nachlaß A: Klepper, 77.4472/2.)

85. Cf. Hans Franke, "Der Soldatenkönig: König Friedrich Wilhelm I. von Preußen," *NSZ-Rheinfront* (Neustadt/Haardt), 23 April 1937; Dr. Erich Valentin, "'Der schweigende Poet': Zu Jochen Kleppers Friedrich-Wilhelm-Roman 'Der Vater,'" *Völkischer Beobachter* (München), 20 August 1937; "Neues deutsches Schrifttum: 'Der Vater,'" *N.S.-Tageszeitung* (Plauen), 14 May 1937; and Arthur Pfeiffer, "Jochen Klepper, 'Der Vater: Ein Roman des Soldatenkönigs,'" *Völkischer Beobachter* (Berliner Ausgabe), 17 July 1937.

86. Jochen Klepper's diary entries during the time of his appeal from late April to mid-June 1937 make clear that he attempted to petition Goebbels personally. However, when he received encouraging news about progress toward rescinding his expulsion, it came from Hans Hinkel, who had read and praised *Der Vater*. Klepper never mentioned any decision by Goebbels—see Jochen Klepper, *Unter dem Schatten Deiner Flügel* (Stuttgart: Deutsche Verlags-Anstalt, 1956), pp. 444-45 and 464-67.

87. See Diller, pp. 79-81 and 163-65.

88. Cf. "Vom Systemfunk zum Volksfunk Adolf Hitlers," *RRG-Presse-Mitteilungen*, No. 493 (1936), p. 3; and Joseph Goebbels, *National-Sozialistischer Rundfunk* (München: Eher, 1935), pp. 7-8.

89. "Dr. Goebbels beglückwünscht den Rundfunk zur 10. Hörer-Million," *Völkischer Beobachter* (Berliner Ausgabe), No. 315 (11 November 1938), p. 6.

90. Diller, p. 166.
91. See pages 16-17 of Goebbels' entry for 3 April 1942 (Hoover Institution: Reel 2, frames 1770-71).
92. Diller, p. 168.
93. Ibid., pp. 360-61.
94. Leonard W. Doob, *Public Opinion and Propaganda* (New York: Henry Holt and Company, 1948), pp. 472.
95. Rundfunkstatistik, in: Hans-Joachim Weinbrenner, *Handbuch des Deutschen Rundfunks 1938* (Heidelberg: Kurt Vowinckel, 1938), pp. 289-95.
96. Cf. page 27 of the entry for 14 May 1943 (Hoover Institution: Reel 4, frame 4653; also in *TGB2*-VIII, 298). For other evidence of Goebbels' rejection of the radio play, see the SS Security Service Report of 5 October 1940 on the declining state of the radio play. The document includes the pencilled remark: "Nothing can be done, Goebbels rejects the radio play as a general principle"— BAK: R 58/1089, fol. 174.
97. Goebbels, "Rede zur Eröffnung der 15. großdeutschen Rundfunkausstellung [1938]" cited in Gerd Eckert, *Der Rundfunk als Führungsmittel* (Heidelberg: Kurt Vowinckel, 1941), p. 179.
98. On this point Goebbels' entries from the war years corroborate the testimony Moritz von Schirmeister gave before the Nuremberg Tribunal on the high priority given to radio and Goebbels' attention to the most trivial details of the program's makeup: "During the war the radio was for Dr. Goebbels the most important instrument of propaganda. He did not keep such a strict watch on any department as he did on the radio department. At meetings over which he presided he personally decided the most minute details of the artistic program. . . ." (*Trial of the Major War Criminals before the International Military Tribunal*, vol. 17, p. 241).
99. In the entry for 2 September 1939, Goebbels recorded his success with Hitler with his law imposing the death penalty for listening to foreign broadcasts— cited in *Der Spiegel*, No. 32 (3 August 1992), p. 69.
100. Cf. Boelcke, *Kriegspropaganda 1939-1941*, pp. 747-48. It is noteworthy that Goebbels' remark comes precisely on the day when all weekly radio program magazines ceased publication in order to conserve resources for the war effort.
101. See page 16 of the entry for 13 February 1942 (Hoover Institution: Reel 1, frame 579; also in *TGB2*-III, 298); see also pages 21-22 of 4 February 1942 and pages 21-23 of 8 February 1942 (Hoover Institution: Reel 1, frames 385-86 and 480-82 respectively; also in *TGB2*-III, 249-50 and 273-74).
102. Page 16 of the entry for 13 February 1942 (Hoover Institution: Reel 1, frame 579; also in *TGB2*-III, 298). For details on this program reform and the

appointments of "Group Leaders" for each of the ten different categories, see Diller, pp. 358-61.

103. A good example is found on pages 25-26 of Goebbels' entry for 22 May 1943, where he criticizes Karl Cerff, a member of the Propaganda Ministry, for advocating a "hyper-National Socialist stance" ("*übernationalsozialistischen Standpunkt*") on the radio's musical program. According to Goebbels, if Cerff had his way the broadcasting industry's repertoire would be restricted to works performed only on the lur, a Nordic instrument from the Bronze Age (Hoover Institution: Reel 4, frames 4843-44; also in *TGB2*-VIII, 346).

104. See pages 23-24 of the entry for 26 February 1942 and page 22 of 27 February 1942 (Hoover Institution: Reel 1, frames 908-9 and 931; also in *TBG2*-III, 377 and 382-83). Goebbels published "Der Rundfunk im Kriege" in *Die Zeit ohne Beispiel: Reden und Aufsätze aus den Jahren 1939/40/41* (München: Eher, 1941), pp. 503-7; and "Der treue Helfer" in *Das eherne Herz: Reden und Aufsätze aus den Jahren 1941/42* (München: Eher, 1943), pp. 229-35.

105. See Hedwig Zöllner, "Klingendes Rundfunkjahr: Eine Rückschau auf die unterhaltenden und künstlerischen Musiksendungen des Jahres 1943," *Reichsrundfunk* 1943/44, Heft 10 (January 1944): 197-202.

106. See the excerpt from Goebbels' entry for 7 September 1944, cited in Reuth, *Goebbels*, p. 564.

107. *Völkischer Beobachter*, No. 42/43 (11/12 February 1934).

108. *Der Kinematograph*, of 4 November 1933, cited in Albrecht, p. 23. On the creation within the Propaganda Ministry of the office of the Reich Film Dramaturgist, whose charge was to prevent films on subject matter that contravened "the spirit of the time," see Joseph Wulf's citation from the *Licht-Bild-Bühne* of 3 February 1934, in Wulf, *Theater und Film im Dritten Reich: Eine Dokumentation* (Frankfurt/Main: Ullstein, 1983), p. 296.

109. Directive of 17 October 1935, signed by Adolf Hitler (BAK: NS 6/11). The text is published in Albrecht, p. 523.

110. Cf. 14, 16, 17, 21, 24, and 26 October; 11 November; 9 and 18 December 1936; II, 697-99, 702, 706, 708, 723, 751, and 760.

111. E.g., Veit Harlan, *Im Schatten meiner Filme. Selbstbiographie* (Gütersloh: Sigbert Mohn, 1966). More recently Leni Riefenstahl generated controversy with her highly unreliable version of her "strained" relationship to the Nazi hierarchy and Goebbels' alleged animosity toward her—L. Riefenstahl, *Memoiren* (München: Albrecht Knaus, 1987); published in English translation under the title *A Memoir* (New York: St. Martin's Press, 1993). On this issue there is a fascinating interview scene in Ray Müller's documentary film on Riefenstahl's life and work *Macht der Bilder* (1993; shown in the United States under the title: *The Wonderful and Horrible Life of Leni Riefenstahl)*. Müller

confronts Riefenstahl with citations from Elke Fröhlich's 1987 edition of Goebbels' diaries, in which Goebbels mentions his high regard for Riefenstahl's work and numerous social and film-related meetings in the 1930s with her. On camera, Riefenstahl vehemently denied the validity of all these entries.

112. Elke Fröhlich, "Joseph Goebbels und sein Tagebuch," *Vierteljahrshefte für Zeitgeschichte* 35, No. 4 (1987): 518-19.
113. See the reports on this visit in the film industry's trade journal: "Dr. Goebbels für Farbfilmverbreitung," *Film-Kurier,* No. 140 (18 June 1936); and "Der Farbfilm marschiert. Wer wagt, der gewinnt," *Film-Kurier,* No. 142 (20 June 1936).
114. See pages 20-21 of the entry for 29 September 1943 (Hoover Institution: Reel 5, frames 5895-96).
115. Bogusław Drewniak, *Der Deutsche Film 1938-1945: Ein Gesamtüberblick* (Düsseldorf: Droste, 1987), pp. 33-34.
116. Cf. Reinhold Keiner, *Thea von Harbou und der deutsche Film bis 1933* (Hildesheim: Georg Olms, 1991), p. 19.
117. Page 22 of the entry for 15 May 1942 (Hoover Institution: Reel 3, frame 2774; also in Lochner, 215).
118. Pages 20-21 of the entry for 19 May 1942 (Hoover Institution: Reel 3, frames 2865-66, also in Lochner, 221).
119. See pages 27-28 of the entry for 29 April 1942 (Hoover Institution: Reel 2, frames 2392-93).
120. See pages 23-24 of the entry for 26 February 1942 (Hoover Institution: Reel 1, frames 908-9; also in *TGB2*-III, 377).
121. The full text of the 107-page typed manuscript is reproduced in Albrecht, pp. 484-500.
122. See pages 25-26 of the entry for 3 March 1942 (Hoover Institution: Reel 1, frames 1030-31; also in *TGB2*-III, 407).
123. When he checked over the film's final revisions, Goebbels noted with satisfaction its "surprising parallels to the present" and the likelihood that it would offend military leaders, which it did during a preliminary screening on 27 January 1942—see pages 33-34 of the entry for 25 January and pages 30-31 of 28 January 1942 (Hoover Institution: Reel 1, frames 132-33 and 220-21; also in *TGB2*-III, 187 and 207-8). The film generated so much controversy with the general staff that it did not premiere on 30 January 1942 as planned and was only released to the public a month later after General Keitel and Hitler had come out in favor of it—see pages 16-18 of the entry for 2 March and page 7 of 20 March 1942 (Hoover Institution: Reel 1, frames 1000-2; also in *TGB2*-III, 400; and Reel 2, frame 1412; also in *TGB2*-III, 499-500).

124. Such thinking came up in almost all of Goebbels' comments on the impact *Der große König* was supposed to have on German viewers. In particular, see page 34 of 25 January; page 31 of 28 January; pages 21-22 of 19 February; and page 8 of 13 April 1942 (Hoover Institution: Reel 1, frames 133, 221, and 756-57; also in *TGB2*-III, 187, 208 and 340; and Reel 2, frame 1952).
125. Pages 30-31 of the entry for 1 March 1942 (Hoover Institution: Reel 1, frames 983-84; also in *TGB2*-III, 396).
126. At one point Goebbels mentioned an attempt by the Finance Ministry to impose a 100 percent tax on theater and cinema tickets. He condemned this move as "the undermining of our cultural operations that the Führer has recognized as essential to the war"—page 20 of the entry for 16 March 1943 (Hoover Institution: Reel 4, frame 3742; also in *TGB2*-VI, 562).
127. Percy Ernst Schramm, "Erläuterungen zum Inhalt," in Picker, *Hitlers Tischgespräche im Führerhauptquartier*, p. 33.
128. E.g., pages 13-14 of the entry for 20 March 1942; and page 110 of 23 September 1943 (Hoover Institution: Reel 2, frames 1418-19; also in *TGB2*-III, 501; Reel 4, frame 5734). See also the entry for 10 May 1943 (*TGB2*-VIII, 265).
129. Cf. Fritz Lang, "Fritz Lang Talks about Dr. Mabuse," *Movie* 4 (November 1962): 4-5.
130. Cf. Gösta Werner, "Fritz Lang and Goebbels: Myth and Facts," *Film Quarterly* 43, No. 3 (Spring 1990): 24-27; see also Nancy Caldwell Sorel, "First Encounters: Fritz Lang and Dr. Joseph Goebbels," *The Atlantic Monthly* 255 (March 1985): 77. According to Lang's account, Goebbels had not considered his "Jewish blood" from his mother's side to be an obstacle to the appointment. Following his emigration, however, Fritz Lang acquired the status of a "Jewish director" in the eyes of the Reich Chamber of Culture when it compiled its data on Lang's former wife, Thea von Harbou, who remained in Germany and pursued an unremarkable though still quite lucrative career as a screenplay author—see the membership data card for Harbou in BDC: RKK/Thea von Harbou.
131. See, for example, Bar Kochba, "Die Frau im Mond," *Der Angriff*, No. 46 (24 October 1929); Hermann Göring, "Film und Nationalsozialisten," *Der Angriff*, No. 59 (8 December 1929); and "Film in der Kritik: 'Siegfrieds Tod,' musikalisch synchronisiert," *Völkischer Beobachter*, No. 129 (9 May 1933). Here we might also mention the subtle tribute to Lang that Goebbels paid in his *Das erwachende Berlin*, a photographic montage with commentary chronicling cultural and political developments in Berlin from the last two decades. A nighttime shot of Berlin's Ufa-Palast cinema advertising the film *Metropolis* is featured prominently among the "positive" cultural achievements Goebbels associated with the metropolis—Goebbels, *Das erwachende Berlin* (München:

Franz Eher, 1934), p. 26. Reuth notes that the publication date of 1934 is misleading, since the volume already appeared in late 1933.

132. Cf. Thomas Mann, *Tagebücher 1933-1934,* entries for 26 October 1933 and 29 January 1934, pp. 233 and 301. For some details on the expatriation action of the Bavarian Political Police against Mann, see Reginald H. Phelps, "Thomas Mann, LL.D., Harvard, and the Third Reich," *John Harvard's Journal* (July-August 1986): 66-67.

133. For further details on the handling of Mann's works within the Third Reich, see Glenn R. Cuomo, "Official and Private Reaction Within the Third Reich to Exile Literature," in *Die Resonanz des Exils: Gelungene und mißlungene Rezeption deutschsprachiger Exilautoren,* ed. Dieter Sevin (Amsterdam: Rodopi, 1992), pp. 168-71.

Notes on the Contributors

EHRHARD BAHR is professor of German and chair of the Department of Germanic Languages at the University of California, Los Angeles. He is the author of books on irony in the late works of Goethe (1972), on Georg Lukács (1970), Ernst Bloch (1974), and Nelly Sachs (1980). He has published extensively on eighteenth- to twentieth-century German literature and philosophy. A book on the impact of the French Revolution on German literature and philosophy, edited by Bahr and Thomas P. Saine, appeared in 1992. From 1990 to 1992, Bahr served as a consultant to the exhibition "'Degenerate Art': The Fate of the Avant-Garde in Nazi Germany" at the Los Angeles County Museum of Art, the Art Institute of Chicago and the Smithsonian Institution in Washington, D.C., in 1991, and at the Altes Museum in Berlin in 1992.

JAN-PIETER BARBIAN studied history, German literature, and philosophy at the Universität Trier. From 1987 to 1991 he participated in a research project supported by the Deutsche Forschungsgesellschaft on the history of German-French scientific relations in the eighteenth and early nineteenth centuries. His dissertation, "Literaturpolitik im 'Dritten Reich.' Institutionen, Kompetenzen, Betätigungsfelder" (Literary policy in the 'Third Reich': Institutions, competencies, spheres of activity) was published by *Archiv für Geschichte des Buchwesens* in 1993 and is now coming out in a revised paperback edition with the Deutscher Taschenbuch Verlag in Munich in late 1995. His other publications have been on mining and iron works in Germany and France in the eighteenth and nineteenth centuries, cultural politics in the Weimar Republic and the Third Reich, and on the history and literature of the Netherlands in the twentieth century. Since 1991 he has been the head of the department for Cultural Education at the Volkshochschule of the City of Duisburg.

GLENN R. CUOMO is associate professor of German language and literature at New College of the University of South Florida. He is the author of *Career at the Cost of Compromise: Günter Eich's Life and Work in the Years 1933-1945* (1989). His other publications include articles on Eich's pre-1945 radio broadcasts, Hanns Johst and the Reich Chamber of Literature, Gottfried Benn, Heinar Kipphardt's play *Bruder Eichmann,* the reception of exile literature within the Third Reich, and George Bernard Shaw's works in Nazi Germany. He is presently working on a monograph on Eich-criticism as well as pursuing projects on Joseph Goebbels and modernism, and the influence of censorship on the process of literary production.

BOGUSŁAW DREWNIAK is professor of German history at the Gdańsk University. He has over 100 publications on contemporary German history, German cultural history, and Polish-German relations. Among his works are the books: *Kultura w cieniu swastyki* (Culture in the shadow of the swastika, 1969), *Teatr i Film Trzeciej Rzeszy w systemie hitlerowskiej propagandy* (Theater and film of the Third Reich within Hitler's propaganda system, 1972), *Das Theater im NS-Staat. Szenarium deutscher Zeitgeschichte 1933-1945* (Theater in the Nazi state: Scenario of German contemporary history 1933-1945, 1983), and *Der Deutsche Film 1938-1945. Ein Gesamtüberblick* (German film 1938-1945: A complete overview, 1987). Under the auspices of the University of Hamburg, he is currently researching German theater in the Free City Danzig and in Poland during the period from 1919 to 1939 for an anthology on German theater in exile, as well as completing a book on Polish-German cultural relations from 1919 to 1939.

JONATHAN PETROPOULOS is assistant professor of history at Loyola College in Maryland. He received his Ph.D. from Harvard University. His revised dissertation, *Art As Politics in the Third Reich,* is forthcoming in 1996 from the University of North Carolina Press. Other works in progress concern the cultural politics of interwar Austria, a biography of the art plunderer Kajetan Mühlmann, and a study of the professions concerned with art in Germany from 1918 to 1945.

PAMELA M. POTTER is assistant professor of musicology at the University of Illinois in Urbana-Champaign. She is interested in tracing the relationship of Western music to its political, social, and economic environment. Her research has mainly focused on music and musical scholarship in the Weimar Republic and Nazi Germany, along with broader investigations into the gulf between popular and high culture in twentieth-century music. Her publications include articles on Richard Strauss and the Third Reich, music and musicology in Germany between the two world wars, the Nazi exploitation of Richard Wagner's symbolic image, and music performance in the Weimar Republic. She is currently writing a book for Yale University Press on German musicology and society from 1918 to 1960.

ALAN E. STEINWEIS received his PhD in German history from the University of North Carolina in 1988, Chapel Hill, and was a postdoctoral fellow at the Freie Universität Berlin in 1988-89. He teaches history and judaic studies at the University of Nebraska, Lincoln. He is the author of *Art, Ideology, and Economics in Nazi Germany: The Reich Chambers of Music, Theater, and the Visual Arts* (1993) and of several articles on Nazi cultural policy. He is currently researching the German occupation of East Upper Silesia from 1939 to 1945.

DAVID WELCH is professor of modern European history and director of the Centre for the Study of Propaganda at the University of Kent at Canterbury, England. His publications include *Propaganda and the German Cinema, 1933-1945* (1983; paperback 1985); editor of *Nazi Propaganda: The Power and the Limitations* (London: Croom Helm, 1983); *The Third Reich: Politics and Propaganda* (1993); *Modern European History, 1870-1980: A Documentary Reader* (1994), and *The Third Reich: Politics and Propaganda* (revised paperback edition 1995). He is currently completing *German Society and the Impact of Total War, 1914-1918: The Sins of Omission* (forthcoming 1996/7), as well as a textbook on the history of political propaganda in the twentieth century.

INDEX

Abetz, Otto, 134, 137, 138
Ahler, Rudolf, 211
Aigner, Dietrich, 158
"*Aktion wider den undeutschen Geist,*" 12, 157, 164, 178
Alverdes, Paul, 176
Amann, Max, 159, 165, 169-70, 172, 178, 181, 201
Amt für Kunstpflege (Office for Promotion of Art), 79, 83, 208
Amt Kunstschutz (Art Protection Office), 134
Anacker, Heinrich, 175
Andersch, Alfred, 3, 178
Andres, Stefan, 177
Anton, Karl, 220
Arendt, Hannah, 140

Baarová, Lida, 172, 203
Barlach, Ernst, 10, 13, 123, 127, 132
Bartók, Béla, 53
Bauer, Walter, 177
Baumeister, Willi, 132
Baur, Wilhelm, 165, 169, 181-82
Bayreuth Festival, 73
Bebel, August, 203
Beckmann, Max, 11, 123
Belling, Rudolf, 13, 132
Benda, Hans von, 52
Benjamin, Walter, 5
Benn, Gottfried, 13, 14, 161, 162, 176
Bergengruen, Werner, 177
Berlin Philharmonic Orchestra
 founding, 41-43
 and Goebbels, 47, 49, 209-10
 and Hitler, 52
 Jewish members, 49, 53, 209-10
 and Propaganda Ministry, 47-49, 51-53, 58
 reorganization, 43-45
 subsidies, 2, 45-67
Berlin Symphony Orchestra, 43, 45-46, 49
Bermann-Fischer, Gottfried, 179
Berndt, Alfred Ingemar, 98-99, 172
Bethge, Friedrich, 85
Beumelburg, Werner, 161
Billinger, Richard, 85
Binding, Rudolf G., 161, 176
Bischoff, Friedrich, 176
blacklists
 of literature, 88, 164, 180
 of music, 54-55
 of "non-Aryan" composers, 88
Bloch, Ernst, 5
Blomberg, Field Marshal Werner von, 205-6
Blunck, Hans Friedrich, 161, 165, 167, 169, 175, 213, 225
Bobrowski, Johannes, 178
Boese, Engelbrecht, 158
Bonnard, Abel, 138

books
 bans of (*Buchverbote*), 180, 214-15
 burning of, 11, 99, 164
 reserves of, 182
Bormann, Martin, 125, 134-36, 138, 140, 156, 169
Börsenverein der Deutschen Buchhändler, 158, 163-64, 170, 178
Böss, Gustav, 43
Bouhler, Philipp, 171, 156, 183
Bracher, Karl Dietrich, 160
Brasillach, Robert, 174
Braun, Eva, 203
Brecht, Bertolt, 5, 6, 41
Brehm, Bruno, 175
Breker, Arno, 3, 129, 133, 138, 139
Bronnen, Arnolt, 176
Broszat, Martin, 140
Brüning, Heinrich, 44
Bürckel, Josef, 130

Carossa, Hans, 174, 176
Casement, Sir Roger, 88
censorship
 of books, 173, 180, 205
 of film, 104-105, 219-20
 of music, 53-55
Churchill, Winston S., 207
Cinema Law (Reichslichtspielgesetz), 104-105, 219
Civil Service Law, 11, 28, 160, 161
Cocteau, Jean, 138
Combat League for German Culture, 13-16, 79, 97, 101, 124-25, 159-60, 165-66
Cultural-Political Archive, 170
Culture, Reich Chamber of (RKK)
 creation of, 1, 12, 23-25, 96-97, 122-23, 166-68
 and "eighth chamber," 208

Dahm, Volker, 2, 158
"Degenerate Art" Exhibition, 1, 6, 11, 13, 16, 52, 121-22, 127, 138
"Degenerate Music" Exhibition, 16-17, 52-54, 129
Derain, André, 138
deferments (*UK-Stellungen*), 139
Deutsche Akademie für Dichtung, 161
Deutsche Arbeitsfront (DAF), 15, 71, 74, 80, 101, 125, 166, 170
Deutsche Schillerstiftung (Schiller Foundation), 26, 175
Deutsche Studentenschaft, 12-13
Deutscher Schriftstellerverein, 163
Deutscher Tanz- und Unterhaltungsorchester, 210
Dietrich, Marlene, 123
Disney, Walt, 220-21

Ditzen, Rudolf, (pseud. Hans Fallada), 177, 214
Dix, Otto, 10, 11, 132, 139
Döblin, Alfred, 11
Doob, Leonard, 217
Dostoyevsky, Fedor, 212
Dreiser, Theodore, 212
Drexler, Anton, 8
Drieu la Rochelle, Pierre, 174
Dwinger, Edwin Erich, 175

Ebermayer, Erich, 177
Eckart, Dietrich, 72
Eggebrecht, Axel, 177
Eggers, Kurt, 175
Eich, Günter, 3, 178
Einsatzstab Reichsleiter Rosenberg (ERR), 134, 136-37
Eisenstein, Sergei, 104
Engl, Adolf, 101
Erler, Otto, 211
Euringer, Richard, 82
Europa Film Gesellschaft, 222-23
Ewers, Hanns Heinz, 162-63, 176

Fallada, Hans. *See* Rudolf Ditzen
Feininger, Lyonel, 10, 127
Feuchtwanger, Lion, 164
Fick, Roderich, 135
Film, Reich Chamber of (RFK), 101-102, 123
Filmkreditbank (FKB), 102-104
Fleischer, Dave, 221
Frank, Hans, 136, 138
Frederick the Great, 203, 212, 215, 223
Frenssen, Gustav, 213
Frick, Wilhelm, 10-11, 13, 131, 140, 159, 205
Friedländer, Saul, 7
Fröhlich, Elke, 197-98, 200, 220, 225
Führermuseum, 134-35, 141.
  See also Sonderauftrag Linz
Funk, Walther, 48, 51, 53, 128, 131, 133, 164
Furtwängler, Wilhelm, 44-52, 57, 72, 123

Galsworthy, John, 86
Garbo, Greta, 104
Gay, Peter, 159
Geertz, Clifford, 199
Geissmar, Berta, 51
Genoud, François, 197-98
George, Heinrich, 85
George, Stephan, 123
Gerigk, Herbert, 83
German Labor Front. *See* Deutsche Arbeitsfront
Gestapo, 74, 83, 130, 135, 137, 170, 173, 176-77, 178, 205
Giesler, Hermann, 133, 134
Giménez Caballero, Ernesto, 174
Glaeser, Ernst, 177

Goebbels, Joseph
  art acquisitions by, 132
  bans of art by, 132
  and book burnings, 11, 99
  as Culture Chamber president, 23-24, 97, 167, 209
  and *Der große König,* 223-24
  and festival performances, 47, 72-73
  film policy by, 100, 104, 106-14, 197
  and "final solution," 202
  and *Kolberg,* 115-17
  role in *Kristallnacht,* 172, 204-205
  literary policy by, 164-65
  Michael, 199, 204, 211
  on modern art, 16, 97, 127-29
  on pensions for artists, 30, 32, 175
  personnel policy by, 171-72
  and purging of Jewish artists, 28-31, 49, 177, 209-10
  radio policy by, 215-19
  rivalry with Rosenberg, 3, 13, 97, 123-25, 166, 168, 206
  and "total war," 89, 115-16, 139, 183, 224
  Vom Kaiserhof zur Reichskanzlei, 199-201, 209, 225
  Der Wanderer, 204, 211
  See also Propaganda Ministry
Goebbels, Magda, 203
Goethe, Johann Wolfgang von, 84-85
Goldberg, Simon, 48
Goldmann, Wilhelm, 179
Goltz, Joachim von der, 176
Göring, Hermann, 14, 74-75, 125-26, 128, 131, 135-36, 138, 140, 205, 207-208, 224
Grabbe, Christian Dietrich, 72
Graff, Sigmund, 85
Great German Art Exhibition (GDK), 17, 121, 129, 132, 138, 141
Great German Radio Exhibition, 217-18
Griese, Friedrich, 213
Grimm, Hans, 161, 176
Gründgens, Gustav, 83, 85, 207, 224
Günther, Hans F. K., 11
Gutterer, Leopold, 88

Haberstock, Karl, 131
Haecker, Theodor, 176
Haegert, Wilhelm, 172, 182
Hagemeyer, Hans, 170
Hamsun, Knut, 213
Hanfstaengl, Eberhard, 126
Hansen, Rolf, 108-109
Hansen, Walter, 16, 128
Happel, Hans-Gerd, 158
Harlan, Veit, 112, 115-16, 220, 223
Hartmann, Paul, 211
Haupt, Gunther, 181
Hauptmann, Gerhart, 161, 213
Heckel, Erich, 10, 13, 126
Hederich, Karl Heinz, 172

Hedin, Sven, 206, 215
Heiber, Helmut, 197
Heine, Heinrich, 6
Hemingway, Ernest, 212
Hess, Rudolf, 14, 72, 134, 156, 170, 208
Heydrich, Reinhard, 134, 137, 205
Hilberg, Raul, 31
Hilpert, Heinz, 69, 78, 211
Himmler, Heinrich, 16, 125-26, 130, 132, 134-37, 138, 140, 169
Hindemith, Paul, 6, 53, 57, 126
Hindenburg, Paul von, 28, 122, 204, 215
Hinkel, Hans, 103, 162, 165-66
Hinz, Berthold, 132
Hitler, Adolf
    aesthetic views of, 2, 5, 140
    art acquisitions by, 132
    and Berlin Philharmonic Orchestra, 52
    and early NSDAP program, 8-9
    and film, 100, 219, 224
    and *Führermuseum*, 134-35, 141
    and Great German Art Exhibition, 17-18, 129-30, 141
    and Haus der deutschen Kunst, 11-12, 98, 121, 129-30
    Mein Kampf, 7, 9-10, 159
    on modernism, 15, 17, 121-24, 140
    at 1934 Nuremberg rally, 15, 124-25
    and plundering of art, 131, 134-35
    and Prussian Academy of the Arts, 207
    on theater, 73, 83
    and "total war," 139
    and writers, 207, 215
Höber, Lorenz, 48-50
Hodge, Merton, 86
Hofer, Carl, 13
Höller, Karl, 210
Honegger, Arthur, 53
Hönig, Eugen, 128
Hopwood, Avery, 86-87
Horn, Camilla, 220
Huch, Ricarda, 11
Huchel, Peter, 178
Hugenberg, Alfred, 159

Institut für Zeitgeschichte, 198
Irving, David, 198

Jannings, Emil, 205, 220
Jessner, Leopold, 69
Jews
    and "Aryanization," 131-32
    and "degenerate art," 6-7, 26, 129
    elimination from film industry, 103
    elimination of Jewish musicians, 47-50
    exclusion from cultural life, 11-12, 27-32, 82, 103-104
    and Hitler, 8-10
    persecution of Jewish writers, 177
    propaganda films about, 111
    seizures of artworks from, 122, 130-31, 135-36
    See also Jüdischer Kulturbund
Johst, Hanns, 3, 82, 84, 160, 162, 169, 175
Jüdischer Kulturbund, 17, 32-33, 84, 103
Jugendfilmstunden, 113
Jugo, Jenny, 220
Junge Kunst in Deutschland, 138
Jünger, Ernst, 176

Kafka, Franz, 17
Kaiser, Georg, 161
Kaléko, Mascha, 177
Kampfbund für Deutsche Kultur.
    See Combat League for German Culture
Kandinsky, Wassily, 10, 13
Karajan, Herbert von, 3, 210
Kaschnitz, Marie-Luise, 178
Kast, Michael, 158
Kästner, Erich, 177
Kerr, Alfred, 162, 164
Kestenberg, Leo, 43, 46
Ketelsen, Uwe-Karsten, 69, 83
Keyserling, Hermann Alexander Graf von, 205-206
Kiepenheuer, Gustav, 179
Kirchner, Ernst Ludwig, 13, 127, 132
Klee, Paul, 10, 11, 13
Klepper, Jochen, 177, 215
Knittel, John, 174
Kochanowski, Erich, 162
Koeppen, Wolfgang, 178
Kokoschka, Oskar, 10, 13
Kolbenheyer, Erwin Guido, 161, 213
Kolberg, Hugo, 53
Kollwitz, Käthe, 11
Körner, Ludwig, 211
Körner, Theodor, 116
Korte, Werner, 56
Kraft durch Freude. *See* Strength through Joy
Krauss, Clemens, 73-74
Kriegler, Hans, 216
Kristallnacht, 6, 130-31, 172, 204-205
Krolow, Karl, 178
Künkler, Karl, 83
Künsberg, Freiherr Eberhard von, 137
Kunst der Nation, 14, 16, 126
Kunst im Dritten Reich, 139

Lang, Fritz, 104, 123, 225
Lange, C. A., 43-46
Langenbeck, Curt, 85
Langenbucher, Hellmuth, 170
Langgässer, Elisabeth, 177
Laubinger, Otto, 76
Law, Reich Chamber of Culture, 96-97, 166-67
Lawrence, T. E., 212
Leander, Zarah, 109

Lehár, Franz, 87
Lehmbruck, Wilhelm, 10, 13
Leiser, Erwin, 6
Lessing, Gotthold Ephraim, 84
Ley, Robert, 74, 80, 125-26, 132, 140, 174, 208
Liebeneiner, Wolfgang, 86
Liste des schädlichen und unerwünschten Schrifttums, 177, 180, 205
Literature, Reich Chamber of (RSK), 2, 123, 165, 172-75, 177-78, 182, 205
Lochner, Louis P., 197-98, 201
Loerke, Oskar, 161, 176
Lokatis, Siegfried, 158
London, Jack, 213
Lowry, Stephen, 110
Ludwig, Emil, 164
Luxemburg, Rosa, 203

Macke, August, 13
McLachlan, D., 197
Maillol, Aristide, 138
Mann, Heinrich, 6, 11, 114, 160, 161, 164
Mann, Klaus, 17
Mann, Thomas, 5-6, 11, 85, 176, 202-203, 226
Marc, Franz, 10, 13
Marcks, Gerhard, 13, 132
Marinetti, Filippo Tommaso, 14
Mason, Tim, 7
Maugham, W(illiam) Somerset, 86, 212
Mechow, Benno von, 176
Mendelssohn, Felix, 40, 53-54
Menuhin, Yehudi, 69-70
Menzel, Herybert, 175
Merker, Reinhard, 127
M-G-M, 222
Miegel, Agnes, 175, 213
Mies van der Rohe, Ludwig, 126, 132
Minetti, Bernhard, 3, 70
Moholy-Nagy, Ladislaus, 14
Möller, Eberhard Wolfgang, 85
Molo, Walter von, 161, 214
Mommsen, Hans, 14
Mozart, Wolfgang Amadeus, 73-74
Mühlmann, Kajetan, 136-37, 138
Müller, Otto, 13
Music, Reich Chamber of, 26, 28-29, 52, 53-54, 71, 87, 123

Nachtkritik, 98, 127
Nazi Cultural Community (NS-KG), 79-80, 124-25, 208
Nazi Trade Union (NSBO), 101
newsreels, 111
Niemöller, Martin, 176
Nolde, Emil, 10, 13, 123, 124, 127, 132, 139
Nossack, Hans-Erich, 3, 178

Oldenbourg, Friedrich, 163, 165

Ortner, Hermann Heinz, 85

Packwood, Robert, 202
Pankok, Otto, 13
Paramount Film Company, 222
Parteiamtliche Prüfungskommission zum Schutze des NS-Schrifttums, 170-72, 180, 183
Pauley, Bruce, 130-31
Paulsen, Peter, 135
Paumgartner, Bernhard, 73
Pechstein, Max, 13, 132
PEN Club, 162, 174
Peterson, Edward, 140
Picker, Henry, 133, 205
Pleyer, Wilhelm, 175
Pohl, Gerhard, 177
Popitz, Johannes, 49
Porten, Henny, 224
Posse, Hans, 134
Propaganda Ministry
  evolution of, 95-96, 122, 166, 215-16
  literature department of, 168-69, 206
  theater department of, 75-77, 210-11
Prussian Academy of the Arts, 11, 132, 160-62, 207-208

Rachmonova, Alexandra, 212
Räther, Arnold, 102
Rehberg, Hans, 85
Reichel, Peter, 5
Reichsmusiktage, 17, 52
Reichsverband Deutscher Lichtspieltheater e.V., 100-101
Reichsverband Deutscher Schriftsteller, 163, 167, 174-75
Reimann, Viktor, 201
Reinecker, Herbert, 178
Remarque, Erich Maria, 164
Reuter, Ernst, 55
Reuth, Ralf Georg, 198
Ribbentrop, Joachim von, 134, 137
Richter, Hans, 163
Riefenstahl, Leni, 3, 111
Rinser, Luise, 178
Rischbieter, Hennig, 70
Rohlfs, Christian, 13, 127
Röhm, Ernst, 14, 200
Rosenberg, Alfred
  and antimodernism, 14, 123-24, 126
  and Combat League, 14-15, 79, 159, 165-66
  as Führer's Commissioner, 79-80, 124, 170
  intervention in theater policy, 74, 89, 213
  and his Literature Office, 157, 168, 170-72, 174, 177, 180-83
  against merger with Culture Chamber, 208
  and Office for Promotion of Art, 79, 83

Index

rivalry with Goebbels, 3, 13, 97, 123-25, 166, 168, 206
  role in plundering art in the East, 134, 136
  and *Thingtheater,* 211
Rothschild, Louis de, 131
Rowohlt, Ernst, 179, 214
Rühmann, Heinz, 3, 86, 224
Rust, Bernhard, 125-26, 128, 140, 161, 169
Ruth, Roy del, 221

Salomon, Ernst von, 176
Schäfer, Hans Dieter, 1, 158
Schardt, Alois, 126
Scheuermann, Fritz, 102
Schiller, Friedrich von, 72, 82-85, 204
Schillings, Max von, 161
Schirach, Baldur von, 125-26, 137, 138, 140, 225
Schlemmer, Oskar, 10, 11
Schlösser, Rainer, 67, 73, 76-77, 83-84, 88, 162, 170, 210
Schmidt-Pauli, Edgar von, 162
Schmidt-Rottluff, Karl, 10, 13, 127, 132
Schmidtseck, Rudolf von, 50
Schnabel, Ernst, 178
Schneider, Reinhold, 176
Schnurre, Wolfdietrich, 178
Schoenberg, Arnold, 11, 40, 54, 57
Schreiber, Otto Andreas, 125-26
Schröder, Rudolf Alexander, 176
Schultze-Naumburg, Paul, 11
Schumann, Gerhard, 175
Schutzverband deutscher Schriftsteller (SDS), 162-63
Schwitters, Kurt, 14
Seidel, Ina, 213
Semmler (Semler), Rudolf, 197
Seyß-Inquart, Arthur, 136, 140
Shakespeare, William, 54, 72, 86, 88, 212
Shaw, George Bernard, 86, 88, 206-207, 210, 212, 215
Sicherheitsdienst (SD), 31, 130, 135, 137, 169, 170, 173, 178
Sinclair, Upton, 212
Solonewtisch, Iwan, 212
Sonderauftrag Linz, 135, 136
Sösemann, Bernd, 199
Speer, Albert, 125-26, 133, 135, 138, 140
Spitzenorganisation der Deutschen Filmindustrie (SPIO), 100, 102-104
Sprenger, Jakob, 206
Stadelmayer, Peter, 201
Stang, Walter, 79, 80, 85
Stehr, Hermann, 213
Steiner, Joshua, 202
Stoffregen, Götz Otto, 163
Strauß, Emil, 213
Strauss, Richard, 26, 48, 57, 123, 225

Stravinsky, Igor, 53-54, 57
Strength through Joy (KdF), 52, 73-74, 79-81, 125-26, 208
Stresemann, Wolfgang, 53, 55
Strothmann, Dietrich, 157
Suhrkamp, Peter, 3, 179
Synge, John Millington, 88

Taylor, Richard, 199
Theater, Reich Chamber of, 71, 75-76
Theater Law, 74, 76-77, 96
Thiess, Frank, 176
Thingspiel/Thingtheater, 68, 82-83, 211
Thorak, Josef, 129, 133
Timmermans, Felix, 174
Trenker, Luis, 104
Trotzki, Leon, 212
troup entertainment, 80-81
Tucholsky, Kurt, 164

Ufa, 100
Ufa-Film GmbH (Ufi), 107
Undset, Sigrid, 206
Union nationaler Schriftsteller, 162
Urban, Gotthard, 165

Verhoeven, Paul, 52
Vesper, Will, 175-76, 177, 213-14
Volckmar-Frentzel, Theodor, 181
Volksempfänger, 216
Voss, Hermann, 135
Vowinckel, Kurt, 165
Vugesta, 137

Wagner, Richard, 53, 72-73, 74, 204
Wagner, Winifred, 73
Walter, Bruno, 47-48
Wedekind, Frank, 206
Weidemann, Hans, 125-26
Weill, Kurt, 41
Weisenborn, Günter, 177
Werfel, Franz, 161
Wessel, Horst, 84, 200
Wessel, Inge, 200
Weyrauch, Wolfgang, 178
Wiechert, Ernst, 176, 213
Wilde, Oscar, 86
Willrich, Wolf, 16, 128
Winnig, August, 176
Wismann, Heinz, 165, 168-71, 181
Wolfe, Thomas, 212
Wolff, Hermann, 41
Wolff-Metternich, Franz Graf, 134
Wulf, Joseph, 157

Yeats, William Butler, 88

Ziegler, Adolf, 16, 121, 128, 129, 138
Zöberlein, Hans, 175, 213
Zweig, Arnold, 164